TO BE NEAR UNTO GOD

TO BE NEAR UNTO GOD

By ABRAHAM KUYPER, D.D., LL.D.

FORMER PRIME MINISTER OF
THE NETHERLANDS

Translated from the Dutch by
JOHN HENDRIK DE VRIES, D.D.

BAKER BOOK HOUSE
Grand Rapids, Michigan

PHOTOLITHOPRINTED BY CUSHING - MALLOY, INC.
ANN ARBOR, MICHIGAN, UNITED STATES OF AMERICA
1979

BIOGRAPHICAL NOTE

DR. ABRAHAM KUYPER was born in Maassluis, Netherlands, October the twenty-ninth, 1837. His parents were
the Reverend Jan Hendrik and Henriette Huber Kuyper.
At Maassluis and at Middelburg, where his father was
called in 1849, he attended school. His teachers, we are
told, took him at first to be a dull boy. They must have
changed their opinion when at the early age of twelve he
was able to enter the Gymnasium at Middelburg. In due
time he was matriculated at the Leyden University, from
which he graduated with highest honors. It was here also
that he took his Doctorate in Sacred Theology in 1863,
when he was about twenty-six years of age.

A year later he began his ministry in Beesd; was then
called to Utrecht, and from there, in 1870, to Amsterdam.
In 1872 he became Editor-in-chief of De *Standaard* (The
Standard), a daily paper, and the official organ of the Anti-
Revolutionary Party, which in politics represents the
Christian contingent of the Dutch nation. Shortly after,
he assumed the editorship of De *Heraut* (The *Herald*), a
distinctively Christian Sunday Paper, published on Fri-
days. For more than forty-five years he filled both these
exacting positions with extraordinary vigor and power.

In 1874 he was elected a member of the Lower House of
Parliament, which office he served until 1877. In 1880 he
founded the Free University in Amsterdam, which takes
the Bible as the unconditional basis on which to rear the
whole structure of human knowledge in every department
of life.

Then followed twenty years of strenuous labor, in the
University and out of it, when some of his greatest treatises
were written covering a period that may well be regarded

5

as having exerted a most important influence on the ecclesiastical and political history of his country. It is by his almost super-human labors, no less than by his strength and nobility of character, that he left "foot-prints on the sands of time" with such indelible clearness, that in 1907, when his seventieth birthday was made the occasion of national celebration, it was said: "The history of the Netherlands, in Church, in State, in Society, in Press, in School, and in the Sciences of the last forty years, can not be written without the mention of his name on almost every page, for during this period the biography of Dr. Kuyper is to a considerable extent the history of the Netherlands."

In 1898 he visited the United States of America, where he gave the "Stone Lectures" at Princeton Theological Seminary. It was then that Princeton University conferred the Doctorate of Laws upon him.

Upon his return to the Netherlands, he resumed his labors as Leader of the Anti-Revolutionary Party, until in 1901 he was summoned by Queen Wilhelmina to form a Cabinet. He served as Prime Minister until 1905. Then a year or more was spent in travel, a graphic account of which appeared in a two-volume work: "Om de Oude Wereld-Zee" (Around the Old World-Sea), the entire edition of which was sold before it was printed.

After that, Dr. Kuyper resided in the Hague as Minister of State, in the public eye the foremost figure in the land, and in some respects without a peer in the world. At seventy-five years of age he began in the columns of De Heraut the series of weekly articles: "Van de Voleinding" (Of the End of the World), three hundred and six in all which took six years to complete. De Maasbode, a Roman Catholic publication in the Netherlands, refers to this work as "most unique and without a rival in all the literature on the subject." References to the end of the world are traced throughout all the books of the Bible, and carefully exposited, while the Revelation of S. John is dealt with section by section. When he was eighty-two years old he was laying out plans for another great work on "The Messiah." But the end came on November eighth, 1920.

During all these years his work was many-sided to an astonishing degree. As has been said: "No department of human knowledge was foreign to him." And whether we take him as student, pastor or preacher; as linguist, theologian or University Professor; as party leader, organizer or statesman; as philosopher, scientist, publicist, critic or philanthropist—there is always "something incomprehensible in the mighty labors of this indefatigable wrestler; always something as incomprehensible as genius always is." Even they who differed with him, and they were many, honored him as "an opponent of ten heads and a hundred hands." They who shared his vision and his ideals prized and loved him "as a gift of God to our age."

What was the secret of this almost superhuman power?

In 1897, at the twenty-fifth anniversary of his editorship of De *Standaard*, Dr. Kuyper said: "One desire has been the ruling passion of my life. One high motive has acted like a spur upon my mind and soul. And sooner than that I should seek escape from the sacred necessity that is laid upon me, let the breath of life fail me. It is this: That in spite of all worldly opposition, God's holy ordinances shall be established again in the home, in the school and in the State for the good of the people; to carve as it were into the conscience of the nation the ordinances of the Lord, to which Bible and Creation bear witness, until the nation pays homage again to God."

Few men have had an ideal before them like this. Few

men have been as obedient to the demands of such a purpose in life as he. He gave himself literally body, soul and
spirit to this high calling. He lived with watch in hand.
Every hour of day and night had its own appointed task.
His writings number more than two hundred works, many
of them of three and four volumes each, and cover an
extraordinary range of subjects.

As a man he was singularly appreciative of a word or
act of kindness on the part of others. The writer of this
note here speaks from personal experience. Dr. Kuyper
knew something of the holy art of love. He prided himself
on being a man of the people. It is remembered by many
with admiration and gratitude, that however pressed by
his multifarious labors, he never refused audience to any
that came to him for counsel and help.

He never claimed originality. His life and labors can not
be explained from himself alone. In connection with what
a reviewer of this book suggests, when he calls these meditations: "Exquisite life-studies in the Word," we confine ourselves here to the more deeply spiritual under-
current of his life, as the secret of his phenomenal power.

In his early years the religious life in his country was at a
low ebb. "Church life was cold and formal. Religion was
almost dead. There was no Bible in the schools. There
was no life in the nation."

But intimations of better things to come were not wanting. As far back as 1830, Groen van Prinsterer, a member
of Parliament, began to protest against the spirit of the
times. "This brought about a revival of Gospel preaching
—that by nature all men are sinners in need of the atoning
Blood of Christ. Great offense was taken at this. It was
not long before Evangelicals could not be tolerated. It
was not irreligion that was wanted, but religion such as
would please every one, Jews included."

Hence when the subject of this sketch was a university student, it was not strange that he felt no inclination toward the Gospel ministry. He had no sympathy, he said, with a Church which trampled her own honor under foot; nor with a religion which was represented by such a Church. He drifted along with the modern stream, and warmly took part in applauding Professor Rauwenhoff, who openly denied the bodily resurrection of Jesus.

A series of experiences, however, made deep impressions upon the young scholar.

The University of Groningen offered a prize for the best essay on John a Lasco, the great Polish Reformer. By the advice of his teachers, Kuyper resolved to become one of the competitors. Imagine the disappointment when an earnest search in all the great libraries of his country and in those of all Europe failed to produce the necessary material for the work. As a last resort, Dr. de Vries, one of the professors at Leyden, who had taken a deep interest in the promising young scholar, advised him to visit his (Dr. de Vries') father at Haarlem, as he was a fine student of history and had an extensive library. He went, but only to hear the venerable preacher tell him that he would look for these books, but that he had no remembrance of ever having seen one of a Lasco's works in his collection. A week later Kuyper returned, by appointment. Let him tell himself the experience of that hour:

"How can I make you share my feelings when, being admitted to the venerable preacher, I heard him say to me in the most matter of fact way, while pointing to a rich collection of duodecimos heaped on a side table: 'This is what I have found.' I could scarcely believe my eyes. Having searched in vain all the libraries in the Netherlands; having carefully examined the catalogues of the greatest libraries in all Europe; having read again and again in anthologies, and in records of rare books, that the titles of a Lasco's works are simply copied, without the works themselves ever being seen; that his works, if any are still in existence, are extremely rare; that most of them are as good as lost; that with a possible exception of two or three, no one has had them in hand for as much as two hundred years—and then as by a miracle to be brought face to face with a richer collection of Lasciana than could be found in any library in Europe; to find this treasure, which was the "to be or not to be" of my prize essay, with a man to whom I had been referred by a faithful friend, but who did not even know that he had it in his possession and who but a week ago scarcely so much as remembered the name of a Lasco—in all seriousness one must, in his own experience, have been surprised like this, to know what it means to see a Divine miracle confront him in his path."

It need scarcely be said that he won the prize. But the experience did more—"it reminded him of God." It threw a doubt upon his rationalism. He could no longer deny that there was such a thing as "the finger of God."

Another experience came to him about this time in the reading of the well known novel, "The Heir of Radcliffe." He devoured the book. It gave him an impression of Church life in England such as was almost altogether lacking at the time in the Church in the Netherlands. It brought him in touch with the deep significance of the Sacrament, with the impressive character of liturgical worship, and with what he afterward used to speak of as "The Anointed Prayer Book." But over and above this, he felt in his own soul an irresistible acknowledgment of the reality of every spiritual experience through which the hero, Philip de Norville, passed. The utter self condemnation of the broken-hearted man, indeed, his complete self abhorrence, the brilliant young student applied to himself; it became to him a power of God unto salvation.

Looking back upon this experience he writes: "What my soul went through in that moment, I have only later fully understood; but yet in that hour, nay, from that very moment, I learned to despise what formerly I admired, and to seek what formerly I spurned. But enough. You know the lasting character of the impression of such an experience; what the soul encounters in such a conflict belongs to that eternal something, which presents itself to the soul years afterward, strongly and sharply defined, as though it happened but yesterday."

But, under God, it was the simple country folk of his first parish that were instrumental in leading him into that fullness of spiritual life toward which his former experiences had pointed. As he ministered to them, they admired his talents; and soon learned to love him for what he was; but they set themselves earnestly to united and individual prayer for his entire conversion to Christ. "And," as Kuyper writes afterward, "their faithful loyalty became a blessing to my heart, the rise of the morning star of my life. I had been apprehended, but I had not yet found the Word of reconciliation. In their simple language they brought me this in the absolute form in which alone my soul can rest. I discovered that the Holy Scripture does not only cause us to find justification by faith, but also discloses the foundation of all human life, the holy ordinances which must govern all human existence in Society and State."

Thus began his Christian life. At the Cross he made the great surrender of himself to his Savior and to His service. "To bear witness for Christ" became the passion of his life.

That Christ is King in every department of human life and activity was the key-note which he kept ringing in all his writings, addresses and labors, whether as theologian or as statesman, as a leader in politics, as president of the Christian Labor Union, as promoter of Christian education, it was all done from the burning conviction stated on page 275 of this book that: Christ rules not merely by the tradition of what He *once* was, spake, did and endured; but by a living power which even now, seated as He is at the right hand of God, He exercises over lands and nations, generations, families and individuals."

Thus the finding of some lost books, the reading of a novel, the teaching of uncultured folk, were experiences which explain in part Dr. Kuyper's great work.

The more one acquaints himself with the vast scope of the varied labors of this man, the more deeply one becomes impressed with the striking significance of the devotional, mystical output of his pen. Profound theological learning, great statesmanship, extraordinary intellectual acumen along any line is not thought as a rule to be compatible with childlike simplicity of faith, mystical insight and sweetness of soul. But in the words of a reviewer: "This Book of Meditations disproves the idea, that a profound theologian can not be a warm-hearted Christian." "Dr. Kuyper must have lived the life of Christ," says another, "else he could never have written up to the title of this Book." On page 230 the author himself tells the story: "By means of these Meditations we are bent upon opening the eyes of as many as possible to the need of making communion with, knowledge of, and love for God, more than ever before, our daily concern;" and on page 354: "The fellowship of being near unto God must become reality, in the full and vigorous prosecution of our life. It must permeate and give color to our feeling, our perceptions, our sensations, our thinking, our imagining, our willing, our acting, our speaking. It must not stand as a foreign factor in our life, but it must be the passion that breathes throughout our whole existence."

In pursuit of this ideal, Dr. Kuyper took time to add to his gigantic labors the writing of a devotional meditation every week. He wrote more than two thousand of them. They are entirely unique in character. They are well said to form a literature by themselves, and are in line with the best works of Dutch mystics, such as Johannes Ruysbroek, Cornelius Jansinius, and Thomas a Kempis.

This book offers one hundred and ten Meditations on this single thought from Psalm 73: "As for me, it is good To Be Near Unto God." The Rev. Edward Everett of Boston writes: "To me this represents a most precious idea in religion, the inexhaustible freshness of a single phrase of Divine utterance. With but a portion of a psalm embedded in one's heart, there is no lack of food for mind and soul. The secret of perennial bliss lies in the art of meditative repetition. The title, 'To Be Near Unto God,' is like an embryo of which the book is a harmonious development. There is nothing in the one that is absent from the other."

It is not strange that it has already been forecast that "a few decades hence this book will be recognized as one of the greatest devotional classics in the world."

With almost unabated vigor, Dr. Kuyper kept up his labors until shortly before the end. Standing by his death-bed, his friend and colleague asked him: "Shall I tell the people that God has been your Refuge and Strength to the end?" Though weak, the reply came at once in a distinct whisper: "Yes, altogether."

With grateful acknowledgment of a debt which can not be paid, these Meditations in their English dress are hereby affectionately dedicated to the memory of their sainted Author by the

TRANSLATOR

Epiphany Rectory,
  Walpole, Massachusetts.
    November 1, 1924.

PREFACE

As in everything that risks itself in the depth of mysticism, so in the preparation of these Meditations, lurked undeniable danger. The soul that seeks God involuntarily inclines to step across the boundary appointed of God, defined by the word "near," and to force an entrance into His Being. From the first I was on guard against this danger, and I believe I have escaped it. On the other hand, fear of this danger could not be allowed to repress that fervor and that spiritual warmth, which refreshes the soul only when the feelings are aroused and the imagination awakened. Mere thinking is not meditation, this is something quite different, and, in view of the wide-awake preparedness necessary to withstand the constant onslaught waged from the gates of hell against the Church of the living God, with a fierceness that neither respects nor spares, this *other something* is an undeniable need of the soul.

This onslaught puts one on his mettle to present counter arguments, philosophical refutation and keen-edged anti-criticism. But this, unless counter-balanced, confines our spirit to the world of thought, and thereby threatens to externalize our creed, our faith and our piety. Intellectualism produces, as it were, beautifully shaped, finely cornered and dazzlingly transparent ice-crystals. But underneath that ice the stream of the living water so easily runs dry. There may be gain in doctrinal abstractions, but true religion, as shown in the warm piety of the heart, suffers loss.

This is not necessary. The Fathers of the Church have set us an example. With them we find a virile gift of argument; but it is always permeated with ardent mysticism.

Contemplative thought, reflections and meditations on the soul's nearness unto God tend merely to correct the above-named error; tend to draw the soul away from the abstract in doctrine and life, back to the reality of religion; tend, with all due appreciation of "chemical" analysis of the spiritual waters, to lead the soul back to the living Fountain itself, from whence these waters flow.

Stress in creedal confession, without drinking of these waters, runs dry in barren orthodoxy, just as truly as spiritual emotion, without clearness in confessional standards, makes one sink in the bog of sickly mysticism.

Only he who feels, perceives and knows that he stands in personal fellowship with the living God, and who continually tests his spiritual experience by the Word, is safe. He exhibits strength, and maintains, for his part, the power of religion in his home, among his associates and in the world at large, and inspires with reverence even those who are despisers of God and his word.

My prayer is, that the Meditations here offered may establish, advance, or restore, such a healthy state of soul with many a child of God.

To have reached this end in the case of even one heart would furnish abundant reason for praise and thanksgiving.

KUYPER

The Hague, Netherlands.
June 1, 1908.

CONTENTS

CONTENTS

To Be Near Unto God

I

TO BE NEAR UNTO GOD

WHEN in holy ecstasy the Psalmist sings: "I love the Lord, because He has heard my voice and my supplication, he pours out his whole soul in this song, but no one can analyze that love.

To have love for God is something altogether different and something far weaker than to be able to say: "I love God."

You have love for your native land, you have love for the beauty and grandeur of nature, you have love for the creations of art, from the sense of compassion you have love for suffering humanity, you are conscious of love for what is noble, true and of good report, and thus in all honesty almost every man can say that he also has love for God, and that his love for God even exceeds all other loves, since all good that inspires love is from God, and God Himself is the highest good.

And yet while this love for God can be a lofty sentiment, can be deeply serious, and can even be able to ignite a spark of enthusiasm, the soul may have no fellowship with the Eternal, and have no knowledge of the secret walk with God; the great God may not have become *his* God, and the soul may never have exclaimed in passionate delight: "I love God!"

Love for God, taken in general, is still largely love for the idea of God, love for the Fountain of Life, for the Source of all good, for the Watcher of Israel Who never slumbers, for the One Who, whatever changes, eternally abides.

But when there echoes in the soul the words "I love God!" then the idea, the sense and the reality of the Eternal Being becomes personified. Then God becomes a Shepherd Who leads us, a Father Who spiritually begat us, a Covenant-God with Whom we are in league, a Friend Who offers us His friendship, a Lord in Whose service we stand, the God of our confidence, Who is no longer merely God but *our* God.

Thus for many years you may have had a general love for God and yet have never come to know God.

This knowledge of God only comes when love for Him begins to take on a personal character; when on the pathway of life for the first time you have *met* Him; when the Lord has become a Personal Presence by the side of your own self; when God and you have entered into a conscious, vital, personal, particular relationship—He your Father, you His child.

Not merely one of His children, no, but *His* child in an individual way, in a personal relation different from that of the other children of God, the most intimate fellowship conceivable in heaven and on earth—He your Father, your Shepherd, your bosom Friend and your God!

He who has not come to this, does not understand this. It goes too deep for him. And yet if he is religiously inclined, when he hears others talk about it, he senses that if he could attain unto such a love, his own love would be more tender than now he feels it to be.

This tells him that as yet he misses something. It may awaken in him a longing for it; a craving in him for that which would be so beautiful to possess.

And this craving can prepare the way for higher things. For when it comes to a meeting with God, the action proceeds from both sides. God comes to him, and he comes to

God. First from afar, then ever closer, until at length all distance falls away, and the meeting takes place—a moment of such blessedness as can never be expressed in words.

, Then, and only then, comes the "nearness." For everything hinges on that nearness, on that feeling, "it is good for me to be near unto God."

He also who has not entered into this secret, may say with others, "it is good for me to be near unto God" (Ps. 73, 27), but as yet he does not grasp it. He says it without thought. He thinks it means a pious frame of mind, but feels no slightest burning of a spark of this mystical, most intimate and personal love in his own heart. Adoration, worship, prayer for grace are there, but no attachment yet of love.

To be "near" is to be so close to God that your eye sees, your heart is aware of, and your ear hears him, and every cause of separation has been removed; near in one of two ways: either that you feel yourself, as it were, drawn up into heaven, or that God has come down from heaven to you, and seeks you out in your loneliness, in that which constitutes your particular cross, or in the joy that falls to your lot.

That word "near" implies that there is, Oh! so much that makes separation between you and your God; so much that makes you stand alone, feel desolate and forsaken, because either God is away from you or you are away from Him, so that it leaves you no rest, and you can not endure it. Then everything within you draws you to Him again, until that which made separation falls away. And then there follows the meeting; then He is near you, and you know once more that you are near Him.

Then there is blessedness again; blessedness that exceeds everything that can be imagined. Then it is good, Oh! so good—above all things else—to be *near* again to your God.

But this blessedness may be tasted only at rare moments in this life.

And then there remains the blessedness in the life that is eternal, when that nearness to your God shall continue forever. Eternally near Him in the Fatherhouse.

Cruel is the way in which the world thwarts you in this.

To escape from the world in hermitage or cell was not the solution, but you can understand what went on in the souls of those who, for the sake of unbroken fellowship with God, took this course.

It might have been the solution, if those who went out from the world had been able to leave the world behind. But we carry the world in our heart. It goes with us, because no hermitage is so well fortified, and no retreat in forests so distant, but Satan finds means to reach it.

Moreover, to shut oneself out from the world in order to be near unto God, is to claim for oneself here on earth what can only be our portion in the Fatherhouse. It is true that in seclusion one escapes a great deal. Much vanity the eye no longer sees. But existence becomes abnormal. Life becomes narrow. The "human" is reduced to small dimensions. There is no task; no more calling; no more exertion of all one's powers. The conflict is avoided, and therefore victory in the struggle tarries.

Nearness unto God here on earth yields its sweetest blessedness when it is cultivated in the face of sin and the world, as an oasis in the wilderness of life. And they against whom the world has turned most cruelly in order to turn them away from God, have attained the highest and the best, when in spite of every obstacle, and in the face of worldly opposition they have continued to hold tryst with God—like Jacob at Penuel, Moses in Mount Horeb, David when Shimei cursed him, and Paul when the people rose in uproar against him.

In the midst of the conflict to be near unto God is blessed, and also apart from the conflict with the world, or sin, or Satan, when clouds gather over your head, when adversity, loss and grief inflict wound upon wound in your heart, when the fig tree does not blossom, and the vine will yield no fruit, then with Habakkuk to rejoice in God, because His blessed nearness is enjoyed more in sorrow than in gladness, this has been the lesson of history in all times.

Not when in luxury and plenty David pleased himself, but when Saul persecuted him unto the death, did he sing his sweetest song for God.

Yet the world continues to be cruel. Its cruelty may assume an ever finer form, but in its refinement it becomes ever more painful.

In former times there were many things that reminded people of the sanctities of life, which of themselves provoked thought of higher interests and called eternity to mind.

All this is different now. In common life there is almost nothing that helps to retain the memory in the soul of the high, the holy and the eternal. In public life, every reflection of heaven is extinguished. No more days of fasting and prayer are appointed. No one may speak any more of God. No *memento mori* now reminds you of your death. Cemeteries are turned into parks. Sacred things are held up to ridicule. In conversation and in writing the dominant note is that heaven reaches no farther than the stars, that death ends all, and that life without God thrives as well, if not better, than life in the fear of the Lord.

And this discounting of God in public life throws itself as a stream between your God and your God-fearing heart. Your faith is strained in the measure in which you try, against the current of this stream, to hold yourself fast by God.

Especially to our young people, and to our dear children, this modern cruelty of the world is unspeakably dangerous.

But be of good courage.

God knows it, and in His eternal compassion He will come nearer, closer, and more quickly to you and to your dear ones, in order that even amidst these trying conditions of modern life you and they may be near unto Him. But then there must be no peace by compromise, or more than ever will a vague love for a far distant God desert you.

That which alone can save is taking part in that life of secret fellowship, which enables you to say "I love God," and then you will not remain standing afar off, but press on to ever closer nearness to God, in the personal meeting of your soul with the Eternal.

II

THE SOULS WHICH I HAVE MADE

THERE is subtle charm about the thing that we have made, and this is by no means always because of its intrinsic value, but rather because we have made it ourselves.

He who has studied portrait painting and for the sake of perfecting himself in his art copies celebrated originals, puts a value on his copy, which, in his estimation, the far more beautiful original does not possess.

Flowers which a lad has gathered from his own little garden are more interesting to him than a bouquet from the florist. The country gentleman prefers vegetables from his own gardens or hothouse, even if the quality is nothing special as compared with that of the produce imported from abroad. A contributor to a monthly or quarterly periodical deems his own article, when it comes out, the best of that number. This holds good in every department of life. There is no end of interest in produce that we ourselves have raised. Cattle bred on our own stock farm are preferred to any other. We are more happy in a house that we ourselves have built.

This may involve a little too much self-complacency, which especially in the transition period of life not infrequently breeds conceit. It must also be granted that affection for our own handiwork may go too far if from sheer egotism it makes us indifferent to better work from other hands.

And yet, though too much self-complacency may play a part in this, this is not the principal trait that dominates the preference that is given to a product of one's own.

This is felt at once when you reckon with mother-joy which revels in play with her own child in a way that no woman can in play with the child of another.

Truly, self-delusion and selfishness play all too frequently anything but a subordinate part in this joy of the mother-heart over her own child; but history of all ages, and folk-lore of all lands bear witness, that an altogether different string from that of selfishness vibrates in this wealth of mother-love, and that the music peculiar to this other string is only understood when the sacred fact is brought to mind that it is she who bore the child.

In her own child the mother sees, and is conscious of, a part of her own life. The child does not stand by the side of the mother as number one alongside of number two, but in the child the mother-life is extended.

This selfsame trait asserts itself in every product of our own, whether it be our own thought, knowledge, exertion, will-power or perseverance; and whether it be our own article that we sent to the press, our own house that we built, our own picture that we painted, our own embroidery that we embroidered, our own flower that we raised, or our own hound or race-horse that we bred, there is always something in it of our *own*, a distinctive something that we imprint upon it, an individual stamp that we have put upon it, something that makes us feel about it as we can never feel about anything that we ourselves have not made.

And by this trait of our human heart God comforts the sinner. That trait is in us because it is in God. And of this trait God says that it operates in the Divine Father-heart for our good, because where there is a soul at stake, God can never forget that He Himself has made it.

For I will not contend forever, neither will I be always wroth; for the spirit should fail before me, and *the souls which I have made* (Is. lvii, 16).

As little as a mother can allow her just anger with the child of her own bosom to work itself out to the end, just so little can God's displeasure with a soul exhaust itself, because *He Himself has made it.*

As a father pitieth his children, so the Lord pitieth them that fear Him (Ps. 103, 13). Though a mother may forget her sucking child, "yet will I not forget thee" (Isa. xlix, 15).

The Father-name of God expresses completely this self-same richly comforting thought. It implies not merely that a father loves, and that God loves too, but that God's love for you springs from the same fact from which springs the love of father or mother for their children, to wit: the fact that God has created and formed you, and has made the soul that is in you.

That you have been created after God's Image, declares that by virtue of your creation, God feels Himself related to you; that He finds something of Himself in you, and because you are His own product, His own creature, His own handiwork, you are, and remain, an object of His Divine interest.

Because God has made your soul, there is something in it of God Himself, a Divine stamp has been impressed upon you; there is something of God's power, thought, and creative genius in you, as in no other. You are one of the Lord's own works of art, precisely like which He created none other. Imagine for a moment that you had ceased to exist, then something would be wanting in the rich collection of the Lord. And from this originates a tie between God and your soul, whereby you are a star in His firmament, which the Father of spirits can not do without.

And therefore God seeks that which is lost.

An artist who had a collection of his paintings on exhibition in a museum, and discovered one day that one of his pictures was gone, could not rest until it had been traced and restored to its place on the wall.

So does God miss every soul that falls away from Him, because it is a soul that He has made; and what Jesus described in such touching and beautiful terms in the parables of the lost penny, the lost sheep, and the prodigal son, was born in His heart from the one thought, that God can not let go of the work of His hands, and therefore can not unconcernedly leave the souls of sinners as the prey of perdition, because they are His handiwork, and because *He Himself has made them.*

And therein consists also the grievousness of sin.

If on entering the museum one morning the afore-mentioned artist saw that under cover of night some ruffian had wantonly cut all his paintings with a knife, his bitterness of soul would know no bounds, not merely because of the treasures of art that had been ruined, but because that which had been ruined was what he himself had made.

And this bitter grief is inflicted upon God, when a soul falls away from Him.

The soul that He has made, has inwardly been torn asunder by sin, and is bruised and wounded almost beyond recognition.

And more than this, as often as by yielding to sin we ruin our soul still further, it is at the same time, an injury done to Him because He Himself has made it.

To ruin your own soul, or the soul of your children, or that of others by your example or by willful seduction, is to spoil the work that God has made, and to wound Him in the likeness of Himself, that He has wrought in it.

It is as though you took a child, and before the eyes of his mother struck him down, and maimed him for life. It is to defy the love of the Maker for His handiwork, willfully giving offense, and grieving the Maker in that about which His heart is most sensitive.

To him, therefore, whose heart is fixed, this saying of the Lord's: "the souls that I have made," has a twofold meaning.

First: the blessed consolation, that, provided you believe, the displeasure of the Lord with the soul that He has made shall not be without end. And secondly: the wholesome stimulus it gives not to restlessly poison the soul by sin, but to favor it, to spare it; not to sin against it, but to shield it from corrupting influences, because your soul is one that belongs to God, because He has made it.

The confession that God created man after His own Image does not fathom the depth of the thought. The plummet goes far deeper. The saving and uplifting power of this article of faith is only felt, when every morning you begin the new day with the fresh realization of the thought, that the soul that dwells within you is a work of Divine art, and that your soul is one that God has made, in which His honor is involved, over which His holy jealousy watches, and which you can not make an instrument of sin, without laying violent hands upon that towards which God sustains a personal relation, because He Himself has made it.

Forsooth, it does not say anything but that you should know that you are a child of God, but it says it in a more gripping way; it tells you that the child that in sin denies his Father, touches Him in His honor, and grieves His Father-heart.

III

NOT RICH TOWARD GOD

JESUS understood the seriousness of the conflict between
God and money, which constantly presses itself upon us;
and one may safely say, that in our Western lands this conflict is more fierce than it ever was in the Eastern regions
where Jesus ministered, and where the ordinary wants of
life are more easily satisfied than with us.

We do not realize how largely life itself is dominated by
money. Put all desire for wealth aside, love simplicity,
and even then life is different and unfolds itself differently
when financially you have a moderately free hand, than
when from early morning till late at night you have to
work hard for sheer sustenance of self and family.

To be intent upon making money may soon become a
sinful passion, and at length may make the slave of money
lose all sense of honor. Yet to be intent upon increasing
one's financial means in itself is easily understood and
entirely above blame. Only think how much this means
with respect to the education of your children, your own.
development and the advancement of the Kingdom of
God.

Money is an extraordinary power; and in times of pressing need the lack of it makes one painfully helpless.

The influence of money, therefore, upon a sinful, unconverted heart is exceedingly great. Again and again you
see even a converted child of God caught in the snares.
What then must be the fatal influence of money upon a
human heart that, even though it entertain intentions that
are more ideal, has never come to a definite choice of God
and of His Christ.

32

To ensnare such people, money and Satan join forces, and this gives rise to Mammon. At first one may try to separate money from Mammon, but in the long run it can not be done. Money is a power in your hand; but before you are aware it becomes a power over you, a power that dominates you and that, whether you will or no, draws you ever farther away from what is high and noble, and subjects you to the power of Mammon.

Jesus saw this. He fathomed to the bottom the deep shamefulness of it, its desecration of human nature, and in Divine compassion for this gilded slavery He again and again called the multitude that flocked to hear Him, from Mammon back to God.

Only in this sharp contrast lies the power of resisting the tyranny of money.

If you are truly subject to God, money will be subject to you and will not harm you.

If, on the other hand, you undertake to defend yourself against the fatal influence of your money and its seductive power, you are lost before you know it, and deeming that you are your own master, you have found your master in the money-power.

Jesus therefore contrasts two kinds of riches with one another—riches in money, or riches toward God.

Not, that the one excludes the other. If you are rich toward God, it will not harm you to be also rich in this world's goods. For then you know yourself as steward of the Almighty, and the money will serve you, and, through you, it will serve God.

You can also be rich toward God and poor toward the world, and be contented and happy, and revel in your far higher riches of soul.

To be poor toward God and rich toward the world, on the other hand, is nothing but a false show, a parade of wealth and pleasures that envelope you without refining your inner self, and which at your death, if not before, fall away and leave your soul empty and shorn.

And it is still harder to be poor toward God and poor toward the world. Then there is nothing to supply the wants of life. Nothing to sustain you. Only a biting discontent, that ruins your entire inner existence. Then full of vexation and carping care, life to you is shorn of every attraction.

What is it to be rich toward God?

To understand this, imagine for a moment everything you call yours in the world as taken from you. Picture yourself abandoned and forgotten of all, in utter isolation alone with your own heart. And then ask yourself: What have I now? What do I now possess?

When dying you will come to this. In solitariness of soul you will go into eternity. What then will you carry with you? Money and goods you must leave behind. You must even part with your body, and retain nothing but your soul, your heart, your spiritual self within. Will you go into eternity poor or will your heart then be rich? It can no longer be rich in this world. It can only be rich in spiritual good. You will die poor, or you will die rich— toward God.

If such will be the case at death, then examine yourself now; think yourself deprived of all you have; take your soul by itself and ask: "What have I now? What do I own? Do worldly possessions impart worth to me as man, or am I something by myself? Do I own anything in the hidden places of my heart, which gives worth and significance to myself, or am I by myself actually nothing?"

Let no one deceive himself in this.

Without avarice, it is possible for any one to enrich his spirit with knowledge, to develop a talent for art, to excel by cleverness and versatility. All this has worth and meaning, and is not apart from God. Only it is all merely concerned with this life, and when life here ends loses its meaning; only so much remains, as has imparted a higher, nobler bent to your character. Whatever has established and enlarged our personality, character and inward strength, that and nothing else has become our personal property, of which neither catastrophe nor death can deprive us.

But without more this will not avail.

A fully developed personality, a well established character, inward strength of spirit, and will-power, all these are only a benefit when you can use them for good. Satan is the most strongly developed personality imaginable. It is seen with great frequency to what lengths a man can develop himself in evil.

Hence the question is, have you developed those powers of personality, and those traits of character, that are adapted to the life of eternal blessedness? If not, at death your other achievements will be of no use to you. There are strongly developed characters and cultivated talents in hell; but these bring no blessedness, they rather add to the misery, because they are apart from God and provide no riches toward Him.

Thus your heart, by itself, can speak of "owning property" only when you have developed in yourself those powers and capacities that will be used in heaven, that will make you feel at home there, and that will enable you to develop still further powers in the heavenly realm.

You can not acquire these powers save as you enter into fellowship with God. Through God the powers of the Kingdom must operate in you, which will fit you for heavenly citizenship. In Christ you must be reconciled to God; the Father must come and make His abode with you;

and then that other life will spring up in your heart that is fed from heaven, that enriches you with higher power, and satisfies the cravings of your inner emptiness—with God.

Then you become possessor of the riches which God pours out into your heart.

To be rich toward God is to own God Himself, to be a temple of the Holy Ghost, to carry about in your heart the Holy and Glorious One whithersoever you go, and every morning and evening to be refreshed anew at the Fountain of the water of life.

There is still on earth, Oh, so much that prevents you from enjoying this blessedness to the full; but it is nevertheless the privilege of being rich toward God that the more you become detached from the world the more these riches increase. And when at last the world fades from sight their increase will still be endless.

It is a wealth that can not be used up, but ever increases itself. It is interest upon interest in the holiest sense. It is always the Fountain and never the cistern—a wealth which always exceeds boldest expectations, because it is to be rich in the *Infinite*.

And then of course there is the inheritance.

Again and again Scripture refers you to it.

There is an inheritance of the saints in light, and he who is rich toward God is additionally enriched with this inheritance.

The difference between being rich in God and this inheritance depends upon the difference between the inward and the outward life.

Riches toward God are inward. "Now already in part. Presently yet more."

But in addition to this inward state of being rich toward God, there also belongs a being rich in an outward state.

And this as long as we are here we still lack; but that shall come when the inheritance shall be divided which now is being kept for you in heaven.

An inheritance of glory. An environment of elect persons and elect angels only. A dwelling in palaces of everlasting light. A fruition in glory such as here has never entered the heart.

No more sin and no more sorrow.

Eternally in Christ with our God in the fullest, richest satisfaction of what our human heart in its best moments can desire or expect.

Rich toward God and therefore rich *through* God.

Oh! how deeply have we fallen, that this being rich toward God charms so few people, and that those who are charmed by it still hunger so often for the things that draw away from God and therefore impoverish our person.

IV

IN THE COVERT OF THY WINGS

THE deepest question that governs our Christian life is that which touches our personal fellowship with God. And in the Book of Psalms, which is the richest outpouring of a devout heart, you see how the inmost longings ever and again go out after this Divine fellowship.

Certainly there is in the Book of Psalms also a mention of *the tie* that binds us to God as the Creator and Supporter of all things; and of the *relation* in which by faith he who fears God stands to the Holy One; but both this tie and this relation are still something else than *fellowship* with the Eternal.

The heart of him who fears God does not rest until it has come to such a conscious fellowship with its God, that between itself and the heart of God there is mutual knowledge, the one of the other—even the clear sense that God has knowledge of us and we of Him.

What we between people call mutual companionship, intimate association, union of soul with soul in faithfulness and in love, is implied from of old in Psalm 25, 14: "The secret of the Lord is with them that fear him; and he will show them his covenant."

Even as two intimately connected friends go through life together, and mutually unbosom themselves to each other, and in this intimate walk through life become the confidents of each other's secrets, so it is told of Old Testament heroes of the faith that they "*walked with God.*"

And although these are but figures and terms borrowed from those that are used to describe human happenings;

and although, when we would describe our appreciation of our fellowship with our God, we should never use these terms and figures except with deep reverence for His Divine Majesty, nevertheless, it is equally certain that God Himself has pointed them out to us for this end.

The Scripture sets the example in this, even to the extent that it borrows pictures from animal-life by which to illustrate this fellowship with God. As Jesus portrayed His tender love for Jerusalem by the figure of a hen that gathers her chickens under her wings, so David not only said that he would abide in the tabernacle of the Lord for ever, but also that he would trust under the covert of God's wings (Ps. 61, 4).

And why not?

Is it not God Himself Who in the world of winged creatures has created this exhibition of tender fellowship, as the expression of what moved His own Divine heart? And is not every such expressive, touching picture of love's fellowship in nature a God-given help by which to interpret to ourselves what we perceive and feel, or only dimly sense, in the mystic depths of the heart?

Even the vast range of creation falls short of material for this, and therefore the Lord has purposely placed still another picture before us, by which to illustrate the intimacy of fellowship with Himself; even that of living together in one house.

The house, or with nomadic tribes the tent, was not, of course, a part of creation, but was mechanically constructed by human hands. When Jabal came to do this, the social life of man took an incredible step forward.

The house, as the family dwelling, was foreshadowed in creation. Jesus called attention to the fact that foxes have holes and birds of the air have nests. And was there no deep sense of want expressed in the words that He, the Son of man, had no home of His own wherein to lay his head?

Intimacy of life is only born from dwelling together under one rooftree; the family home is the nursery of love; it is the external hedging in, with the tie of the most intimate fellowship of life.

And in Scripture the house, or dwelling, is presented as a means by which to make our fellowship with God assume a definite form. God also has a house; and the idea of dwelling in the house of our God is the richest thought that is given us, to set forth the most intimate and tenderest fellowship with Him.

Purposely, therefore, the Tabernacle of the Lord is erected in the wilderness, and presently it is rendered permanent in the Temple on Mount Zion. Moreover, it is stated, that at Horeb God Himself showed Moses the pattern of the Tabernacle. Hence Tabernacle and Temple were actual representations of what exists in heaven.

And in connection with this, the ardent longing to dwell in the house of the Lord finds expression in the Psalms. The Psalmist would rather be a doorkeeper in the house of God, than dwell in the palaces of the ungodly (Ps. 84, 10).

"One thing have I desired of the Lord, that will I seek after; that I may dwell in the house of the Lord all the days of my life; to behold the beauty of the Lord, and to enquire in his temple" (Ps. 27, 4).

But this was not permanent. Tabernacle and Temple rendered only temporary service. They were a transient form in the rich unfolding of consecrated life. And when Jesus came He said: "Woman, the hour cometh, and now is, when ye shall neither in this mountain, nor yet at Jerusalem, worship the Father, but when true worshippers shall worship the Father in spirit and in truth" (John iv, 21, 23). This means that without emblems, symbols, or outward forms, worship shall be spiritual, as from heart to heart.

If, therefore, we feel a holy sympathy for David's burning desire, to dwell in the house of the Lord, we may not apply this to any earthly house, not even to the visible Church. That would be the return to the dispensation of shadows. That temple is no longer a symbolic house of God made of wood and stone, but the majestic palace of God in the heavens.

God dwelleth in the heavens. *There* is the Tabernacle of his Majesty. *There* is the Temple of his Honor. When Jesus teaches us to pray, "Our Father, who art in Heaven," He detaches the soul from everything earthly, and lifts up our heart on high, in order that we shall no more think in earthly terms of the Majesty of our God.

To dwell in the house of the Lord all the days of our life, means: every morning, noon and night to be so clearly conscious of our fellowship with the Living God, that our thoughts go out to Him, that we hear the sound of His voice in our soul, that we are aware of His sacred presence round about us, that we experience His operations upon our heart and conscience, and shun everything we would not dare to do in His immediate presence.

The Psalmist goes one step further, which plainly shows that already under the Old Covenant, amid the shadows, the faithful grasped the higher reality. For, he adds, "I will take refuge *in the covert of Thy wings*" (Ps. 61, 4. R. V.)

To think of the glory of God above, to picture life in His holy Temple, to have walks among angels and saints before the white throne, is not yet enough. The house of the Lord may enclose our fellowship with Him, but in that house we shall look for God Himself.

One must live with a person in his house, in order to enjoy his company, the house is nothing to us without him, and he is our first and chief concern in it.

Such is the case with our search after fellowship with God.

"*Sursum corda!*"—lift up your hearts. I will lift up my heart to the trysting-place of Thy holiness.

But this is not the end. In order to find God, we must dwell in His house. To be near unto Him in His house is the sole end and aim of all godly desire and endeavor.

And to express this in terms of passionate tenderness and daring boldness, David exclaims: "I will take refuge in the covert of Thy wings." Here soul meets soul; here is the sacred touch; here one perceives, and experiences, and realizes that nothing stands between ourselves and our God; that His arms embrace us, and that we cleave unto Him.

But his imagery is attended with danger lest it be taken too literally, and God, in an unholy sense, be interpreted in terms of matter. False mysticism has shown to what errors this may lead.

But if you realize this, and are on your guard, this imagery is supremely rich and superbly glorious.

It means that you possess God Himself, and that you have made fellowship with Him a reality. Provided that it is in Christ, by your Savior alone, that you, the impure and unholy, are initiated into this tender fellowship with your God.

V

WHEN HE TURNETH HIMSELF UNTO THE PRAYER

How is this? Does the Lord turn Himself unto our prayer only after long delay? Is not He omnipresent? Is not every whispered and stammering prayer known to Him, before there is yet a word in the tongue? How then can the All-knowing One at first indifferently stand apart and only gradually become aware that we are praying to Him, and turn Himself to the prayer which He temporarily ignored?

And yet without doubt this is what is meant. The Psalmist stands before a closed heaven. In sorrow of soul supplication is made, but trouble is not removed, and God contends against the prayer of His people. The arch enemy does not pray, does not understand God, but in this he is encouraged by Jehovah. God's own covenant people continue to be repulsed. God hides His face. And the Psalmist cries: "O Lord hear my prayer and let my cry come unto Thee. Hide not Thy face from me. In the day when I call, answer me speedily" (Ps. 102, 1, 2).

This relieves his troubled mind. With prophetic daring he forecasts the day when the Lord will hear the prayer of his people again, and inspired by this thought declares: "When the Lord turneth him unto the prayer of the destitute, and despiseth not their desire, then all kings of the earth shall fear him" (Ps. 102, 17, Dutch Ver.).

Thus in fact he was still in a period, when the Lord holds Himself deaf to His people, and the future still holds the moment in which the Lord shall turn Himself unto the supplication of His people.

What do you think? Has not the Psalmist felt and known the objections that rise from the very Being of God against this human representation, and do you stand on a so much higher plane that thoughts arise in you, that were foreign to him?

But pray, who has portrayed in terms of finer imagery than he the omnipresence and omniscience of God? Are not the expressions in which you clothe your prayers borrowed for the most part from his writings? Did not he propound the question: "Shall he who planted the ear, not hear?" and did not he say in the hundred and thirty-ninth Psalm, "There is not a word in my tongue, but, lo, O Lord, thou knowest it altogether. Thou hast beset me behind and before. Such knowledge is too wonderful for me; it is high, I can not attain unto it?"

In fact, it is the Psalmist who has described the virtues of God in behalf of all Christendom, and the secret things of the Almighty are nowhere placed before us, veiled or unveiled, more clearly than in his language.

And when this eminently saintly poet over and over again speaks to us of God, also in connection with this matter of prayer, in a way that is so purely human, what else then can it mean, save that the terms of intimacy between man and man retain their significance in the secret walk with God; and that therefore there are moments, when God turns Himself away from our prayer, and that, Praise His Name, there are moments when He turns Himself unto our prayer.

You believe in Christ, and in the truth of His saying: "He that hath seen me, hath seen the Father, and how sayest thou then: show us the Father?" You yourself kneel down before Him, saying: "My Lord and my God," and what is the Incarnation of the Word other than that God became Man? And what profit can this be to you, unless you feel that, in Christ, God has come to you in a *human* way.

Until the birth in Bethlehem, God spoke to you in *human words*, but in Christ God appears to you in *human nature*. He reveals Himself to you as the Son of Man. A human heart here speaks in human language and in human motions. S. John declares: "In Jesus we have seen and heard not only what is God's, but we have touched and handled, and actually seen before our eyes the eternal-Divine in human stature and in human form."

The whole Christian faith, the entire Christian confession rests upon the clear conviction, that God has not laid it upon you to lose Him in endless abstractions, but, on the contrary, He would come to you ever more closely in human form and in human language, in order through your human heart to make warm, rich fellowship possible with Himself.

Moreover, you must understand that all this rests upon sober reality. It is not semblance, but actual fact, because God created you *after His Image*, so that with all the wide difference between God and man, divine reality is expressed in human form. And that, when the Word became Flesh, this Incarnation of the Son of God was immediately connected with your creation after God's Image.

And you would undo all this when in the place of this warm, rich fellowship with God which can not be practised except in a human way, you would put a whole system of abstract ideas about the immensity of God, and so create a distance between Himself and you which excludes all intercourse and fellowship of soul.

Leave this to philosophers who do not practice prayer; to theologians, dry as dust, who are no children of their Father in heaven. As for you, love God with a love, of which childlike fellowship with Him is the warm expression.

You know yourself that the practice of prayer puts the seal upon the words of the Psalmist. At one time, heaven is open to you, and as you pray angels descend and ascend to present your petitions at the Throne of God. At another time your prayer is formal and your words come back upon yourself, and the circuit of heaven, as Job (xxii: 14) calls it, is closed against you.

Then the turning point is reached in this oppressive isolation, and you perceive that the gate of heaven opens once again, and your prayer obtains free access to the Throne of the Almighty, and you understand from your own experience what the Psalmist here affirms regarding the blessedness of the moment in which the Lord turns Himself again unto the prayer of a soul that is utterly destitute.

But is the solution of this apparent contradiction as impossible as it seems? By no means, provided you have eyes to see the workings of God in your prayer-life.

Yea, when you deem that prayer originates with yourself; when you do not believe that the spirit of prayer goes out from your God within you, and you think that God's active part in your prayer only begins when He hears and answers it, then indeed you face here an insoluble riddle.

But if you take it in the other, truer way, and make it clear to yourself that your prayer-life too is quickened, directed and carried on in you by God, then light shines in upon you.

The farmer sows the seed in the newly ploughed furrows, and leaves it quietly to do its work, in order that when dew and sunshine from heaven have caused the seed to sprout and send the blade upward, and ripen the corn in the ear, he may return to the field and gather in his harvest.

And is not this the case in our prayer-life? Here too our Father Who is in heaven takes the initiative by sowing the seed of prayer in our heart. Then follows a slow process. That prayer-life must come to development in us, and prayer in our soul must ripen. And only when this result has been obtained, and prayer has unfolded itself in us into that higher form, the heavenly Husbandman turns Himself again to the prayer-life in us; and then comes the rich hearing and answering of what went up from our soul to Him.

Such is the case with our prayer-life taken as a whole. Through foolish prayers we come to purified prayers. Through earthly prayers we come to those holier ones, which have been watered with dew from above and which radiate sunlight of a higher order.

And such is the case with individual, particular prayers. These, too, are not at once purified and made perfect. These, too, go through a process in the soul. These, too, spring up from a root, and only by degrees develop themselves into prayer such as our Father Who is in heaven expects of His child; prayer which is not merely a sound of the lips, but rises from the depths of the heart; prayer, in which one's own sense and inclinations agree; prayer in which not merely a spontaneous thought but our whole person expresses itself; prayer, in which in very truth the soul pours itself out before the Holy One.

For this, God allows us time. It is not done all at once. If His response were immediate, no prayer-life would be developed within us, and no single prayer would be sanctified in us. Weeds that spring up between our prayers must first be rooted out. Every sort of infectious germ that creeps in must be removed. And prayer must refine itself, it must sanctify itself, so that in a heavenly sense by faith it may be able to ripen.

Therefore God leaves you to yourself for a time, so that by the trial of His seeming indifference the development may the better be prospered. And when at length your prayer has reached that degree of perfection which renders it meet, as a prayer of a saint of God, to be laid on the altar, then He turns Himself again to your prayer; and you offer thanks to your Father in heaven, that He has trained you in that holy school of prayer.

VI

HEARKEN UNTO ME, MY PEOPLE. GIVE HEED TO ME, O LORD!

In times past it was commonly believed that sound itself came from the throat, and that its power was but limited. Hence a word could only be heard at a short distance, farther away it could not be heard, and so we were cut off from those with whom we desired to speak. He who had anything to say from a distance, sent a messenger, and later, when the great invention of writing was made, the message was carried by a letter.

Since then, however, all this has been changed. Now it is known that our throat has no sound of its own, but it enables us to make vibrations in the air, and these vibrations find in the ear of him who listens an artistically constructed instrument that receives them.

When we speak, we transmit our thoughts in these vibrations. Along the airwaves they glide to the ear of him who hears us, and through the ear they quicken the selfsame thoughts in him. Thus we speak.

But this is not all.

It was discovered that apart from throat and ear, and at a very much farther distance, communication could be established by means of visible signs, and thus telegraphy originated. Then it was found that a like contact of throat upon ear could be obtained along an extended metal thread; which discovery brought us the telephone.

And now still greater advances have been made. It has been demonstrated that intelligent communication can be transmitted through the air, without the aid of wires, and thoughts have been exchanged at distances of thousands of miles.

Thus things which in former times were altogether unthinkable have now become reality. And when we consider how quickly these more and more wonderful inventions have followed one another, it is plain that still further developments can be looked for, and that dealing with people at incredible distances will yet, perhaps, become the common practice.

This now comes to the help of our weak faith.

That the Lord is simultaneously a God at hand and a God afar off (Jer. xxiii, 23) expresses in prophetical language the fact that before God all distance falls away, and that He can speak to us and can hear our voice, even though heaven is His throne and we kneel here on earth; yea, though we whisper a prayer under our breath, which he who stands by our side can not hear.

Faith had no other explanation for this than the question: "He that planted the ear, shall he not hear?" and "shall He Who formed the voice, not speak?" (Ps. 94, 9).

Confidence was based upon the confession of God's omnipresence, and upon the fact that He is the *All-knowing One;* but there was nothing in this that supported and carried the imagination.

And it is *this* which has become altogether different.

Now that it has become possible for us, impotent creatures, to extend our voice across whole continents and make ourselves intelligible to one another; now that, even without the help of wires, exchange of thought has become possible at distances of many thousands of miles; and everything tends to show that this is but the beginning of a communication which shall be yet further developed, we now can have some idea of the way in which this communication can at length endlessly extend itself, and how the

Lord our God, Who has the absolute disposal of all these means, inasmuch as He created them, from the Throne of His Glory can look down upon us and can whisper to us in the soul. And how, on the other hand, when, however weak, our voice goes out to Him in supplication, it can be heard by Him, since all distance that separates us falls away.

As regards the life of glory among the redeemed, it becomes more and more clear to us, that in that life communication shall not only be possible from time to time with a few, but that when once every limitation of our temporal life falls away and that life of glory begins, communication with all God's saints shall be possible at one and the same time.

Even then, it will all be the expression and the working out of the fact of our creation after the Divine Image. It will not be in the same way that God has communication with us now, but it will be a communication in a *similar* way. And now that even we ourselves can speak with our fellowmen at such incredible distances, it seems to bring us closer to God in our prayer, and God Himself closer to us when He speaks. And the "*Hearken* unto me, my people," followed by the prayer, "*Give heed* to me, O Lord," has become more real to us.

In our secret walk with God, if we may so express ourselves, there is still a wholly different phase, even that of sacred ardor that springs from the indwelling of the Holy Ghost in us. As often as this indwelling operates, there is no distance between us and God. Then the Lord speaks to us in the inner chamber of the heart; then we are aware of His holy presence, not afar off, but close by, and our speaking to Him is the confidential whisper as from mouth into ear. Such is the case at close of day, when higher peace fills the heart, and the blessed enjoyment of being God's child brings us a hushed ecstasy.

But we do not deal with this phase now. We here speak of the man who truly believes, but who, either by sin or trouble, has in part lost the consciousness of being God's child, and finds himself at a far distance from God, and God far distant from him; a condition of the soul that constantly presents itself in this life, even with those who are most saintly. And then it seems that at first God does *not* hear, and as though we have to call on Him that He may hear again the voice of our supplication.

"Give heed to me, O Lord," is the soul's cry of him who feels as though God pays no attention to his prayer. And in the same way, when by Isaiah God says: "Hearken unto me, my people," it means that at first the people give no heed to the speaking of the Lord.

Both these cries, therefore, belong to the phase of temporary estrangement, when fellowship between God and our soul, and between our soul and God has been interrupted by sin or by sore trial. Then communication must be established again. In the parlance of the telephone, God then rings us up, and we call up God, that He may listen to us. And so the broken connection restores itself.

Communication, fellowship with God, is the great sanctifying and protecting power, that holds us up in life. It is not we apart here below, and God far distant in heaven above, so that but a few moments of the long day we remember Him on our knees; but it is constant, continuous fellowship with our Father in heaven, as little as possible disturbed or broken, and this is the secret of the faith-power of God's child.

In former times, when life was less hurried and less busy, this was easier than now. Life in the present time subjects our nerves to so great a strain, and overwhelms us restlessly with such new sensations, that the quiet collecting of the soul before God becomes ever less frequent; and it is for this reason that in our times the hidden walk with God suffers loss.

But there lies a counterpoise in these new discoveries of world-wide communication. They help to impart a feeling of reality to our effort to restore the broken connection, in a way that was not possible before.

And so these discoveries of science become a support to the life of our devotions. Our hearkening unto God can gain by them, and our prayer, "O Lord, give heed unto me and hear the voice of my supplication," can derive strength from them in our approach to the Throne of God.

VII

THAT WHICH I SEE NOT TEACH THOU ME

THE knowledge which you have of yourself, or of your inner existence, differs according to its source; a part of it you acquired yourself, and a part of it you received from God.

If you ask wherein these two parts of your self-knowledge differ, then call to mind *this* difference. You diligently acquire knowledge of the good there is in you, whereas the evil that dwells in you must be brought to your remembrance and pointed out to you by God.

You see this in a child. The praise he receives is readily accepted and fondly cherished; but when he is corrected, he resents it, does not believe that he did wrong, and makes light of it. And he continues in this course until his conscience taught by God, awakens his self-accusation.

In later life, this goes on more covertly, but in reality the process is the same. The heart then is not so much carried on the tongue as in childhood's years, though some succeed in making their inner life manifest to the eyes of others. But no sooner is the personal life disclosed to the ear of a friend, than the same result is reached. There is a part of our self-knowledge which we have acquired ourselves; but there is also another part, which we ourselves perhaps had neglected, but which through hard lessons in the conscience has been taught us by God. At times this difference is strikingly evident, because for the most part we begin not only by not seeking this instruction from the conscience, but by not desiring it, and we only submit to it when God inculcates this knowledge against our will.

In some instances God is obliged—we say it reverently —to force this self-knowledge upon people all their lives; they simply will not learn it; yea, and even worse than this, they deliberately reject a part of what God taught them about themselves, by forgetting it.

There are others, on the other hand, men and women who in all honesty want clear self-knowledge, and who sincerely seek to know the truth regarding themselves. Nathaniels, who do not court flattery, but shun it; who hate the false image of themselves which they see dimly in the glass, and who can not rest until they know themselves as they truly are. When God speaks in the conscience there is with them a willing, listening ear. They take this lesson of God as a warning, and they profit by it.

Add higher grace to this, and the gains will be still greater. Then the ear is not merely willing to listen when God speaks, but the lesson of God in the conscience is earnestly sought, and the level is reached of the pregnant prayer: "Aside from what I myself see and discover in myself, *teach thou me*, O God." (Job xxxiv, 32, Dutch Ver.).

You find these two parts of our knowledge in every domain. There is always on the one hand a part that we acquire ourselves, and on the other hand a part that God gives us.

To *see* is to observe, and commonly therefore we call this first part of our knowledge that which is founded upon observation. By the side of this stands another part of knowledge, which man never could have acquired of himself, but which God has taught him.

This is the case with all human knowledge. Everywhere and in all ages man observes, gains information, investigates, enriches his experience, and thus acquires a certain knowledge of nature and of life, which he turns into profit.

With respect to this, one nation has a keener eye, a finer ear, higher powers of invention and more perseverance; in consequence of which it makes greater strides in development. But in the main all this knowledge rests upon what man sees. It is founded upon observation. It is developed by thought.

In addition to this there is a further knowledge which God imparts directly, and in a twofold way. In the first place, by raising up among nations men of genius; and in the second place, by the grant of discoveries. Men of genius are creations of God which he bestows upon a people, and by these men of superior endowment human knowledge has been deepened and enriched in a measure such as would never have been possible without them.

The same is the case with the great discoveries, in which there is always a mystery; discoveries which open up entirely new realms of knowledge; discoveries which we owe to what unbelief calls chance, but which he who believes gratefully attributes to Divine appointment.

Here another thought presents itself.

When idealism is shown by individuals or peoples, that high aim is one of the strongest possible motives to seek after truth and knowledge. He who misses this idealistic sense may have a thirst for plain, materialistic knowledge, but the knowledge of the higher things in human life leaves him cold and indifferent. A money-fiend is an adept in the knowledge that promises gain; but what does such a gold-slave care for the higher knowledge of the nobler elements of our human life? As little as a deaf man cares for the wondrous creations of a Bach, or a blind man for the art of a Raphael or Rembrandt.

As this is true of individuals, so it is also true of nations. When a people fail of this idealistic sense they degenerate into materialism and sensualism, and shut themselves off from all higher life. They make no advance and can not enrich other nations. They even deteriorate, and not infrequently in their own decline drag other nations down with them.

In this, one age may differ from another in the same nation. In the sixteenth century the Netherlands stood especially high and was an inspiration to all Western Europe. In the eighteenth century, on the other hand, they degenerated, and have in no way blessed other nations.

Whether such an idealistic sense operates strongly and inspiringly in a people, depends upon God. When He sends forth the breath of such higher aims upon a people, they begin to live for nobler ends, and become enriched with the knowledge of purer human existence. When He takes that breath away, understanding is dulled and all nobler knowledge fails.

Through this idealistic sense, God can draw a people unto Himself, and can communicate to them something of the warmth of His own Divine Life; but He can also withdraw Himself from a people, surrender them to themselves, and then they must pay the price of the loss of all higher and nobler knowledge.

So we arrive again at the same result. There is a part of our knowledge, which we, looking around and observing, have in our own power; but there is also a part of human knowledge, even a knowledge of a higher and nobler order which God alone imparts unto a people.

Apply this to yourself, to individual persons, and you feel at once that the knowledge which God brings springs by no means exclusively from the conscience, but altogether differently and on a far larger scale it comes to you partly from God's counsel, and partly from the relation which He sustains to your spirit.

You may have been born of your parents and find much of them reproduced in yourself. Yet it is the Lord Who created you, and the formation of your person, together with your disposition, your character and predominating tendency is His work.

Hence, when you discover in yourself a thirst after higher knowledge, and a predisposition to nobler learning, the impulse that is born from this is an impelling operation of the Spirit of God in you, and thereby you obtain the fruit of a knowledge that does not come to you by your power, but by virtue of the higher impulse which He quickens and maintains in you.

Circumstances co-operate with this. You may have a friend whose nobleness of character becomes your inspiration. You may have experiences and contact with people which stimulates you to study higher things. Onerous duty, bitter grief, or grave responsibility may be laid upon you by which you make unusual advances. And again it is God alone Who appointed all this in your behalf.

But above all else, you may feel the rise of a strong drawing in yourself after God, so that He leaves you no rest, liberates you from earthly vanities, and in a mystical way makes you aware of an inward Divine insistance, which compels you to concern yourself with the higher things of life, causes you to mature therein, and over and over again enriches you with them.

If this be so, it is not you who have thus lifted up yourself to God, but it is God Who has thus drawn you up to Himself, even you, not someone else. Why you, and not another? This is a mystery. We know not.

Nevertheless the fact remains, that in this way you too possess two parts of your knowledge; that which you owe to your own sight and observation, that other and higher knowledge, which God has taught you.

This unfolds itself most richly when higher grace operates in your soul. Not that every grace-endued child of God advances thereby to such higher learning. Here too there is diversity of gifts. Some believers lack almost every capacity to enter into the mysteries of the higher life. Some practice mysticism along the way of the emotions, but continue limited in knowledge. Some acquire a wealth of learning regarding the way of salvation, but remain indifferent to the higher, nobler knowledge of human life. But there are others, too—and this is most glorious—who, of warm sensibility, rich mysticism, and clear insight into the knowledge of salvation come in addition to that inner unfolding which extends their knowledge to the nobler parts of human learning, and makes them not only deeply religious, but also men of exalted idealism.

Then such a one stands at the summit of the mountain of God's holiness. A light above the light of the sun dawns upon his horizon, and his knowledge becomes that of the saints made perfect.

This goes hand in hand with the deepest sense of absolute dependence and a thirst after ever larger knowledge; a longing which utters itself in the prayer of God's child: "O God, aside from what I myself see and discover, teach Thou me. Instruct me ever more in Thy holy fellowship."

VIII

GOD, MY MAKER, WHO GIVETH SONGS IN THE NIGHT

NIGHT is a mystery in our life, and remains a mystery.

For years together, sleep to most people is a provisional going out from life, in order after some seven or eight hours to come back to it. When they fall asleep, which most people do immediately after their head touches the pillow, *they are gone*, and when the hand on the dial of the clock has moved on a given number of hours, they rise and resume their part in life. At most they have an occasional remembrance of a dream that entered into their sleep, but for the rest it is all a blank. The seven hours during which they were lost in unconsciousness passed by unobserved, and as far as their remembrance of them goes they amounted to no more than two or at most three hours.

Thus a third of life is taken out of their existence. When they are thirty years of age, they have actually lived but twenty, and the other ten years are wrapped in the haziness of sleep.

This sleep, however, was not devoid of purpose. He who was weary on retiring, rises girded with new strength, though as far as his consciousness goes, he was idle. His thinking, feeling, willing, working, have all been at a standstill. This absolute surcease of life is the normal state of things, for as long as man is well, in the fullness of his strength and not oppressed by cares, he sleeps as long as nothing disturbs him from without.

Why this was so ordained, remains a riddle. For though it is true that after hours of work our strength becomes exhausted and demands rest to recuperate, this does not solve the problem. For at once the question arises: "Why this exhaustion of strength?" God, our Maker, after Whose Image we are created fainteth not, neither is He weary. The heavenly hosts of angels do not sleep. Of the New Jerusalem we read: "And there shall be no night there" (Rev. xxii, 5). Thus, a being who does not continually exhaust his strength, and hence is in no need of sleep, is conceivable. Why God, our Maker, appointed a life for us with continual exhaustion of its power to be restored by sleep, remains a mystery. This ordinance of the Lord has not been promulgated without a purpose and a wise design, though no one understands it.

A third part of our earthly existence is subtracted in unconsciousness from life that is known without our knowing or understanding why.

But does not Scripture say that in the night our reins instruct us, and does not sleep obtain from this a higher significance?

Undoubtedly! But though such was the case with David, it is by no means ordinary experience; and if it were, a regularly returning period of seven or more long hours for a spiritual instruction in the secret places of the soul would be out of all proportion. Only think how large a part of the day it is from nine o'clock in the morning until four in the afternoon. And yet, this is but seven hours, and these, out of every twenty-four we sleep away.

This is only modified by sickness, by pressing cares or by old age. By these three causes, sleep is shortened or disturbed or deferred, and a part of the night is struggled through without sleep. Then, indeed the night obtains an entirely different significance, because one can not get to sleep, or because sleep is too frequently broken, or too soon ended.

Dreams also can not be said to have no significance.

There are dreams that show us what we are; and others from which a helpful thought goes out with us into life; dreams again, that afford us momentary fellowship with our beloved dead, which gives us a sad pleasure. God may even use a dream by which to reveal something to us. But in spite of all this, most dreams are forgotten on waking and when they leave a memory, nothing but vague, vanishing and mixed images float before the mind. Even the petition from the ancient evening hymn: "O God, in sleep let me wait on thee, In dream be thou my joy!" does not define, save in rarest instances, the content of our dreams.

This does not deny, however, that without our being aware of it, the Spirit of God works upon our spirit while we sleep, and builds up our inner life. Here again the mystery of our life by night hides the mighty workings of God. We can not count with them, because they go on outside of our consciousness. At times on waking, an insight may come to us into difficult problems which troubled us the night before, and he who fears God will praise Him for it, but this also is a work of God which eludes our grasp, and of which we can but say with the Psalmist: "We see it, but we understand it not" (Ps. 118, 23, Dutch Ver.).

No, our life by night obtains a conscious significance for us only when sickness, care, or age come to disturb our ordinary sleep, and Scripture witnesses to this when it says: "My reins also instruct me in the night seasons" (Ps. 16, 7); and "In the night I commune with mine own heart" (Ps. 77, 6); and when Isaiah (xxvi, 9) with his soul desires the Lord in the night; and so likewise when Job (xxxv, 10) confesses: "God is my Maker, who giveth songs in the night."

This constitutes a school of learning, which should be reckoned with more seriously.

Sleeplessness is an apprehensive phenomenon, that casts its shadow upon all of the next day; but it is an evil that leads either to sin or to glory according to the way in which our faith-life spends such sleepless hours.

If sleeplessness makes you do nothing but utter gloomy and peevish complaints by day, and rebelliously turn yourself over and over on the bed by night, then it becomes sin to you. If, on the other hand, such hours of wakefulness are used to confirm your fellowship with God, to make it more intimate and to strengthen it, then it glorifies the inner life of the soul. Moreover, such devotional use of sleeplessness is medicine that invites sleep, while rebellious restlessness only increases wakefulness. To struggle against God in such an hour makes for restlessness and feelings of oppression, which drive sleep ever farther and farther away from you; while, on the other hand, conversing with God in such a sleepless hour, brings restfulness and calm and induces sleep's approach.

This result, however, is merely a by-product; the main thing is, that a sleepless night is of itself an appointed time to seek the Lord, and to apply to your wakeful hours the Psalmist's word: "It is good for me to be near unto God."

That which in our busy life draws us continually away from God and estranges us from Him is our strenuous activity, the multitudinous sounds on every side, the constant interviews with people who address us. All this ceases at night. The absence of things that absorb attention gives rest to the eye. The stillness of night puts the ear out of commission. No work presses in upon us. Chase and hurry have given place to calm. There is nothing to divert us, no one to tire or to detain us. All the conditions are there, a hushed mind, and this stillness, to help us to hold converse with our God. Such an hour of night invites us, more than any other, to enter into the

Tabernacle of God. The night-time has something in it of the solemn stillness of the Sabbath.

This stillness is introduced by your evening reading of God's Word, by your evening prayer, when on your knees you have poured out your soul unto your God. And now you are at rest, and your one concern is, either to set aside the cares of the day which you brought with you to your couch, or, in fellowship with your God, so to take them that He carries them for you.

But this is not in your hands.

It is not enough that you think of God and make approach to Him. Fellowship must come from both sides, and if God does not simultaneously draw near to you, you can not enjoy His intimacy.

To think: "God is always ready, He is waiting for me, so that it depends on me alone whether I will meet Him," shows no dependence on your part upon Him, nor sufficient humility. To think of God is no enjoyment yet of His fellowship. Fellowship is something far more ardent, and whenever it falls to your lot, it is an operation of grace, a favor extended to you, for which you owe Him thanks. It is not that you are so good and devout as to lift up yourself to God, but it is of His Divine compassion that He comes down to you, in order to enrich and bless you with the consciousness of His nearness.

The gain is so great, when your last feeling before you sleep is that of joy in the tenderness of the Lord, and when on waking in the morning you feel your first conscious thought to go out to God. This accustoms you to God, and prepares you to go into the night of the grave, in order that you may never more be disturbed by anything in your fellowship with God.

In the night, upon our bed, when we can not sleep we feel small, far smaller than by day when we are adorned by our garment, and our word makes our influence count as we struggle to make or maintain our place in life. But we lie upon our bed and stand no more upright. We are motionless and do not move. And this smallness and insignificance of our appearance makes us more fit to meet our God.

Then God becomes so great to us. Then we feel indeed that He is our Maker. His faithfulnesses present themselves to us. The arms of everlasting compassion underneath bear us up and encircle us. Joy expels the somber temper of the soul; gladness the carping cares. We come into the atmosphere of the worship of God's everlasting love, and when His Spirit inwardly imparts His touch, the note of praise rises from our inmost being, and it becomes a literal fact with us that "God our Maker giveth us songs in the night."

IX

I CRY, BUT THOU HEAREST NOT

To get no answer! when we stand at a closed door and it is not opened, makes us feel anxious.

We then knock harder and harder, and when this brings no response, we call louder and louder; and when still no sound is heard, and there comes no answering voice, fear strikes the heart that something has gone wrong with the child, or perhaps brother, whom we know must be inside the room.

To get no answer! when in need and distress we have called for help and have waited, and still wait for an answer that does not come, how often has it turned hope into despair.

To get no answer! It makes us so restless, when there are fears about the welfare of child or brother far distant, and we write, and write again for information, and the information does not come; and then we telegraph with answer prepaid; and still no answer comes.

To get no answer! It sends a chill to the heart, when one of the family is dangerously ill, and we approach his bedside, and call him by name, first in a whisper, then louder and find that he does not hear us.

To get no answer! It is overwhelming in the case of an accident in a mine, or a landslide in the digging of trenches when victims are entombed, and people from without call, and call again, and listen with bated breath for some sound or answering sign of life, and the silence continues unbroken.

To get no answer! It caused such anxious fears when not long ago Martinique was overturned by an earthquake, and telegrams were sent to inquire about the condition of things there, and no sign of any kind was returned.

On Carmel the Prophets of Baal knew what this meant, when from morning until noon they cried: "O, Baal, hear us! and they leaped upon the altar and cut themselves with knives, but lo! there was no voice, nor any that answered" (I Kng. xviii, 26). And their hearts were more troubled still, when Elijah from his side cried out: "Hear me, O Lord, hear me!" and obtained the answer, and fire from above consumed the sacrifice.

And yet he who loves God has not always obtained an answer.

Read the complaint of Asaph in Psalm 83, 1, "O God, keep not thou silence; hold not Thy peace as one deaf and be not still, O God!" Consider David's distress in Psalm 28, 1: "Unto thee do I cry, O Lord, my Rock, hold not thyself deaf to me; lest, if thou hold thyself silent to me, I become like them that go down into the pit."

Or, what is stronger still, remember the *Lama Sabachthani* of Golgotha, echo of the prophetic complaint of Psalm 22, 2: "O my God, I cry in the daytime, but thou hearest not; and in the night season I will take no rest."

Here is the difference between the nominally religious man of the world and the devout believer in God. We have nothing to say of one who is an out-and-out man of the world. Such a one does not pray at all. Still less does he "cry to God," or expect an answer. But the people of the world are not all like this. A great many are not wholly irreligious. That is to say, they are still attached to some form of religion. They have not wholly abandoned prayer. True, it is mostly a matter of habit. They may say grace at meals, which consists mainly in a whispered utterance, and upon retiring at night a prayer by rote, of thanksgiving and petition.

In days of trouble, however, and in moments of anxiety (when a loved one at home is sick unto death, or reverses in business bring one low) this sort of prayer revives itself. Then such a one does really come to pray and to cry unto God. And when that cry proves of no avail, and the danger is not averted, the prayer that has proved futile falls back heavily upon the heart embittered by disappointment.

With the devout believer in God, it is altogether different. He *seeks* his Father. He knows by experience that it is possible, even here on earth, to hold fellowship with that Father Who is in heaven. He has knowledge of "the secret walk with God." From blessed experience he knows that in this secret walk, fellowship is mutual, so that not only he seeks his Father, but the Father also lets Himself be found of His child.

Then although he can not say "God is *here*, or *there*" he feels and senses that God is close by. He can not prove that God addresses him, and yet he knows that he hears the voice of the Lord. Here is no semblance, but reality; no self-deception but rich actuality. And in the lead of the Good Shepherd he follows on, comforted by the rod and staff which he hears ahead of him.

With the nominally religious man of the world this is pure materialism; with the devout believer in God this is sacred and most blessed mysticism.

But in this holy mysticism there is a tale of suffering.

Not once, but constantly it happens that the fellowship with God is broken off.

In times gone by there was no way of illustrating such invisible communion. Now there is, since we are in touch with people thousands and thousands of miles away from us, and can speak from a great distance with those whom we do not see, and hear the voice in return. Now we have advanced so far that wireless telegraphy permits communication apart from any visible, tangible guidance, and now we can understand how such communication can be disturbed, interrupted and broken off.

God's saints on earth have such a mystical communication with their Father Who is in heaven; a mystical telegraph, a mystical telephone, a mystical communication without wire or any guidance. And as little as primitive man can understand our telegraphic communication, so little can the man of the world understand the mysterious communion of the believer with his Father, Who is far off and yet close by.

But for this very reason it is true, that this communion can be interrupted, and sometimes entirely broken off. There are moments when the soul cries after God, seeks Him; the heart goes out to Him, and nothing comes back; no sign from above is vouchsafed, it seems that God is away; nothing but silence remains, and no voice comes. There is no answer.

Why at such times God withdraws Himself from His child, can be surmised but never can be fathomed. The cry of Jesus: "My God, my God, why hast thou forsaken me?" remains an impenetrable mystery.

Yet even here surmise may prove of value.

You awake in the morning, and ordinarily your first thought directs itself to God. This gives you a blessed sense of His nearness, as at His hand you begin the day. But see, one morning it is different. You are not aware of God's nearness. There is no connection between your heart and the Eternal. And pray as you may, there is no fellowship. "O God! hold not thyself as one deaf, why dost thou not hear me!"

Yet even in this feeling of desertion you are aware that grace operates, for the loss of communion with God makes you unhappy.

This break may be accounted for by sinful inclinations of the heart, secret sins which disturb communion; or, your heart may be troubled about many things, so that the Lord has been removed from the center of your inner life. Then this loss is for your good; it makes you turn in upon yourself and bring your heart again to fear His Name.

Physical conditions also can interrupt this feeling of fellowship, as when a headache depresses you, and hinders the free utterance of your spirit, or lessens your susceptibility. This provides a motive for not neglecting bodily rest and calm.

At other times, again, the failure to get an answer can not be explained from any cause whatever; there is nothing in your inner life that enters a complaint or an accusation against you, and yet God withdraws Himself from you.

Even then, we may make a conjecture as to the cause.

All too readily the believer overestimates his piety, becomes accustomed to the love of God, and begins to take it as a matter of course that he is granted this secret walk with Him; sometimes he may even count it as a special holiness that he seeks this fellowship.

This can not be tolerated, for this would make of grace a common thing, whereas it is, and must always be, *holy grace*. And it is the lesson of experience that the full appreciation of this fellowship with God is strengthened by nothing so much as by the temporary want of it.

When for a long time the soul has had no hearing, and at length an answer comes again from God, then there flows into this hidden tryst a still more intimately tender blessedness, and the soul bathes itself in the fullness of the love of God.

X

SEEK YE MY FACE

In bygone days nothing was more common than to hear an aged, godly man tell with affectionate delight how he came to know God.

At such and such a time "I learned to know the Lord," was then the manner of expression.

Afterwards this changed, and they would say: "in such and such a way I was discovered to myself;" or, "I was converted then and there;" or, "it was then that I surrendered my soul to Jesus;" or, "it was thus that I found my Savior"—or whatever terms they might choose by which to tell what had transpired in their soul.

Every one of these forms of expression has its own significance, but it can scarcely be denied, that the former way of saying, "I learned to know the Lord," is by no means inferior to the later ways in truth, depth and fervor.

Jesus himself said: "This is life eternal, that they know thee" (S. John xvii, 3), and He thereby but confirmed the plaintive cry of the Prophet about this decline in Israel, that there is no *knowledge of God* in the land (Hosea iv, 1).

And yet, it can not be denied, that in the long run the saying: "I have learned to know the Lord," can not satisfy because, without being observed, it has been separated from its mystical background and made to consist in external, intellectual, doctrinal knowledge.

To know God has more than one significance.

Surely he does not know God who lacks all knowledge of His Being, Attributes and Works. Neither can he be said to know God who has not learned to worship Him in His Holy Trinity. Again, in connection with this, the saying of our Savior should not be lost sight of: "No man knoweth the Father save the Son and he to whom the Son will reveal him" (S. Mat. xi, 27); a revelation which must undoubtedly be taken to include the light that shines out upon us from the Gospel of Jesus Christ.

But as readily as we grant this, it should be maintained with equal stress and emphasis, that this does not exhaust the knowledge of God; that it contains a spiritual reality which goes deeper than intellectual acumen, and employs the abstractions of dogma and doctrine merely as a means by which to clarify impressions received, the perceptions of the soul and spiritual experience.

The latter has gradually been forgotten, although knowledge of God in the abstract has been retained. This knowledge became a collection of formal and doctrinal expositions. And at length he deemed himself as most advanced in sacred learning, who was able to give the most impressive, clever and exhaustive interpretation of some dogma regarding God.

This could not permanently satisfy, and then the soul's experience of the life of grace passed to the other extreme and mysticism began to seek religion altogether, or nearly so, in the work of redemption by Christ, in conjunction, of course, with what applied to oneself.

Was this a gain?

Undoubtedly in part. Far better an inward condition of soul that warmly refreshes itself in the work of salvation and glories in the walk of the way of redemption, than a sort of Christianity that merely weaves webs out of doctrinal intricacies.

But it is not the highest way.

Old time worthies occupied a far more exalted vantage-ground when they learned to know the Lord both in a doctrinal and mystical way. From this viewpoint it was

God Himself Who ever remained the center, and religion (which is *the service of God*) came far more completely, more fervently, into its own.

Created after the Image of God, it is natural and necessary that in our relation to Him, as far as possible, we should have apperception like to that in our relation to our fellow man.

There is a language in nature; there is a language that addresses us from the animal-world, but altogether different and far richer is the language that is addressed to us by man, even though his voice be silent.

The face, the countenance speaks; speaks by its entire expression, but especially through and by the eye. The eye is as a window of the body through which we look into another's soul, and through which he comes out of his soul, to see us, scan, and address us.

The rest of the body in comparison to the face is dumb and inanimate. It is true, expression is effected by means of the hand, and especially the people of southern Europe have the habit of emphasizing and guiding every word with a motion of the hand; and it is also true that with violent emotion the whole body acts, giving expression to feeling. All this does not alter the fact that the higher a level a man has reached, the more the rest of the body remains composed and calm, letting the face alone do the speaking, thereby imparting to it a far richer and finer expression.

A ruffian in the market place speaks with both hands and feet; a prince upon a throne says far more by look, and majesty of face.

From this it necessarily followed, that in speaking of our intercourse with God, "the face of God" was given the prominence, and that distinction was made between what proceeds from His mouth, what expresses itself through His eye, and what breathes in anger from His nostrils.

We reveal ourselves in the highest sense by speaking face to face, and so our walk with God could not be illustrated otherwise, than by the privilege of being permitted to meet God face to face.

This may not be taken in a materialistic way, such as has even led to the representation of God, the Father, in the form of an aged man.

It is known that even Moses fell into this snare, when he prayed that he might see God's face. A bold prayer, that received as answer: "Thou canst not see my face, for there shall no man see me and live" (Exo. xxxiii, 20).

Thus this remains forbidden. Never should we think of the holy God in an earthly way. The imagery which here must lend support remains wrapped in mystical dimness. A visible face exhibits what is corporeal, and God is spirit.

The fact is this.

When we look any one in the face so intently that at length we grasp his inner self, then the external face has only been the means by which to attain knowledge of his internal existence, and it is conceivable that if all the external fell away, we should still retain the knowledge of his person.

Knowledge of God is reached in another way. Here no physical auxiliary enters in between. Here our spirit enters directly into the spirituality of God as soon as God's Spirit enters into us. In like manner, nay, far more effectively, we obtain a spiritual knowledge of the being and nature of God; and in order to describe this knowledge we merely use the imagery of the face.

The main thing is that we no longer satisfy ourselves with a conception of God, a scientific knowledge of God, or a speaking *about* God, but that we have come in touch with God himself; that we have met Him, that in and by our way through life He has discovered us to ourselves, and that a personal relation has sprung up between the Living God and our soul.

This mystical knowledge of God is expressed in Scripture in all sorts of ways. We read constantly of the secret walk with God, of dwelling in His Tabernacle, of walking with God, and so on; and the Gospel itself unfolds this in the rich, glorious thought that the Father comes and tabernacles with us. And yet the most frequently used term to express the higher knowledge of God is, "the face of God."

Of Moses, the man of God, this stands recorded as the highest distinction that marks him off from all the Prophets, that God spoke with him face to face, as a man speaketh with his friend.

What face here signifies is obvious.

Hence when Scripture brings us the Divine exhortation: "Seek ye my face" (Ps. 27, 8), it contains a profound significance.

We can perceive one at a distance, we can hear him spoken of, we can become aware of his presence without yet having approached him, and placed ourselves before him, so that he looks at us and we at him.

But there is a moment in the life of the child of God when he feels the stress of the inability to rest, until he finds God; until after he has found Him, he has placed himself before Him, and standing before Him, seeks His face; and he can not cease that search until he has met God's eye, and in that meeting has obtained the touching realization that God has looked into his soul and he has looked God in the eye of Grace. And only when it has come to this the mystery of grace discloses itself.

XI

MY SOLITARY ONE

SOLITUDE is something that has to be reckoned with, when you consider the effect it has upon the mind.

This is most evident with a little child, who in solitude becomes afraid and begins to cry. If less striking, yet this impulse to seek or shun solitude marks itself with adults with sufficient clearness, for us to infer from it something about their character.

Some people, whenever possible, escape from their busier surroundings in order to bury themselves in solitude; while others, when left alone, feel oppressed, and only find themselves again in the company of others.

This portrays itself in a threefold way.

The most striking example may be borrowed from the choice that the heart has made at the cross-road of good and evil. In order to do wrong, one hides and conceals oneself. Evil works by night. But when the wrong is done and the conscience is awakened, solitude becomes oppressive and diversion is sought in others' company.

Less striking, yet sufficiently evident is the way the liking for or dislike of solitude shows itself respectively in the more meditative or more active disposition. One lives more within himself, thinks and ponders and feels deeply; another lives in externals, runs and slaves, and likes to make a show of his activities. Even among nations, this difference is apparent. One people lives within doors, another, whenever possible, in the street; a difference for the most part determined by climate and nature.

And in the third place, this seeking or shunning of solitude finds its cause in the consciousness of power or the lack of it. Diffident, awkward, inwardly cowardly natures are almost afraid of company, and draw back with downcast eyes; while he who is clever, energetic and courageous, mingles freely among all sorts of people.

There is more to it than this. Solitude is loved by the man of study; it lures the old man more than one who is in the strength of his years; in feeble health, with weakened nerves, people shrink from too much excitement. These causes, however, are accidental, and are no index of character; but in connection with them it is striking that the Psalmist twice calls his soul "the solitary one;" once in the passion psalm, prophetic of Golgotha (22, 20): "Deliver my soul from the sword, my solitary one from the power of the dog;" and again in Psalm 35, 17: "Rescue my soul from their destructions, my solitary one from the young lions."

Your soul is—your *solitary one*.

This expresses its preciousness. To parents that have but one child, this solitary child is more precious than the seven of which another may boast. If this solitary child dies, the generation dies and the lifeline of those parents is cut off.

Applied to the soul, your soul stands apart from your property and your body. However much you are attached to your goods, if they are lost other goods can replace them, and though once your body shall be lowered in the grave, presently you will rise in a glorified body.

But such is not the case with your soul. Your soul is your *solitary one*. It can not be replaced. If lost, it is lost forever. For this reason, Jesus warns us so solemnly: "Fear not them that can kill the body, but rather fear him who can destroy your soul, yea, I say unto you, Fear him" (S. Luke, xii, 4, 5).

All loss can be made good except the loss of "your solitary one."

And therefore here the consciousness of your self separates itself from your soul. You, who view yourself, who think about your self, find a busy, active world round about you, and see yourself in a decadent, visible body that grows and flourishes, or is sick and pines away. But you have still something else within you, hidden in your inward being, and that hidden something, that "solitary one" within, is your soul, which you must love, and which at your death you must return to your God in honor and holiness, because from Him, and from Him alone, you received it.

From this comes the sense that the soul within you dwells alone.

Truly, your soul can approach the world and the world can approach your soul.

God endowed you with senses, which, like so many windows, enable you to look out upon the world and communicate with it. God has endowed you with feeling and fellow feeling, whereby, though others may be far away, you can sympathize with them, rejoice with them, and suffer on account of their sorrows. God has endowed you with the gift of speech, whereby your soul can express itself, and the soul of another can speak in your ear. Speech has been committed to writing, and, thanks to this glorious invention, which likewise has been given us of God, your soul can have fellowship with preceding generations, or with contemporaries whom you have never met. And, not least, you have a sense and knowledge of a higher world above, and it is as though angels of God descended upon you and from you ascended again. And best of all, in your heart you have a gate that opens into your soul, through which God can approach your soul, and your soul can go out to God.

But in the face of all this, your soul itself remains distinct from that world, from that nature, from those angels and from God, and in a sense separated. And so, taken by itself, your soul within you is your solitary one, that *is* something and *has* something which purely and solely is its own, and remains its own, with respect to which the loneliness within can never be broken.

One of two things here happens.

Either the soul is too lonely, or you yourself have too little knowledge of the soul in its loneliness.

The soul is too lonely within you, when you are bereft of what supported you and gave you companionship. This is the loneliness of sorrow and of forsakenness, which oppresses and makes afraid.

Your soul is disposed to sympathy, to society, to give and win confidence, to be man among men, and to spread wings in spheres of peace and happiness.

And when these do not fall to your portion, when hate repels and slander follows you where love should attract and sympathy refresh you, then shy and shrinking your soul draws back within itself. It can not unburden itself nor express what it feels. Shut up within itself, it pines away in sadness and grief.

Or when the joy of life takes flight, and care makes a heavy heart, and sorrow comes upon sorrow, and the outlook darkens and the star of hope recedes behind ever-thickening clouds—then, in oppressive isolation the soul is thrown back upon itself and pants for air, while Satan sometimes steals in with the suggestion of suicide.

But as the soul can be troubled and oppressed by too great solitude, it can also suffer loss when you do not fully appreciate the significance of its solitariness. This is the common result of a superficial, thoughtless existence that is weaned of all seriousness.

Then the soul is not understood nor honored in its own

solitary, independent existence. Then there is the chase after diversion and endless recreation; with never a turning in upon oneself, never the collecting of the soul for the sake of quiet thought, never a seeking after the soul for the soul's own sake, while the soul itself continues always haunted, always a slave to its environment, never coming to rest, inward peace and self-examination.

And so you see people in the world go out in two directions. On one side the wretched and distressed pining away in inner solitariness; on the other side, the laughing, always busy, hurried and self-externalizing crowd, which neither ever seeks solitude nor harbors a thought about its own solitary soul.

Against this giving way too much to solitude, and this not entering far enough into the appreciation of the soul's solitariness, one remedy alone is offered unto us, and that is, the coming into the loneliness of our soul of the fellowship of our God.

In our soul there is a holy of holies, a holy place and an outer court.

The world makes no closer approach to our soul than this outer court. There it remains, and neither observes nor understands anything of the deeper secrets of the soul.

Intimate, spiritual friendship makes a closer approach; a small circle of individuals about us, who understand us better, who see through us more clearly, and thereby are able so much more tenderly to sustain and comfort us, enter the holy place. But even they do not enter the holy of holies. There is always a deep background, where they can not enter in, and where in utter solitude the soul abides.

There is only One Who can enter this holiest and most intimate recess of our soul, and He is God, the Lord, by His Holy Spirit.

And therefore He alone can break the soul's loneliness, and comfort him who is caught in the snares of death, and save the soul of him who diverted himself in the interests and pleasures of the world.

XII

GOD CREATED MAN AFTER HIS IMAGE

FROM the fact of your creation after God's Image springs all true religion, all genuine piety, all real Godliness.

You have passed the stage of the milk-diet of little children, and live on solid food. Thus you understand that calling upon God and walking in the way of His commandments does not by itself make you religious, devout and godly, and that the secret of salvation in all its hidden amplitude is not revealed, until your soul has come to fellowship with the Eternal Being, and you abide in the covert of His wings.

The more outward form of worship is not devoid of worth. Provisionally it is even the only attainable one; and if it does not build for heaven, it exerts a binding influence upon thousands and thousands for the life that now is, and prevents the dissolution of society.

But the plant of genuine godliness outgrows at length the outward form, and in the words of the Apostle goes on unto perfection. It comes to blossom in the gleam of God's Majesty. It is fostered by the outshining of His glow and watered with dew from above. Thus it comes to a personal knowledge of the Lord, as a man knoweth his brother; to a dwelling of the soul in the Tabernacle of the Lord, and to an indwelling of the Holy One in the temple of the heart.

This requires fresh emphasis.

Every outward form of religion can change and pass away, but that which remains the same and which till the end of your life does not weaken but gains in strength, is the blessed fellowship of your soul with your Father in heaven; so that by night you retire with God, and at early dawn find Him again, and follow after Him as your Good Shepherd all the way of your pilgrimage here below.

In this alone consists the more intimate communion of saints.

Truly, it binds you to others when you learn that they are one with you in the faith, that they belong to the same Church, that with them you break one bread and pour one wine.

But yet on the great journey to the courts of everlasting Light you prefer as fellow travellers those who, under whatever form, have intimated to you that they live in the communion of holy converse with the living God.

This goes back to your creation.

This means that real religion, yea, the possibility of genuine godliness, springs solely and alone from the fact that you have been created after God's Image and after the likeness of God Almighty.

That you have been conceived and born in sin does not alter this in the least. There is no genuine religion without regeneration, and in re-birth the fundamental trait of your creation after God's Image revives again.

Hence the fact that you have been born in sin needs no consideration here. The subject in hand is the conscious, actual fellowship with your Father in heaven. And this rests upon the necessary harmony which prevails between the *original* and that which the *image* shows of it.

The solidarity of the *original* and the *image* is felt and understood at once. There is no image apart from the tie that binds it to the original.

See it in the case of a portrait or picture. If the portrait is good, it is so because it is like the person whom it represents.

You feel this even more strongly with a photograph than with a painted portrait or marble statue.

With a painted portrait, or with a bust, the painter or sculptor comes in as a third between you and your picture. But not so with a photograph. Then it is you yourself who by the operation of light upon the sensitive plate create your own picture and form the features after those of your own face.

And what in this way your own person effects in photography expresses only very inadequately what God did when He said: "Let us make man after our likeness," and then so created him.

Only with one's equals one has close fellowship.

But there is also a more distant kind of association. When spring opens, an impressionable mind holds conscious communion with nature in her nameless beauty. This communion is more tender with the world of plants and flowers and fruits than with the starry hosts of the firmament. It is closer still with the world of animals, especially is there a fellow feeling for the horse that you ride, the dog that meets you with a joyful bark, the lark who sings his morning song with tremulous beat.

But yet, with mountain and stream, moon and star, flower and domestic animal it always remains a fellowship at a distance. However intelligent and expressive a look a faithful animal may give you, you do not understand his life, because it is of a different nature from yours.

It only comes to actual fellowship when you come in touch with man. "What man knoweth the things of a man save the spirit of man which is in him?" S. Paul asks the Corinthians (I Cor. ii, 11). And this is so. Man alone can understand a man, and the more human you yourself are, the better you will understand humanity in others.

The more you are like another, the more the two of you

exhibit a selfsame likeness, the more intimate your fellowship will be. A compatriot comes closer to you than a foreigner. One of the same generation, of like business, of like position, of like circumstances and experience in life, comes closer to you than one who in all these particulars differs from you. Among men, like alone fully understands like.

Hence when God said: "Let us make man after our Image and after our Likeness," this expressed of itself the Divine intention, to create beings that would be able to practice fellowship with God, and that would be capable of receiving His glorious communications. If then it is so, that genuine, exalted, glorious religion consists in this mutual fellowship, then it follows that when God created a being after His own likeness He thereby at the same time created religion.

In the creation of nature God glorified His omnipotence, and the more this life in nature was refined from its chaotic state till the splashing of waters ascended to the wing-beat of the nightingale, the more majestically Divine omnipotence revealed Itself in splendor. The whole earth is filled with His glory (Ps. 72, 19).

But in all this, there was as yet no self-conscious, responsive fellowship for God with his creation.

God stood above nature and nature was subject to His Majesty, but there was no comprehension, no knowledge, no understanding of God in it, and from it rose no note of thanksgiving, of worship and of fellowship that went back to Him.

There was *Power* there; but what was still lacking was the thrill of the fellowship of *Love*.

And this also the Holy One desired, His creation must needs address Him, and He it. Intimate, hidden mutual fellowship with His creation had to come. Knowing, loving, seeking—the Eternal Father willed to be known, to be loved, to be sought. The flame of religion must inwardly gleam through His creation as the sun gleams through the earth in the sphere of externality.

And this *could* not be, this was neither conceivable nor possible unless He created a being after His own Image and after His own Likeness, a being that would be of Divine generation, that would be His child, and would cleave to Him as Father.

A being that although separated and distinguished from the infinite Majesty by unfathomable depths would yet in its own life feel and know the life of God, would company with God as a friend with his brother, having been introduced and initiated into the secret "walk with God."

Thus, not for your sake but for God's sake, religion is founded in your creation after the Image of God.

Your serious practice of the hidden walk with God is to realize the purpose that was expressed in your creation after His Image.

For though it is true that this exalted endowment renders you supremely rich, happy and blessed, though it anoints you priest and king, baptizes you as child of God, and ennobles you as a princely creature in the sanctuary; yet you fail dismally if you take this to be the root of the matter.

First in rank and order here also is, not, what makes you blessed, but that which causes your God to accomplish His purpose; and that purpose always is that He wills to be known, loved, sought and worshiped; that He wills to have conscious, worshipful fellowship offered Him at the hand of His creation; that He wills not merely to be great, but to be known, *as such,* and believed, and loved.

For this He created man. For this also He created you. And for this also He created you after His Image and Likeness.

XIII

NONE OF ME

THE new paganism, which is broadly on the increase, is in one point altogether different from that against which prophets and apostles joined issue: *it has no idols*.

Metaphorically it has. It is said with good reason, that a mother makes an idol of her child, a wife of her husband. One worships his idol in art and the other in Mammon. But however common it may be to speak in this way metaphorically of an idol, yet all this is something entirely different from the heathen's idolatry, which has visible idols, builds temples and pagodas for them, appoints priests in their honor, burns sacrifices and orders festivals.

Ancient paganism with its visible idolatry was *personal;* modern paganism soars in vague enchantments.

In Paris and London and, as report has it, in New York, societies have been formed of men and women that hold meetings in pagan-like chapels, and kneel down and mutter prayers before images of idols. But these are not the people who lead the new pagan movement. These, for the most part, are persons who have spent part of their life in heathen Asiatic countries, and now in Europe or America imitate what they have seen in Asia, and in which they took part while there. This is a little oil flame on top of wide waters, and is utterly without significance with respect to the great movement of spirits.

The modern heathen movement, on the other hand, is driven by an entirely impersonal object, has no thought of setting up images of idols, and scorns idolatry proper as it is still known in India, China and Japan.

That which drives this new heathen movement is two-fold; negatively, it is the denial of a personal living God; positively, it is the doting either on vague ideals, or on sensual pleasure and money.

This makes warfare against this new form of heathenism far more painful and difficult than that which Prophets and Apostles waged against idolatrous heathendom.

Of old it was name pitted against name, person against person, image against image.

Not Baal, but Jehovah.

Not Jupiter, but the Lord of Hosts.

Not the image of the great Diana, but Christ, the Image of the Invisible God.

Thus the personal character which heathendom borrowed from visible idolatry compelled the setting up by the side of it an equally personal object of worship.

It was Zion pitted against Basan, Jerusalem against Gerizim, priest against priest, and, in the same way, God, the living God, the eternal and adorable Jehovah, against Moloch and Baal.

Hence the scorn of idols: "ears have they, but they hear not. Eyes have they, but they see not. Mouths have they, but they speak not. They who make them are like unto them; so is every one that trusteth in them. But thou, O Israel, trust thou in the Lord" (Ps. 115, 6, 9).

But now this fails us.

The modern pagan dotes on humanity, is zealous for art, feels impulse and love for high forms of life, or takes part in the chase after sensual pleasure and wealth, and obeys the spur of passion.

This has the sad result, that they who in other ways are still faithful Christians have too largely abandoned the personal element in their worship of the living God, and in turn dote on the beautiful ideals of love and mercy, of peace and higher good, without feeling any longer that deep, personal communion with the personal, living God, in which lay the power and strength of the faith of our fathers.

Of course it is entirely true that the immortal ideal of love and mercy means nothing else than the expression of Divine attributes; but the trouble is that instead of confessing, God *is* love, or love is *God*, one forms an *idea* of love for himself, turns it into an ideal (behind which the living God is lost from sight), dotes on that creation of his own thought, and becomes a stranger to God.

Apply this more closely to Christ, and you reach the same result.

In the place of an image of an idol, God has set up the Image of Himself in His only-begotten Son, as the Christ is revealed in the flesh.

By this, the *idea* is repressed, the *ideal* is relegated to the background, and in the foreground, in clear and transparent light, stands the *Christ*, the incarnate *Word*.

All the enthusiasm, wherewith Christianity was carried into the world, sprang from this heaven-wide difference.

With philosophers of Greece and Rome, it was zeal for beautiful ideals, but with the Apostles, it was passionate love for the living Christ, the tangible Image of the living God.

It is this personal attachment of faith to the living Christ in very Person, in which the secret of their power consisted. It was a love of heart to heart, by which the world of that age was won. It was love and affection for the Mediator between God and man, that brought heathendom to its fall.

When S. Thomas kneels down and exclaims: "My Lord and my God!" there reveals itself all the power of the personal worship of God in Christ by which the Church of Christ became what it is.

But this too is being lost.

First it was weakened by a sentimental holding fast to Christ as man, whereby God, if not forgotten, was obscured in His Majesty.

And now even among Christians it has come to this, that putting aside the Person of Christ, an ideal in Christ is loved, presently to develop into a stronger tie than that to the Person of Christ Himself.

Admiration of the ideal breaks down the *faith*.

This now is the complaint of the Lord in Asaph's song (Ps. 81, 11): "*They would have none of me.*"

It can not be put more personnally than this.

They love my creation, they enjoy the world which I called into being, they admire the wisdom which I made to shine as light in the darkness, they dote on love and mercy, the feeling for which I made glow in their heart; but Me they abandon, Me they pass by, of Me they have no thought, to Me they give no personal love of their heart, with Me they seek no fellowship, Me they do not know; my personal converse does not interest them; they have everything that is mine, but they would have none of me.

The complaint is often heard that an acquaintance enjoys what is yours, satisfies himself with your goods, honors your ideas, adorns himself with flowers from your garden, even praises what you do, but remains a stranger to personal attachment, no trace of affection for you is discovered in his heart, no sympathy with you is shown, and of yourself he desires to know nothing.

The reason for this is found all too frequently with the person himself; so that one admires him, honors him, praises his deeds, and yet feels bound to say: he is not a man to invite personal affection.

But of course, with God this does not hold. He alone is

adorable, the highest Good, Love itself, in every way love-able, eternally to be desired.

And when in the face of this a complaint comes from God: "they would have none of me," it is a piercing complaint against our heart, against our faith; it expresses deepest feeling aroused by gross misappreciation. "I am the Only One Whom they should desire, and lo, they would have none of Me. They love Me not, they cleave not unto Me with heart and soul. For their personal affection I, their God, am not the potent, all compelling point of attraction."

Here is complaint against the superficiality, vagueness, and unreality of our piety, against the diminished and ,weakened conception of our religion, against the actual faithlessness of our heart; in brief, against a religious decline which expresses itself in our lack of holy ardor, in the quenched fires of our higher enthusiasm, in the congealing of the waters of holy mysticism.

This is partly a personal wrong, springing from too high an opinion of self, from too potent a self-sufficiency, from lack of dependence and proper trust; but it is also an evil of our times, a common, contagious disease, whereby one poisons the other; an apostasy of the world of spirits, which turns our heart away from the living God.

This must be resisted.

The struggle must be begun against our own heart first, that we may attain again personal fellowship with the living God.

This struggle must be extended over our entire environment, in order to repress all false religion, with its vague ideals, and replace it by personal affection for the living God.

This battle must be waged with enthusiasm and untiring fidelity in our preaching and devotional writings and in ardent supplications, to call the living God back into our personal life.

And then this struggle must be carried out into the world to call it back from fancy to reality, from the idea to the essence, from religion to the Only Object of our worship, from doting on the abstract to the love of the faith that directs itself solely to Him who has revealed Himself in Christ as the personal living God.

XIV

A SUN

OF a dear child, especially if it is a girl, father and mother often say: "Our little darling is the sunshine of our house and of our life."

But however grateful one may be who may own such a miniature sun to brighten the home, especially in seasons of trouble, infinitely higher is the praise in which the Psalmist indulged when he gloried in Jehovah as the Sun on his pathway of life, and sang in the ear of the saints of all time: "The sun of my life is my God."

To this tender, deeply passionate language of Scripture-poetry our Western heart should be more accustomed. The music of the Psalter is always uplifting and inspiring. "The Lord God is a sun and a shield" (Ps. 84, 11). Whenever read or sung it finds an echo in our heart. But this does not come to us from ourselves. Everywhere, among rich and poor alike, a sunny child in the home is a ready topic of conversation, but when do you ever hear one tell from deep, personal experience: "My God has been a sun unto me all my life, and will be till I die."

The figure is still in use, but preferably in a doctrinal way, almost exclusively in the limited sense of "Sun of Righteousness," whereby righteousness is given the emphasis at the expense of the rich imagery of the sun.

And yet, this luxurious imagery of the sun contains such transcendent riches. It is not a mere comparison, for when you truly realize that God is the sun of your life, this blessed knowledge is a treasure, that brings you closer to God, casts a sheen upon all of life, and imparts a reality

93

to your Christian knowledge which liberates you from barren abstractions.

Truly, the sun is not to us what it was to the Psalmist in the East.

The firmament there glows and glitters with sparkling radiancy, the splendor of which our Western eye does not surmise from afar.

The skies flooded both the land from which Abraham emigrated, and the land God gave to him and to his seed, with a sheen of heavenly brightness, compared with which our sky seems wrapped in twilight.

A sky such as the shepherds saw by night bending over Bethlehem, was, as it were, prepared and appointed for the arrival and reception of the angelic hosts, and where the stars enchanted the eye in such a way by their magic beauty, and the moon filled the mind with such ecstatic animation, what in such a country must the sun be, of which the Psalmist sang (19, 6): "His going forth is from the end of the heaven, and his circuit unto the ends of it; and there is nothing hid from the heat thereof."

If then there ever was an idolatry that is intelligible, it is not the worship of images, nor of spirits, but that hushed worship, in that glorious region, with which the wandering Bedouin by night looked up to the stars, and by day looked up to the dazzling brightness of the sun; in his *rapture* at length imagining that that wondrous, majestic, all-pervading and all-governing sun, was not a mere heavenly body, but even God Himself.

This error the Psalmist in Israel has righted. That sun in the sky is not God, but God is my Sun, even the Sun of my life. The sun has been appointed of God Himself to bless us in nature, and also to provide a glorious, rich imagery of what God is to us in the emptiness of our life.

It is not original with us, to compare God with the sun;

we have not chosen the sun as an image of God, but the sun is the image in nature of what God is to us in our life. He himself speaks to us in that sun and in His operations in the whole round of our existence. And when with all your analytical studies of the virtues of God, and with all your reasonings about His Providence, you have at length reached barren, distinctive definitions, and are past feeling and can no more get warm, it is as though suddenly the glow of the higher life communicates itself to your entire inner being, and you epitomize everything in this single phrase of delight: *"God is my sun, he is the sun of my life."*

This holy imagery is peculiarly effective in this particular, that it places before our eye so clearly and vividly the penetration of the hidden power of God in our inner existence.

The sun is heaven-high above you, and yet right by you, round about you; you feel and handle him; you escape him in the shade, and shut him out of your room by blinds; he is a power far off and equally close by; and of this power, this working of the sun, you know that it enters into the earth, and there underneath the ground, hidden from every human eye, it causes the seed to germinate and sprout.

And the same workings and the same contrast apply to God. In the heavens, far above you is His Throne, and yet the selfsame, exalted God with His Presence everywhere is even close by and round about *you*, and enters into your heart, fills its deepest places, works within you with hidden power, and if ever holy seed has germinated in you or ever a sacred flower has budded on the stem of your soul, it is God, your Sun, who with power worked this in you.

Imagine for a moment that the sun had gone out of your life, and a condition such as is found at the north pole would prevail in nature round about you. Everything that lives would die, every plant and every herb; every tint would pale, and all would be covered over with one immense shroud of snow and ice. And that this is not so, that everything lives and pulsates, and exhibits color and glow, that food springs from the ground and the flower-cup bends upward, and sweet loveliness breathes throughout the whole of nature, yea, the whole of life—is the result of the sun alone that pours out life and warmth, and by it, as by magic, brings life out of death and turns the barren wilderness into a fruitful land.

And such is the case with your soul and God.

Think for a moment of your bereft and desolate soul deprived of the gracious inward shining and working of your God. It would be for your heart as though life were departing from you, and all glow and warmth were leaving, and that icy cold would cause your soul to freeze. Not one flower more would unfold in the garden of your heart, no holier motion would anymore stir itself in your soul; all would wither and die, and the heart within you would cease to be a human heart.

Whether it is said: "With thee, O Lord, is the fountain of Life," or whether the Psalmist cries: "In thy light shall we see light," or whether the heart exultingly sings: "God is my Sun," one dominating thought is expressed: *With* God there is life, *without* God there is death in my soul. From Him, and from Him alone, I derive all life, power and animation.

That which makes the sun so rich toward the whole creation, enriches my heart, and my whole human existence. With Him I am aboundingly rich, blessed and supremely happy; without Him I am poor, empty and cold.

But there is more.

The sun not only cherishes life by his warmth, he also colors and exhibits it by his splendors of light. With the lengthening of shadows by night everything becomes pale grey, and vague and nebulous till dissolved in darkness, but sunrise brings friendly light, which makes you see proportions, measure distances, perceive forms and tints and colors, and nature catching these splendors speaks clearly to your heart.

And this is what God, your Sun, effects for you in your inner life. When He is hidden to your darkened eye, your life is nothing but somber greyness, a life without point of departure, direction or aim. Then all knowledge and insight fails, there is no courage to go forward, no inspiration to finish the course—a groping for the wall as one blind, a being shut up as in oneself, without cheerful, friendly association, without knowledge, without self-consciousness, without color or form, a life as among tombstones where weeds thrive, snakes lurk about and the shriek of the night-bird startles.

But when God breaks through the mists, and the sun rises again in your soul, then everything becomes different as by a holy magic wand. Light dispels your inner darkness. Peace in its kindly way rids your troubled mind of oppression, and seeing with heavenly clearness, by the light of God's countenance, the way before your feet, bravely you walk on while the Sun from on high cheers and sanctifies your heart.

The image of the sun is also significant in that the shining of God on the heart is no unbroken brightness.

As day is followed by night, and summer by winter, it has ever been the same in the life of God's saints.

Now a time of clear conscious fellowship with God, so that life from hour to hour was, as it were, a walking with God, and then again, a time of overwhelming activities which exhaust mind and body—difficulties that absorb the soul, cares that burden the heart. Then a change in the spiritual life as of day and night. And it is well with him who can say, that in every twenty-four hours his estrangement from God has lasted no longer than the hours of his sleep.

But apart from this rise and fall almost every day in the intimacy of our fellowship with God, there is a drawing back of the shining of this Sun, and then again a drawing near, whereby also in the life of the soul summer and winter alternate one with the other.

Blessed, uninterrupted, ever equally intimate fellowship with God is not of this earth; it only awaits us in the palaces of everlasting light. Here on earth there have always been and always will be changes and turns, whereby one year yields a far richer harvest than the other; difficulties through which the soul struggles in order to climb from a lower to a higher viewpoint, trials which make it pass through the depths of gloom and darkness, whereby for weeks and months the soul is covered, as it were, by a layer of ice.

The sun then is not gone, but thick clouds prevent his breaking through. And this keeps on until God's hour is come. And then gradually the clouds dissolve, until at length they entirely disappear. It becomes spring again in the soul. That spring is the prelude to a glorious summer. And in the end we thank God for that cold dearth of spiritual winter, which now makes our enjoyment of both spring and summer so much the richer.

There is still another trait of comparison that should not be ignored.

In nature the selfsame heat of the sun has this twofold effect upon the ground that, on one hand it warms and cherishes, which causes germination and fruition, and on the other, that it hardens the clod and scorches it, and also singes the leaf and withers the blossom.

This describes God's working on our conscience.

When we glory in God as the Sun of our life, it implies that the love and the grace of God are never abused with impunity.

Hardening of the heart is a thing to fear, and yet it came upon Israel and frequently comes upon us now. Hardening, because the heat that radiates from God upon us does not soften and inwardly warm us, but repulsed by resistance within us attacks and sears our outward religious life.

Here we would rather not mention that mortal hardening which leads to an eternal ruin. He who is in this state will not read our devotional meditations.

But there is also a temporary hardening which as long as it lasts dangerously retards the process of our spiritual life; and it is this temporary singeing by grace, this temporary hardening by God's love, this temporary scorching by the outshining of God's faithfulness, which is all too frequently observed.

Then it is either a sin from which we will not break away, a sacrifice we will not bring, a step we will not take, an exertion from which we shrink or a sin in the sensual, domestic, public or church life, which we try to unite and harmonize with the enjoyment of God's grace. And this is not possible, in the nature of God it is unthinkable, and when we go on in this, the sun keeps on shining, even fiercely sometimes, but the result is that there is no more striking of root, and the very heat of God's grace hardens us.

"Thou Lord art the Sun of my life!" Oh, it is glorious language wherewith to enter eternity; beware, lest at some time it will witness against you.

For the "fall and rising again" applies here also.

XV

UNDER THE SHADOW OF THE ALMIGHTY

EVERY creature is the product of a thought of God; hence all created things can serve as emblems of the Divine.

It is not of ourselves that in winged creatures we hail a figurative expression of the Divine life; but Scripture does it, and now, accustomed to it, every devout believer readily acknowledges that this imagery warms the heart and enriches the mind.

In what Jesus said of Jerusalem this comes within every one's comprehension. The hen with her chickens is a figure of Divine compassion, which moves every one by its beauty and tenderness. "Jerusalem, Jerusalem, how often would I have gathered thy children together as a hen gathereth her chickens under her wings, and ye would not" (S. Mat. xxiii, 37).

Yet this word of Jesus has a far deeper meaning than he who merely admires it imagines. Truly it speaks of protection and compassion, for this is the purpose here of the gathering together. But there is more in it than this. It also implies that the chickens belong with the mother-hen; and that nothing else than return to her can render them safe against the dangers of cold, and prowling vermin. Yea, it also contains the striking figure that by nature the chickens are appointed a hiding place close by the mother-hen, and that they find shelter and protection of life only in the immediate nearness of the mother-life, under the outspread wings that will embrace and compass them.

Thus, this striking saying of Jesus is taken bodily from Old Testament imagery and in turn is explained by it.

When in Psalm 91 it is said: "He that dwelleth in the secret place of the Most High, shall lodge under the shadow of the Almighty," we deal with the selfsame figurative representation.

It is the epitome of what the Psalmist elsewhere expresses (61, 4): "I will make my refuge in the covert of thy wings."

It is the same thought that was expressed by the wings of the cherubim over the mercy-seat of the ark of the Covenant.

It is ever the one idea: God created a fowl that gathers her brood under her wings and with these wings covers and cuddles them; and now this richly suggestive picture is held before us in order that our soul might seek refuge under the shadow of the Almighty and hide in the covert of His wings.

Not from what moves in the waters nor from what creeps or prowls on the ground and hardly ever from four-footed beasts is this imagery borrowed; but, in the main, only from *winged* creatures that can lift themselves *above* the earth and, as it were, live between us and heaven.

Angels before God's Throne are pictured with wings as Seraphs. With the descent of the Holy Ghost upon the Son of man, there is mention of the form of a dove. That it might have wings to fly upward is the secret prayer of the soul that is bound to the dust. And so it conforms to the order of creation, it corresponds to the Divinely ordained state of things, and it therefore appeals to us as something that is entirely natural that in order to express the tenderest and most mystical kind of religion, the *winged* creature is held up to us as a symbol, and that boldest imagery serves to picture to us what it is "to be near unto God," to make it, as it were, visible to our eyes and perceptible to our feelings.

But this symbolism must not be carried too far. Our heart must ever be on its guard against the danger of all sickly mysticism that interprets the holy things of God in a material way. God is a Spirit, and every effort that seeks contact, fellowship and touch with Him in any other than a purely spiritual way avenges itself.

This exaggerated symbolism leads to idolatry by which one makes a material image of God out of stone or precious metal; or makes one lose himself in pantheistic mud, mingling spirit and matter, and at length in sensual excesses, first defiling and then smothering what began spiritually.

But however necessary it is, for this reason, to keep fellowship with God purely spiritual, spirituality must not be confused with *unreality*, and this, alas! is the mistake of many a soul, in consequence of which it withers away.

For then we only see what is before our eyes; nature round about us; the blue heavens above us; our own body with its powers; and all this is considered real; this has form, body and matter; this is tangible and has actual existence. And then, in addition to this is what we think, what we picture to ourselves, what we work out in our spirit; this is the abstract part of it, our world of thought; a world without reality; and the center of this unreal world is then our God. A God Who exists merely in our thought, in our spirit, in our idea, and with Whom fellowship is only possible through our processes of thought.

In this case there is no mysticism of the heart; no uniting of our heart to fear God's name (Ps. 86, 11); no experience of the hidden walk with God; then God has no independent existence for us outside of our thought; and for this self-sufficient soul there is no "being near unto God" nor dwelling in His tent.

Against this danger, every deeply spiritual life in Holy Scripture protests, to wit: the lives of Psalmists and Prophets. They did not find God to be a product of their own thought. They found Him to be a real, living God, Who drew near unto them, compassed them with the arms of His everlasting compassion; a God Whose holy glow they felt burn as a fire in the marrow of their bones, yea, a God with Whom they found peace, rest and cheer of soul, as they realized how wondrously they were privileged to hide in the covert of His wings, and to pass the night under the shadow of the Almighty.

You can not analyze this thrice blessed state of mind. You must experience it. You must enjoy it. Having it, you must watch lest it slip away from you again or be interrupted, but analyze it, dissect or explain it, you can not. This would allow the wedge of your critical judgment to enter in, which would chill the glow that comforts you.

The way to obtain it is to learn that your *self-sufficiency* deceives; that highminded self-sufficiency is the canker that gnaws at the root of all religion. It is the futile dream of a small insignificant world, of which our little self is the great person, whose mind understands everything, whose will disposes everything, whose money governs everything and whose power carries everything before it. Thus your own self becomes a miniature god in a diminutive temple, and then in your sinful isolation, of course, you are deathly cold—frozen—away from the living God; and all passing of the night under the shadow of God's wings is impossible.

If you can truly say: "such is not my case, I realize that I am powerless, forsaken and in need of help," then the way to fellowship with God is to learn that to lean upon people for support is sinful. Not by any means all leaning upon your fellowmen. The faith of others is a prop to your own faith; the courage of others shames your cowardice; the example of another may double your own strength. By nature we are disposed to be gregarious in matters of life and belief. But what you must rise above is the *sinful* leaning on others; and sinful in character is the kind of leaning on people that sees in them something else than an instrument for our help, appointed of God, for as long as He allows it. Never should it be a leaning upon man as long as one possibly can, without seeking help from God until all human help fails. From God must be our help at all times, whether power to save springs up from within ourselves, or comes to us from others. Even when at length all human succor fails us, we have yet lost nothing whatsoever, because our God is the Unchangeable One, and unchangeably remains the same.

And in this confidence of faith you will stand, provided you are continually bent upon eradicating, root and branch, the *doubt,* which gloomily makes you ask, whether in very deed there *is* support and help, whether there *is* deliverance and salvation, for you. This doubt, allowed but for a moment, unnerves you altogether. Then you are as the little chick that anxiously looks around and no- where sees the mother-hen and now helplessly flies hither and thither, until the hawk observes it and snatches the lost fledgeling away. Then all your feeling of lofty assurance is gone—gone your perception of your calling in life, gone your faith that God has hitherto led you and shall lead you further still. Then all your strength fails you. The prophecy in your heart is dumb.

And at length your fellowship with Satan becomes more intimate than your hidden walk with God.

Notice carefully that the Psalmist does not merely glory that he rests in the shadow of his God, but that he hides in the shadow of the Almighty.

This must needs be added.

The symbolism of the helpless chick that the mother-hen protects from the hawk—even to the extent of flying at it and chasing it away—is the image of a power that makes us think of the Almightiness of God.

Otherwise your resting on the Father-heart of your God avails you nothing. He who *rests* under the shadow of God's wings but does not *trust*, puts his God to shame. For what else is it than to entertain the fear that one mightier than God will snatch you away from under the Divine protection?

Unbelief, when you are far distant from your God, can be atoned for, insofar as you fly to Him; but still to harbor it in the heart after you have sought refuge with God, is a fatal wrong, which profanes the love for which God looks to you.

Hence blessed peace, hallowed rest, quiet and childlike confidence, such as even in seasons of bitterest trial God's elect have enjoyed, is not the result of reasoning, not the effect of deliverance, but solely and alone the sweet returns of taking refuge in the covert of the Most Highest, of holding close to the Almighty, of the knowledge and enjoyment of being near unto God.

Do not imagine therefore, if thus far you have been a stranger to this fellowship with your God, that when danger comes and storm gathers over your head and all human help fails you, you shall at once be able to find your hiding-place under the shadow of the Almighty. In the hour of calamity and dismay this has been tried by those of a transient faith, but they have never succeeded.

The way to find it is the reverse of this. Not in the hour

of need, as a means of deliverance, does one find the secret walk with God as it were ready at hand, but he who in happier days has practiced it knows the wings under which deliverance can be found, and when snares are laid for his soul finds rest and safety under the wings of His God.

It is not a mother-hen with no brood of her own, that spreads her wings for whatever will seek refuge beneath them, but it is her own chicks, which she herself has hatched, whom she knows, and for whom she will risk her life, that will find help and protection with her.

And such is the case with this shadow under the wings of the Almighty. They are his *own* whom He calls and awaits; they that are *known of Him* He will cover with His everlasting love.

He who is at home under the wings of God, shall in the time of danger pass the night under the shadow of the Almighty.

XVI

WHEN THE AIR IS ASTIR

VIOLENT storms did not rage in Paradise. In the garden of Eden no other breeze blew than the soft stirring which in softer climate brings morning and evening cool. Hence in the narrative of Paradise nothing is said of a quickly rising wind, but of a fixed, periodic stirring of air (in Gen. iii, 8, it is called "the cool of the day," and in the original, as given in the marginal reading "the wind of the day") which announced to Adam and Eve the approach of God.

The symbolism is still intelligible. Amidst the luxuriant stillness of Paradise, where everything breathes rest and peace and calm, suddenly a soft rustle is heard, sighing through the leaves, just such a sound as strikes the ear, when, seated near a grove, we hear one come through the underbrush, whose tread pushes light twigs aside, makes the leaves quiver and causes a soft noise to go before him. When in Paradise this rustle is heard through the leaves, a soft breeze caresses the temples, and it seems as though Adam and Eve feel themselves gently touched. And with this quiet rustling and this touching emotion comes the inward address of the Lord to their soul, and thus the representation arose that the voice of the Lord came to them, walking in the garden at that time of day when the air was astir.

To look upon "the wind" as a bearer and symbol of what is holy, has thus gone forth from Paradise into all of Revelation. Of God it is said (Ps. 104, 3), that He walketh upon the wings of the wind; and in Ps. 18, 10, that He flew quickly upon the wings of the wind. When at Pentecost the Holy Ghost came to the Church, a sound was heard

from heaven as of a rushing mighty wind (Acts ii, 2); and
when Nicodemus received instruction regarding regeneration, the Savior purposely applied the symbol of the wind
to God the Holy Ghost.   Thou hearest the sound thereof,
but knowest not whence it cometh, and whither it goeth"
(S. John iii, 8), and thus it is with the Holy Ghost.

In a northern land like ours where the wind is a common
phenomenon, this is no longer so deeply felt.   But in the
regions from whence sprang Revelation, where weather
conditions were more quiet, and the rise of the wind,
therefore, more noticeable, the wind in its stirring has ever
spoken of higher things.

Natural philosophy had not yet come to analyze atmospheric currents.   The storm, as it arose with black
clouds in the sky, and with its violent boom and roar made
the whole forest tremble—that terrible windpower was
still explained as coming from above.   It came as a mysterious, inexplicable force; it was felt but could not be handled; it was heard, but could not be seen; it was an enigmatic,
intangible force, pushing and driving everything before it;
and the impression went forth that it acted upon man
immediately from God, without any connecting link, yea,
as though in that gale God with His Majesty bent over
him.   "The Lord hath his way in the whirlwind," said
Nahum (i, 3), "and the clouds are the dust of his feet."

This symbol of the wind is the reverse of that of the
temple.

The temple speaks to us of a God Who dwells in us as
His temple; Who is not afar off, but close by; Who has
chosen His abode in our heart, and Who from its depth
quickens, reproves or comforts us.

Thus the temple symbolizes the indwelling of the Holy
Ghost in the secrecy of the heart.   It represents the intimacy, tenderness and closeness of fellowship.   And though

there may be a veil in the temple, and fellowship with the indwelling Spirit may sometimes be interrupted, the renewal of love never comes from without, but always from the depth of our own being. It is and always shall be: "Immanuel, God *with us;*" *in Christ* with all His people; *in the Holy Ghost* personally with His child.

In contrast with this is the symbol that is borrowed from the wind.

Softly the wind of day, as a slight stirring of air, enters Paradise from without; it approaches unobserved, but always comes from without, and thus comes to man who at first does not even perceive it.

Here also it begins with a distinction. As symbolized by the wind, man at first is without God; God is separated from man. And not from man in prayer, but from God in the air astir, proceeds the motion whereby He approaches man, awakens him, and at length entirely fills him.

Both of these symbols have the right of existence; our Christian life must concern itself with both; and only he who allows these two to come to their own, lives in vital fellowship with the Eternal.

Between God and us the difference is so radical in every way, that we can never think of God in His Majesty otherwise than as highly exalted above us; He as having established His Throne in heaven, and we kneeling on this earth as His footstool.

This is the relation pictured in the symbol of the wind; the wind striking us from the clouds, and we sometimes feeling the cutting effects of it in the marrow of our bones.

But between God and His child there is also a free fellowship which defies distance; which removes every estrangement, and presses toward intimate union. And this relation is pictured in the symbol of the temple.

Our heart is a temple of the Holy Ghost, God Himself indwelling in the inner life of our soul.

The temple represents the overwhelming wealth of all-embracing love. The gale remains the symbol of the Majesty of the Lord. And only where these two operate completely, each in its own domain, is there both the most blessed worship of God's Majesty, and, at the same time, the most blessed enjoyment of His eternal Love.

Thus let the pendulum in the inner life of the soul ever move to and fro.

When you feel that for a time you have abandoned yourself too lightly and too easily to the sweetness of mysticism, and in dreamy communion with God might lose the deep reverence for His Majesty, then with one pull snatch your soul loose from this easy familiarity, in order that the greatness of the Lord Jehovah, in contrast with the smallness and the nothingness of your creaturely existence, may appear again in all its sublime loftiness.

And, on the other hand, when for a time you have been strongly affected by the Majesty of the Lord so that you know full well the Holy One above, but feel yourself at heart deserted of your God, and that all the more intimate love of God in the soul threatens to die, then likewise with supreme effort you must bring your frozen heart under the glow of the everlasting compassions, that fellowship with the Eternal may be tasted by you again.

But it is a gain when this swinging of the pendulum is not continued with too much force, and the intimacy of the "Our Father" and the reverence of the "which art in heaven" follow each other rhythmically in the daily experience of our inner life.

A life of mere dreaming and super-tender perceptions will not do; he who abandons himself to this weakens and slackens his spiritual existence, becomes unfit for his Divine calling in the world and forfeits the freshness of the life of his piety.

With a healthy state of heart there is here constant and regular alternation. There is constant and serious application to our calling, and with it God above us from Whom comes our strength and in Whom stands our help; and then again the search after God in prayer, the losing of oneself in the Word, the becoming *inwardly* tender by a feeling of sacred love.

Our God a God afar off and yet a God near at hand!

Taken this way, the wind obtains still another one than a natural significance.

Every day of your life forms a whole by itself, and every day of your life in everything that happens to you, that impresses and affects you, there is a plan and direction of God's. First those hours and moments when nothing speaks to your heart and everything loses itself in the ordinary run of things, and it seems that this day has no message for you. And then sometimes in the most trifling matter there is something that strikes you, that arouses your attention, that makes you think, and causes thoughts in you to multiply; something that a child calls out to you, a friend whispers in your ear, something that of itself comes up from your own soul; or something else that you hear, some message that is brought to you, something that brings color and tone into the dullness of the day and is for this particular day "the stirring of the air" in which the Voice of God comes near unto you.

Thus God the Lord comes every day seeking after us. So the Voice of our God follows after us throughout our life, to draw us, to engage our interest, and to win us for Himself.

And therefore lost is every day in which in the stir of the air the voice of your God truly passes by you, but does not affect and awaken you.

And also blessed is each day of your existence in which in the gentle stir of the air God makes His approach to your soul, and that approach bears fruition with such intimacy of fellowship that with fresh draughts you may enjoy again the eternal love of your God.

XVII

THOU SETTEST A PRINT UPON THE HEELS OF MY FEET

It always affects us like a discordant note when in Ps. 39 we read those grievous words of David: "O God, turn away from me, that I may refresh myself!"

Is there a more unnatural cry conceivable?

Man and God constitute the deepest contrast, and all true religion, springing from our creation after God's Image aims solely to put man into closest communion with his God, and where this is broken to restore it. And here the Psalmist, who still counts as the singer who has interpreted the religious life most profoundly, prays and cries, not for the approach of God; but that God will go away from him, leave him to himself, give him rest, and thereby refresh the closing hours of his life: "Hear my prayer, O Lord, hold not thy peace at my tears, *turn away from me*, that I may be refreshed, before I go hence, and be no more seen."

In Psalm 42 he says: "As the heart desireth the water-brooks: so longeth my soul after thee, O God," and here the very opposite: "*Turn thee away from me*, that my soul may refresh itself."

On one hand, deepest longing for the joy of the presence of God, on the other, the agonizing cry for deliverance from God's presence. Confess, does it not seem at first hearing as though the one literally contradicts the other?

And yet this bitter wail of David does not stand by itself alone. In Job you find an expression, that is even still more painful, of this crushing consciousness of the presence of the Lord, when in order to pour out his consuming anguish in fullest measure, he despairingly exclaims: "Thou puttest my feet in the stocks and thou settest a print of thyself upon the heels of my feet" (Job xiii, 27).

By itself there is nothing strange in this. The ungodly, too, are familiar with this agonizing dread. When unprepared, suddenly a mortal danger overtakes them, they handle, as it were, with their hands the power of God that forces itself upon them. In case of shipwreck out at sea it is seen over and over again that godless scorners, who but a few moments before over their wine-cups were making light of everything that is holy, suddenly stricken with terror spring from their seats with the cry: "O God, O God!" and pale with fear struggle for their lives.

And aside from these, with people who do not make a mockery of religion but in reality live without God—when serious sickness comes upon them or disaster overtakes them we see the same effect; to wit: that they also at such a time become suddenly aware that they have to do with the dreadful unknown power of that God Whom they have long ignored, and they tremble in their heart.

In ordinary circumstances we are sufficient unto ourselves. We extricate ourselves from trifling difficulties. We know how to rise above reverses of lesser magnitudes, and when they are overcome, the triumph heightens the sense of our self-sufficiency.

In such circumstances we feel free, unconstrained and unencumbered; we are our own lord and master. We are conscious of a lesser power that opposes us, but we push it aside and bravely continue the tenor of our way.

But all this becomes different when anxieties, dangers and disasters come upon us that overwhelm us, which we can not face, which nothing can avert, and which render us painfully conscious of our helplessness.

Then we feel that we are attacked by a higher power, that casts us down and makes all resistance futile and absurd.

This power places itself before us as an unseen and unknown opponent, who in a mysterious way cuts the tendon of our strength, binds us as with bands of death, mortally distresses and perplexes us, and leaves us nothing but a shriek of terror.

And however much the world has become estranged from God, at such times there is even in the most hardened heart still some tremor in the face of the Majesty of God. They have no faith in Him, but an anxious feeling steals upon them that now they must deal with Him, and the reproach that increases their terror is that they have so long ignored Him.

But this sense of dread most strongly affects the godly man in the moment that his faith fails him and God loosens His hold of the soul.

Then it seems not only that God abandons the soul but at the same time tightens His grip upon the body.

A man such as Job could not imagine anything that did not come to him from God. He had partaken of peace as from a cup handed him by God. And now that the evil day had come, and calamity upon calamity struck him, he could not explain it otherwise than that each of these disasters was a new arrow from the bow of Divine displeasure, aimed to strike and mortally wound him.

But just because Job was genuinely pious, this could not be the end. While at first he had the impression that God in anger stood afar off and with arrow upon arrow wounded him from a distance, he now sees God coming nearer to him, and at length, as with the hand of His Almightiness lay hold of him.

And at the moment when he feels that God has approached him in anger, as man against man laid hold on him, and is ready to throw him, his fear assumes a yet more striking character.

A tyrant who attacked Job and overcame him might at most put his feet in stocks and thereby render him powerless, but now that God does this it can not be all.

Now he perceives something that makes it seem as though God not merely stands before him and attacks him from without, but as though with His Almighty Power God enters into his very being, goes through him altogether and causes him to become rigid, so that at length he feels himself penetrated to the very heels of his feet by the Almighty One and crushed by the anger of the Lord.

Such mortal agony as this can only overtake the saint.

God in his anger is only felt like this by him who all his life most deeply realized the power of his God.

Thus there is a twofold perception of God's august presence: at one time in the blessed fellowship which the soul enjoys with God, and at another time in the awful consciousness of God's dreadful presence in the fears that assail us.

If now we were dealt with according to our sins and according to our deserts, this latter fellowship exclusively would be our portion, even the fellowship with the Holy One in his Divine displeasure.

Thus it will be forever in hell.

This *is* hell.

Here on earth diversion, pleasure, all sorts of means are at hand to put the thought of God far from us, and in addition to this, the godless here enjoy the terrible privilege, that they can sin, excepting at rare moments, without being troubled in their conscience by the presence of God Almighty. While here on earth they can put a screen between themselves and God and thus be far distant from Him.

But in eternity this is not possible. There they stand from moment to moment in the presence of their God.

And this awful consciousness of the presence of their God will be "the worm that dieth not, and the fire that is not quenched."

It is different with those who already here on earth have known God in His peace. They have received grace. In their behalf, God withdraws Himself in such a way that He covers His displeasure, veils His terrible Majesty, and, in spite of their sins, makes converse and communion with Himself possible without mortal fears.

Then between God and the creature there does not stand the screen of worldly vanities, but Christ, the Reconciler, the Redeemer, the Mediator of God and man. Hence already here on earth blessed and sweet communion with God can be enjoyed in Christ.

But if for one moment faith fails you, the shield of Christ is removed, and you feel yourself suddenly face to face again with the naked Majesty of God in His anger, and then the agony of soul in God's otherwise devoted children is more awful than the children of this world ever experience on earth.

Then for a moment the child of God is caught as in the snares of hell.

Such was the case with Job.

That was when he exclaimed: "O my God, thou brandest thyself in the heels of my feet."

That was when David prayed: "O my God, turn thee away from me, that I may refresh myself before I die."

And herein is grace, that at such moments the Comforter comes to our soul, that again the shield of Christ is put before us and God, Who made His anger flash for us, again reveals Himself to His tempest-tossed child as Abba, Father.

XVIII

MY SHIELD

IN the national hymn of the Netherlands the words are still sung by patriots in public assemblages, and in the streets: "My Shield and Confidence, Art Thou, O Lord, my God." And they but echo the utterance of the Psalmist's soul of thirty centuries ago: "The Lord is a Sun and Shield" (Ps. 84, 11).

With us the shield no longer plays any part. A battle now is fought at a great distance, with cannon and rapid-firing guns, against which soldiers to protect themselves cover themselves in the ground or behind breastworks.

But in those days when David wrote his psalm, fighting was mostly done man to man, at close range, sometimes foot touching foot, the sword of one clashing against that of the other; a struggle that could not end until one of the two was bathed in his own blood.

And of course in such a struggle the shield was one's life. Without a shield, while in contest with another who had a shield, one was lost.

Hence among the nations of antiquity it was the main thing in fighting, even as to this day it covers the African savage.

The shield caught the arrow; it broke the blow of the lance, and parried the stroke of the sword.

Therefore when those thousands and thousands in Jerusalem who had handled the shield themselves, and owed their life to it, raised the song of praise in the outer courts of Zion, and gloried in Jehovah as "the shield of their confidence," they felt, in a way we can never fully know, what it means to rejoice in God as in one's Shield.

A shield was a cover for the body which, mark you, was not held in front of the combatant by another, but even in extremest danger was handled by the man himself.

The shield grasped by the left hand was held before the arm and was in fact nothing else than a broadening of the same. In case of assault one involuntarily raises his arm, and at the risk of having it wounded, tries to cover his face and his heart with it. In order in such encounters not to expose the arm and to cover the larger part of the body the passionate desire to save life invented the shield; first the long shield, which was as long as one was tall, and then the short shield or buckler, with which to parry the stroke of the sword.

But always in such a way that the man who handled the shield moved it himself now this way, now that, and held it out against the attack.

"The Lord is my Shield" does not say, therefore, that God protects us from afar, and covers us without effort on our part. "The Lord is my Shield," is the language of faith. It sprang from the sense that God is close at hand, that our faith lays hold on Him, that we use Him as a defence against the assailant, and that thus by faith, *one* with God, we know and feel that we are covered with His Almightiness.

In a time of mortal danger a mother can stand before her child, so as to cover her darling with her own body, and then it can be said that that mother is a shield to her child. And so God is still the shield of the little ones who as yet do not know Him, and can bring no faith in Him into action.

But this holy imagery did not come from this. It originated with the man who in hard and bitter struggle had handled the shield himself and had saved his life by it.

The shield is to the man what the wing is to the eagle.

It belongs, as it were, to the body of the warrior. It is one with his arm, and his safe return from war hangs by his dexterous use of it.

And so the Lord God is a Shield to those who trust in Him, to those who believe, to those who in times of distress and danger know the never-failing use of faith, and who by reason of this faith understand that God Himself gives direction to their arm.

The shield points to battle and to struggle.

To the struggle against everything that rises up against us to destroy us in body and in soul.

He is our Shield against contagious disease, against the forces of nature, and against danger of death by accident. But, mark you, not in the sense that we should passively submit to it, and leave it to God to cover and protect us. The imagery of the shield allows no such interpretation. On the contrary, that God is a Shield against disease and pestilence, against flood and fire, implies that with utmost exertion we must use every means of resistance that God has placed within our reach; that by prayer we must steel our nerve to act; and that in this way by faith we have God for our Shield, a Shield that we ourselves must turn against the assailant.

And this is not different with our soul.

No weak interpretation has a place here. We should not say that we must *avoid* sin, no, we must *strive* against it. We should know that in sin a hostile power turns itself against us; that back of this power lurks the planning spirit of Satan, who stealthily presses upon us and aims to kill the soul, and who, if we have no shield to lift up against him and no skill to handle it with dexterity, will surely overcome and throw us.

Truly, still more than in the struggle for the body, God is your Shield in the struggle to save your soul; but then this demands, that you yourself must fight for your soul; that you yourself must catch the eye of the assailant who aims to destroy your soul, lift up the sword against him and meanwhile cover your soul with your Shield.

That God is your Shield in the struggle for your soul means that you yourself must stretch out your hand to God, that you yourself must engage in this warfare with every spiritual means of resistance at your command, and that then you will find that God is your Shield, Who by faith you hold up against Satan.

We speak of an escutcheon (by which we mean a shield) on which the man who owns it has engraven his blazon. This is a sign of personal recognition to those who know him, telling who it is that hides behind it. Thus the shield expresses the person; it becomes something by itself; a personification; by it is known the greatness or smallness of the power of defence.

Thus God is the Shield of those who trust in Him, a Shield on which human pride has not engraven for itself a lion's or a bull's head, but one on which in deep humility, in trustful meekness, looking away from self, and in confidence in his Father Who is in heaven, he who believes puts nothing but the name of Jehovah.

To take the Lord as your Shield, is to hold before the forces of nature and of Satan the Name of the Lord; to show to the world in characters of flame that we belong to the hosts of the living God; that we do not fight by ourselves, but that the Hero who leads us is the Anointed of the Lord; a proclamation that ours is the highest power of every human soul, the invincible power of faith.

Thus you see how far this scriptural imagery reaches.

We saw it in the confession that God is our Sun, the Sun of our very life. Here you understand that God is our Shield and our Buckler in the struggle to save our life.

And then you also feel and know that it means nothing if exultingly you sing of God as your Shield, unless in every emergency, in every form of struggle, instead of leaving this Shield hanging on the wall, you put this sacred Buckler to use by a living, zealous and heroic faith.

XIX

IMMANUEL

With many, nothing stands quite so much as an obstacle in the way of the practice of intimate fellowship with God as the saying of Jesus to the Samaritan woman at Sychar "God is *a spirit,* and they that worship him must worship him in spirit and in truth" (S. John iv, 24).

In all our attempts to make representations of things, and no less in all our processes of thought, we begin with what we can see, hear, smell or taste. Our thought has no grip on that which is not material, and when we want to talk about it, and try to picture it to ourselves, we have no way of doing it except as we compare what is invisible with something that is seen.

We know that we have *a soul,* but no one has ever seen his own; and even the question in which part of our person our soul dwells, can only be answered approximately.

It is the same with the spirit-world and with the spirits of the departed. Good as well as bad angels are bodiless. They have neither shape nor form by which they can be recognized. Whether an angel needs space in order to exist, no one knows. Whether in illness our sick-chamber can hold a thousand angels or not, no one can tell. Only when in order to appear to us an angel receives form is the difficulty lifted. As long as he is pure spirit without form, he utterly escapes our observation.

And it is not otherwise with those who have fallen asleep in Jesus. The dead exist until the return of the Lord in a purely spiritual state, in separation from the body, and we can form no idea about the souls of the departed.

And we are troubled by this selfsame obstacle when we try to lift up our heart unto God.

God also does not discover Himself to our visible eye. He is Invisible because He is Spirit and the Father of spirits. And for this reason, in the way of our ordinary knowledge and discovery, God is never found or met.

The touch of our soul with God takes place in a spiritual manner.

It takes place of itself in Immanuel.

What is it that makes us feel at once at home, when in foreign parts we unexpectedly hear others speak our own language?

Is it not the sense that this language is common property with us and our fellow-countrymen, a language by which we live, and by means of which we come into closer touch with others than is possible in a foreign tongue?

We are similarly affected, only far more strongly by the company of animals. Highly organized animals approach man at a high level of intelligence. In the association of a shepherd or hunter with his dog or of a horseman with his horse, it comes not infrequently to a very significant relation. And yet, however close sometimes an animal may come to us, when we join company again with a fellow-man, at once another and a far richer world discloses itself to us. He is flesh of our flesh, bone of our bone, a soul like our soul. This creates fellowship and makes it more intimate.

This is especially marked when we come in touch with people who are of the same mind and aim with us. There are groups among us, classes, professions and a number of other distinctions. And if one desires to become acquainted with us and to know us more closely, so that there is a mutual opening of heart to heart, he must belong to the same group, to the same kind, and, as it were, be embarked with us on the sea of life in the same boat.

And this is the significance of "Immanuel."

In the Babe of Bethlehem God Himself makes approach to us in our human nature, in order in our language, through our world of thought and with the help of our imagination, to make Himself felt in our human heart according to its capacity.

In our nature: This means that it is not required of us that we shall go out from our nature in order to find God by a purely spiritual existence. No, God, *our* God, wills to bless us, and from His side makes the transition which is spared us. Not that we go to Him but that He comes to us. Not that we must lift ourselves up to Him but that He descends to us, in order afterward to draw us up to Himself. He enters into our nature, takes it upon Himself, and lies in the manger in the ordinary condition of our human nature.

Here the distance between God and ourselves is taken away. The effort is spared us of trying to grasp this by becoming purely spiritual. What we receive, is human nature. What we hear, is human speech. What we observe, are human actions. Through and behind all this, there plays and glistens an unknown brightness, a mysterious loftiness, a transparent holiness, which now does not repel us, but rather attracts and fascinates, because it approaches us in our human nature.

So the human nature of Immanuel is not merely a screen to temper the too dazzling glories. No, it is *the* means and instrument to bring the Divine life naturally and intimately close to our own heart.

It is as though the human nature in *us* identified itself with the human nature in Jesus in order thus to bring God and our soul into immediate contact one with the other.

We do not say that this by itself was necessary. It

rather seems that the fact that we are created after God's image supplies us with everything that is indispensable to our fellowship with God.

But bear in mind that sin ruined this image of God.

And now in this weakened, undone estate only a gift of holy grace could fill in the gap, and this has taken place in Immanuel, in the coming of our God to us in the auxiliary garb of our human nature.

That this was necessary, even idolatry affirmed when it imaged the Lord of heaven and earth after the likeness of a man; and therefore the Christian religion could undo idolatry and paganism, since in Immanuel it alone presents the true Image of God anew. Is it not true that only under Christ this intimate fellowship with the living God has been brought about, which has so gloriously expressed itself in psalm and hymnody?

Apart from Immanuel, there is merely a philosophy about God, denial of God, or, at most, idolatry and cold deism.

In and through Immanuel alone there is a life in and with God, full of warmth, uplift and animation.

In Immanuel God draws near to us in our own natural existence, and through Immanuel our soul spiritually mounts up from this nature to the Father of spirits.

In Immanuel is the passage, not the goal.

It begins with Jesus but it ends with the fact that the Father Himself makes tabernacle with us, when also the day breaks on your soul of which Jesus said (John xvi, 26): "In that day I say not unto you that I will pray the Father for you, for the Father himself loveth you."

Then unfolds itself the rich activity of the Holy Ghost the Comforter, Who could not come until after Jesus had been glorified.

Let there not be anything artificial, therefore, or conventional, in our seeking after God. No intentional, pre-meditated, going out after Jesus with our suppositions, in order thus to find fellowship with our God.

What Immanuel brings us is reconciliation, so that we *dare* draw near again, and, at the same time, the Divine in human nature, so that we *can* draw near again. What we owe Him is the *Word*, the rich world of representations and thoughts, the result of His work as our heritage, the supply of powers of the Kingdom which inwardly renew us.

But with all this, it is always the personal touch, the actual fellowship with our God that remains a hidden spiritual motion, so that inwardly we hear His voice, and we can say with Job (xlii, 5): "Now mine eye seeth thee."

This is fellowship with our God as man with man.

Jacob at Peniel!

XX

IN THE LIGHT OF THY COUNTENANCE

In moments of tense joy the human face is radiant.

When the soul is cast down the face expresses gloom, the eye becomes darkened, and it seems that instead of showing itself in the face and speaking through it, the soul turns the face into a mask and hides itself behind it.

So there is a relation between color and states of mind: with joy we associate light, with sorrow somber shades, and mourning expresses itself in black.

This same contrast presents itself when we enter the world of spirits. Satan is pictured in greyish-black tints; good angels appear as kindly appearances of light.

In the Father's house above there is everlasting light; for Satan is reserved the outer darkness. The righteous shall *shine* as the sun in the firmament, clothed in garments of light. And when on Patmos the Christ appears to S. John, the Apostle beholds a sheen of glory that blinds him.

Could it be otherwise than that this selfsame rich thought of light as the expression of what is exalted, holy and glorious should likewise find expression for itself in the world of our worship by application to the Majesty of God?

God is light, and in Him there is no darkness at all. He dwelleth in light unapproachable and Father of Lights is His name.

Hence after the creation, God could not appear in the world that He had made save as He first sent out the word: "Let there be light." The Majesty of God revealed itself in a column of fire at the Red sea, in a cloud of light in Jerusalem's temple. When Moses is marked as ambassador of the Lord, a blinding splendor shines forth from his face. On Tabor the Savior showed Himself as in a radiating light enveloping His entire Person. When the new Jerusalem is portrayed, its highest glory is that there shall be no sun and no moon there, because of that world of glory God Himself shall be the Light.

Sacred art for centuries expressed this by portraying the head of Christ and of saints surrounded by a *halo*, and their person in glistening robes.

We do not treat this from its material side.

It is well known that certain people are strongly impregnated with magnetism and can make electric rays of light to radiate from their finger-tips; and doubtless in moments of great joy, the radiancy of face is connected with material operations; while the source of this facial light is not in the magnetic current but in the spirit, in the soul, in the hidden self, and all the rest is merely used as vehicle and means of direction.

He who carefully watches a child—who never conceals anything—in moments of its exceeding gladness, observes in the outward play of countenance that the eyes dilate and increase in brightness; that the complexion heightens so that it glows; and that it is by supreme mobility that this expression of the soul portrays itself in the face.

In part, this portrayal of the soul upon the face is even permanent. In contrast with the noble countenance of self-sacrificing piety, there is the brutish, dull, expressionless face of the sensualist.

Especially with young persons of constitutional delicacy, with the fire of youth in their eye, and of transparent complexion the expression in the face of true nobility of soul is sometimes unsurpassingly sympathetic.

Thus the language of Holy Writ that speaks of "walking in the light of God's countenance" (Ps. 89, 15), receives a voluntary explanation from life itself.

With God everything material falls away, but what remains is the utterance of the spiritual, the rich, full expression of the essential. God can not step forth from His hiding, save as everything that reveals itself of Him is Majesty, animation and glory.

It is evident that this revelation may also be an exhibition of anger, but this we let pass. We here deal with a soul that seeks after God; a seeking soul that finds God; a soul which, happy in this finding, looks into God's holy Face, in order to watch in blessed quietness everything that goes out from it. This brings but one experience, to wit: that that which beams out from God is never darkness, never somberness; that it is all light, soft, undulatory, refreshing light, and in that light of the Divine countenance the flower-bud of the heart unfolds itself.

This is the first effect.

Gloomy people may be pious but they do not know the daily tryst with God. They do not see God in the light of His countenance and in its brightness they do not walk.

When they who are otherwise brave of heart get hard lines in their face, it only shows that they have wandered out from the light of God's countenance—and how difficult it is to regain it!

A human face that beams with genuine kindness and sympathy is irresistible, and draws out the glow from your face which expresses itself first of all in a captivating smile.

But this is far more strongly the case with God the Lord.

You can not look adoringly at God in the light of His countenance without the gloom in your face giving way to higher relaxation.

In the light of His countenance you learn to know God. When this beams forth, His Spirit emerges from its hiding and approaches your soul in order to make you see, perceive and feel what your God is to you. Not in any doctrinal form, not in a point of creed, but in outpourings of the Spirit of unnamable grace and compassion, of an overwhelming love and tenderness, of a Divine pity which enters every wound of your soul and anoints it with holy balm.

The light of God's countenance which shines on you also envelops you. It encloses you. It lifts you up into a higher sphere of light, and you feel yourself upborne, as it were, on the wings of this light by the care of your God, by His providence, by His Almightiness. In the light of God's countenance everything, including your whole life, becomes transparent to you, and from every Golgotha experience you see glory looming up.

Also this:

The light of God's countenance penetrates every part of your inmost self and leaves nothing of your sins covered in you, though these are covered by grace.

Of course it can not be otherwise than that as soon as you are aware of the light of God's countenance shining through your person, every effort to hide sin is futile; altogether different from X-rays, the light of God shines through your entire self, your life, including your past. Nothing is spared. It is an all-pervading light which nothing can resist.

The light of God's countenance ought to frighten you, but yet—it does *not* do this. It can not do this because it lays bare to you the fullness of the grace that is alive in the Father-heart of God.

Hence, if there is one who does not yet believe in the perfect forgiveness of his sins, from him God hides His

face; only when fullness of faith in the Atonement operates in you, does the light of God's countenance shine
out to you, compass and penetrate you.

And then follows the walking in that light.

Walking here implies that not only occasionally you
catch a beam of that light, but that it has become constant
to you. That it is there even when you do not think of
it, and that it is ready at hand whenever your soul longs
for it.

And then you continue the walk on your pathway of
life from day to day in that light.

No longer led by any phantasies of your own, or
spurred by worldly ideals that have proved themselves
false, with no more darkness of sky above you in which
at most a single star glitters, you pursue your way by the
light that is above the light of the Sun—even by the outshining of ever fuller grace in the light of the countenance
of your God.

XXI

SEEK THY SERVANT

A SEARCHLIGHT projected from a tower over city and plain is a striking image of the flashing out of the All-seeing Eye.

Amidst shades and darkness with the velocity of the twinkling of an eye, a ray of clear white soft light darts out from a single point as its source, spreads itself over an ever increasing surface of country below, and immediately every object and form in the track of that light stands out in sharp outline. Nothing remains hidden.

So from the All-seeing Eye above, heart and soul-searching light beams forth, laying bare the deepest folds of the conscience.

It is not this seeking and searching, however, which the Psalmist refers to when he prays (119, 176): "Seek Thy servant." Scripture here employs the figure of the shepherd who is out on the hills seeking the lamb that wandered off from the flock and is lost. The Psalmist himself tells the story: "I have gone astray like a sheep that is lost; seek Thy servant; for I do not forget Thy commandments."

This figure from country life stands far higher than that of the searchlight.

Here is love, the yearning to possess again what was lost; and then the inability to let go what belongs to the flock; the motive of the search, or, if you will, the stirring, impelling passion of the heart.

Here also is reciprocity. The lost sheep bleats helplessly for the shepherd the while the shepherd scans the mountain side to find it.

The lost sheep wants to be found, and the shepherd wants to find it.

The bleating is the call: "Seek me, O shepherd!" and by bleating, the sheep itself co-operates in the finding.

So here we have the beseeching cry of the soul: "Seek Thy servant;" the prayer to be found, and at the same time an outpouring of soul, which itself makes the finding possible.

He who prays like this is not the child of the world, not the man who, far distant from God, is engrossed in the pursuit of worldly wealth, or who in his heart worships himself as his idol.

There is no reference here to the unconverted. He who here prays knows that he is God's servant, that he has entered upon the service of the Almighty; that he has been with God, from Whom now he has wandered away. This is clearly expressed in the image of the shepherd with the lamb. He who has wandered away from the flock has been with it; he who calls for the shepherd has known him.

"Seek Thy servant!" is the direct cry of God's child that has known his heavenly Father in His love and for want of this love feels himself lonesome and sick at heart, and longs for the tender enjoyment which it has tasted in the nearness of God.

Hence do not misunderstand the mystical sense of this cry of distress. It is not a call for conversion, but for *return*. He who is not converted *can* not pray like this. He who so calls, fell away from a love that was once known, and with all the tender yearnings of that lost love he longs that he might have it back.

This is a frequent occurrence.

One had entered in through the narrow gate; he had seen his path sown with higher light; the sense of new life had thrilled the heart; powers of the kingdom coursed through the arteries of the soul; he knew that he was alive, for the cup of reconciliation, full to the brim, had been handed him; he rejoiced in God his Savior; blessedly within him unfolded the intimate fellowship-life with God in Christ.

But it did not last. Fogs rose across the inner sky. From walking in the way he began to wander in by-paths, and presently lost it. Things began to be uncertain, and the heart restless and comfortless. Influences from beneath repressed holy influences from above.

How far God seemed to be distant again! how weakened the tie of faith in Christ which was once so firmly strung.

So it was all dark again for the soul, a feeling of loneliness and of being forsaken took possession of the heart, until it could endure it no longer, and yearning again after God, it set itself assiduously to the task of seeking after God.

This seeking, however, did not bring the finding. No sign marked the way. Going now in this direction and now in that, he remained equally far away from God, or wandered off still farther.

No, it has not been put in your power when once you have tasted God's love, to make light of it; first to win it, then to let it go, and then to take it again.

He who has known God and has forsaken Him, does not of himself find Him again.

So you learn to understand your utter impotence. Of yourself you can do nothing. But this you know, you can not do without God. The absence of His love creates an aching void in your soul.

Until at length it is realized: "I can not seek my God again, but He can again seek me."

And then comes the anxious bleating of the stray sheep, the call from the depth of the soul to the God that has been lost.

The suppliant cry: "O God, seek Thy servant!"

This deep longing to find God again can sometimes take a wonderful hold upon a man's heart.

There are those who in childhood were graciously permitted to enjoy the love of God, even though they were then but partly conscious of the fact; they were regenerated but conscious faith never reached the fuller knowledge of His Name.

This obtained the unusual condition of soul that, though God operated in it by His power, yet doubt entered the mind and the heart.

You know certain people who have not as yet been able to grasp the faith, but whose noble qualities of mind and heart render them peculiarly interesting and refreshing; frequently they are far more attractive to you than many a confessed believer. They are as flowers in the bud that can not come to bloom, but this half open bud exhales exquisite fragrance.

They are souls that are inwardly consumed with longing after God, and do not understand the nature of their longing. They are not aware that already they belong to God, they are only deeply conscious of nameless drawings after Him.

They do not pray themselves, but others who can pray, pray for them: "Lord seek this Thy servant—this Thy handmaid—for every utterance of their lives indicates that they rightfully have a place in the ranks of Thy servants and handmaidens."

They are children of the family who have not yet discovered their Father.

And such prayer is heard; not prayer from the lips, but from the soul, in behalf of ourselves and of those whom God has laid upon our heart.

Then God seeks them, and finds them, and lets Himself be found of them.

How this proceeds no one can tell. To bring it about, God employs a man's natural lot in life. He uses a written thought which He makes us read. He works this by means of affliction that heavily burdens the heart, hard and perilous times which try us to the utmost, contact with different people who meet us by the way, impressions of angels which He makes to hover round about us, inworkings which He causes to operate immediately upon our heart. It is the embroidering of God upon our soul of an holy work of art in all sorts of colors and in all sorts of designs.

But however different and inscrutable these operations may be, the outcome is assured. God seeks us, and finds us, till at length we discover that we have been found, and the nearness of God is enjoyed vitally, strongly and sweetly again in our heart.

Only, in this seeking of God, do not hinder the finding.

Not merely doubt, but the very inclination that prefers doubt is sin against God's love.

When God seeks you and places His hand upon your shoulder do not draw back, but fall to your knees, offer thanks and adore.

XXII

STRENGTHENED WITH MIGHT

No one questions any longer that the atmosphere in which we breathe and live exerts an uncommon influence upon our health. Fresh air builds up and invigorates. You see this with mountaineers, how the fresh mountain air puts iron into their blood; and, in the same way, with those who dwell in marshy regions, how the air, charged with poison from the swamps, keeps them below par and makes them pine away.

How can it be otherwise? Is not breathing a restless inhaling, always with full draughts, of what swarms about us in air and atmosphere; and not alone our breathing, but, if in lesser measure, the absorption also of the thousand and ten thousand pores in the skin is a drinking in of the atmospheric elements, and this opens the way to influences that affect our entire system?

Hence the pale and the anaemic are always urged to seek fresh air and to breathe more healthy atmospheres. Hence, equally, in hot, sultry summer days the panting for relief which evening brings, and, if within easy reach of the shore, the longing for a breath of the cooler, more invigorating air of the sea.

Now, we consist of body and soul, our being is twofold; and so this mighty influence upon our constitution of the atmosphere in which we live naturally finds a counterpart in the strong influence which the *moral* character of our environment exerts upon our own moral development.

This, too, is above question. Sad and joyous events continually show both how injuriously low moral standards affect character, and how life amid moral and healthy surroundings quickens one's moral sense.

Education is, perhaps not altogether, but very largely influenced by the surrounding atmosphere—the light and shadow of environment; and the secret of our mother's influence upon the formation of our character is largely due to the fact that as children we were longest in her presence.

The moral life, too, has laws and ordinances. It expresses itself in facts and deeds. It reflects itself in writings and conversations. But apart from all this, moral life is still something else, a sort of spiritual air, a moral atmosphere which is either healthy and bracing, poisonous and injurious, or neutral and weakening. And though your character may be strong you, too, undergo these several influences to your spiritual profit or loss.

This is not all.

There is not only in the air you breathe a power that affects your bodily health and, in your moral environment, a power that operates upon your moral life, but there is also an atmosphere of *person* which counts.

Constant association with a sensually disposed person of little elevation of character has a depressing effect upon your own. On the other hand, daily intercourse with a person of higher principles, of more seriousness of thought, of holier aim in life, stimulates you. Such a one is like a good genius to you. Such environment holds you back from what would otherwise pull you down.

This is especially evident when this person is indeed a man of sterling character or a woman of a dominant spirit. Persons exercise an attraction upon one another which has a leveling effect. The one is stronger than the other, and the stronger molds the weaker into uniformity to his own nature. Imitation lies at the bottom of human

nature, and unobservedly and unintentionally the weaker
inclines to be and to act like the stronger, even to the
extent sometimes, of the inflection of voice and kind
of conversation.

And this personal influence of itself leads to the influence of the religious atmosphere, which is distinctly
different from the moral.

All religion is *personal* at the core.

Moses has put the print of his personality upon all
Israel. Christendom has been carried into the world by
the Apostles. S. Augustine has inspired the Middle Ages.
The Reformation on the Continent of Europe and in the
British Isles bears the stamp of its spiritual fathers. And
in every community, to this day, in which a strongly
animated religious life is dominant, you can point out the
persons from whom this bracing atmosphere has emanated.

It is, then, fire from the heart of one that kindles fire
in the heart of the other.

The child of God that is robed with the beauty of holiness, as with a garment, also wins souls for God in his
environment.

Now we come to the highest rung of the ladder which, as
a rule, is too little reckoned with.

There is a breathing-in of mountain air and sea air.
There is a drinking-in of the moral atmosphere that surrounds us. There is an appropriation in ourselves of the
animation that comes to us from a finely-strung heart
with which we are in touch. But there is also, and this is
the highest, *a hidden walk with God Himself;* and it is the
influence that goes out from this hidden walk which for
the strengthening of our heart far excels all others.

S. Paul prays for the Ephesians (iii, 16), that they might
be "strengthened with might by his Spirit in the inner
man."

This, then, is the highest, richest, holiest atmosphere that can and must work upon you inwardly.

Suppose that Jesus were still on earth and that you, say for the space of a month, could see Him every day; you would feel yourself transferred thereby into an atmosphere of noble and holy living which in an unequaled way would strengthen you with might in the inner man.

To live for three long years in this holy atmosphere was the all-surpassing privilege of the Apostles, so that afterwards, strengthened in the inner man, they were enabled, even without the visible presence of Jesus, to witness against the world.

This is not possible now. We know Jesus no more after the Flesh. But through Him we have access to the Father Himself, and the daily, personal, hidden converse with God is open to us.

If, now, you take this to mean that it all ends with the short moments that you pray, then you remain in this holy atmosphere only a short time. All your prayers together, as a rule, do not occupy more than one half hour in every twenty-four.

But this is not the way the Scripture takes it. Already David sang (Ps. 23, 6): "I will dwell in the house of the Lord forever." And all the saints who before and after the royal harpist have sought, found, known and enjoyed this hidden converse with God, understood by it, a frequent thinking of God, a continual lifting up of the soul to Him, a pondering on all things with an eye to Him Who loves us, an ever being near unto Him, and a continual experience of blessedness in His holy, courage-inspiring and animating nearness; a personal appreciation of His omnipresence; our whole life and our whole existence being immersed, as it were, in the holy nimbus that shines

out from His Divine Being—a feeling in our own heart of
the throbbing of the Father-heart of God.

Churches with such a motive-power are alive; others
that lack this, though dogmatically they may be sound,
are dead. A preacher who brings this atmosphere to his
congregation is an ambassador of God. Preachers who
have no eye for this, because their heart does not go out
after it, are as tinkling cymbals.

When to be near unto God is your joy and your song;
when you dwell in His tent, and the hidden converse with
Him is daily your delight, then your whole person undergoes day by day the mighty, strengthening influence of
the holy atmosphere above; of that atmosphere in which
angels breathe and from which departed saints drink in
the never-fading freshness of their soul. Thus the powers
of the kingdom communicate themselves unto you in the
inner man. This is heavenly ozone that fans your soul;
power that restrains in you what is impure and unholy;
draughts from the Fountain of life which make your
breast swell with vitality and vigor; even the Holy Ghost
in whom God Himself touches you and inspires you to
nobler exhibits of power.

O! what a change would overtake all of social life if
every soul could breathe this holy atmosphere.

But this is the sin in point. When you say to one who
is anæmic: "seek mountain air," or "seek sea air!" he
at once considers the means to do it. Everyone is willing
to do this!

But when you say to one who is spiritually weak:
"Withdraw yourself from your surroundings and seek an
atmosphere of a higher moral character," then you may
move a single individual, but by far the greater number
continue to delight themselves in their own evil ways.

And when you go further and say: "Practice the hidden

walk with God, and drink in the atmosphere of the life above!"—then no one moves except as God Himself draws him.

This is a proof of the very high grace that has been ministered to you, if you indeed do know this secret walk.

O, bend the knees, even as S. Paul, unto the Father of our Lord Jesus Christ, that this glorious privilege may not be taken from you, but that rather from this hidden walk you may continually obtain might *to strengthen you in the inner man.*

XXIII

TO WHOM IS THE ARM OF THE LORD REVEALED?

THERE is no thought that lifts us more effectually above the power of the dust, and consequently, also, above the temptation of the senses, than the confession, that God is *a Spirit;* and from this a second thought follows naturally: that they that worship Him can not and must not worship Him otherwise than "in spirit and in truth."

This leaves no room for introducing anything whatsoever into the worship of God's Name, that is material, sensual or bound to form.

God is a Spirit. That is the truth which liberates your existence, your soul, your spiritual being from every tie that inwardly would bind and distress you; always, of course, on this condition, that you worship also personally in spirit and in truth with all the love of your heart this God, Who is Spirit.

God is a Spirit. That is the undoing of all idolatry, of all worship of the creature, of all homage paid to images in unholy form and the expulsion of all the sensual cruelty which idolatry brought with it, and which hastened the downfall of the nations of antiquity.

God is a Spirit. That entails a lifting up of your human existence above the whole visible world, and a lifting up of your spirit to those higher spheres of the invisible world, where God dwells in unapproachable light. For if God is a Spirit, then He is independent of this whole visible world; then He existed before the mountains were brought forth; then there is an eternity in which nothing material had been created; and then it follows that all things visible occupy a secondary place. Then the dying of your body is not the dying away of your existence. Then you can continue to be, to exist, even when for a while you yourself will be nothing but spirit. And then you can enjoy already here on earth the deep satisfaction that, if necessary, you can afford to despise the whole world, and yet maintain high spiritual standing, and spiritually be supremely rich in God.

But however potent and superlatively rich the confession that God is a Spirit may be, it, too, has been corrupted by sin.

You feel this most strongly when for a moment you think of Satan and of the whole world of demons. It is true that some people who take pride in the thought that they are "civilized" and "highly developed" take Satan and his demons as mere fabrications of weak minds. All they who believe, agree in this matter that Jesus knows better than these quasi enlightened minds, and that in the Our Father He taught us to pray: "Deliver us from the Evil One," and wove the good rule into it, when He put the prayer in our lips: "Thy will be done on earth as *it is in heaven.*" "In heaven" must mean, "by thy angels."

What are angels, except bodiless beings who are only spirit? And if Satan, as can not be otherwise, was not created evil, but was originally a good and brilliant creature of God, who belonged to the world of angels, what else can we do than confess of him that he too is a spirit, and that his demons also are spirits?

Does this make sin purely spiritual, and does this exclude it from the world of sense?

By no means. It does say that all sin, including voluptuousness and drunkenness, originates in the spirit, and that the Psalmist was correct when he prayed (Ps. 19, 13):

"Keep back thy servant from presumptuous sins; let them not have dominion over me; then shall I be upright, and I shall be innocent from the great transgression."

Nothing is more deplorable, therefore, than that in society at large "immorality" is taken almost exclusively to consist in drunkenness, riotous living or adultery, and that pride, self-glorification, and the consequent low estimate of others, bitterness, anger and the passion of revenge in nowise seem to detract from the good name of celebrated men.

According to this theory, the glorious confession that God is a Spirit, is then abandoned to the most dreadful pantheism, presumptuous pride leading at length to such an exaltation of self that one dreams that he himself is God.

And from this, and this alone, even among christian people the monstrous madness has evolved that having "the new man in the spirit" all responsibility for whatever sensual sins "the old man" might have committed can be thrown to the wind.

This is precisely the error which is now alive again in the school of Maeterlinck—that the pure soul within obtains no stain from the sensual misdeed done by the body.

All this Holy Scripture subverts, by impressing upon the soul, on one hand, that God is a Spirit, and on the other hand, with equal emphasis, that all the doings of God are *personal* doings, operations of a Person Who stands over against and alongside of us.

God is a Spirit, and therefore not a latent force, not a spiritual impulse pervading the whole creation, not a vague, elusive, inapprehensible working. No, thrice no; but a God Who is our Father Who is in heaven, Who speaks to us, Who listens to our prayer, in Whom throbs a heart full of Divine compassion; a personal God, Who companies and converses with us as friend with friend, Who turns in to pass the night with us, and Who allows us to dwell in His holy tabernacle.

Hence the constant picturing to us of the works of God as personal deeds, and the references to the *face* of God, to the *mouth* of the Lord, to the *ear* He inclines toward us, to the *footsteps* of the Holy One, to the *hand* which He lifts up in blessing upon us, and to the *arm* of power wherewith the Lord our God breaks all resistance.

All this is to a large extent personification, *i.e.*, an application to God of what is found in man. But there is more in it than this. "Shall not he," the Psalmist asks (Ps. 94, 9), "that planted the ear not hear? Shall he that formed the eye not see?"

Our eye, ear, mouth, hand and arm are nothing else than bodily manifestations of our inward powers, even those which God so created in us because He fashioned us after His Image. Hence when we say that God hears, sees, speaks, blesses and fights, this is not metaphorically expressed after the manner of men, but it means that all this is original in God, and appears in us merely after His Image.

When Scripture therefore makes mention of an "arm of the Lord," it means that there is not merely a vague outflowing of power from God, but that God Himself governs this indwelling and outflowing power, that He directs it to a given aim, that He uses it or leaves it unused according to His good pleasure; and that when God employs His power, either in our behalf or against us, this is equally, and in a still higher sense, a personal deed, as when we men lift up our arm in order to protect the helpless, or to ward off an assailant.

When Isaiah (liii, 1) asks: "To whom is the arm of the Lord revealed?" and we direct this question personally to you: "Is the arm of the Lord revealed to you?" then this does not mean the general, vague question as to whether you believe that there is a God, and that there is a power of God, and whether you acknowledge that this power of God operates; but the question means whether in your experience of life and in that of your soul, you have come to the discovery that this Almighty God deals personally with you, that as God He has turned Himself personally to your person, that He has come in touch with you as a man deals with his friend or with his adversary, and whether in this severe personal relation you have discovered the *arm of the Lord*, at one time lifting up itself to cover and to protect you, at another time turning itself against you to resist and to vanquish you.

And this is what is lacking in the spiritual life of most people, alas, even among professed followers of the Lord. They lack that which is recorded of Moses; that he endured *as seeing* the Invisible. They do not understand when of Jacob it is written, that he wrestled with God as with a man. They have a vague sense of influences, of operations, of powers that go out, but they do not *see* the Holy One, they have no dealings with God as with their Father Who comes to His child, looks upon that child with His eye, listens to it with His ear, lays His hand upon that child and covers it with the arm of His power. They pray to God, they praise Him, but do not meet Him on the way, they do not feel Him near upon their bed, they do not feel His holy breath go out upon them, they do not see that "arm with power" in which lies all their assurance and salvation.

Hence, it can not be insisted upon with sufficient urgency that Bible reading be made a more serious business; that we wean ourselves from the false tendency to take everything in Scripture *metaphorically*

The Scripture, the Word of God, is the lamp before our feet and the light upon our path, because it alone engraves these two things upon our soul, both that God is *a Spirit* and that this God, as our Father Who is in heaven, comes to us by the way, meets us face to face and deals with us as a man with his neighbor.

Invisible and yet seen.

XXIV

THAT THEY MIGHT KNOW THEE

"THIS *is life eternal, that they might know thee, the only true God!*" (S. John xvii, 3). No deeper meaning nor more exalted aim can express itself in human words. Indeed it is not spoken by a seer to us men, but by the Son to the Father; a word that must ever be overheard anew by him who seeks God, since for this purpose it was intended, and for this purpose has come to us.

Of the prayers that Jesus prayed here on earth during more than thirty long years, in Joseph's home in Nazareth, on the mount, or in desert places, in the morning and when the sun inclined to set, by day and at night— nothing has been handed down to us save a few outpourings of soul, and the cry of distress in Gethsemane. Here, however, in this chapter of S. John the high-priestly prayer of the Savior is given us in all its sublime tenderness, and He Who has given us the Scripture as a *vade mecum* on our pilgrim journey, has appointed and ordained that what Jesus here prayed to the Father can evoke an echo from our own praying heart.

Suppose that all the prayers of the Savior had been preserved in book-form, it would be a treasure that could not be exhausted. First the child-prayer from the newly unfolding soul-life which already at the age of twelve had opened up so divinely that, even in its still limited form, it immediately breathed and grasped perfection. Then the period in the prayer-life of Jesus from the twelfth to the thirtieth year, spent in retirement and preparation for the undertaking of the great work of redemption. And then that third period of three years, so brief, so quickly past, and yet by far the richest because of the storms that raged and were battled with through more than a thousand days; and who shall say how many hours of the night were spent in agonizing prayer each week that linked one Sabbath to another.

And yet, of all this wealth of prayers nothing is given us to overhear, nothing has come to us, practically nothing has been recorded, save this one: "I thank thee, O Father, Lord of heaven and earth, because thou hast hid these things from the wise and prudent, and hast revealed them unto babes. Even so, Father, for so it seemed good in thy sight."

And now, here, in the high-priestly prayer, this holy diadem that has been handed down to us unimpaired and unabbreviated, is at heart the selfsame thought: "This is eternal life that they might know thee, the only true God." In S. Matthew (xi, 25): "Not the prudent and the wise, but babes:" here in S. John (xvii): "Not the world, but those whom thou hast given me out of the world."

In each case: *The knowledge of God*, that which has been revealed of the Holy, is taken as the highest.

And in all this the one thing to be adored is the *good pleasure of God*.

An act of prayer, not as criticism of what is holy, but a receiving, a drinking in of holiness, and by this entering in of holiness into our life, to live not merely eternally, but with a life that in its own nature is eternal.

There is life when something stirs within us and when, from this inward stirring, something enters into being. So it is with the pregnant mother who feels life because she is aware of motion within herself and by this knows that presently life is to be born from her.

So, and not otherwise, it is with our person, with our self, with the inward existence of our soul within us. If everything remains quiet within you, if you hear nothing from your soul, if nothing stirs within your inmost parts, then it remains a secret to you whether or no your soul *lives*. You have a part in the life of the world, as the undulation of the waters at sea leaves no single drop at rest, but shares constant, restless motion with it. But this is for you no life as yet of your own; no inward stirring, the impetus of which springs from within yourself.

Such undulation in conjunction with the undulation of the world can truly develop warmth within you and enrich you either intellectually or in the range of your affections, but it lacks in you any individual impulse, and therefore can give you no lasting possession. And when at length the moment arrives, in which death lifts you out of the undulation of the life of the world, you shake off this impersonal life that has been lived along with others, and you have nothing.

The individual, personal life in you springs from a germ which God caused to germinate from the seed implanted in you, and this germ demands, in order to be able to develop itself, constant *feeding*, with nourishment suited to its nature. If this germ in you does not find this food, it becomes impoverished and shrivels. That it is surfeited with food foreign to its nature is no help. This it can not assimilate, can not digest. And in so far as it does enter into it, it is thereby denaturalized.

Neither is it any help that, only once in a while and in certain measure, it receives food suited to its nature. To develop itself in full measure, it must be fed regularly and continuously with proper food; and this must not end until its growth and unfolding is completed.

This is "eternal life" for the soul. Not merely a life hereafter, but an unfolding of your inner being according to its disposition, its nature and destiny; an unfolding whereby whatever poisons the inner life blood is expelled; whereby there is never lack of what the life blood needs; and whereby this inward feeding, strengthening and sanctifying is so constant, so permanent, so essentially eternal, that complete fruition is attained.

This is eternal life.

Eternal life for the inner being of the man created after God's Image.

And this is the word of Jesus, that your soul finds; this feeding for eternal life only and alone in *the Eternal Being Himself*.

"God Himself is my portion, my everlasting good" (Ps. 16, 5). "What can my heart desire on earth beside thee?" (Ps. 73, 25).

God is the highest good!

"In thy light we see light, with thee is the source, the fountain of my life" (Ps. 36, 9).

Undoubtedly, everything is continually coming to us from God, everything is owing to Him, every good and perfect gift cometh down from the Father of Lights. From Him, through Him and to Him are all things. But the end and aim is that God Himself shall be all and *in all*.

Glorious is the confession that our God is Lord of lords, King of kings, that He appoints, allows and governs all things; but deeper, infinitely deeper, is the experience of the entering in of God the Holy Ghost, who tabernacles in you, chooses you for His temple, prays in you and prays for you with unutterable groanings.

In this alone the heart finds rest.

All that grace apportions unto us is but *outshining* of brightness and glory; the burning hearth itself of all heat and glory is in God Himself.

Every drop of the water of eternal life refreshes us, but

the Fountain from which these waters spring is the Divine heart of the eternal Being.

And, therefore, throughout the entire Scripture, throughout the whole Church, and in the souls of all saints, it is ever and always this one passionate outburst of song: "It is good for me, it is my blessed lot, to be near unto my God."

Him the eye seeks, Him the heart desires; and only when the soul within us has found in God its highest good, the germ within us revives from its withering, and the developing, the unfolding begins, whereby from the bursting bud appears the blossom of everlasting life.

This can not be otherwise because of the nature of your soul.

You have not made that soul yourself. The world has not formed its nature. Neither has it become what it is by chance. What the soul of man should be, God alone has determined. And as God has appointed it, so is the soul in its nature, and so it continues to be, irrespective of whether it be the soul of a Judas or the soul of a S. John.

It can develop itself in a holy way, it can also wither and canker away in sin; but whether it develops in glory or by poison becomes corrupt, this development and this corruption both are what they are by reason of the nature of the soul as God has planned it.

From God every creative plan has gone forth; a plan for the stars in the firmament, for the corn in the ear, for the lark that sings among the branches, for the angel that sings the "Holy, holy, holy," in the sanctuary above. But the creation of man's soul was of a different nature.

With charming clearness the Scripture defines the nature of the soul in the single phrase, that you have been created after the Image of God. This includes everything. From this everything explains itself. From this it follows that the soul can never have its "highest good" otherwise than in Him after Whose Image it originated. And for this reason the further truth, that everything that directs the soul to another good, rather than to God, as the highest, wounds, corrupts and poisons it.

It is painful to see that the nations in their seething masses understand nothing of this. More painful it is to see how many there are among serious people, who reach out after everything but God. And most painful it is to see that there are even many Christians who chase and press after everything, but show that they have never enjoyed their highest good.

Yet Jesus does not despair.

He continues even now above to pray for His saints here below: "Father, this is eternal life, that they might know thee, the only, true God," and ever and anon the inner soul-life in a child of God discloses itself, and responds to that prayer an: "Amen, yea, Amen!"

XXV

SHOW US THE FATHER

IN this meditation also the main thought is the striking word of Jesus: "*This is eternal life, that they might know thee, the Only true God.*" The meaning of this saying is too profound, too rich to be fully thought out at one time. So we come back to it now, and will do so again presently.

We tried to make you feel what *eternal* life is. We did not undertake to epitomize it in one idea, neither have we analyzed the conception of it. We tried to interpret the idea of the life that is *eternal* more fully than as if it were merely a life without end. A life extending without end would drive you to hopeless despair; *eternal* life, something entirely different, inspires and rejuvenates.

Now to the point.

It does not say that he who knows the Father shall *receive* eternal life. It is not said: If you are religious and zealously seek to know God, your reward after your death shall be eternal life. It states altogether differently that, to know God is itself eternal life. And you realize that the difference is heaven-wide. Eternal life, taken as a reward for your painstaking efforts to learn to know God, is a superficial, mechanical and unnatural interpretation. On the contrary an eternal life that itself consists in knowing God is a thought so deep, that you, peering into it, see no bottom.

Eternal life, interpreted as a reward for knowledge, represents it as a sort of school discipline. Much study, much memorizing, much taking notes of dictations, and then, as a reward, promotion from a mortal and passing existence into an ever-enduring, never-ending one—a kind of higher life-insurance.

It then comes to consist of a piece of memory-work. A study of a subtly composed work on dogmatics, every part of which has been traced out in all its particulars, and which presents in an orderly form what in the course of ages has been systematized regarding the Being and work, the Person and attributes of the Infinite. And when at length everything has become dry and barren to the eye of your soul, till no more fragrance of life is perceptible anywhere, then this barren, dead knowledge is to receive the reward of eternal life.

But the knowledge of God itself is eternal life. He who possesses this knowledge already possesses this eternal life *now*. On the other hand, he who dies without having found this knowledge of God here, will not find it in the hereafter. On him the eternal morning never dawns.

You feel, you handle it. So interpreted (for so it must, so only it may be taken) this word of Jesus presses itself upon you as a power, as a strong power that enters into your very being and conscience, and asks you: "Have you already obtained this knowledge of God?"—as a power that urges you, now, before it is too late, to reach after this knowledge, until in the stirring of your soul you feel the swell of the undulation of this eternal life.

And now comes Philip and asks naïvely: "Lord, show us the Father" (S. John xiv, 8).

This was childlike in its simplicity, and yet he took the proper starting point from which to advance. He who so asks shows that he is in earnest. He wants to attain unto the knowledge of God. It is evident, from his saying that he desires no book-knowledge but life-knowledge of God. He wants to know God, God Himself. And what more natural than that he begins by asking: "Show me the Father."

In some quarters the religious life has developed itself too dogmatically. This was inevitable, it could not be otherwise. Doctrinal expression was indispensable. But yet it is not without risk when it appears too onesidedly in the foreground. It is the selfsame difference as between the Gospels and the Epistles; in the latter, dogmatic conflict is already in evidence. And even in the Gospels you have the same difference between the Sermon on the Mount and the controversy of Jesus with the Scribes.

The early periods of Christianity were better than the later. What rapture marks the language of early creedal statements and liturgies, and offices of Holy Communion, and how comparatively barren and emaciated are later formulas. At first, life runs like a river. Later on there is nothing more than drained river-beds, with only some weak rill coursing through the sand. Oh, who can say how greatly this has impoverished the people of the Lord!

Now, Philip knows nothing of these contrasts. He still faces it with childlike ingenuousness. God is to him really the Eternal Being. God is his desire, he seeks after God, and therefore it is the prayer of his heart that he might see God. And so in stress of soul he says: "Show us the Father."

When some person is mentioned, and you are asked, "Do you know him?" then, if you do not know him, nothing is more natural than that you say: "I have not even seen him."

Seeing is of first importance. To receive an impression by seeing, speaks for itself. This accounts for the fact that both in the Old and New Testaments this seeing of God appears always in the foreground. Even as early as Moses when he prayed: "Show me Thy glory!" and Jehovah answered: "No man shall see my face and live" (Exo. xxxiii, 18, 20). And you know how later on S. Paul exulted in the fact that: "We all, with open face, *behold-ing as in a glass the glory of the Lord*, are changed into the same image from glory to glory (I Cor. xiii, 12). This takes place in a measure here; but more fully hereafter. "We shall see face to face. Now I know in part; but then I shall know even as also I am known."

The life of Scripture throbs with such words as these. Here all barrenness is gone. It is full of reality. It is all for the sake of God, the living God; to see Him, to behold Him; and then ardently to rejoice in this life-giving insight.

And therefore what Philip asked ("Lord, show us the Father") was a well chosen beginning, springing from the deepfelt thirst after the living God.

But, alas! outside of you, God can not be seen, and why He can not be, is perfectly plain.

You can only see that which is outside of you, when it presents itself to you in the world as a separate object, and is sufficiently defined to fall within the range of your vision.

No one can see the world, but only such pieces and parts of it—now this part, now that—as may fall within your reach. But even if you could see the whole world, which is impossible, you would not be able to see God; for the world is finite, and God infinite, and the broadest conception you make of the world, sinks away into nothing when compared with the infinite God.

And then you can only see whatever has form, figure, appearance, and falls within your range; and "God is a *Spirit*, and they who worship Him, must worship Him in spirit and in truth."

To see God *outside* of yourself is therefore impossible. To want to see Him outwardly is to belittle Him, to give Him material form, and to deny Him as Spirit.

And here idolatry comes in.

Idolatry was this: that the nations "changed the glory of the incorruptible God into an image made like to corruptible man" (Rom. i, 23).

This did not spring from wickedness, but from piety. It was not the worst but the best people of a nation that built temples and placed an image of God in them. From among these nations the cry went up: "Show us God." And the priest did show them their God in an image that they made.

They thought in this way to bring God closer to the people; and yet by that miserable image they caused all knowledge of God to be lost.

With every *representation* of God, God Himself is gone.

Hence the judicious warning of S. John, before he died: "Little children, keep yourselves from idols!" (I John 5, 21).

And so the two continue to stand over against one another.

On one hand, the urgent call: "Show us the Father!" The soul-cry which is not satisfied with a dogma, a conception, a formula; which wants to possess God himself; the truly pious, childlike thirst for the living God: on the other hand, you can not represent God to yourself as an object, nor see Him with your eye. He is the Invisible One. And with every effort to represent Him in an image, you lose the Infinite and wander ever farther away from Him.

The reconciliation of these mutually excluding perceptions—that you are inwardly driven not to rest till you see God, and that you, by representing God to yourself, lose Him altogether—lies in what Jesus replied to Philip: "He that hath seen me, hath seen the Father; and how sayest thou then: Show us the Father?" (John xiv, 9).

But how?

There is a perception *outside* of you, but there is also a perception *within* you. Not within yourself alone, but within you *in your human nature*.

Now, in the Son of man, God Himself appears before you in this human nature. And by your fellowship with the Son of Man you also see your God, in Jesus, through Jesus, and in yourself by the Holy Ghost.

Not the image of God in the temple of idols, but the Image of God in the Messiah!

XXVI

HE THAT HATH SEEN ME HATH SEEN THE FATHER

More than once there flowed from Jesus' lips expressions, declarations, words, which still in reading them make you tremble, and shrink back, *except you worship Him.*

As for instance, when Jesus says to you, and to every one: "He that loveth father or mother more than me is not worthy of me" (Matt. x, 37).

Imagine some one in our days at a public gathering daring to say anything like this. Every hearer would count him insane. Or still worse, if some one entered your room, and in your presence thus addressed your child— would you not be bent upon finding the surest means of keeping this corrupter of your child away from him for the future?

Yet Jesus spake thus; and you yourself impress it upon your child that this is true, and must be so, *because you worship Him.*

And in the same way with what Jesus answered Philip: "He that hath seen me hath seen the Father," there is the selfsame difficulty.

Whoever spoke like this, you would at once endeavor to render harmless by putting him away among the insane, except you yourself worshiped and adored God in Him.

Choice there is none.

Against a man of such blasphemous pretension, public opinion among any people not dead to religion would demand measures of protection. But your heart gives an echo that says Amen to this striking word of Jesus, because you yourself worship Him. It all depends on this.

The Sanhedrim, the vociferous Jews in the court-square at Jerusalem, acted logically from their point of view when they saw in Jesus a blasphemer and cast Him out—*so long as they* themselves did not worship Him.

As long as their eye was closed against Jesus' divine Majesty, they could not do otherwise. And their fault, their sin, their mortal guilt was not that they cast Jesus out, but that they did not see God in Him. That is to say, their mouth was full of talk about God, but when in Jesus God appeared before them, they knew Him not and denied that it was God.

Such is still the case.

In times when the religious capacity of observation is illumined, thousands again see God in Jesus, who were not aware of it before. And, again, in times like ours when this religious capacity of observation is limited and weakened, the masses die to the faith, and soothe themselves by heaping honorary titles upon Jesus, such as: "the ideal-man," "the example of true piety," "the hero of faith," "the martyr of a sacred cause." Altogether words—and again words—to hush the conscience, and to evade the inevitable consequence of an acknowledgment of His Deity, that with Thomas they kneel down and in ecstatic adoration exclaim: "*My Lord and my God.*"

Voltaire fell into the frenzy of daring, when "L'Infâme" flowed from his reckless pen. And yet, Voltaire was braver than these irresolute spirits; and so far as the root of the matter is concerned they stand where Voltaire stood.

They also do not believe that he who saw Jesus saw God. Only, they take no chance by saying how Jesus Who dared to claim this must be judged.

This seeing of God in Jesus is the highest act to which the spirit of man can come.

Many accept this while they are still children, but do

not think about it much as they grow older. As for the rest, they leave this conviction uncultivated and do not apply it to their later developed consciousness, but leave it alone as something alien.

You should not judge these people too severely. Many are not able to do more. Their hand reaches no farther, and they no doubt have a sensation of moral uplift from this immature conviction.

But the thrice blessed, who have been initiated into an intimate and more ardent piety, can not rest content with this. They ponder and meditate, and undergo sensations and experiences of soul which cause them to enter more deeply into the mystery than is ever possible, without this activity of soul, by mere analysis of doctrine.

To them, seeing is something other than sight with the sensual eye, because this is not the richest, not the clearest, not the fullest seeing.

God saw before we saw, without the eye of sense, purely spiritually and immediately.

When God imparted the gift of sight to man, by creating him after the Divine Image, it could not be otherwise than that in man, too, this sight originally must also have been spiritual, internal and immediate. And only because God clothed man with a body also, and placed him in a material world, did He form for him the eye by which to see this world.

But for this purpose alone; for nothing else. And therefore this material eye could not do service for any other perception than for that of this *visible* world. In behalf of the other, deeper, much richer and far more extensive world, which is not visible, this bodily eye is of no avail. For this, man received another eye, the eye of the soul, to which the eye of the body, as a subordinate instrument, only renders auxiliary aid.

Hence there are two worlds: the spiritual world and the visible world, and in connection therewith, two kinds of eyes: the eye of the soul and the eye of the body, and consequently two kinds of sight, the seeing *immediately* by the spirit, and the seeing *mediately* through the eye; a seeing *inwardly*, and a seeing *outwardly*.

An ideal perception, of which we even now have such a clear sense that nothing is more common than the saying: "You see that I am right,"—"the seeing" referring to something that has been said, argued, explained, and not to something that has been shown to the eye of sense.

To see the Father in Jesus was, from the nature of the case, no primitive action of the sensual eye. God is a Spirit. He who in Jesus would see the Father, must therefore in Jesus see that Spirit which is God.

And therefore there can be no other meaning here than of a spiritual sight with the eye of *the soul*.

First you may only become aware that in Jesus there is something spiritual, much as in other holy persons. By further study of His inner Self, you perceive that what is spiritual in Jesus stands at a higher level than with any one else, and that in Him it is clearer, fuller, richer.

But this does not as yet explain Jesus to you, "higher, richer, fuller spirituality" than in others, even the best, does not as yet say enough. There discloses itself in Jesus a still more unfathomable depth, so that at length you must acknowledge that in Him the spiritual lives and glows more richly than you could ever picture it in your imagination. In Jesus it exceeds what was deemed possible, it surpasses the conceivable, and thus your spiritual observation of Jesus passes over into the infinite. You make no more distinctions. From the background of His being eternal perfection shines out toward you. And now everything shifts before the eye of your soul. Unconsciously you have passed from the finite into the infinite, and thus you feel that it is God Himself Whom you perceive through Jesus and in Jesus—and you kneel down, and you worship.

Yet this experience of yours is not independent of what your eye of sense sees in the *Incarnated Word*. In thus scrutinizing Jesus you do not separate His spirit from His personal appearance. You do not eliminate the body in order to penetrate to the soul. You take Jesus as He was, spoke, appeared and labored.

It is a complete manifestation, a whole, a mystery that stands before you.

And as, even among ordinary people, sometimes a moment comes when they appear radiant, and their face, their eye, around their lips, in their word, their appearance, their act, allow their soul to shine through, so that through their outward form you look into their inward being—so it was with Jesus, only infinitely more strongly, and with Him at all times.

His appearance must have been overwhelming. The impression which He made must have been full of surprise. And when you think what soulfulness there was in His holy eye, what impressiveness in the features of His face, what sympathy and power in His finely modulated voice, you feel at once that the physical appearance of Jesus was no hindrance to a perception of the Divine in Him, but rather a vehicle by which to approach it. It was as though through Jesus, God Himself came out into the visible world, inviting and alluring all who saw Jesus, to admire and to worship God in Him.

If when Jesus appeared on earth, man had been as he was before the fall in paradise, in Jesus every one would at once have recognized God to the full.

But with the darkened eye of the soul of sinful man this was not possible. God was there in Jesus, but the world could not see it. There was a veil before the eye of the soul, and only when God Himself lifted this veil, did man see Deity in Jesus.

This eye in the soul is not a separate thing. It is rather the sum-total of all the powers in the soul which enable it to become aware of, to perceive, to discover and to enjoy. This spiritual sight is a feeling, a perceiving, with all the powers that slumber in the soul. It is a waking up of the entire human nature that is within us, which, created after the Image of God, goes back to that original Image, clearly perceives the relation between the Image and the original, between the original and the impression, imprints it upon its own sense of self, and so knows God with an inward knowledge.

So alone has the human nature in Jesus grasped and known God to the full. In each and every one of us is not human nature *as a whole*, but this nature in one variation, in one special, definite form. In Jesus, on the other hand, this human nature *itself* was embodied. Therefore was He called *the Son of Man*. And because of this, Jesus was not only God, but as man also He alone of all others entirely grasped and understood the Father.

"No man knoweth the Father but the Son, and he to whom the Son will reveal Him."

Thus you can not of yourself, and when left to yourself, with your inner soul-perception *grasp* God, and with the eye of your soul *see* God. Jesus could and can do this well, but not you. And for you the way thereto is opened only when you go to Jesus, when you become adopted in Jesus' fellowship, so that you become a living member of this mystical Body of which Jesus is the Head. And then you not only *see* God in Jesus, but God also comes to make tabernacle in you through the Holy Ghost.

For this indwelling of God in your soul is for you the disclosing of the Divine mystery to your own hidden *self* within your inmost hidden parts.

"Philip, have I been so long a time with you, and do you still say: Show me the Father?

"He that hath seen me he *hath* seen the Father"—in me and through me, your Savior!

XXVII

WITH ALL THY SOUL

WHEN the question is raised, whether there is one that seeketh after God, the Psalmist disputes it, and bitterly complains: "They are all gone aside. . . . there is none that doeth good, no not one" (Ps. 14, 3). There is *none* that understandeth, there is *none* that seeketh after God.

Did the poet then dissemble, when in the ear of all the ages he sang so touchingly: "As the hart panteth after the waterbrooks, so panteth my soul after thee, O God!" (Ps. 42, 1). Or did Asaph only pretend a state of soul, which was nothing but self-deceit, when he exultingly exclaimed: "Nevertheless, I am continually with thee" (Ps. 73, 23).

Certainly not.

The question is, whether by nature in the heart of even *one* person the magnetic attraction still operates, which draws toward God and overcomes every hindrance, every resistance. The answer to this is no, and ever again, no; there is no such drawing in the human heart, damaged and maimed, it no longer is what it was by Divine creation, but what it has become by self-corruption. You see it before your eyes.

Or is it not a matter of tears that outwardly the great mass of people have no feeling for God, and thirst not after Him. By itself the number is small of those who take their religion with any seriousness, and smaller still the number of those in whom true piety is revivified. Mingle among those who are still in every way religious, see them, study them, listen to their talk, in their company do as they do; and how surprising it is that everything

is done in so external, artificial and mechanical a way;
and how rarely you feel, that you deal with a soul which
makes it a business to make approaches to God, to come
closer to Him, and to *find* Him.

Even in worship, in church or elsewhere, frequently the
question can scarcely be repressed: "Does he or she, when
the Amen has been said, come away from the presence of
God; or even in worship has this soul been as far absent
from God as ever?"

Doubtless, there are always some who in prayer and at
other times, seek fellowship with the Eternal in their
soul. Only, upon inquiry, it appears again and again,
that the magnetic attraction did not originate with them,
but that with magnetic power God Himself drew them.

Why this power operates on one, and does not affect
another, we do not know. But the fact remains that, as
the magnet attracts steel, so God can attract the soul.
And when He does, this drawing is irresistible. Then the
soul seeketh God, because God draws it.

How does this operate?

Does the soul make its approach to God through the
understanding, through the will, through the feeling,
through the imagination, or by an unexplainable mystical
working for which there is no name?

And the answer differs according to the character of
those who make it. One attributes it to intellectual and
doctrinal knowledge of God; the other to the intimacy of
love; a third to the concurrence of the will; a fourth to
dreams and visions; a fifth to inspirations; and the more
you ask, the more the answers differ. Disposition and
temperament here play the chief rôle. The subtle dis-
sector of ideas and definitions entrenches himself in vigorous doctrinal confession. The man of action, in his devotion to practical results. He who by nature is finely strung,

in the note of pensive longing which he elicits from his emotional temperament. And likewise imaginative minds and those inclined to phantasies, in representation and ingenious imagery. Every one after his own kind, we may say. So it is now, and so it was in ages past. From old writings you see people of long ago still alive before you, and it is evident that things generally are as they were; all sorts of currents, all sorts of schools, all sorts of tendencies—one this way and the other that. You never find unanimity. Never is God sought after with all the soul.

This shows that the choice of one particular method of seeking after God shuts off ways to God, which truly could bring you into His fellowship; and, that the children of God must maintain free walks in all these ways, so that nothing shall limit their communication with the Father's House.

The reason for this is, that the finding of God is not effected by any one power of the soul, but by the whole soul itself. It is not our knowledge, it is not our will, it is not our imagination or our thought, that grasps God and possesses Him; but it is the knowing, the willing, the pondering soul in its totality, in its inner unity and soundness, in its inner reality. Ray by ray enters in, but each ray is caught up in the one focus of the awakening life of the soul; and this action is called *faith*.

The difficulty here, too, springs from the ruined conditions within, occasioned by sin.

This ruin we do not take into account sufficiently, because we place it too exclusively in the domain of *morals*. And yet, the whole loss which it entails, is only known when you trace it in its fatal workings in the spiritual life.

In your relation to God things count so much more seriously.

This concerns the first and great commandment; loving God with *all* your soul, with *all* your strength. And this is possible. The soul is disposed to this. Yea, it can freely be said, that your soul, as soon as it works normally, can not do otherwise than direct itself to God, in all its entirety and with all its strength. But nowhere does it show more strongly than in this very particular how abnormal in every way the soul has become by sin. And the worst of it is that with respect to this the soul itself is so little aware of its abnormality.

He who has done wrong, especially when it is a heinous wrong, at least knows it, and does not find it difficult to kneel before God and confess his guilt. With more refined forms of transgression, even in the moral sphere, this inner sense may fail us; when gross sin is committed, the conscience speaks in almost every man.

But with respect to the violation of the first and great commandment almost no one has any feeling about it.

Thousands upon thousands, by day and by night, deny God all love, withdraw their whole soul from Him, and rob Him of all their strength—gross transgressors in the spiritual domain, who do not even think that they sin.

And even with those who have been discovered to themselves, the redeemed, the saved, who have confessed to have love for God, conditions are about the same. Among them also you frequently find those who, over and over, for a whole day at a time, have given at most a small fraction of their soul to God, and feebly, with perhaps only one of their powers have consciously worked for God; and who, when they kneel down at night, do *not* feel it as sin that they have violated, let us say, nine tenths of the first and great commandment.

This same tendency operates so fatally with the one-sided activity that is brought about by reason of our disposition and temperament, and inclines us to use those powers which come most naturally into action, and therefore exact least self-conquest.

Thus, an intellectually disposed man, when he becomes pious, seeks his strength, in his search after God, in dogmatics.

If this is eternal life, "that they might know thee, the only true God," well, then, he will apply himself to this. Of another knowledge save that which is acquired by intellectual analysis he has not the faintest idea, but in his own department he is proficient. So he exhausts himself in tracing what the finest thinkers have embodied in their doctrinal systems regarding the Nature, the Work, the Person, the Attributes—and so on, of the Divine Being. In this he absorbs himself. This appeals to him. Above others he prides himself on it. And now he actually thinks that in this way the real knowledge of God has become his portion.

"No," says another, "Jesus has said, that he who doeth *the will* of his Father who is in heaven, shall know the glory of the faith;" and he, as a man of action, gives his money, is zealous as few are, brings willingly one sacrifice after another, devotes himself to the affairs of the Kingdom with all his strength. But he has a dislike for all doctrinal distinctions. The creed does not do; with him the main thing is the practice of life.

A third has neither pleasure in doctrine nor in works, but is of an emotional temperament, and he seeks his strength in tender sensations which he arouses, in soulful utterances, in mystical perceptions of love, and so deems that he comes closer to God.

Imagination is the play of phantasy on the part of him who rather seeks his strength in visions and representations, and enjoys himself most in what his idea paints before the eye of his soul. Has not even S. Paul gloried in ecstacies of spirit and in being caught up into higher spheres?

Add to this, inspiration, the bringing to remembrance, the perception in the soul of sudden emotions, and so on, and you feel, how widely among men the sensations and motions of the soul diverge, when a thirst after God awakens in the soul.

And this now is the pitiful fact, that instead of understanding that *all* these workings, all these powers and exertions together must be used in love for God, in order to make real the loving of God with all one's powers— God's children for the most part hold themselves each within their own domain, and seek God with *one* of the powers of their soul, thus leaving the others unused, and then frequently oppose a brother who seeks his salvation in the exercise of another power of soul than theirs.

"With all thy soul," said Jesus. They say: "With a fraction of the life of my soul;" and just because they are truly pious and sincere of purpose, they do not tremble at the thought of how dreadful it is to have all the rest of their soul remain inactive for their God.

XXVIII

I SAW ALSO THE LORD

"THIS is eternal life that they might know thee, the only true God;" but then it must also be a knowledge of God not merely with the intellect but with every means at man's disposal by which knowledge may be obtained.

It must be a knowledge which is the result of every observation and apperception.

With this the question at once comes to the fore as to whether our imagination or, taken more broadly, our power of *representation* also plays a part in this.

Superficially one would be inclined to answer this question with a decided *no*.

For God is a Spirit; and if the expression "spirit" here means, that we must exclude all corporeality or materiality, it is not seen how with the Lord our God there can be any mention whatever of an *appearance*. And if all *appearance* is inconceivable, how then would one be able to make a *representation* of God? Truly one can, as the heathen did in many ways, make a form, a figure of an idol, but then this remains purely a contrivance; and naturally with that knowledge of God which shall be to us eternal life, a cunning device does not interest us; we want reality.

According to this, one would have to say that there can be no representation of God, nor can any bodily manifestation show itself, because, by reason of the absolute spirituality of the Eternal Being, every idea of matter, form or dimension with regard to Him is altogether excluded.

And yet, however convincing this may seem, this does not end it.

What is there to say of what Isaiah tells us in his narrative of his vision (ch. vi, 1)?   Even mentioning the year in which it took place, he says: "*I also saw the Lord sitting upon a throne, high and lifted up, and his train filled the temple.*"

Let the question here rest as to whether Isaiah saw something that was outside of himself, or something that thus presented itself only within the field of his inward vision. It is enough here, that Isaiah had a *vision* of God, and that he was able, in his prophecy, to give some *representation* of it. It was a *vision*, which so forcibly took hold of him, in which so much happened, and which resulted in so important a prophecy, that it wholly dominated all of Isaiah's later life.

For us, who honor the work of the Holy Ghost in Isaiah's unction, inspiration and Divine utterance, it is impossible to take this call-vision merely as the product of an unhealthy imagination. There was reality in it, and an act on God's part. And so we come to the conclusion that, among several means by which to make Himself known to man, God also has made use of perceptible manifestation, even though this was transient.

There is more.

In the New Testament as well as in the Old Testament we read repeatedly of angel-appearances and of appearances of the Messiah previous to His Incarnation.

Are not the angels spirits, even as God Himself, incorporeal and immaterial? And yet you read again and again that there are angels who appear, who speak, who do something. The angel that smote the armies of Sennacherib stands on a par with the angel that led S. Peter forth from prison.

Moreover, previous to the Incarnation, Christ existed purely spiritually; and yet, the appearance, the mani-

festation was so apparent with the Messiah in old days,
that the Patriarch receives Him in his tent and makes
Him enjoy food at his table.

And now it is well known that in our days all this is
scoffed at and is said to be innocent fiction; but less superficial psychology is not satisfied with this, and attaches to
such a narrative a far higher intrinsic worth.

If, now, you observe how Christ Himself, when on
earth, literally accepted Old Covenant records in which
such appearances are mentioned, and confirmed their
direct significance, who, then, can reach any other
conclusion than that a certain appearance and thus
also a certain manifestation of a being that by itself is
purely spirit is not inconceivable, even though it be
of God.

This play in Scripture of making images and representations of spiritual subjects, has this peculiarity,
that the traits of them are always borrowed from man.
With the Cherubim we read of animal forms, of a lion and
suchlike, which serve to represent great power and glory;
but in every meeting with man the appearance of an angel,
of the Messiah, and also, as in Isaiah (ch. vi) of the Eternal Being Himself takes place in human form, in human
dress, and with the use of human language.

Even of wings (which are borrowed from the animal
world) there is no mention in any record of the appearance of an angel; though you read of wings in connection
with the Seraphim above that hover about the throne of
God.

This fixed use of the *human form* here is significant.

For this appearance in human form is immediately
related with the creation of man after God's Image.

Christ Himself is called the *Image* of the Invisible God,
and also the "express *Image* of his substance." And after

this Image, as we learn, *man* is created, in such a way that there originated a certain likeness between man and this Image.

What then was more natural than that the Eternal Being, in order to reveal Himself to man, either directly by Himself, or through His angels, passed over from Himself to His Image, and from His Image to man?

The very thought that there is an Image of God implies that he is mistaken who thinks that in a spirit there can be no distinction and no expression. It shows that by Himself God does not exist as an even Sameness, but with an infinite fullness of distinguished and yet undivided life, and that this, as it is ever present in the Divine consciousness, is to God the Image of his Divine Being.

In any event, this is certain, that when God created man after His Image, this Image must have existed before He could create man after it. And also, that in this Image always lay the vehicle of transition by which to reveal Himself to man in human form.

This was only consummated in the event at Bethlehem, but it had been foreshadowed in the preceding manifestations; and on this ground it can not be denied, that with a view to a better knowledge of God, which is eternal life, the representation-making and image-forming life of our spirit can be taken into account.

The key to this secret is that spirit and matter, God and the world, stand over against one another, so that the distinction between the two must never be lost sight of, because then, willingly or otherwise, we are irresistibly drawn into Pantheism; while, on the other hand, it can never be denied that God Himself has created the world, so that whatever is in the world can not do other than express what in God was the Thought, the Word from eternity.

And so as to what in ourselves concerns soul and body, it must inexorably be maintained that soul and body are two, in this sense, that after death the disembodied soul continues its life until the resurrection; while, on the other hand, it may not be forgotten that soul and body in every respect are counterparts of each other, and that the soul can only reveal its power in full through the body.

This gives rise to a threefold realm of activity. One of purely *spiritual* activity; one of activity through and with the help of the *body;* and a third, which may be called a mixed realm, in which the spirit operates purely spiritually, but with data from the world of sense.

With this, the use of figures in our spoken language can not be included. For then we know very well that we mean something metaphorical, something outside of reality.

When the righteous is said to be courageous as a lion, everyone knows that there is no mention here of a real beast of prey. But it is altogether different in our dreams. Then we see visions, but we ourselves co-operate. We carry on conversations. We feel when others touch us. And everything seems so real that we find it difficult to believe that the burglar who threatened our life does not actually stand by our bed when we wake with fright.

This selfsame thing, this being real to our senses of an imagined something, is far stronger and more acute in a vision. Such visions are, one can almost say, dreams which one dreams, not in sleep upon one's bed, but by day, while one is fully awake. And although this vision-life is far stronger in the East than with us, yet he who deems that it does not exist among us is mistaken.

Meanwhile both dream and vision are far excelled in clearness and reality by an *appearance;* and that we feel ourselves so little at home in this sphere, is only owing to the fact, that science as yet knows nothing of these spiritual operations. She lacks sufficient data for her observation, and therefore is not able thus far to enter this mysterious realm. There is here a world of real operations in the face of which science stands impotent. This brings unbelieving science, in its exalted self-esteem, curtly to deny the reality of all this, while believing science, confessing its inability to explain the phenomenon, thankfully accepts what Scripture teaches concerning it.

We therefore carefully refrain from saying that the image-forming and representation-making life has nothing to affirm with respect to our knowledge of God. The man of intellect who asserts this, contradicts Scripture all too boldly.

Only this much is certain, that the second commandment binds us; that is to say, that we ourselves must not make a concrete image of God, not even in our imagination.

In behalf of the knowledge of God, the image-forming life may only operate when God Himself quickens it within us; as in the call-vision of Isaiah, or in the appearances to Abraham. This image-forming factor in the knowledge of God has in the end found its completion in the "human nature" of the Christ; and the Christ in His human nature, after having entered into glory, has appeared to S. John on Patmos, and the image of this appearance has been described for us in the inspired record.

This is the only appearance that has been given to the Church of Christ, and this alone may and must govern our imaginative life.

To this is added, in the second place, that also in the child of God is seen something of his Father.

The higher God's children stand, the more this is visible.

The more barren they are, the less this is seen.

When the life of a child of God is deeply spiritual, then some other child of God of like spirituality may see in him something of the Image of the Eternal Being.

From which it follows, that you also, if you are a child of God, have the high calling, not now by the play of your imagination, but by the image-forming appearance of your whole personality to cause something of the Father to be seen by those who are of the family of God.

XXIX

IF ANY MAN WILL DO HIS WILL

In behalf of the growth in the knowledge of God there is great strength in conforming oneself to God's will.

There is a knowledge of God which comes to us by our thought, by our imagination, by inward experience, and so on; but in nowise can it be denied, that there is also a part of the knowledge of God which comes to us *through our will*.

The will of later times has come mightily to the fore as a means of explaining many things, in connection with which in former times no one thought of applying it.

An influential school of philosophy, which still holds its own, put the will so prominently in the foreground, that all other activity of our spirit appeared insignificant by the side of it.

The fundamental thought in connection with this is, that the will alone brings everything to pass, creates reality, and reveals itself as a power; and the deeper one enters into the question, the more forcibly one is brought to acknowledge, that the *will* is the power, the only power, which governs and employs all other faculties.

This is confirmed by history; it is observed again and again in the present time. In every department of life the strong-willed man exercises authority and overrides the weak. It was in man that one became acquainted with this wonderful power of the will. In the animal-world also a similar phenomenon could be discerned; but our knowledge of animals is too limited, and so it seemed safest to start out from the power *to will* as it showed itself *in man*.

But of course one could not stop with this. The phenomenon of the *will* is too great, and its dominance too prevalent, for it to exist in man otherwise than derivatively. Primarily—*i.e.*, in the original state of things—the will existed outside of man, and man himself was the product of the great, supreme, *Universal-will* that brought all things to pass.

What until now had been worshiped in the world as God, or had been denounced as Satan, was nothing else than this *Universal-will*, *i.e.*, the gigantic will-power, by which everything is that is.

The world least of all exhibits Wisdom, far less Love; it is nothing else than the product of a monstrous will-power. Hence the unsatisfactory condition of the world.

And since in us also, on a small scale, there is a will with power to will, the supreme duty of human life is that we should train our will, develop it, apply it to mighty deeds, and that with this strongly trained human will we maintain ourselves in the face of this *Universal-will*.

So everything that is, and everything that is called history, reduces our whole life to one power, and the only thing that is noble, and the only thing in us that can be called holy, is our personal will.

That the philosophical school, which spoke thus oracularly, is radically opposed to all religion, and particularly to the Christian religion, needs no further demonstration.

But it is noteworthy that in the Christian Church religion simultaneously exhibited an allied tendency which likewise put the will to the fore and, in the end, made every other utterance of the Christian faith subordinate to it.

We refer to that tendency in the religious world which is more and more lax in its interpretation of the Creeds, which allows feeling and sentiment ever less opportunity of being heard, and evermore shows the need and the inclination to exhibit Christianity solely in works and in display of power, *i.e.*, in utterances of the will.

This idea and inclination, however, were not born nor borrowed from this philosophic school which interpreted the universe in terms of the will, but with it owed their rise to a general phenomenon which shows itself in human life.

In the Church, after the Reformation, there was first the barren period of *dogmatics* in the seventeenth century, and after that the period of emotional religion in the eighteenth century. And since neither of these brought satisfaction, and it became evident that with both of them Christianity was heading toward the shoals, it came about of itself that with the depreciation of doctrinal statements and an increasing distaste for emotionalism, the other extreme was reached, namely, from now on to interpret Christianity exclusively in *works of the will:*

Not the hearer, but the doer of the law shall be holy.

Not every one that sayeth, "Lord, Lord, . . . but he that doeth the will of my Father who is in heaven," shall be saved (S. Matt. vii, 21).

"If any man doeth his will, he shall know of the doctrine, whether it be of God" (S. John vii, 17).

In brief, a number of clear, strong utterances of Holy Scripture can be cited in support of this new effort.

And so, a tendency developed everywhere which excelled in that it could boast of its exhibition of Christian works, and fell short in that it underestimated the creeds and mysticism.

A powerful aid in this direction was the well known fact that in the Christian conflict of the nineteenth century, English Christians took the lead.

The period of terse credal formulas was dominated by Switzerland, France and the Netherlands. The emotional period had come into power through German and

French Sentimentalists. But with the nineteenth century, England came to the fore, England with its matter-of-fact system, with its commercial spirit, with its indomitable power of will.

From England this passion for good works crossed over to the continent of Europe, and what this *will-tendency* has accomplished in the sphere of philanthropy and missions can never be sufficiently appreciated.

It has given birth to a new life, and given rise to a newly-felt need to exercise power. . . . It simultaneously put to shame the barren and meagre results of intellectual orthodoxy and the weak and sickly fruit of sentimental mysticism. There was evidence of a readiness to give, of a devotion, of an energetic faith, such as had not been seen among us since the days of the Reformation.

And even in the Salvation Army, which is the most sharply defined example of this will-tendency and at the same time its most spectacular expression, there revealed itself a manysided activity in behalf of the unfortunate, which aroused sympathy even in unbelieving circles.

What remained, however, a matter of regret was the onesidedness of such an endeavor, which from the first incurred the danger of forsaking justification by faith, and of putting in its place salvation by good works.

The center of gravity was removed too far away from God and placed in man. The outward supplanted the inward life of piety. And as in unbelieving circles much self-sacrificing philanthropic activity was seen, soon the strange relation arose, that the men and women of this "Gospel of Works" felt themselves more closely related to unbelievers who found their ideal in similar endeavor, than with believers on Christ who fell short in acts of mercy.

Moreover, and this cut deeper still, it could not be

denied that in this Gospel of *the will* real religion, *i.e.,* the search after fellowship with the Eternal Being, was more and more lost.

Tender piety was sadly missing, and the plant of Godliness became more and more encrusted with mold.

The hidden walk with God, the quiet ways of the "being hid in Christ" were ever less considered, both in preaching and in the walks of life. In fact, no more was heard of it.

It must all be *deeds*, nothing but *deeds*, always *facts* and once again *facts*. And it even became the habit to estimate good deeds by numbers, and from these statistics, if they were favorable, to infer that God's blessing rested on one's works.

There were reports of the numbers of converts, reports of moneys raised, reports of the membership of one's society, reports of the hungry that had been fed, the naked that had been clothed, the sick that had been healed. Even flattery in regard to such reports was not always unacceptable.

And when you objected that in this way Christianity was externalized and the knowledge of God which is eternal life was relegated to the book of forgetfulness, the answer was that your surmise rested altogether upon a misunderstanding, because that very knowledge of God does not come to you through the intellect or the feeling, but through *the will.*

Only he who doeth and will do the will of God, knows the Eternal.

This pretext can not be dealt with now. We will do this in a following meditation.

XXX

INCREASING IN THE KNOWLEDGE OF GOD

HE who doeth the will of God, by the very experience which this brings, increases of himself also in the knowledge of the Lord.

When there are two persons, one of whom is strictly *orthodox* in his faith but indifferent as to his manner of life, and the other strict as to his *manner of life*, but careless as to the faith, then he who doeth the will of God, has a better chance of knowing God, than the confessor who surprises you by his accuracy of detail in doctrinal knowledge.

The so-called "Christendom of the deed," the "practical Christianity,"—this tendency to seek salvation in "Christian works"—was entirely right, in so far as the doing of God's will is certainly one of the means which is indispensable, if one would attain unto the full knowledge of God.

If the knowledge of God is eternal life, then this knowledge of God can not be something apart from life. Bring to mind again and again that eternal life is not life in the hereafter, but in the present. And this life does not come from the cistern, but from the Fountain. A knowledge of God which itself is this eternal life, can, therefore, not be thought of apart from your practical doings, your actual existence, your plans and your deeds.

If in all you do there is a will, and if your deeds are only right when they conform to the will of God, then you can not help seeing that there is a connection between the knowledge of God and the doing of His will.

The ox knoweth his owner, says Isaiah (i, 3)—but Israel does not understand. In our country we would say: a horse knows his rider. The draft-ox is not largely in use among us. But how does the draft-ox know his owner, how does the horse know his rider? Certainly in part by the eye and in part by the ear, but surely not least by the manner in which they are treated. When the rider comes up from behind, so that the horse sees nothing of him, and he utters no word or sound, so that the animal hears nothing, the thoroughbred knows his rider at once, and is immediately aware whether his owner or a stranger springs into the saddle. That horse, if he is at all trained, knows the will of his rider and conforms himself to it, even so perfectly that at length he becomes one with his rider, and—as on the field of battle—will of himself do his rider's will even with loosened bridle. Thus the animal, by allowing himself to be carefully trained, has so far attained unto the knowledge of his owner, that it has become a living, subordinate instrument to him.

Thus also the child of God who has lived according to the will of God—and has conformed himself to God's will, by the help of that will alone has come to an instinctive knowledge of God, such as no catechism or creed can give him.

We do not say, that the knowledge of God thus obtained is the only knowledge, nor that it is sufficient, nor that it gives complete insight; what we do say is, that the doing of God's will brings a particular trait into the knowledge of God, which is indispensable if it is to be a living knowledge, and which can not be replaced by anything else, be it understanding or feeling.

Take the forgiveness of him who has wronged you.

As a child of God you know full well that this is your duty, even to this extent, that you are not done with it, when outwardly you restrain yourself, and requite no evil for evil. Christian forgiveness reaches much farther and goes far deeper. It must be an honest forgiveness, without any reservation. Not one single seed of anger or bitterness must remain in you, or it is not the forgiveness that God commands.

Thus, you must forgive your very worst enemy, and forgive in such a way that you bless him who cursed you and that you truly love him.

Mark you: you must *love* your enemy. Not show him love in order to show him how generous you are, and so by your show of love actually humiliate him. No, you must love him as yourself. This is almost incomprehensible, and yet absolutely necessary.

You pray in the Our Father: "Forgive us our trespasses, as we forgive those that trespass against us."

To forgive you from love is thus the measure of the forgiveness of sin which you ask of God for yourself.

Not as though God would be bound to your measure, or that He should forgive you because you forgive. All this is subversion of the Gospel. No, it means, that you dare not ask more of God, than you know is in your heart to give to your debtors.

And what does all this mean, save that in doing the will of God by forgiving your enemy, you feel what forgiveness means, that you receive from God the sense and the will to forgive, and that thus you come to the knowledge of your God, as regards His will to forgive you.

He who himself does not forgive, who in spite of God's will continues to harbor hatred, and thus, in this matter of forgiveness fails of conforming himself to the will of God, lacks this particular knowledge of God which makes it clear to him how his God forgives him.

You see, therefore, from this one illustration, how the

doing of God's will makes you increase in the knowledge of God in deed and in truth.

At the same time, you learn from this still something else.

The "practical Gospel of works" puts special stress upon doing something extra, something outside of the ordinary life. It speaks by preference, therefore, of "Christian works," of "Christian activities," by which it means, things that go on outside of the everyday life of one's business, family and society. Zealous missionary activity, promoting the interests of Christian education, visiting the poor, caring for the sick and blind, and so on, are the things which are called "Christian works."

And in part this interpretation is instinctively correct.

When, full of life and power, Christianity goes into the world, none of these things can remain untouched. It all belongs to it. Genuine, true Christianity can not satisfy itself with inspiring ordinary life. It brings with it all sorts of things that would remain unknown without it.

Only this: it is a great fault to suppose that it is all for the sake of the roses that grow against the wall, and that that wall back of the roses can be left to fall into ruins.

No, the doing of God's will covers *the whole* of our life, our ordinary as well as our extraordinary life, and the knowledge of God in the ordinary life is far finer, far more intricate, far more difficult than in those extraordinary things.

To know God's will in regard to your personal life, your calling, your life's task, your family with all its relationships—in regard to society and your touch upon people, is a life-study with which you are never done, which goes on until your death. And to acquire the power, not only of seeing in all this what the will of God is, but also to bend your mind to it, and to conform your life to it in everything, down to the smallest detail, is not only a daily study, but a daily struggle, in which he alone who is led by God's Spirit, triumphs.

He who applies himself to this and busies himself with it every day, learns ever more and more to understand God's will, and with every victory which he gains, he also daily increases in the knowledge of God, a knowledge which he acquires not with his understanding alone, but with his whole person.

The more you begin to feel as God feels, and become minded as God is, the more truly you become the child of the *Father Who is in heaven*. It is not the will of God that only for a single time, against your inclination, you should curb yourself heroically, and yield yourself to God; no, to do the will of God, is, so to become transformed in your mind and inclination, that you yourself will what God wills. And he who attains unto this, and is daily concerned therewith, increases in the knowledge of God, by increasing in the knowledge of himself.

You will appreciate this when you call to mind that in God, Being and Will are not two, but one.

God's will is the crystal-pure expression of His Being. Knowledge of God's will thus becomes of itself knowledge of His Being. The one is not to be separated from the other.

Only, the will of God can only become completely known along the way of the will. For should you recite the Ten Commandments, and gather every utterance of God's will from the whole of Scripture, this would not give you the least right to say that you therefore know the will of God. You may know it by rote but the will is within, and can only be known within, by having your personal will enter into the will of God.

What it means to pilot a ship through the channel into a safe harbor can not be known by him who has merely read a book on the art of navigation; it is known only by him, who has himself been at sea, has commanded a ship in the storm, and has safely brought it to port.

In the same way, the knowledge of God's will is not acquired by learning lessons in morality by heart, but with the organ of your own will you must so grasp the will of God, that you yourself fulfill it.

You need not for this reason censure this "practical" Christianity as though it were of no use. On the contrary, it is absolutely indispensable. Only, you must add depth to it. You must apply it to your whole life. And, further, you must clearly see that the knowledge of God which comes by doing his will, far from being the whole knowledge of God, is only a part of it. A part, which certainly must not be wanting, but which, only in connection with that other knowledge of God, which you acquire by the understanding, feeling and imagination, together constitute one whole, and together form that full knowledge of Him, which is eternal life.

Only do not lose sight of the fact that the daily "increase in the knowledge of God" (Col. i, 10) is acquired preeminently along the way of the will.

There is a twofold will of God.

There is a will of God concerning you, which determines your life, your career and lot in life. It was in regard to *this* will of God that Jesus prayed: "Not my will, but Thy will be done."

There is also a will of God for you which tells you *how* you must will, and what you should do and not do; and it is this will of God, of which it is said in the Our Father: "Thy will be done, as in heaven by Thy angels, so on earth by me."

And it is this latter will of God, which, if you live by it and conform yourself to it little by little makes you *increase* in the knowledge of God.

XXXI

BESIDE THE STILL WATERS

THE will should be considered still more closely, if you would attain unto the knowledge of God. The field in which our will operates, was not sufficiently plowed and harrowed in the days of our fathers. The great question then was, whether the will is free or bound. Beyond this, even in preaching and catechising, the great significance of our will was ignored. Yea, are there not many people now, by whom the whole realm of the will is left fallow?

This does not mean to say that in the time of our fathers, and in our own past, there has been no increase in the knowledge of God through the will. How could that be? The will does not only come into action by what is written about it in a book, or taught from the pulpit. It is the Lord, Who makes your will to operate, and direct itself for good. It is He Who worketh in you both to will and to do his good pleasure (Phil. ii, 13), and how could your God be bound to sermon or book?

We only mean that he who is so blessed and fortunate as to be refreshed every morning and evening with a drop of grace from the Fountain of Divine Compassion, and has time and insight to ponder and meditate on holy things, does wrong, when he leaves so important a component part of his soul's power, as resides in the will, almost if not wholly uninvestigated. This can not help but impoverish him in consequence. Our will is something inscrutably wonderful, so Divine a product of creation in our soul, and so deeply engraven a trait of the Image of God that reflects itself in us, that lack of reverence and of admiration betrays itself when we do not lift the veil from before it.

Moreover, our will is so powerful an instrument, that he who handles it thoughtlessly, readily wounds himself therewith.

We should also distinguish between times and times.

There is a time of childhood, followed by a time of early youth, in which one lives by instinct, and does what he does without knowing why he does it.

But there comes a time when, as it were, the sediment disappears from the waters, and the mirror of the consciousness becomes clear, and then comes reflective thought. Our age is farther advanced than that of our fathers. The former instinctive life becomes more and more the conscious life. And he who takes no part in the transition falls behind.

The whole Church will become aware that she loses power, when she adheres to the old without harmonizing her insight into the past with the claims of our clarified consciousness. She then gets out of touch with life; her preaching does not concern itself with what stirs and moves in life. She does not arm the faithful, and amid the great conflict of spirits it comes to pass that in her ever weakening condition she at length passes out of the fight.

Will it do then, for a time like ours, when in every way the will is the object of investigation and thought, for Christians to act as though the study of the will did not concern them?

Yet we must confine ourselves to our subject.

These meditations aim to lead the soul closer to the *hidden walk* with her God; to bring her such knowledge of God as is itself eternal life. In this knowledge of God we must increase. And this increase in the knowledge of God is effected more through the will than through our understanding.

This is the point which we now press.

The holy Apostle expresses it so clearly: "Walk worthy of the Lord unto all pleasing, whereby we shall be fruitful in every good work, and at the same time increase in the knowledge of God" (Col. i, 10).

He who so bends his will that at length he himself has no other will than to forgive his debtor, comes through this his will to the knowledge of the compassionate God Who forgives him.

To God, forgiveness is no outward rule which He applies. Forgiveness comes from His will to forgive, and this will to forgive comes from His Being. If now you come to will like this of yourself, then you become conformed in this to your Father who is in heaven. What Jesus said: "Be ye perfect, as your Father who is in heaven is perfect," is in this particular point then realized in you; and feeling thus that you yourself are of the family of God, you come to a knowledge of God that is not a lesson learned by heart, but one that springs from your relationship to God itself.

Do you understand the beauty, the intimacy, the Godliness of this?

Now this.

All men are not alike in power of thought nor in freedom of time. There are those who are able to analyze deeply and sharply and to look into questions. But there are far more who can not do this. We would not call the latter dull, but, for all that, it is a fact that, for the most part, people are not able to scrutinize to the full every part of our glorious Creed. They simply can not do this. They lack capacity.

Freedom in the matter of time also differs with one man and another. A laborer who leaves home at early dawn and comes back tired at night, what time has he for study in sacred things, especially compared with a clergyman or a professor in theology who can spend all day in it? For such study requires preparation, books, and retirement. And what a difference there is between a farm hand at the plow, and a minister with a university training, a well supplied library and a study of his own.

If now you seek the knowledge of God mainly in education, and if you say that this knowledge thus obtained is everlasting life, how cruel you become. As though eternal life came for the most part to people of study, and as though the shepherd wandered aimlessly behind his sheep.

You feel yourself, this can not, this must not be.

If knowledge of God is eternal life, then increase of this knowledge must be obtainable by some means within everyone's reach—the scholar in his study, the laborer at his work, the busy mother in her home.

Then of itself you discover the importance of the will, and the relative unimportance of mere intellectual *attainment.* Do not many learned people give the impression of standing almost altogether outside the knowledge of God, while numbers upon numbers of hard-working, simple souls exhale a fragrance of eternal life?

And here you touch the sensitive nerve of life itself.

A will works in every man. The will is in action every day. The will is active in, and with, everything. The work, the act, the power of the will, its impulse and passion may be widely divergent, but without the will there is no act, no deed, no career in life.

Here every difference between man and man falls away. Every one faces it daily for himself. In whatever retirement or simple position in life one may find himself, there is a will that wills, a will that operates.

It is not a something apart, something added to life; it is the urgency of the soul itself that throbs in every artery of the life.

Quietly, by the side of still waters, this action of the will goes on all day long till the very end of life—with every one; at every moment, on every occasion. It is a never resting, ever newly-fed stream of will-choice, will-decision, will-action, which continuously, quietly ripples along, bearing life company and in part carrying it.

Thus it is in everyone's power, by this continual exercise of the will, to increase continually in the knowledge of God, and thereby to attain unto an ever fuller possession and enjoyment of eternal life, provided we separate this exercise of the will ever less from the will of God and derive it ever more from God's will.

Thus all cruelty disappears. Whether you have a limited life or a large one makes no difference; even though it continue on its way like the quiet flow of a gentle stream, the knowledge of God can daily be enriched by it, and you can daily increase in eternal life as well as the queen on her throne, or the farm-hand behind the plow; and the professor in his study is not then necessarily better off than he who moves the shuttle in a loom.

All this goes on quietly as by the side of very still waters; and the best part of it is that it asks for no extra time outside of the daily life.

All intellectual training demands special time. In behalf of it the daily task must be abandoned. Time must be set apart for it. For most people this is almost impossible. For most of us life is a mill that never stops.

But as regards the knowledge of God through "the willing of your will" all this is of no account.

The will never operates outside of the life, but always within it. Whether you walk behind the plow, or stand behind a school desk, care for your children in the home, or nurse the sick, it is all the same. It is all the expression and activity of the will. And provided you do not go counter to the will of God, but make your will coincide with His, it is all one process of activity whereby you can increase in the knowledge of God, in order by this knowledge to mature in the eternal life.

XXXII

WHO WORKETH IN YOU TO WILL

By being willing yourself to do what God wills you to do, you increase in the knowledge of God; not in barren book-knowledge, but in that living soul-knowledge of your God, which itself is eternal life.

This springs from all sorts of causes, but not least from the fact that your willingness is not born from yourself, but is wrought in you by God. He it is, writes the Apostle (Phil. ii, 13), "who worketh in you both to will and to do of his good pleasure." First therefore the willing, and only afterward the carrying out; and although you yourself work this whole will-motion and will-action in your soul, yet it is God Who works them in you.

This distinction, as is self-evident must be made, otherwise your own willingness would be mere semblance, and in good works God's child would be merely a puppet mechanically moved into action. This distinction therefore must be sharply defined and clearly grasped. Your own self wills, not because it wills of itself, but because God so works within, that, truly and actually it is you yourself who wills thus and not otherwise.

It takes some exertion on your part to see this clearly, and you may readily be inclined to accept the advice that someone may give you, not to weary yourself with all these distinctions; but if you heed this advice of spiritual sloth, you are not fair to yourself.

Ask your physician how many distinctions he has to make in a single group of nerves; or how many varieties of disease-germs he observes in the blood.

And is it fitting, that man should exert himself so

greatly in behalf of the body that perishes, and not in behalf of the soul which is so much more precious? And yet,
such is the prevailing tendency. Almost every one has
some sort of manual, illustrated if possible, from which
to learn how the body is constructed; but no one reads
about the soul. With the great mass of people all investigation and study of the soul is wanting.

And then a man speaks at random about his soul, his
will, his understanding, himself—it is all chaotic; and in
this way he remains till death a stranger to his own inner
self. He can talk about everything else. He knows his
house, his village, his town, and frequently even foreign
lands, but the key to the chambers and vaulted corridors
of his own soul, he never so much as handles. And since
the penalty for the lack of self-knowledge is a very meagre
knowledge of God, one lessens thereby his own part in
that eternal life which far excels all else.

We therefore urgently exhort, that the above distinction be carefully considered.

When a martyr says: "I will die for the Name of the
Lord Jesus," he must truly will to do this himself; and
then this willingness to die for Jesus must be, and must
continue to be, an act of his very own. But that his *ego*
thus wills it, does not come from himself by nature, but
is wrought in his own self by God.

An illustration here may not be out of place, and you
can represent this to yourself most vividly when you think
of a ship.

At the stern of that ship is a rudder, and attached to
this rudder is the tiller, and this is held by the hand of
the helmsman.

Should there be no steering when at sea, this boat moves
under the action of the wind and waves, then when the
ship turns the rudder turns, and when the rudder turns

the tiller turns, and with it the hand and the arm of the man at the helm moves involuntarily back and forth.

Behold the image of a will-less man.

He is adrift upon the sea of life. As wind and waves drive, so he is driven along, under influences from without and from within—of circumstances, of his passion. And as life makes him go, now in this direction, now in that, so he goes; and so turns the rudder in his inward purpose, and so turns the tiller and the hand at the helm; *i.e.*, his will.

The will-less one!

But it is altogether different when there is steerage in the ship. Then the man at the helm keeps the course. He knows where he wants to go. And when wind and wave would drive him out of his course, he works against them. Then his hand grasps the tiller firmly, he turns it, and therewith the rudder itself, against wind and wave. And the ship that responds to the helm, cuts through the waves, not as tide and wind would direct it, but as the helmsman wills.

Such is the man of character, the man with will-perception and will-power, who does not drift, but steers.

But there is still a third point.

On the bridge of the ship, far away from the helm, stands the captain, and he has placed a helmsman at the tiller. Now the captain on the bridge must know what course the ship must take. On the bridge he stands much higher, and therefore knows far better how the ship must point to the right or to the left. And so the helmsman has but this single duty, namely, that he listen to what the captain on the bridge commands, and that he carries out those orders.

Applied to the soul, God is this Captain on the bridge, and we are the man at the helm. And if, with the tiller of the small boat of our soul in hand, we but will what God wills, and so turn the helm to right or left as God commands, then no danger need be feared, and presently through wind and wave the little boat enters safely the desired haven.

If this goes on through the whole of life, we grow accustomed to it; we know at length by anticipation, whether the Captain on the bridge will command left or right. Thus, of ourselves we come to know God's will more and more. And this knowledge of God brings us nearer to the haven of salvation,—to eternal life.

Now to the matter in hand.

When God so works in upon our self that at length we will what God wills, the process is not external but internal.

It is not, that we are down here on earth, and that, far away from us, and high above us, God is enthroned in the heavens, and that from this infinite distance, God imparts a mechanical impulse to our soul. No, in order to do this, God enters into us.

To a certain extent this is even the case with the captain on the bridge, who calls out to the mate at the helm.

What is it to call?

He who calls makes air-waves vibrate. The vibrations extend themselves to the spot where the man at the helm stands. This vibrating air-wave enters into the ear of the mate and touches the nerve of his hearing. This auditory nerve carries the motions over into his brain. Thus there is direct, continuous motion, which from the captain penetrates to the brain of the mate.

And thus the figure illustrates the point.

But here it is yet stronger.

When God works upon our soul, and within it upon us, He is the omnipresent One, Who is high above in heaven, and yet close by us. And even "close by" is still too weak, because God is *in* every one of us. There is no part in our being where God is not present.

This is so with all men. But when God has dealings with one of His children this internal presence is still far closer and more intimate, for then He dwells in such a one by His Holy Spirit. If now you believe that this Holy Spirit is Himself God, then you understand how God Himself indwells in His child, has His Throne in the inmost hidden part of His child's being, and thus, not from afar, but within the sanctuary of His child's own person has fellowship with its self.

There God works upon this self. He labors on it day and night, even, when we know nothing of it. He is our Sculptor, who carves the Image of Himself in our soul, and causes us ever more and more to resemble His own Being.

Thus He transforms our self and our will.

And so it is God Who works in us, and on our will, by transforming the *self* that wills.

Taken in this way, it becomes a steady, a holy entering in of God's will into our will, thanks to the refining, purifying and transforming of this self.

It is a work which for the most part goes on unobserved within us, so tenderly and gently does God's hand conduct this inner work. Yet the process is not always so. Sometimes the sculptor is forced to strike off a piece of the marble, so that it crashes and splits and splinters. These are the periods of violent conflict within, when everything trembles and reverberates with moral shocks.

But whether gently, or violently, it is ever the process of sculpturing. And this Sculptor does not work after a model which He puts before Him, but is Himself the Model. He forms us after His own Image.

So this Divine labor in the realm of our will brings us into ever closer likeness to this Image of God. And this continuous process of being ever more nearly transformed after the Image of God, what else is this, than that God's will enters ever more deeply into us? And what is this ever more deeply entering in of God's will into our will, but an ever better understanding of God, a better knowledge of Him, an ever clearer insight into His will and purpose?

So you see that there is still an entirely different way of learning to know God from learning to know Him through books or sermons.

Later on, we will show why also this knowledge of God from books and sermons is absolutely indispensable. For the moment let it rest. The need is great and pressing that the eyes of many, that are now closed against seeing God's work in the inner life of the soul, be opened to see the beauty and the glory of it.

Without entering into the reality of the life of the soul and of God's work therein, there is no strength, no outshining of power, and no constructive results of this power in the life. It is then a dead Church which only sends out sounds when it deems that it sings psalms unto God. Then the world pushes us aside, and not we the world.

Attention must therefore be concentrated upon the will, upon willingness, upon the self that wills, and upon God Who in the self works the willing.

For feeling, imagination and heroic courage, the poets prayed in behalf of their songs.

For feeling, will-power and heroic courage, every child of God supplicates his Father.

XXXIII

WHAT I WOULD THAT DO I NOT

THE distance from the Lord our God, at which even the noblest, the most gifted and the mightiest man on earth stands, is so immeasurably great, that it is readily understood how one can almost despairingly exclaim: "why should we try to know God!" The Lord is great and we understand Him not (Job xxxvi, 26). All we can do is to kneel in worship before the unknown God.

This is what the doubters meant, who at Athens reared an altar to the "Unknown God" (Acts xvii, 23). They did not mean thereby that, besides the many gods who already had their altar, there was still another God whose name they did not know, to whom therefore as an Unknown God they offered their sacrifices. No, this altar to the Unknown God stood for a system, a viewpoint.

They would say thereby: "Our fellow-citizens in Athens who kneel before Minerva or Jupiter, are mistaken when they accept all the narratives concerning the gods as valid currency. All that is said about knowing God, rests upon self-deception. Of the Infinite, nothing can be known. True, there is One who is Infinite, or at least there is something Infinite, but who and what this Infinite One is, remains for us men an impenetrable mystery. Worship this Infinite as the great Unknown; do it with the confession of your ignorance; openly recognize that all knowledge of God is withheld from you; and holy mysticism will refreshingly affect you. But do not pretend to have what you have not, and never make it appear that you have been introduced and initiated into

knowledge of God. For what else is this but self-deception, which must lead to the deception of others, and is
the key to all priestcraft."

This was the thought of that small group of men in
Athens. Among the ablest and noblest of our race many
are of such mind now. "Agnostics" is the name by which
they call themselves. And their aim and intention is to
have you understand well that they are by no means godless, and not in the least irreligious; that among the pious
they are the most pious; and that for this very reason, in
deep humility and candor, they confess that the God Whom
we worship is One Who by His Supreme Majesty withdraws His knowledge from us men.

However pious this may sound, at heart this viewpoint
is untenable.

Christianity stands diametrically opposed to these
people.

The declaration of S. Paul at Athens: "This God,
whom ye ignorantly worship, Him declare I unto you,"
remains unchangeably the standard of Christian doctrine, which has been raised in the face of these mis-
guided ones.

Surely, had God not revealed Himself, no one of us
would know Him.

But God *has* revealed Himself. That He has done so,
is the glad tiding which every christian brings to the
world.

And therefore in the face of this seemingly pious ignorance of the Agnostics, we boldly, and without one moment's hesitation, emphasize the word of Christ: "*This
is eternal life, that they might know thee, the only true God.*"

But there is also exaggeration on the other side.

There are leaders and laymen who without scruple and
without the slightest bashfulness, argue familiarly about

the High and Holy One, the Everlasting God, and in their public prayer show such lack of reverence, that it arouses aversion.

These are men and women without the fear of God in their hearts, who think that they know everything about the Most Highest that can be known, and are not even faintly aware that all our reasoning *about* the Eternal, and all our talking *to* Him, is nothing but so much stammering.

It is indeed true that love casts out fear. But then fear must first be there, and against it love must have struggled, for only thus is the victory gained of the childlike, "Abba, Father!"

But when one hears God spoken of in a way which shows that there never was any fear of His Name, nor any love to repress that fear; that there never was any conflict and therefore no victory gained; then there is nothing of the childlike: "Abba, dear Father!" but only an indiscreet airing of knowledge and pedantry, which exhales no fragrance of piety, but rather chokes the germ of vital godliness.

To avert this, it is exceedingly needful that the knowledge of God be brought into relation with our whole inner existence, our creation after the Divine Image with the fact of our being the offspring of God, and especially also with our intentions and purposes.

Bare intellectual knowledge of God, which is not applied by the will to our life, is a frozen ice-crust under which the stream has run dry.

But with this *willing* a twofold distinction must be observed.

There is willing and willing.

There is a willing which remains what it is. And there is a willing which translates itself into doing. And especially in our days the tendency is to attribute inward worth only to this second willing, which knows how to put its will into execution.

There is something bold, something brutal, in this will-life of our times. All that is wanted is to will. He who wills must be daring, let come of it what may. But in any case the will must be the expression of a power that is able to do everything. Where there is a will, there is a way. And under the leadership of such men as Ibsen this effort of the will has been driven so onesidedly that many now make it a point of honor to pay no attention to anything or anybody, and in the face of every form of opposition irresistibly to endeavor to carry their will into effect.

Compared with these present-day heroes of the will a weakling like S. Paul truly cuts a poor figure!

He comes out squarely with the statement that ever and anon he knows moments in his life when he has to confess (Rom. vii, 15): "What I would, that do I not; but what I hate, that I do."

These are honest words, which age after age have been shamefully and dreadfully abused, in order that with pious confessions on the lips, men may quietly persist in sin, and yet silence their conscience.

An abuse which God shall judge.

But apart from this abuse, what S. Paul said is the honest language of everyday life; a stating the fact that our ideal always stands above us, and that we ever have to mourn our inability to reach it and to make it actual in life.

There is a willing in the heart, and there is an effort to realize this willing of our heart in our life.

This willing in our heart is for the most part free. He who restrains his evil inclinations, and conforms his inner will to God's will, fosters in his heart a holy intention.

This, too, involves conflict, but only with the stirrings of the old nature in us. And as long as we stand aloof from life, and counsel with our heart alone, a child of God triumphs inwardly, and at length comes to will only what God wills, and, in this unity of his will with God's will, he finds happiness.

But there follows a second struggle which is far greater.

Now it comes to the point of carrying out the inner intention of your heart against the world, the flesh and the devil. And here it constantly happens that, with the best of will at heart, you meet with stubborn resistance; that you find no power in yourself to cope with it; and that at length you leave undone what sacredly and honestly you purposed in your heart to do and still desire to do.

This tempts you all too frequently to deny all worth to this inner willing of your heart.

What good is it, it is asked, whether you foster the best of intentions and aim at holiest ends, if, when it comes to action, you fail?

This, however, must be resisted. This is debasement of self. It not only brings failure in life, but cuts the vital nerve which binds you to your Divine ideal.

Ten times better fail, and be punished in your conscience by God's judgment, than in every ordinary way to sin along with the world without knowledge of this conflict with your conscience.

Moreover, this inward willing in your heart of what God wills, is of supreme worth, even though strength fails you as yet to carry it into effect.

Already this willing is a quickening of your childship, a coming into closer fellowship with your God, an increase in your knowledge of God, an inward refining which keeps your conscience awake, causes your ideal to remain bright, and helps you to progress.

Of course you progress much farther, when, from being willing at heart, it becomes action in the accomplished deed and eventually becomes a part of life. Then the moral power of faith operates, then the hero-nature awakens in you, and the all-conquering power of the Almighty becomes manifest in you.

Only, it does not begin with this.

It begins with the transposing of the *willing* in your heart.

Then comes the sad, painful experience, that the willing is there, but that the doing still tarries.

But, even in that stage, the powerful, the penetrating working of the conscience performs wonders. And it is this working which at length leads you into the last stage, and brings you from the bare *willing* of what God wills, to the *doing* of His holy pleasure.

XXXIV

NOT AS I WILL

In the Our Father, and in Gethsemane, it is the same prayer: "Thy will be done," but, though on both occasions the emphasis and the words are alike, the meaning in Gethsemane is altogether different.

"Thy will be done!" in the Our Father means: "Thy will, O God, *be done by me;*" in Gethsemane, on the other hand, it means: "Let Thy will, O God, *come upon me,* let things happen with me not as I will, but as thou wilt."

This latter prayer also supplies so large a part of that knowledge of God which is eternal life.

We increase in the knowledge of God, when our will conforms itself to God's will in such a way that we do not think, speak and act otherwise than in harmony with the ordinances of the Lord. This makes us to increase in the knowledge of God, because then God's will enters into us, He Himself transforms our will, and uniformity with the Image of God becomes ever more clearly visible.

But there is also an increase in the knowledge of God which comes when we ourselves will what God ordains concerning us; when willingly we adapt ourselves to what He has determined for us in His council and by our lot in life; and when we accept everything that our lot in life brings us, not only without complaint and murmuring, but with the heroic courage of faith.

But *this* increase in the knowledge of God progresses differently and in a far more painful way.

The painfulness consists in this, that when we accept God's will in our lot, we suffer that will passively. When, "Thy will be done!" means: "Let me do Thy will as the angels do it in heaven," it stimulates our energy, imparts tension to the will, and when we triumph over sin, great gladness fills our heart. But when: "Thy will be done!" means: "Let things happen with me not according to my desire but according to Thy decree," then there is need of submission, of resignation to suffer what God ordains and appoints.

Then there is, at least in the lower school of suffering, no development of energy, but inward enervation; no stimulus that tightens the will, but a stressing cord that binds it; a total loss of self; not the smile of heroic boldness, but the tear of poignant sorrow.

And this indeed leads to deeper knowledge of God, but often in a way that is most grievous because it is attended by such unknown and unsolvable enigmas.

Problems then especially cast their gloom upon the heart; not when it is a matter of undergoing a sorrow, but when it comes to the carrying of some bitter cross from one's early years to the end of his life.

Again and again *this* happens in life: A woman was most happy; hers was a pure delight in the possession of husband and child. Neither was she irreligious. An overwhelming sense of happiness found frequent expression in thanksgiving and praise. The love of her Father in heaven was so great. He made her so happy, her cup was full to overflowing.

But things change. Serious illness breaks up the quiet of her peace. And husband and child are snatched away by death.

Now everything is gone. Now she can not be comforted. Now her deeply wounded soul rises up in rebellion against God.

It has all been self-deception—misleading. No, God can not be Love. How could a God who is Love be so

cruel as to cast her down from the heights of her great
happiness into the depths of bereavement and grief?

And in this bewilderment of affliction, words of despair
and of defiant unbelief flow from her lips. "Talk no more
to me of God. Cruelty can not be love. There is no God."

So the break of happiness in life becomes the break of
faith in the soul.

She fancied that she knew God, and now that He appears different from what she had imagined, she gives up
all faith.

With her husband and with her child she also lost her
God.

And what is left in the soul is but a burned-out hearth
from which the last spark has been extinguished.

This makes you feel how hard the lesson is which
through the school of suffering must make us increase in
the knowledge of God.

When for the first time in our life the cross with its full
weight is laid upon our shoulders, the first effect is that it
makes us numb and dazed and causes all knowledge of
God to be lost.

The psalm of love was so beautiful, it glided of itself
into our soul so sweetly. A God who is only Love, love
for us, in order to bless us, to make our life rich and glad,
Oh, who would not willingly attain unto the knowledge
of such a God?

In our life among men it is indeed glorious when love
and nothing but love is shown us. And how rich, then, our
heart feels in the possession of a God, who causes only
love, only streams of happiness and peace to flow out
after us.

But now dawns the day of adversity, the day of trouble
and disappointment, the day of sickness and grief. Where
now is the love of my God? Where now is that outflow

of love from the fatherheart? For not only has God not spared me my dying husband and my darling child, and has left me praying without coming to my aid, but He has deliberately taken *them away* from me. He sent the sickness into my home, and, O, too cruel almost for words, He himself has killed my husband and my dear child; He has torn them from my heart, to be carried out to the grave.

And of course, in the end, this must bring it about, that we attain to another, a better knowledge of God, which explains His dealings with us. But at first what our heart feels is that we can not square this with our God as we had imagined Him, as we had dreamed Him to be.

The God we had, we lose, and, then it costs so much bitter conflict of soul, before refined and purified in our knowledge of God, we grasp another, and now the only true God in the place thereof.

The first lesson, then, consists in this, that in actual life, with our whole outward and inner existence, we give in to a higher decree, and bow before an All-power, against which we can do nothing.

And this *seems* dreadful, but yet this very thing is the discovery of God as *God* in the reality of your experience.

As long as we are but just started on the way to the cross we fancy ourselves the main object at stake, it is our happiness, our honor, our future—and God added in. According to our idea we are the center of things, and God is there to make us happy. The Father is for the sake of the child. And God's confessed Almightiness is solely and alone to serve *our* interest.

This is an idea of God which is false through and through, which turns the order around, and, taken in its real sense, makes self God and God our servant.

And from this false knowledge of God the cross removes all foundation. Cast down by your sorrow and grief, you become suddenly aware that this great God pays no heed to you; that He does not measure nor direct the course of things according to your desire; that in His plan there are other motives that operate entirely outside of your preferences; that, if needs be, His Might crushes you with one blow; and that in the working of that Plan and of that Might you are nothing else and nothing more than a particle of dust which cleaves to the driving-wheel and is driven before the wind.

Then you must submit, you must bend. You stand before it in utter impotence, and from this selfsame heaven, in which thus far you saw nothing but the play of light and clouds, darkness now enters into your soul, the clap of thunder reverberates in your heart, and the flaming bolt of lightning fills you with dismay.

This is the discovery of God's reality, of His Majesty which utterly overwhelms you, of an Almightiness which absorbs within itself you and everything you call yours. And for the first time you feel what it is to have to do with the living God.

Such is God.

Now you know Him!

And then begins the new endeavor of the soul, to learn to understand this real God thus known. Then begins the query, the guessing, the pondering, *why* this Almighty God should so be and do. Then the troubled heart seeks an explanation. It seeks this in its guilt and sin. It seeks this in the after-effects of the past. It seeks this in the purpose wherewith the cross was laid upon us, and in the fruit which it shall bear in the unraveling of eternity. For a long time it still remains the endeavor of finding the explanation of God's doings solely and alone *in ourselves*.

Until the soul makes a still further advance, and abandons the theory of Job's friends, and, like Job, receives the answer from God Himself out of the whirlwind, and now learns to understand how God's appointment covers all suns and stars, all hours and centuries, and causes all creatures to revolve themselves around Him, the Eternal One, as the one and only center; so that therefore His council and plan are as high as heaven and consequently exceed our comprehension; and that not the verification of His council, but the entering into the life of it, whether it be through joy, whether it be through sorrow, is our honor and the self exaltation of our soul.

This breaks the passiveness which enervates, and quickens again the stimulus which imparts heroic courage willingly to drink the cup, to drink it oneself, and not let it be forced upon us. To will to drink, as Jesus willed to die on Golgotha—with a broken heart, to co-operate in God's work, and in this suffering co-operation with God, Who slays us, to find eternal life.

The soul is thus like the sentinel who lets himself be shot down at his post and, in dying, enjoys the approving look of his general.

And he rejoices therein, because he knows, and now sees, that the general, who doomed him to death, yet loved him.

XXXV

I LOVE

ESPECIALLY in the first stage, the love which a young man feels for the maiden of his choice and this maiden for the elect of her heart, is sometimes so overwhelmingly extravagant, and surpassing all reason, that one feels that there is a mysterious power at play, which sets all composure at defiance.

This is not always so with two young people who are betrothed; such eccentric tension of the mystery of love is rather the exception. And let no one think that the doting, intoxicating love which we are here considering has anything in it of sinful, sensual inclination or of unholy voluptuousness. The ecstacy of love we here refer to occurs only with those who are in love, and courses through soul and body both; but, even in our sinful life this love can well be free from every fleshly motion.

When this ecstacy flames from both sides with equal faithfulness and warmth, then the world hears nothing of it. Then only the nearest relatives are in the secret. Tragically public, on the other hand, it frequently becomes, when it glows overwhelmingly in the heart of a young maiden, but does not find response in like measure in the heart of him she loves. Hardly a day passes but here or elsewhere the papers report the case of a girl who became betrothed and who ardently loved, but presently discovered that her lover was unfaithful, so that life itself became too much for her—she preferred death to life, and sought it in self-destruction.

This ecstacy of love is an abnormal kind of affection, because it withdraws the person whom it masters from his normal existence, and transports him into a condition of soul, which without being insanity, yet shows signs that are similar to it. Therefore we began by saying that it is outside of all reason. One who is in such a state of ecstacy can not be reasoned with; and as Burger in his "Leonora" tells us so graphically, for those who so love, only one of two things is possible; either their love must be reciprocated, or they can not find rest till they find it in death.

Do not take this too ideally.

It does not follow that such a young maiden stands exceptionally high as a woman. Rather, the contrary; such ecstacy not infrequently takes hold of otherwise ordinary girls, who are at times even very egotistical. This ecstacy also passes away frequently after a certain number of years, and nothing remains save an ordinary, sometimes a very common, person.

Passion in the ordinary sense is not what overpowers such a girl, and it is best interpreted as an ardent longing, bordering on insanity, to wrap up her whole existence with that of another.

It is and will remain a remarkable phenomenon.

A flooding power in the heart which, when it suffers disappointment, makes one quickly and decisively seek death, is an expression of human life, which deserves attention from all.

The Song of Songs sketches such an ecstacy of love, and aims thereby to outline an image of the love of the soul for God.

The whole Scripture stretches the canvass on which, at length, the Song of Solomon in striking colors embroiders the figure. Wedlock on earth is an embodiment of the tie that binds God and His people—God and the individual soul together. Jehovah even calls Himself Israel's husband, and says that He has betrothed Israel in righteousness. Infidelity toward the Holy One is called a whoring in idolatry. And so it is ever again the God-given love between man and woman, which in colored imagery becomes the standing expression of the love which binds the soul to God. And though in the New Testament this is more applied to Christ, yet He, the Son of God's good pleasure, is called the bridegroom of His Church, and His Church is the bride who invokes Him.

Still farther.

When Jesus analyzes for us the great commandment of love, He thereby directs soul and senses to the Eternal Being, and defines to us his love in terms which describe the ecstacy as it is found in life. For what is it to love God with all the heart, and all the soul, and all the mind and all the strength, other than to be entirely lost in, and consumed by, a higher attraction, which makes us pass by everything else, and causes us to know, to find and to enjoy an object for our love, in which we lose ourselves altogether?

The great significance, which the love between husband and wife should always have, and sometimes has yet, is only to be explained from the fact that God Himself in this love has imaged the highest love between Himself and the soul.

This lends to this high-strung love a holy and exalted character. This brings it to pass that this love develops harmoniously and nobly, creates the purest happiness that is tasted on earth; and that in sensual degeneracy it works terrible ruin and corruption. And from this it is likewise explained how, when suddenly and unharmoniously it takes hold of a receptive mind, it wrests such a soul away from itself and throws it into semi-frenzy.

Back of all this pushes and presses the higher love which God formed in the tie between Himself and His creature, and it is only the sinful character of our earthly existence that brings it to pass that what does not belong together is united, that soul and body separate themselves, that the equilibrium of the inclinations of the soul is broken, and that thus the best and holiest corrupts itself in sensuality or frenzy.

It is like the snow-flake, which comes down from the clouds pure-white, but becomes soiled through contact with the impurity of this world.

And yet ever and anon we must go back to conjugal love, if we would understand, what our love for God should be.

In our version, Psalm 116 begins with the song "I love the Lord;" but in the original it is different, much more gripping; it only reads: "*I love.*" We would say: "I am *in* love." It is an utterance of the soul, which from an inward glow perceives that, by the power of love, it has in an irresistible way been apprehended; it feels that an inner motion has been quickened in the soul, which was thus far strange to it; that now it is driven by an inward pressure which thus far it has not known, at least not in this measure. And now it knows and realizes that this is it; yes, this now is love, and therefore in ecstacy it exclaims: "I love! I love! I love!"

And as this wondrous inward motion transports the heart of the maiden, when this love directs itself to the young man of her choice, so here the selfsame irresistible pressure operates, but now in an entirely holy manner lifting the soul above every other thing, directing it solely to the Eternal Being.

With the maiden it was but the faint *copy* of the highest, here it is the highest *itself*. The eternal love which at last sets the pure tie between God and the soul into full, harmonious operation, now causes the soul to love with all the intensity to which it is disposed, all the intensity with which it can love.

This is not the mysticism of imagination. It is not knowing God by your own act of the will. Neither is it knowing God by the analysis of credal statements. It is the close approach to God with the warm, inward feeling of the thrilling, love-seeking heart.

It is to have longed and languished for what could quiet the home-sickness of the heart, to have tried everything that could be tried, and to have been disappointed with it all; and now, at length, to have found the true, the perfect, the holy Object of the love of one's heart, to receive God Himself in the soul, and in this love to be supremely happy.

You feel at once the difference between this love and what commonly passes as love for God.

Who does not love God? Every one, indeed, who is not a perfect atheist. Why should you not love God? Him in whom everything is holy, pure and exalted. In Whom there is nothing unworthy of love, and of Whom every one feels that He is worthy of the love of all men.

And so the great mass of people love their God. They are not opposed to Him. They find in God their ideal of everything that is beautiful and right and good. As they love virtue and right, so they also love God, but without the glow of a tiniest spark of personal relationship or attachment in this platonic love.

It is called love for God, but without the presence of God in the soul and in the mind, and without inclination and drawing of the heart after Him. So there is nothing in this love of that passionate thirsting after God, such as that of the hart that panteth after the water-brooks.

And therefore by the side of this cool, measured, pseudo-love of the world which has no heart in it, the Scripture puts the soul's utterance of tender piety, which sought her God, found Him, and now is aflame with warmest love for Him; can not do without Him; of herself thinks of Him, is continually busied with Him; and directs every utterance to Him and Him alone.

In this love there is a knowledge of God, such as no analysis of idea, no work of imagination, nor power of will, can bring us.

It is *to love*, and in this love itself to enjoy eternal life, and so know God with an intimacy, such as you would deem might not be seemly in a creature. Until, in the hereafter, the wall of separation falls away; and God in us, and we in Him, shall become the perfection of holiest love.

XXXVI

THOU HAST NOT LAID ME UPON THINE HEART

To the superficial mind nothing seems so easy as to love.

One naturally loves himself; to love God requires no slightest effort. And the only thing that at times costs trouble is to love one's neighbor as himself; and this not because will and power to love are lacking, but because the neighbor at times can almost be repulsive.

Yet he who so reasons is altogether mistaken.

To love God is far more difficult than the loving of one's neighbor; and it may safely be said that to ten who really show that they have love for their neighbor, there is at most but one who is consumed by love for God.

Jesus has therefore expressly put the loving of God in the foreground as the first and great commandment, and more than about the lack of brotherly love, Scripture complains constantly about forgetfulness of the Holy One. And that this was no Jewish exaggeration the Apostle shows full well when he repeats to those in Rome the bitter complaint of the Psalmist (Ps. 14, 3): *"There is none that seeketh after God, no, not one."*

This does not exclude the fact that love for God can be imparted to the soul. You sometimes clearly see how this love which at first was small, afterward becomes stronger and more tender. But take a man by himself, as he grows up by nature, not only from among good-for-nothings and criminals, but even from among cultivated and honorable people, there is no love alive in that man for God. He does not seek God. Nay, there is no one who really loves God, as God wills them to love.

For a long time this seemed different, but this semblance was deceptive.

At the beginning of the last century, it was still the
rule among the rank and file of our people to favor religion
and to abhor every form of atheism.

Without desiring to be called pious, no one cared to be
thought irreligious, and on solemn occasions the Name of
the Lord was still held in remembrance.

Are most people in these selfsame circles now worse than
formerly? Certainly not. They have become more
emancipated. But taken in general, people now are what
people were before.

Only with this great difference, that unbelief is preached
now more unblushingly from university chair and pulpit,
in the press and open meeting. And what has been the consequence? Has one serious protest been made on the part
of honest and cultured people against this profaneness?
Not in the least.

On the contrary. In one generation all faith has been
abandoned in ever widening circles, and with it there is a
shameless lack of resentment at the imputation of free
thought.

And this is by no means anything new. This selfsame
condition prevailed in Israel in the days of its spiritual
apostasy.

This is convincingly evident when, by Isaiah (lvii, 11,
Dutch Ver.) you hear God Himself reproach His people of
those days: "Thou hast lied, for *thou hast not laid me upon
thine heart.*"

It is so necessary, therefore, to enter more deeply into
the meaning of the love for God. Supremely necessary
in the case of believers, for even among these there is so
much that glitters like the gold of love, which is nothing
but imitation-gold.

The first step is, then, that you begin to see that to love God is not the *lightest* but the *heaviest* task to which faith calls you.

Ordinarily love is taken to mean that we practise much consideration for others, and that we do all we can to make them happy.

This is seen on every hand, where philanthropy is practised. Love then directs itself first most generously and easily to the unfortunate, and it is a matter of great gladness that this generously expressed philanthropy flourishes so vigorously in our days.

This teaches us to make sacrifices, it invites devotion, it alleviates much suffering.

But of course with this side of love one does not touch God.

Your God is blissful. In no single particular is He in need of anything. In no way is He in need of you. And there is nothing you can bring him. The feeling of pity from which this kind of love springs, can for no single moment govern your attitude to God, the Blissful One.

Here a wholly different kind of love is concerned; a love which springs from the sense that *you belong with God.* That you belong with Him by reason of your origin and your existence itself. That you belong with Him because you are His creature, and that therefore you have no other reason for existence and can have no other destiny in your own future, *save in Him.*

Every vain notion in you, as though you had a reason for existence in yourself, is therefore robbery committed against your God. It is the wheel which loosed from the wagon wills to roll on by itself.

And when in this way one has actually loosed himself from his God, and now from his imagined independence turns himself to God, in order to love Him as something beside himself, and calls *this* "love," then this is worse than a caricature and a mockery; is the outrage of love, and does not make us pious in God's eyes, but accuses and condemns us.

To love God is to take away everything that makes separation between us and Him and thus to come to an existence in which we live for God alone.

Love for God is the drawing back to God of what in the creature became separated from Him.

It is a motion born in the soul, when the magnetizing power goes out from God, which draws us to Him.

It is a pressure, an inclination in us, which allows us no rest for a single moment, and always pushes aside, pushes back and drives out everything that separates or draws us away from God, and so leaves us free again to have fellowship with Him.

In prayer we observe this first. "Take heed," says the Apostle (1 Pet. iii, 7) "that your prayers be not hindered." You observe this yourself, when you want to pray and can not, because there are things that stand between your heart and your God. Then you must first detach your thoughts, inclinations and perceptions from all this, dismiss it all from your spirit, and then God comes back to you, then there is fellowship once more, and you can pray again.

And this very thing, which you experience for a moment in prayer, must be extended throughout your whole life; and when this happens, the true love for God begins to awaken in you.

It is this that Jesus willed and had in view, when he explained it to you as follows: "Thou shalt love the Lord thy God with all your *heart*, with all your *soul*, with all your *mind* and with all your *strength*.

These four together constitute the whole inner organization of your spirit. These four become implicated ever and

anon in other egotistical or worldly interests. Then they
operate conversely. Then they operate away from God.
Then they separate you from the Holy One. And this now
is love, that again and again you loosen all four of these
from these wrong implications, and turn and direct them,
not in part, but altogether, toward the Lord your God.

This is no sacrifice in the real sense, for by sacrifice we
understand that there is something of our own, which
we could keep for ourselves, but which we willingly give
up in behalf of some one else. But this can not be spoken
of in this sense here.

Your heart is God's, your soul is God's, your mind is
God's, and all your powers are God's property.

Hence you bring God nothing. You merely return to
Him that of which you had robbed Him.

And if you do this, and do it in such a way, that all
these four—your heart, soul, mind and strength—direct
themselves to Him again, and altogether serve Him, then
the separation is broken and love celebrates her triumph.

Then it becomes the shamefacedness of the thief, who
returns what he had stolen, and now makes no boast of
anything, but prays to be forgiven.

This is what the Prophet calls: To lay God upon the
heart.

Love is a tender, gently stirring motion, which loves
symbols. Hence among lovers it has long been the custom
to carry each other's picture, or any costly ornament one
had given the other, on the heart.

The idea of this is, that one has given heart and hand
to the other, and now carries this symbol on the heart as
a continual reminder not to let the heart thus sealed go
out to another for one moment, but faithfully to keep it
for the one it loves.

And so; *to lay God upon the heart* means, that one has

made the choice, that one has come to give his heart to God, and now puts the symbol of God's Name upon the heart, in order to seal his heart for God, and strictly to see to it that his heart continues to be kept for God and for God alone.

Thus it is always the same.

Not, to love God thinking thus to bring God something, but quite the contrary, to lose oneself in God because we are His property, and because only by consecrating ourselves to Him to Whom we belong, can we realize the end of our existence.

And to do all this, not in a coldly calculating way, but through a melting of ourselves in the glow of tenderest love. This is the first, this is the great commandment, this is to know the Lord, to feel oneself as a child with his Father, this is to be inwardly consumed by the love of God that is poured out into our hearts.

All that remains is the question, how many there are, even among the pious in our land, who have thus laid God upon their heart.

XXXVII

WITH ALL

THE commandment to love our neighbor as ourselves, receives so great an emphasis in our time, that among the rank and file of people the first and great commandment has more and more passed into oblivion. At least, that it should be put first as every one's highest calling, not merely to serve the Lord our God, but also to love Him —who among the great masses of people think of this?

This substitution of the second in place of the first commandment has obtained such a hold upon people, that even among believers, loving God has lost devotion and warmth.

There is more response when, from the pulpit, pity, generosity and self-sacrifice in behalf of one's neighbor are entreated, than there is when the far higher calling of loving God is urged.

This reversal of order is fatal.

For he who loves God, also loves the brother; while, on the contrary, it is by no means the rule, that he who loves his neighbor also loves his God.

The first commandment guarantees the second, but not, likewise the second, the first. To be warm toward God and cold toward the brother, is simply unthinkable; but innumerable are the men and women who in all sorts of societies for the sake of aiding the neighbor put themselves to the fore, but who are stone-cold toward God, not infrequently even denying His existence.

It is, therefore, supremely necessary, that a counterpoise be put into the scale, and that, with emphasis and seriousness, the great commandment, to love God, be bound again upon the heart of all Christendom.

This call must again be sounded loudly in the Church, and the preacher would rightly understand his duty, who, week by week, would so warmly and eloquently bind this love for God upon the conscience, that, at length, the entire congregation would feel constrained to say: "How warmly does our pastor love his God!" and as though ignited by fire would itself revive in its love for God, with, perhaps, the entire board of officials in the lead.

The press also can and should co-operate in this. And by means of these meditations we are bent upon opening the eyes of as many as possible to the need of making communion with, knowledge of, and love for, God more than ever before our daily concern.

Soundness in the faith, a blameless walk and many good works are undoubtedly indispensable, but the marrow of all religion is blessed fellowship with the eternal Being, and in this fellowship it is only the *love for God* that makes gold glisten.

And yet, why conceal it? as soon as one seriously tries to make this love for God real, he stumbles at once upon a very great difficulty.

This difficulty lies in the two words that stand at the head of this meditation, or really only in the last of the two—in this painful word *all*.

"Would you love God?" says Jesus, "then you must love Him with *all* your heart, with *all* your soul and with *all* your mind." And to this, let us humbly confess it, it does not come in this life even with the holiest of saints. Not by a long way.

Sin and the world have so far estranged us from God, that sometimes it requires an effort to lift up the soul in a conscious utterance of love to God three or four times a day, apart from our prayers. Would it be saying too much, if we add to this, that there is a great deal of prayer made in church and at home, during which the soul has no dealings with God?

And when you do succeed, at least a few times a day to feel your soul go out in love to your God, what then is the degree of tenderness in your love, and how long does this exaltation of soul continue? Still more, how often does this become in you a thirsting after God?

But suppose you have come thus far, not every day, but most days—how far do you even then fall short of this loving of your God with *all* your soul, *all* your heart and *all* your consciousness? For this *all* must doubtless include *all* the day, so that at no time the love for God escapes, or is asleep in you.

Now here, of course, a distinction must be made. The love for God can well up in your heart, it can scintillate in your word, can hold you back from sin and selfishness, and can inspire you to deeds of devotion and heroic courage; and it is entirely true, that the inspiration of this love can operate in us, without our being aware at the moment of a conscious feeling of tender love for God rising in our soul, or without becoming aware of a reciprocal working of His love in our heart.

A martyr from love for God can go into death, and yet at the moment of dying be so distracted by mortal pain, or by the taunts of his executioners, that all tender love-fellowship with his God falls away.

It is also true, that our business, our intercourse with people, and the cares that fill our mind, so engage our thoughts, that we perhaps—yes, *are* able—to send up to God a passing utterance of soul, and yet are utterly unable, to concentrate our soul and senses upon God and center them in Him.

A mystical love for God, which would lose itself all day

long in contemplation, would end in neglect of business, and thus be in conflict with love for God.

But even though you bring all this into account, it is still the great commandment, that you shall love your God with *all* your heart, with *all* your soul, and with *all* your mind; and who of us ever accomplished more than a small part of the whole?

There has been One, who has not failed even in this first and great commandment, but no more than one: even *the Christ.*

Of the second commandment, of neighborly love, you feel that Jesus alone fulfilled it completely, and yet, with respect to love for their fellowmen, although at a great distance, many saints have pressed His footsteps.

But when you go back to the first and great commandment, Jesus stands in the fulfillment incomparably alone. Yea, He, and He alone among all, has loved God with *all* His heart, *all* His soul, *all* His mind and *all* His strength, always, till the end, without one moment's interruption.

This is His crown of glory.

Therein is the life of the world.

Apart from Him, the whole world, with its thousands of millions of people, stands before God, without there being one among them all, who has ever kept the first and great commandment.

But now comes Christ, and now there is indeed *one.*

Now comes from a real *human heart,* from a real *human soul* and from a real *human consciousness* this pure, full, unalloyed love, for the enjoyment of which love offered unto Him by His creature, Almighty God has created the vast multitude of children of men upon this earth.

This is the shield that is lifted up over us.

This is what brings it to pass, that God can still tolerate this world and carry it.

With us, too, this love will come. Many of our beloved ones, who in this life did not reach it by a long way, in the realms of everlasting light now bring this perfect love-offering to God.

And we also will come to it, when in death we shall fully die unto sin, and shall know God, even as we are known.

At least if we fall asleep in Jesus. That is to say, if in our dying hour there shall be nothing, nothing more, that makes separation between us and Jesus.

And what is the cementing power that causes you to cleave to Jesus? Is it not that you love your God; that this love for God has been poured out into your heart, that it has operated in you; that you esteem it of foremost significance; that with all your lack and with all your shortcomings, you have willed, that this love for God should impart unto you your highest inspiration, and should enable you to attain the best?

This is the mystery of being a Christian, that as you hide in the perfect love wherewith Jesus has loved your God, through this glow of *His* love you feel love for God kindle in your own heart, and that whenever this spark of love goes out again, Jesus rekindles it.

XXXVIII

WITH ALL THINE HEART

UNDERNEATH, deeper yet than your heart, lives your soul.

When God searches a man, He not only tests his heart, but enters deeper still into his being; something which Scripture plastically expresses by saying (Jer. xi, 20) that God, after He has tried our heart, also trieth our reins, in order thus to examine us in the innermost parts of our being.

In moments of high tension it is sometimes felt even among men, that the heart is not all, and that, through the heart, the very center of our *self* must be reached. See it in the case of Jonathan. When David swore to him that he would always be faithful to him and to his house, in that moment of violent and deep emotion Jonathan replies (I Sam. xx, 4): "Whatsoever thy soul desireth, I will even do it for thee."

When you consider it seriously, the only thing of worth in your life is that which comes into your heart from your soul, and what by way of your heart enters into your soul.

What goes on outside of your soul can also have considerable attraction for you. In lesser degree when only the outward appearance interests you; in greater degree when you admire in some one his courage and energy, devotion and self-sacrifice. But all this passes away. You do not assimilate it into your *life*. And, as a rule, the emotions and utterances of your heart, which go on outside of your soul, do not rise higher than the feelings—sometimes even not above the dream life—of the sentimental.

The function of your heart derives all real, permanent worth only from the relation in which your heart stands to your soul.

This, however, must never be taken as though your heart were something superfluous, and as though the soul alone were of consequence.

Rather the contrary is true; your heart has been given you by God as an absolutely indispensable organ of your soul.

Only by means of your heart can that which stirs in your soul come to this supreme perception and lofty utterance which we glorify as *love*.

In the great commandment, therefore, Jesus puts the heart in the foreground. First: "Thou shalt love the Lord thy God with all thy *heart*," and only then, "Thou shalt love the Lord thy God with all thy *soul*."

This could not be otherwise.

Love does not begin in our soul, but in God. It comes from God to us. Our heart drinks it in. And thus only when this love of God, by way of the heart, enters into our soul, there wakens in our soul the life of reciprocal love for God, which now presses from the soul into the heart, and causes us to love God.

This last stage is reached only through our heart. Only in our heart is the spark ignited and the fire of love made to glow.

The love of the soul partakes more of the character of worship. Only the heart gives out the tenderness and the warmth.

Only when it becomes a loving of God with all your *heart*, does this love begin to glow in you with real human feeling.

This love of the heart is an irresistible mutual attraction. More than once, therefore, it is described in the Scriptures as a *cleaving* of the soul unto God.

When the magnet draws the steel so closely to itself that there is no air between, then the steel cleaves unto the magnet. When, therefore, between people, there springs up so tender an attraction that at length everything that separated them falls away, then heart cleaves to heart, soul cleaves to soul. And so there is no perfect love for God, until everything that makes separation between us and God, is taken away. And then it is true of this love also, that our heart, and, through our heart our soul, cleaves to God.

A strong, forcible expression, which Scripture uses again and again. So strong, that you ask yourself whether it ever will prove true with you. And yet, to God's child this is not open to doubt. As a rule there lies such a mountain of hindrances between our soul and our God, that there is no mention of a cleaving unto God. But this does not alter the fact that every child of God has known brief moments, in retirement and solitude, in which the love of God drew him so mightily and so irresistibly, and God's blessed fellowship in Christ overwhelmed him so blessedly, that, truly, everything fell away, and the cleaving of his heart to the heart of his God, was the only true expression for what his soul enjoyed, and felt for God.

What in nature is called *power of attraction*, in the spiritual life is called *love*.

Love is not something manufactured, something studied, but is something in itself.

You feel whether some one loves you or not. You feel whether this love wherewith he interests and draws you is strong or weak. And when a great love directs itself to you, goes out towards you, and begins to work upon you, then you likewise feel the irresistibility of this drawing.

"Drawing" is what Jesus Himself calls this outgoing of love. The Father "draws" His elect. Of Himself the

Savior declares: "I will draw all men unto me." That is to say, "I will play upon your heart with such a superpower of grace and love, that you will come to me, surrender yourself to me, and be won by me."

Thus there is a superpower in this love, but superpower through a violence which does not hurt, but blessedly refreshes. As the sun draws the flower-bud upward, and at the same time, by its cherishing warmth makes it to unfold, so this love of God draws you up to itself, and at the same time courses through you with most blessed sensations which cause the heart to swell with holiest joy.

You drink in this love, or, if you will, it is wealth for your soul, and in this wealth of God's love which you enjoy, awakens of itself, pure and tender, the love in your heart for your God.

There is also love for the impersonal.

So we speak of love for nature, when it attracts us by its beauty or awes us by its sublimity. In the same way we can love science, love right, love everything that is noble and of good report.

But all this is a vague, general love which finds no rest, because the soul, which personally lives and loves, can only satisfy itself in a personal love.

Therefore love for a song-bird or domestic animal is of a tenderer nature. For here love concentrates itself upon a definite object, and there is reciprocal expression. The attractiveness of a dog can be very great, because there is personal response. You do not find this in mere nature, in science—in law; but you do find it in a dog who risks his life for you.

All this, however, is but the prelude to higher love, and only with man does love begin to speak its richer language and to reveal its higher character. Here too are different grades in the ascent. The love of mother and child, of father and son, of brother and sister, of friend and friend —till you finally come to marriage; sometimes, Oh, so degraded by sin, and yet in its ideal interpretation the highest love on earth, and therefore, marked by God Himself as the symbol of the love which binds Him to His people, to His elect.

But even in marriage, love can not find its consummation. In accordance with its nature it feels within itself an impulse which goes higher. Only when, at last, love begins to reach out after the Highest Being, and when you feel that the spark of love for God has been ignited in your heart by God Himself do you become aware that now love in you has reached its greatest height, that it can rise no higher, but also that it has no such desire, and consequently is most blessed.

The conflict which then ensues lies in your inequality with God. He is everything, you nothing. He the High and Lofty One, you the insignificant creature of His hand. You, owing thanks to Him for everything; He, heeding nothing, and, therefore, can receive nothing from you.

With men our love is mutual, as between equals. Between a great man and a little child no high personal love can develop itself. The little child can not reach up to the broadly cultured man; the man can not come down to the child, otherwise than in simple kindness.

But this is what God has done for you.

He has done it in Christ. He came in Christ as Man to you, in order to make the inequality equal, to unite Himself to your life, to fit Himself to your existence, in everything to become like unto the brethren—only excepting sin.

Here now is the mystery. The great mystery, whereby with him who joined himself to Jesus, and believed in

Jesus, and in soul became one with Jesus, the true love for God could develop itself without the disturbance of inequality.

And when you say that Jesus has given you everything, and that you can place no crown upon the head of your Savior which He does not already have—then know that there yet remains one thing, that God can demand from His elect; and this one thing, what is it but the love of your heart? But, then, of *all* your heart, till at length your heart draws after God, as God's heart drew after you.

XXXIX

WITH ALL THY SOUL

If it begins to trouble you, yea, to become guilt, that after all the years that you have lived, you have made so little advance in this loving of your God, then consider with more care than you have yet done the rule your Savior has given you regarding it.

You have known the great commandment from your childhood. You have learned it by heart, and no word of it is unknown to you. And in your conscience you have admitted unconditionally that your Savior was right. O, surely, in your love for God nothing could be wanting. It has to be a love with *all* your heart, your soul, your mind, your strength. A love without bounds. Everything for your God, even as for yourself you have to expect everything from God.

But Jesus did not make it a general declaration. Jesus did not say: "Thou shalt love the Lord thy God in everything." No, Jesus has made distinctions—distinguished the heart, the soul, the mind and the strength. And did you do well to pass this by? In this distinction Jesus had a purpose. He has deemed this distinction necessary for His whole Church. He has willed that the ministers of the Word should bind this love for God, severally with the heart, the soul, the mind and the strength, upon the conscience of the congregation of the Lord. And likewise He has willed, that every child of God should continually examine himself, whether his love for God has been practised in this fourfold way.

The root of true piety would have taken hold far more vitally in the sub-conscious life of the Church, if both preaching and self-examination had applied themselves more seriously to the cultivation of this rich, warm love for God, and had drawn vital strength from the keeping of the first and great commandment.

There is no holier power that can inspire us than love; and of all love, the love for God wears the crown.

Therefore love is the bond of perfection, provided you do not volatilize it into a vague conception of ideal love, without rule or object.

All that is noble and lofty in love, and can be lauded and celebrated in song, has reality in it only when it is a love that first loves God, and for God's sake loves the neighbor.

It at once attracts the attention, that in commending the love for God, Jesus puts the *heart* first and not the *soul;* any one of us would have done otherwise.

We would first have named the soul as the center of our whole inner life, and after that, from the soul as the center, we would have gone on to the loving with the heart, with the mind, with all the strength.

Jesus, on the other hand, begins with the heart, then comes to the soul, and only then points to the mind and to the strength.

From what the Lord by Jeremiah says to Israel, this difference between heart and soul can be made plain.

It is in the fourth chapter of Jeremiah that at one time it is said to Israel, that the terrible outpouring of God's wrath shall reach her *heart*, and that at another time it shall reach her *soul;* but with a sharply marked distinction.

When the suffering, that comes upon Israel, is outlined in its first threatening reality, it says (vs. 18): "This is thy wickedness, it is so bitter that *it reacheth unto thine heart.*"

When the suffering continues, and at length becomes fatal, then it says (vs. 10) that: "the sword *reacheth unto the soul.*"

Thus the heart is the seat of the emotions and sensations, the soul the seat of the life itself.

Now apply this to love, and here also it is the heart that receives the impressions and causes the stirring feeling of love to flow forth; but it is in the soul that the love which is received settles, and from the soul springs the impulse of the stirring of love.

Without the heart there would be no enjoyment of love and no exercise of love conceivable, but neither the love enjoyed nor the love exercised would touch your *self*, if there were not behind and underneath your heart something deeper, even the source itself of your life, and if the tie did not operate which binds up your heart with your soul.

You can not hear save with your ear, nor speak save with your voice; but it is nevertheless the soul which uses your ear as instrument of hearing, and likewise it is your soul which must speak in your voice, if your word is to be heard.

And so you can not drink in love and can not show love save with your heart, and yet it is the soul which uses your heart as the instrument, by which with its deepest and hidden life to enter upon the wealth of love.

Hence it will not suffice for you to say that you love God with your heart.

With the heart one can feel himself sweetly affected by the enjoyment of love, and be conscious of the rise within himself of reciprocal feelings of love, without any really true love, simply because the *soul* does not enter into it.

In art, especially, this is strongly evident.

One hears in music and song a touching recital of human suffering, and is at the time deeply moved and carried away. One has felt the sensations of mortal agony, which were uttered in song, go through his heart. One has lived

and suffered along with it. But presently the play is over.
For a moment the impression remains. But an hour after,
everything is forgotten, and, as though nothing had happened, we pursue our course. Not that the heart had not
been affected, for even pseudo-feelings touch it. But the
soul had no part in it, and therefore it did not touch us.

You constantly see this thing in life. With many a
mother it happens that she can not endure the sight of a
tear in the eye of her child. When she sees it she is at once
deeply moved, and at the moment will do everything to
make her darling forget his trouble and to comfort him.
But this also frequently amounts to no more than a pressure of the heart. When the child that wept laughs again,
everything is right once more, and because her love for
her child does not spring from the root of her soul, she
does not know how to love the soul of her child, and instead of saving him, she ruins him!

There is also a loving of God with the heart which makes
it burst into flame when God's honor is attacked, which
enjoys tender emotions toward the Eternal Being, and
which still holds self in sight and not God, because, though
there is love, it is not love that reaches the soul.

Your soul is in your *self*, and your self stands before the
face of your God. Therefore in your soul the question
must be settled, whether your God exists for the sake of
you, or whether you exist for the sake of your God alone.

If, now, you say: "The latter is my case"—Glorious!
But now comes the second question: Is such the case with
you from submission, from the sense of your own insignificance in the face of the Majesty of the Lord, or is it thus
from love?

Do you will to exist for God alone, because you can do
nothing else? Or, did it come to this with you, that you
would not will it otherwise, since God is the dearest

Object of your love, and because you feel your whole existence to go up into this love for Him?

By the heart it will then be enjoyed, and through the heart it will come to utterance. For this you received this costly instrument of your heart. But he who uses this heart and plays upon it in blessed love, is your own self, in the center of your soul, where your person lives in the holy presence of the Triune God.

Have you perceived something of such a love for God within you? If so, do you then understand what it means to say that you love God in the inmost of your being, of your self, of your person, with *all* your soul?

Not that there are merely times when this is so with you, but that this love has become altogether continuous.

Not that with a part of your soul, with a part of your self, you give yourself up to this love for God, so that, for instance, you want to be saved in order yourself to be happy, rather than to glorify your God forever.

And, likewise, not with a division of your soul between your God and your self, so that you still continuously commit robbery in your soul, by withdrawing a part of your desire, of your future, of your self-perception from God.

The demand is so awe-inspiring, it is so all comprehensive: "Thou shalt love the Lord thy God with *all thy soul*," *i. e.*, there shall no more be the least outgoing of life from you, except such as springs from love for God.

And to this you reply: "I should have to be an angel and no man to do this in all its fullness;" and you are right, provided you add: "no sinful man."

But for this you have your Savior, Who as Man has accomplished this perfect love for God in your behalf; and there will be peace in your soul, in spite of all your lack of love, if by a true faith you are hidden in this Savior.

XL

WITH ALL THY MIND

It is singular that Jesus included in the first and great commandment (S. Matt. xxii, 37), the injunction that we should love God also with *our mind.*

When Jesus holds before us the high ideal, that we shall love God with our heart and with our soul, we accept it at once, for at the first hearing we understand that our heart and soul are disposed to love. But how can you love with your mind? Your mind has been given you that you may think, ponder, and understand; but how, involuntarily you ask, can the mind be an organ of love, an instrument by which love can execute its glorious operations?

That so many fail to see this is because it is read thoughtlessly, and no serious work is made of investigating this first and great commandment in each of its parts. With hurried reading, it is taken as though it said that we must put our mind in the *service* of God, and leave it to the heart and the soul to do the loving.

Yet this is not so. It does not say that we must serve God with the mind; that we must center our thought upon God; that we must come to an intelligent confession of God with our understanding, or however one may think he ought to direct the working of his mind toward God. No, it declares clearly and plainly that we must also *love* God with our mind. Our whole religion is focussed by Jesus on this one mighty conception of *love*, and this love must permeate our entire human personality. From the soul, not only in our heart, but also in our mind, it must have dominion, and must bring it to pass, that all our vital powers are led by one supreme motive, to wit: the love for God.

The mind here by no means signifies our logical processes of thought, our clear judgment, our learned understanding; no, our mind here means the whole glorious gift of our *consciousness*, including our creative ability, our imagination, our reflection and meditation.

Powers work in nature far more strongly than in men. But nature, though it lives, is altogether *unconscious*. And though in the more highly organized animals you observe a small beginning of consciousness, yet even with the most highly developed animal it is extremely weak. And the glory of the *conscious* life, which in God alone is perfect, is among all earthly creatures found only in man, because man, in this particular as well, has been created after God's Image.

This consciousness may not come to the highest degree of development with many people. With the insane it may become confused, and the pitifully unfortunate idiot shows, by contrast, what an unspeakably rich gift even the very ordinary man has received from God, in his consciousness, in his self-consciousness and in his conscious life, so that you have no right to consider the consciousness inferior to your heart, and that all religion, which would focus the service of God solely upon the heart and upon good works, and excludes from it the glorious human consciousness, maims itself, robs God of His gift, and must degenerate into false religion.

Thus, you feel at once, that it is indeed Christian duty, that our human science also should direct itself to God, not only that a part of science, to wit: theology, should choose as its object the knowledge of God and leave no path untrod along which this can be enriched; but that science as a whole, in every domain, should ever cause the glory of God to become manifest.

However thoroughgoing and learned science may be,

the moment it leaves God aside, awakens doubt about His existence, or undertakes to deny Him, it is no longer science, but sin; for it sins against the great commandment, that mankind with its whole mind, shall first love God. And since it is contradictory to every idea of love, to be indifferent to its object, or to ignore it, it follows that the scientist, who in his scientific pursuit does not feel himself drawn toward God, and who, before all things else, with his scientific knowledge does not seek to enhance the glory of God, violates the first and great commandment.

And this is the curse, which rests so heavily upon the science of our times, that in its veins it does not feel the throb of love for God, and that it behaves itself as though the great commandment, that we must love God with all the mind, had never been given.

The same applies to our doctrinal standards.

Students of science are but few in number, but every one is called to confess the faith.

What this means, is not difficult to understand.

Every man has a standard, a system of main ideas, from which he starts out, a world of thoughts, however small, by which he lives, for which he contends, from which he acts.

To say, therefore, that every one is called to confess the faith, means, that no one's standard of life must leave out God; that in this standard of life God must be the center; that this standard of life must cleave unto God, must go out from God and go out after God; and that in this life-view, all the rest must adapt itself to the love, the ardent love for God, Who demands it.

Not every man can make this clear for himself. In every other respect, the great mass of mankind borrows its main ideas and fundamental convictions from the knowledge that has been acquired by former generations.

And so here, too, the Church of Christ with her Creeds of age-long standing comes to the help of the plain man. In the Church every one receives with respect to the knowledge of God the result of the experience of faith of by-gone centuries, and no condition of a people can be healthy, if its thousands and tens of thousands do not have these confessional standards of the Church as starting point of their life-view.

Hence, it is the ruin of the love for God with all the mind, when these confessional standards are removed from the life-view, and people are falsely instructed that everything hinges on the mysticism of the love of the heart and on the deeds of the will.

He who drives in this direction, impoverishes the love for God, by excluding from it all the mind, and treads not in the footsteps of Jesus, but goes directly against His great command.

But with this also the love for God with all the mind has not reached its limit.

Apart from Science and Church Creeds, there is still the *common daily consciousness*—in our daily calling, in our associations, in our conversations, in the plans we make, in the line of behavior which we lay out for ourselves, in the intentions which we foster, in our reading, in our thoughts about persons and affairs, in our convictions, in our imagination, in our appreciation of art and literature, in our passing of judgments, in our review of the past and in our thoughts about the future.

All these together form the many-sided activity of our consciousness; it is the daily sphere of the work of all our mind, the school and workshop of our thinking, investigation and reflection; and all this can go on apart from God, or be animated and dominated at every point by the thought of God and love for His Name.

Therefore, with every one of us, Jesus lays claims upon all this for His God and our God. He wills that in and with all this, the love for God shall not merely lead, direct and rule us, but that, from an inner impulse, all this shall form and clothe itself in the way that we know is well-pleasing unto God. Above all we should do this in this way, not merely from the sense of duty, because we must, even when we will it otherwise. And also that we are not merely to do this in order not to invoke the wrath of God upon us, nor for the sake of meriting heaven thereby. But purely from the love of God, because for God's sake, we can not persuade ourselves to use this costly gift of our consciousness to plan or work out anything that would grieve God.

And though in regard to all this we stand in our actual life still far distant from this high ideal, a child of God, who loves his God, by the reading and re-reading of this first and great commandment, will, by this claim that he shall love God with *all the mind*, be brought to a halt. He will thereafter in a different way practise control upon the life of his consciousness. And if he succeeds in this way to cause the love for God to enter more fully into everything he studies, plans and meditates upon, yea, in every word he speaks, then the deeper experience of the love of his God will be his daily gain, and the fellowship with the Eternal Being will ever become more blessedly known within his inmost self.

XLI

WITH ALL THY STRENGTH

NOTHING so offends the Christian soul as the superficial fencing and excited boasting about love which is still counted good form in our loveless social life. This playing with what is highest both in heaven and on earth, becomes specially offensive when, in unbelieving and semi-believing circles you hear time and again the high ideal of love abused, especially by entirely or partly emancipated women, in order effectually to resist therewith every honest confession of the Gospel.

Love is then said to be the whole of religion. Nothing more is needed. The Old Testament is far too unmerciful. S. Paul with his anathemas could at times be far too harsh, and has saved his honor only by his hymn of love in the thirteenth chapter of I Corinthians. S. John, the Apostle of Love, alone is a man one can idolize, for it is probably not true that he wanted to see fire come down from heaven to destroy the opponents of Jesus, and that he should have advised not even so much as to receive in one's house a person who denied the doctrine of Christ, is certainly recorded in the tenth verse of II John, but his epistles are unauthentic. Moreover, as lovers of love, they hold themselves alone to Jesus, who never allowed Himself to be led by anything except gentle, tender love. Though it is true that Jesus could be hard, even sharp, with the Pharisees, but this they themselves are too, for the Pharisees now are the orthodox Christians, and these they themselves do not spare. In their opinion, these slaves of the letter stand outside the law, hence also outside the law of love.

Do you not feel, and taste, that this false love-mania is inexorably judged by Jesus in what He said concerning the first and great commandment?

Oh, surely love alone — and nothing else than love counts. Love is what is highest, love is the one and all. But upon one condition, to wit: that all your love goes out from your love to God, that is to say, that in your love-life the love for God stands in the foreground, and that this love for your God shall so dominate all your love, that you love Him with all your heart, all your soul and all your mind.

Yea, as though this were not expressed clearly and definitely enough in such a way as to cut off the least misunderstanding and misapprehension, Jesus adds to this still a fourth claim, and binds it on your conscience, that this love for God only corresponds to the high ideal when it is a loving of God *with all your strength*.

Thus Jesus does not do what, altogether wrongfully, many a professed Christian does. He does not say: Yes, God is *love*, but you must also count with His *holiness*. No, your Savior places nothing above or beside love. Love to Him is all-sufficient. Only, He objects that this love as a rule is only shown towards *the neighbor*. He demands and wills that in your love, the love *for God* shall be the all-dominating starting-point, and He does not let you go, until you understand that to your love for God no boundary may be put, and that it must also be a love for God with *all your strength*.

Love for God with all your soul, all your heart, and all your mind, may yet stop at the feelings, or be confined to the ideal, but when you must love God also *with all your strength*, then it claims your actual life, your whole personal existence, all the output of your person and life.

Strength is everything that goes out from you, by

virtue of the endowment God has entrusted you with; as the expression of the talents that have been given you, of the powers and qualifications you have at your disposal, of the means at your command, of the influence you exert, of the time that is granted you, of the circumstances which make the exhibition of your strength possible.

And all these powers at your command, which are entrusted to you, under responsibility to Him Who gave them, Jesus demands that you shall exercise in such a way that in the working of them all the love for your God shall be the dominating element.

Do not take this in a false spiritual sense.

The idea is current that, in the virtue that goes out from us, the love for God only finds expression when we apply our strength exclusively to religious and spiritual things.

Consequently it is thought that he who becomes a Minister of the Word, loves God more than he who studies law or medicine; that he who devotes himself to Missions is more consecrated to God than he who spends his powers on the press; that an institution for saving unfortunates is of a higher order than an institution for scientific investigation. In brief, that love for God is more adequately expressed by service in the realm of particular grace, than by life in the broad domain of common grace.

This is all wrong. God's greatness and almightiness do not limit and bind themselves to the narrower domain of salvation of souls, but permeate our whole human life; and with every one of us, according to our talents and calling, love for God must express itself in every department of life with equal zeal and power.

A painter or sculptor can and should, just as consciously and just as intentionally, glorify God from love, as a missionary or a philanthropist. Nothing, not even the humblest calling, is here excluded. A farmer who holds a church office, should serve God from love with all his strength in stable and granary, as well as in his duties as church official. A mother in her family has as sacred a calling to love God with all her strength as a trained nurse in the home or as a woman missionary in the foreign field. False dualism, which relegates mother or servant to common life, and pronounces the nurse sacred, does not cherish love for God, but corrupts it.

Three sins here ensnare our life; the *non-use*, the *wrong* use and the *abuse* of powers entrusted to us. In each of these three the love of God is denied.

As there is no star in the firmament that is not called to shine for God's glory, so God has imparted no grain of gold to the soul of any child of man, but that the glow thereof must be brought out and glisten for God's honor.

But what the stars do not do, indolent man does do. Again and again you see people who have talent but bury it rather than make gains with it for God. Where then is the love for the Eternal Being? Surely it would require effort and self-denial to improve each latent talent to the full. But where is their love for their God when they can not afford this effort, this sacrifice, this self-denial for the sake of their dear God?

God's honor would be exhibited far more gloriously, even among Christians, if all these grains of hidden gold glistened in public sight instead of remaining covered by the dust of self-sufficiency and indolence.

The *wrong* use of talents is different, but it is equally sinful and loveless before God. In this case no efforts are spared, no sacrifices are counted too great, but the object is to secure position for oneself, to get on in the world, to please others, and to become rich, not toward God, but in public esteem.

Then one works and labors early and late, but without God; and from selfish motives—not from love of God. It is not a "working while it is day," and as a child from love for his Father, knowing that this Father shall supply all his needs; but it is a slaving that one may himself provide for his needs. It is all for the sake of lucre, and not for God.

And along this line one comes so easily to the third and still worse sin, namely: the *abuse* of one's gift, in opposition to God and His holinesses. Oh, who can count the men who might have shone as stars of the first magnitude, in honor of God, and who have abused their brilliant talents to break down what is holy, to attack the Word, to oppose religion, and at length, in rash arrogance, even try to destroy the faith in God of others? Who does not know them, the singers and artists, who have abused their talent to encourage wantonness and vanity and to draw souls away from God? How much wit has been abused to mock what is holy and make it appear ludicrous? How much keenness of insight has degenerated into cunning and slyness by fostering lies and dishonesty? How much maidenly beauty and loveliness have been sinned away in impure intention and passion to please?

Not love for God, but enmity *against* God has come to baneful expression in all this abuse.

Over against all this *non-use*, this *wrong* use, and this *abuse* of gifts and talents loaned to us, Jesus places before you nothing else than the claim of love for your God.

He binds this claim not upon the conscience of the world, for the world does not know the real love, because it does not know God, and all real love goes out from the love for God.

But Jesus puts this full claim unabbreviated and without any limitation before you who confess His holy Name; and He does not let go of you until the scales fall from your eyes and you begin to see that it is a sinning away of your life if you do not know homesickness for this full love for the Eternal which can not rest until it loves God *also with all its strength.*

XLII

HE THAT LOVETH NOT
KNOWETH NOT GOD

The knowledge of God is eternal life.

Eternal life is not added to this knowledge, but this knowledge is itself eternal life. This knowledge therefore can not be limited to what the mind grasps or does not grasp, nor to what our intellect sees through, nor to what is imprinted on our memory. The knowledge of God is a knowledge which surely casts an ever clearer image into the mirror of our consciousness, but which can never be an external, abstract jugglery with words.

It is a knowledge which comes to us from our second birth, as a child knows his father and mother; boldly speaking one may say, a knowledge whose seat is in the blood, a Divine atavism. It is a knowledge that is grasped in our will, when our will grasps the will of God. It is a knowledge which comes to us from spiritual experience, almost from inspiration. It is a knowledge which steadily increases in the hidden walk with God, and ripens in the prayerlife. It is a knowledge which experiences enrichment in the dark depths of sorrow, and on the sunny heights of joy and prosperity. It is a knowledge which, unobserved, constantly comes to the surface from the stream of life itself; a knowledge which uses our very person as its organ, and sometimes knows moments when it seems that "seeing face to face"—as through the veil of the sanctuary, as through an opening of a curtain — is already granted us here.

Of course this rich, ever ripening, ever more and more full and overflowing knowledge of God, must ever and anon be caught up in the clear consciousness, and be expressed in the creedal statements of the Church, as well as in our own personal profession; unless this is done, quickly mystical corruption enters in, imagination-mania and sentimental softening. But yet, it offends, and affects one with a chill, when in the Church and out of it, barren scholasticism is seen taking the place of life, and one hears the knowledge of God discussed as though it were an inanimate thing, and no elastic, soul-permeating life.

This is not according to the Scripture but in direct opposition to it.

Hear what the Apostle of the Lord says to you: *"He that loveth not, has not known God, for God is love"* (I John iv, 8).

Though this puts it strongly, yet so it is: by doing ourselves what God does, do we enter most fully into the knowledge of God.

Consider this with a view to the forgiveness of sin, and you will understand the mystery of this particular knowledge of God.

Whether God forgives you your sin is now and for ever for you personally the main question of your existence and of your future. It is now preached differently, as though the main question were, how we can rid ourselves of sin, and work out our own sanctification. But this is all self-deception. As S. Paul and the Fathers bound it upon our soul, so it is and will continue to be. The supreme life-question is: "How can I be just before God?" Forgiveness of sins is the way to dying unto sin; there is no other way. How we, who till death continue to be beings conceived in sin, can be called unto sonship of God, and to dwell forever in the Father-house above, this and this alone is the mighty life-problem, which immediately touches our relation to God and our knowledge of the Eternal. And so the world-riddle and the riddle of our soul ever and always comes down to this one thing: Is there grace, forgiveness and perfect reconciliation for me?

And now it is most noteworthy that the Our Father links, as with an iron hand, the short prayer for forgiveness to the provision that we *ourselves forgive*.

Give us this day our daily bread, is immediately followed by the prayer for the daily bread of Divine forgiveness, for the life of your soul, but this is bound to the honest assertion: "as *we forgive those that trespass against us.*"

In other words: You must love with that deepest love which makes you forgive from the heart those that have wronged you, and only he who so loves, knows God. He knows God, in this His highest love, that though your sins be as scarlet, He makes them white as snow, yea, though they have risen mountain-high, He casts them away into the depth of the sea.

Actually, therefore, in the Our Father itself, is expressed the significant thought, which it seemed so bold to utter, that, by forgiving, we learn to understand how God forgives us; that is to say, by loving we learn to know God in His love for us. And he who loves, not in phrases and in play of the emotions, but so that from the heart he forgives his enemy, entirely, altogether and in full, because he loves his enemy also, thereby increases in the knowledge of God, learns to know God, and learns to understand that God is love, love toward himself, too.

Does this originate from within yourself, so that *you* love *first*, and afterwards, *God* loves *you?* Far from it. In you nothing ever begins with love; and back of the first spark of love that ever glowed in your soul, it was always the hand of your God which caused it to ignite.

Just as little can you ever forgive of your own initiative. You can forgive in such a way that your forgiveness itself becomes new sin to you, but you can never forgive in such a way that it releases your soul. Frequently you hear of a man of the world who forgives, and you yourself have done the same, from a sense of *superiority*, to show that you thought too little of your enemy to hold him up to his misdeed; to show how virtuous you were in that you harbored no hatred; in order to rid yourself of him in your mind and to be no more bothered by him.

But of course, such forgiveness has nothing in common with real forgiveness, except in the name; while what the Our Father intends is a forgiveness from such a genuine, real, affectionate love, that you feel, "if God forgives me like this, then I am saved." For then it is God Himself Who has quickened this love in my heart, who from His own love has caused this love to forgive to flow over into my soul, and thus, in my forgiving of my enemy makes me to know God as having mercy from eternal love for me, once His enemy, but now His child.

At the sound of the apostolic word: "He that loveth not, knoweth not God," the conscience, as a rule, falls asleep with self-satisfaction. For what man is there who loves nothing, no one? Even criminals have been known to love an animal, or child or wife, sometimes at the sacrifice of self.

But what does it signify, when it says: "He who loveth not?" It means, he who does not live from love, he who is not ruled by love, he who has no joy in loving, he who has no love that can stand the test of fire.

And to this fiery test love is put, not in regard to one who is necessary to us, or one who is agreeable to us in life, but even with one who stands in our way, one who in fact we can call our enemy; and, therefore, the genuineness of your love only becomes evident in forgiveness. In the forgiveness of him who offended you, hindered you, embittered your life. And to forgive such a one from love for him, and not because it was your duty, this alone is proof that there is this love in you which makes you learn to know God.

But this is unthinkable, this is impossible, it simply can not be done, you say. To forgive for God's sake, to forgive because I myself am sinful, to forgive from Christian duty, yes; but to forgive from preceding love, how is that? And yet, Jesus demands it: "Love your enemy, bless him who curses you."

Further entering into the root of the matter is necessary here.

"Thou shalt love God with all thy soul, all thine heart, all thy mind and all thy strength, this is the first and great commandment" and then follows: "And the second is *like unto it:* thou shalt love thy neighbor as thyself," and this neighbor shall every time be your enemy.

How can this be? Not merely that I must also love my neighbor, but that this second commandment is like, altogether like unto the first?

And then the answer is: Thus only, when you love in your neighbor what there is of God in him. Nothing else. Hence, not his sin, and not his sin against you. These you should rather hate. But as you love nature, because God's Almightiness and Divinity express themselves therein, and you love an animal, because God hath organized it so wonderfully and provided it with instinct, so you shall much more love your neighbor, as man, because God has created him after His Image; because of the gifts and talents which God created in him; and because of the *germ of essential being* that has been implanted in him.

If all this has been spoiled, everything corrupted, become poisoned and hopelessly satanic, then there is nothing more of God in him, and love ceases, and turns into hatred, which it is bound to do. Satan was a wonderful creature, but he has sinned his divine endowment all away, and, therefore, every child of God hates this monster.

But however deeply fallen, man is never such as he in this life. The murderer on the cross rejoices before the Throne. The most distant wanderer, Jesus has renewed unto life. Hence all your Gospel, in its application to you, is, that in every man, hence also in your enemy, there still remains a point of connection, where grace unto life may enter in. Thereby alone is the Gospel your salvation. And he only who with the love of his heart, for God's sake, continues to love that spark that remains even in one who has wandered farthest off, loves with a love that learns to know God in this His eternal love, wherewith He also loves you as sinner.

XLIII

CLEARLY SEEN AND UNDERSTOOD BY THE THINGS THAT ARE MADE

FROM of old the question, from what source the knowledge of God flows out toward us, has been answered by the Church of Christ in this twofold way: from *nature* and from *Scripture*.

This points to the knowledge of God which comes to us from without; which can be expressed in an abstract idea; and which, therefore, has a place in the Creeds of the Church. But this does not include experimental knowledge of God which comes to us personally from spiritual experience, from the communion of saints, and from the hidden walk with God.

Meanwhile there is majesty in this first knowledge of God which comes to us from without; and in order now to confine ourselves to what *nature* brings us, it is so beautiful and so true that as one Confession of Faith declares, the whole creation round about us is as a living volume in which individual creatures are the letters. Yet, the book of nature brings us no nearer than the recognition of the attributes of God, His Almightiness, His Wisdom, His Goodness, and so on. Of a life in the spiritual Kingdom, of a being driven by the Holy Ghost, of an entrance with our will into the will of God, of a being filled with love by which to come closer to Him Who Himself is Love, even of mystical contemplation, it has nothing whatever to say.

The Creed of the Church is a banner, with a clear inscription, lifted up before the world, by which to declare what Divine glory full of majesty we worship; but it is not the more intimate expression of the knowledge of God as far as this has come to us from self-knowledge, from one's own soul's experience.

In these meditations we have placed this more intimate knowledge of God in the foreground, since devotional writings do not address the world, but speak from the midst of and to the fellowship of the saints, out of experience of soul, to those who themselves have enjoyed like experience, or at least know the home-sickness.

But we have sounded again and again the note of warning in this sanctuary of mysticism not to lose ourselves in sickly emotionalism; and, therefore, we now come to the knowledge of God from nature, not in order to take it objectively, but rather to weave it into our spiritual life.

Here, too, the wandering soul not infrequently impoverishes itself in a pitiful way.

It is then said: "I have learned and have given consent to the fact that in the works of nature the Attributes of God express themselves. I can infer from it that God is great in power, in wisdom and in goodness. But now that I know this, I am through with the book of nature. The sum of the knowledge of God, which comes to me from this, is made up." So the book is closed, and there is no personal, deeply penetrating impression that nature gives us of God's Majesty. One does not look for it. One takes no further count of it. And one almost feels a sense of anger, when, in behalf of their superficial religion the people of the world by preference appeal to *nature*.

It truly gives offense to hear it said, with a certain kind of exaltation, that the Church has served its day and that the Word has lost its significance, and that there is far richer religious enjoyment "in the temple of uncut wood."

But the faithful too are here at fault.

However praiseworthy their appreciation of Christ's Church is, and however rich the treasure that comes to them from the Word, they should not forget that it is equally bound upon our heart that "the invisible things of God from the foundation of the world are clearly seen and understood from the creatures (from nature), even His eternal Power and Godhead" (Rom. i, 20).

Here we observe three stages in the progress of the knowledge of God.

There is a knowledge of God which begins with nature, but which afterward advances to *man* as created after the Image of God, and which at length reaches its zenith in Christ, since He is the express Image of God's Person.

This knowledge of God begins with nature; expands itself in man; and is perfected in the Messiah; and these three do not stand loosely side by side, but form, if we may so express it, a rising pyramid. Nature forms the broad ground level, it ascends in the rich unfolding of human life, and reaches its highest point in the Incarnation of the Eternal Word.

The Christ is not clearly seen nor understood apart from the knowledge of man, and man is not clearly seen nor understood apart from a sympathetic touch upon unconscious nature. If then things are to be right, believers must ever be aware of God's Majesty in nature; believers must feel the life or history of mankind live itself over again in themselves; and so only can they attain unto that clear, full, living impression of the Christ, who in the riches of His grace reveals God unto them.

That this should be the case with believers, rests upon the fact that thus it went on from God's side in His Self-revelation, and still goes on.

God Almighty began to reveal Himself in unconscious nature. Only when that revelation was completed, did He create man after His Image and Likeness as a richer Self-revelation; and only when man had corrupted his way and nearly destroyed it in sin, did God send us as His richest Self-revelation the *Christ*.

And now see how these three links of the sacred chain fit into one another.

First there is the material world. Then from the dust of this world man is created. And only afterward comes as Man, in our flesh and blood, the revelation of the Son of God. The starting point here is that God is invisible.

Understand us well. In Himself the Eternal Being is not invisible, and we are definitely told, that some time we shall see God face to face; yes, that we shall know Him, even as we are known.

Not intellectual, nor even spiritual knowledge is the highest. The highest is *vision* — clear, immediate sight. Seeing without intermedium; even without mirror. Seeing into essential Being itself.

How this shall be made possible for us, is the mystery of eternity, though it is certain that, however dormant, the organ for this is even now present in the soul.

But it is equally certain, that in this dispensation it is not given us to use this organ. This is the dispensation of limitation, of the finite, and of that which is bound to form, color and dimension. And since God the Lord has neither boundary nor end, form nor dimension, He is in this dispensation to us the Invisible.

We do not come to a clear vision of God in this life.

Hence the question was, how God in His Majesty could, nevertheless in this life so reveal Himself, that at length we could come to a clear, fixed impression of His Being. And God has reached this end, first, by revealing to us in nature the working of His Almightiness and Divinity in dimensions which make the impression upon us of the infinite, although we know that they are finite. This is what we call the *sublime*. And in the second place, by putting a pattern of His personal life in the personal existence of man, creating him after His Image. And thirdly, in the end by fully restoring this Image, corrupted and broken by sin, to its original purity, and showing it to us in Christ.

But then, in and behind nature is God Himself.

Hence nature is not a completed work of art which, outside of Him and without Him, exists by itself; but it is God Himself Who shows you every night His starry heavens; and every day, His majesty in the colors of the light, in the wonders of the plant and animal world, in the glory of the sea, in the roar of the hurricane, even causing you to hear it sometimes in the rolling of His thunder.

In all this, is and lives the God of your worship. In the thrill of the life of nature, His own Divine life thrills. Whatever stirs in this Creation, whatever courses through it, whatever wells up from it toward you, is the inner motion of God's own life. Yea, all nature is nothing else than a living throbbing veil, behind which God hides Himself, and yet in whose folds and undulations He reveals Himself to you, clothed with Majesty.

The Apostle puts it so profoundly when he says that in nature the Invisible God is not only understood, but *clearly seen*.

And this clear sight is the main point. Through this screen, through this veil, through this investiture of nature, you must *see* your God in His Almightiness and Divinity.

Not to gaze at nature as at a dead palace with its vast variety of lines and forms, but to feel and to know that, standing before the firmament and the cloudy hosts and before the creation here on earth, you stand before God; that it is He Who, in all this, presses in upon you; in all this, addresses you; and, through all this, lets the fingers of His Majesty work before your eye. It is God who causes the lark to sing for you. It is God who cleaves the sea so that its waters foam. It is God who calls the sun from his tent, and at eventide directs his return thereto. It is God Who, every evening, lights the twinkling fires in the stars. It is God Whose voice rolls down upon you in the thunder. And only he who in all this feels the life of God, and in all this clearly sees the Divinity of His Almightiness, understands the glory of the Invisible.

XLIV

AND THE SECOND IS LIKE UNTO IT

GOD is invisible. He hides Himself behind the veil of nature. But the folds of that veil move themselves in undulations and vibrations whereby we perceive that God Himself behind that veil of nature is close to us. In everything that in nature lives before our eye, murmurs, throbs and moves itself, we feel the pulse-beat of God's own Life. Scripture has no knowledge of a dead nature, and in all sorts of ways it makes us hear in nature the voice of God, and listen for His footfalls. When the earth trembles, it is because He is wroth and makes the foundations of the mountains to shake. In the darkened firmament, "God bows the heaven and comes down." In the whirlwind, "God rode upon a cherub and flew." When "the deep abysses of water" foam, it is God Who rebukes them and drives them forth with "the blast of the wind of his nostrils." The flashes of lightning are arrows which He shoots forth into the firmament. The stars appear when it becomes dark, because God calls them, and behold not one faileth. He waters the mountains from His heights. He sends forth fountains, so that they walk between the hills. He makes grass grow for cattle, and for man bread come up from the ground. It is He Who cleaves the sea, so that the waves foam. And he who has a spiritually trained ear, observes how God as his Good Shepherd goes before him on the way, and hears God's rod and staff beat upon his life's-path, and is comforted thereby.

Hence, all this is not for the sake of a poetic, vivid view of nature; heathen poets also have given us this. No, even in nature everything is for the sake of religion, to reveal

to you the glorious presence of God, and to bring you the
warm, fostering sense, that in all this life of nature the
living, Almighty God is round about and with you, in
order to fill you with the sublime impression of His Almightiness, His Divinity and His Majesty.

But this is not all.

This same living God, Who in nature always envelops
you and presses Himself upon you, reveals Himself in a
far richer way to you in *man*, whom He has appointed as
lord of creation.

Yea, His revelation of life in man is so wonderfully
Divine, that after saying: "Thou shalt love God with all
thy soul, all thy heart, all thy mind and all thy strength,"
He transposes this great commandment into an altogether
different one, to wit: "Thou shalt love *man* as thyself,"
and in this second commandment declares *that it is entirely
like unto the first* (Mark xii, 31). To love God in His
Majesty and to love God in one's neighbor, is one and the
same commandment.

To love God in God Himself and God in man, or in one's
neighbor, differs in form and in fulfillment, but, as commandment, it is one.

Errable science more and more forces the idea upon us
that, as though from dead matter, gradually, of itself, the
plant has been evolved; presently from the plant, of itself, the animal; and finally from the animal, of itself, man.
This wisdom has been christened with the name of Evolu-
tion and Darwin is called the prophet of this new evangel.

This whole system is nothing but the self-deception of
unbelieving thought. But there is this truth in it, that
the whole creation seems built up round about us as a
temple in which man should minister as priest. Everything points to man; calls for man. And when at length
man appears in this temple of nature, everything that went

before, seems to have served to prepare for his arrival. Not for naught has man been called a world in miniature. Only in man does the creation reach its consummation. Almighty God Who in nature hides Himself as behind a veil, appears in man in personal revelation, not alone in His Power and Majesty, but, what means far more, as Spirit. In man is self-perception, clear consciousness, a thinking out of God's thoughts after Him, a revelation of will, a thirst after holiness, the spark of genius, an appreciation of the beautiful, the grasp after the ideal, presentment of eternal existence, the totality (embodiment) of being in one personal existence, the imprinted, innate knowledge of the Eternal Being. And all this is in him solely and alone because God created him after His Image.

You can know a masterbuilder by the palace he has built; a poet, by his songs; a mighty thinker, by his works; but altogether different is the impression that remains of him, when you have seen his likeness and have watched therein the features of his face, the flashing of his eye, the expression of his person.

Such is the case here. The supreme Masterbuilder and Artist shows you first His works in nature; but then He comes a second time, and in man shows you His Image, the image of His own Being.

Not in *one* man, this is impossible; but in man, as in the course of centuries, by millions and millions individual men have been born, have lived and died. But among these millions, there was the hyssop and the cedar. In these few mighty examples which as cedars stood out prominently above the forest of men, the revelation of His Being drew itself ever clearer together; and when you take all virtues and excellencies and choice gifts together, which have been evident in the best of the children of men, then this mighty, this overwhelming whole gives you a revelation of God, which very far exceeds the revelation of God in nature.

Such is the case now. What would it not have been, if no sin had marred and ruined the features of the Divine Image in man?

Now there is disturbance. The mirror in which the Image is reflected, is torn by a thousand cracks. It is time-worn, it is darkened. Some lines and parts of features you still discern, but no more the Image in the beauty of its unity, nor in the clearness of its tones. And when, even so, this Image still interests you and attracts, and ever continues to fill you with warm sympathy, what must it have been to Adam, when in Eve he beheld this Image inviolate before him, and how deep has been the fall into sin, which at once and irrevocably marred this holy Image.

It is true, your experience of people can be so bitter that hatred rather than love of those within your environment springs up within you. But then there is history, which renders permanent for you the best the centuries have to give, and this superlatively rich revelation of human life at its highest reconciles you again to man. Consider the picture-gallery of history, of the heroes of common life and of the heroes of faith. As the Apostle declares (Heb. xii, 1), "we are compassed about with so great a cloud of witnesses, wherefore we should lay aside every weight, and the sin which does so easily beset us."

This now is Divine revelation, revelation of God even in fallen man, and if love awakens within you—real drawing love for man as man—it is in virtue of the glory that is seen in man, glory of God in human talent, in human genius, in human heroism, shining out toward you in human love.

Human *love*, that is the zenith!

Then there is something mysterious in your own self which draws after something equally mysterious in another whom you meet on the highway of life, whereby you overlook failings, forgive sins, no more notice plainness, and with the mysterious power of love envelop him in the hiddenness of his being.

And though this love can become untrue, yea, this love itself may become sin, yet it is in this love for one who loves you, that the warm glow of Divine sympathy overpowers your heart, and the mystery of the love in God reveals itself to you.

At first this is governed by choice. Your love is then limited, narrow-hearted, and at the same time repels others. It is a light, highly illuminant in the measure in which it casts as a deep shadow around itself the darker indifference for others. It is love still captive in selfishness. Love from God, but not yet for God's sake. Love for a few, whom we count worthy of our love, but not yet love for neighbor, *i.e.*, for man as man, for man as the creature of God and created after God's Image.

But the Spirit purifies, the Spirit refines this love. Love for man must be like the love for God. There must be no conflict, or else the love for man would put back the love for God in your heart.

So it becomes a sifting more and more, a loving in man of what there is of God in him; and likewise a hating in man of what there is of evil in him; an incapacity to tolerate it, and with all the seriousness of love, repressing it, until it vanishes from his heart.

And this opens the way by which to search out in every man whatever of God, however hidden, still glows in his soul, and to increase the volume of this spark, and not suffer it to be extinguished.

Until at length love for neighbor loses itself in that most tender appreciation of the fact that in every man on this side of the grave, however deeply fallen and however dead in sin, there always remains the evidence that he has been created after God's Image and that it is still possible for this Image to be restored. The lover of choice porcelains gathers with great care the shards of the broken dish, recognizing their worth, in the hope they may be put together again.

Even so, love for neighbor has become nothing else than love for whatever of God there still remains in him.

The second commandment is like unto the first.

XLV

THE IMAGE OF THE INVISIBLE GOD

GOD is a Spirit. God is invisible. But yet the Invisible God reveals Himself with increasing clearness.

Glimmeringly through and behind the veil of nature; more transparently in *man* created after His Image; and with full clearness in *Christ* Who is the express Image of His Person, the Image of the Invisible God (Col. i, 15).

Image, not likeness. What has been sculptured conveys more reality than what has been pictured in lines and tints; it gives the full appearance; in marble or in metal the image imitates the massive form of life. And while the likeness that is drawn with pencil or brush conveys in turn the warmth of life, the glow of soul, the mobile features, which the cold, hard marble refuses to express, yet the image is more impressive, is more overwhelming by its mightier reality and tangibility.

The Scripture therefore does not speak of the likeness, but of the Image of God Who is invisible, and in this expression the whole action of religion centers itself. God gives His Image; man corrupts this Image; man wants himself to make an image of God. This desire *himself* to make an image of God is grievous sin; and in the end this sin reaches its utmost height, when Satan, as the Beast, as the man of sin, as the Antichrist, himself erects an image, for which he demands worship which alone is due to "the express Image of God's person"—the Christ.

This revelation of God in His Image must not be taken in a figurative or metaphorical sense. On the contrary, it is supernatural reality. Hence the saying of Jesus to Philip (John xiv, 9): "He that hath seen me, hath seen the

274

Father." And hence the hope of glory for every child of God, that one day he too shall see Christ as He is, and that in seeing the glorified Christ, he shall see God Himself face to face. He shall not see Christ, and afterward and alongside of Him see God, but he shall see God in Christ.

Sin has marred the Image of God in the unregenerate beyond the point of recognition. And now God gives in Christ, in *one* person, His full Image in perfect clearness. And this was possible in our human nature, because from all eternity the Son was the Image of the Father, and, as by the shadow of this Image, our human nature was formed from the dust of the earth.

He, therefore, who rests content with the revelation of God in nature, depressed as it is by the curse; or he who rests content with the revelation of the spiritual being of God in man, as he is dead by sin; can not attain unto the true knowledge of God, but must fall away into idolatry or false philosophy.

"No man knoweth the Father save the Son, and he to whomsoever the Son will reveal Him (Matt. xi, 27).

Therefore Christ remains the center of our Divine worship. Not only by what He spake, by what He did, by what He suffered, but by His own Person. The glory of the Apostles lies in what they have heard, seen and handled of the Word of life.

Christ is not merely the highest Prophet among the prophets, and the Head of the Apostles, He Himself is the personal embodiment of everything that is comprehended in the glory of our religion. "In Him dwelleth the fullness of the Godhead bodily." We name ourselves after Him. In His Name salvation is given us. From His Person and Name goes out the regenerating, life-renewing power, which has changed the fashion of this world. Only where He is worshiped, real christianity is. He rules not merely by the tradition of what He once was, spake, did and endured, but by a real power, which even now, seated at God's right hand, He still exercises over lands and nations, generations, families and individuals. To be for Him or against Him, decides the course of the world's history, the final destiny of every individual life. With Him the world shall rejoice in peace, turned against Him, it will be troubled and will continue to be vexed, until either it returns to Him, or in resisting Him works out its own destruction.

Every effort to weaken the Christian religion and to detach it from Him, or to mingle it with philosophical and heathen inventions, must therefore lead to spiritual and moral retrogression.

He who in any wise puts the supreme name of Christ on a line with that of Buddha, Confucius or Mohammed or names them in one breath, undermines the Christian religion and all religion, and with it the happy development of our human race. For all this leads away from the knowledge of God, falsifies the same, and causes the real knowledge of God to be lost; and while to know God is itself eternal life, to be enjoyed here and in the hereafter, all alienation from the Christ, all beclouding of the name of Christ, is no search after life, but after death.

To seek Christ for the sake of salvation is the beginning; but he who understands what salvation *in Christ* is, will for its sake cultivate the knowledge of God.

It is true that in Christ is your surety, that one day your soul will be pure from all sin; the assurance that then no guilt of sin will any more distress you; the promise that you shall one day receive your body back in glory; and, in Christ no less, is the hope of a home in the Father's house of many mansions, of sacred joy in the halls of everlasting light, of an endless fellowship with all God's saints; in brief, of an inheritance that will bring you what no ear has ever heard, no eye has ever seen, or has ever entered the heart of man.

And yet, all this is nothing else than the glory of the palace and of those who may enter therein; the *supreme* glory, which is and remains salvation, is to be sought in God Himself. To own Him as your God, to know Him with clear-sighted understanding, in blessed adoration to enjoy soul-fellowship with the living God—this, and this alone, is the kernel and the pith of all everlasting salvation.

And therefore there is salvation in Christ, both because He delivers you from sin, and because He guarantees the inheritance among the saints in light; but yet, salvation in Christ in only grasped in full, when in Him, as the Image of the invisible God, you lay hold on God Himself, and in this knowledge of God, which shines out toward you from this Image, you imbibe eternal life.

It is not a salvation which Christ but prepares for you, brings down to you, and into which He once shall lead you, simply in order that, after this mighty work has been con-summated, He may retire from the scene. No, even in the realm of glory there would be no blissfulness if Christ were not to be forever there, as the One in Whom you can see, know and enjoy God.

You do not have to wait for this until you have entered the Father-house above.

In the heavenly life the knowledge of God will be con-summated, but it begins here and now. We have not merely a promise of future revelation, but a revelation of God in Christ, which already here falls within our reach.

The Image of God is sketched for us on the Gospel-page in Christ. God is a Spirit, and the self-revelation of God in the eternal Word is expressed for us in the written Word.

Even after His Ascension, Christ still lives on in this Word. With this Word the likeness of God's Image has gone forth into the world. His figure lives on among us, and thanks to this Word, we are so familiar with the Person and the Appearance of Christ, that He accompanies us by the way. As Christ moved among the people of His time, so the imagination brings Him into our own environment, and we apply His word of the long ago to ourselves, in such a way as to make us feel that He Himself addresses, admonishes, encourages and comforts us.

Even this is not all.

There is not only a likeness of Christ in the Word, but powers also, operations and influences have gone out from Him, which, as sparks emitting fire, have transplanted themselves from soul to soul, have kindled fire in the human breast, and thus have caused a flame of love, of sacred purpose, of spiritual consecration to glow, which has extended through the ages and still burns today, and which, when we are privileged to live in it, cherishes and warms us, and brings, as it were, the very breath of Christ close to us.

And all this is not merely the passive result of His appearing twenty centuries ago, but in all reality it is fed and strengthened day by day by Christ Himself, and, immediately from Christ, urges itself upon us. Every soul that is born anew, every holy thought that comes into our mind, all good work that we are enabled to do, it is all His work through the wondrous indwelling of the Holy Ghost.

He would come and take up His abode with us, and He is come, and still comes, every day and every night, to confirm this indwelling in the congregation of His saints. He knows and calls us by name, and adapts Himself to the need of every heart.

So He Who is the Image of the Invisible God, continually urges Himself upon us, continues in us the work He has once begun, and through ebb and flood, makes the ocean of God's unfathomable mercies glisten for us ever more gloriously.

Truly, there is knowledge of God which we take from Him and derive from Him; but far more there is knowledge still of God which He Himself imparts unto us, which He brings into us, and in the hidden depths of our soul makes fully clear to us.

The mystery of it is, that He Who is the Image of the Invisible God, not merely shows this Image unto us, and fascinates us with it, but chisels this Image in ourselves, in our own person, in our own soul.

Our own inner life is made conformable to the inner life of Christ. His Image imprints itself in God's saints.

And this is the highest knowledge of God, which we can attain here on earth, when thus the Image of God in Christ renews the Image of God in us.

XLVI
HALLOWED BE THY NAME

TRUE knowledge of God is not the product of mental discipline.

Also the knowledge of God only becomes real, when it finds its starting-point in what your soul inwardly discerns and experiences. Everything here must go out from a contact, which you know took place personally between you and God. There is no knowledge of light possible for one who was born blind. And likewise no true knowledge of God is possible for you, as long as you do not perceive the existence of God within yourself, there discover it, and truly feel it by the operations that go out from God. Not, of course, by your sense of touch, but by spiritual, immediate perception, so that, not on the ground of reasoning and not from what others tell you, but immediately from your own self you know that God *is*, and that God is great.

This is what our fathers steadily held to the fore in the heroic struggle for the faith, which they went through. And how could this be otherwise with men, who in the midst of oppression and distress, each day in worship before the stupendous Majesty of the Lord felt their soul give way within them, and who, therefore, insisted so strongly on the fact, that God Himself had imprinted in man the sense of God (*sensus divinitatis*), and that this sense of God contained the seed of all religion (*semen religionis*).

But when persecution ceased and peaceful conditions prevailed again, this spiritual, real background of all true knowledge of God was wantonly forsaken, and far too much place was given to intellectual abstractions.

Thus abstract knowledge — knowledge drawn away from the true God — superseded that knowledge which is eternal life. And the necessary result of this was that book-learning supplanted true piety and that the life of the Church became weak.

The Church stood not alone, in this. The retreat from reality to the paper-world of abstract inventions of the mind, became evident in every department of the higher life. Even art, and with it, poetry, became at length infected with this evil virus. Forms, words, phrases, and rhymes took the place of golden speech which wells up from the fountain of life itself.

And then there came, as could not be otherwise, the equally onesided reaction against it. This brought nothing but emotions, simple impressions, pure sensations, ever changing opinions. And as necessary result of this there was beclouding of the consciousness, obscurity of the inner perceptions, confusion in thought and chaos in language.

Such was the case in poetry and literature, and not otherwise in religion. Here too there was nothing but perceptions, sensations, impressions, which with unbelievers led to a falling away into pantheism, and made believers lose themselves in sickly mysticism.

For let it be well understood, that in every sphere, including that of religion, all this is dominated by mighty currents in all of human life.

Things are only good, when the workings of the emotions and of the mind unite in proper equipoise and in pure harmony.

But this, sin will not tolerate. It continually breaks the equipoise, it banishes harmony. And then comes, first, a time when the intellect kills the feeling, and from this period another arises, in which the feeling dooms the intellect to silence. And in the face of all this it ever remains the sacred calling of the preacher to form just estimates of every abuse, and to zealously urge the restoration of equipoise and of pure harmony.

In this series of meditations on the knowledge of God, the working of the hidden fellowship has been exhibited, therefore, from every side. What the imagination, what inspiration, what the working of the will, what love, what the impression which we receive from nature, from man, and finally from Christ, contribute to the true knowledge of God, has duly been considered.

First, the reality of God's hidden walk had to be made palpable, and this was done the more readily, because our age has a leaning in this direction. Wherefore, this urging of the reality of inner motions agrees with the popular notion of our times. Also in the realm of religion, barren trifling with ideas has at length repelled the common mind. Men crave what can be felt and handled and immediately enjoyed, and can sweetly affect our entire personality.

But yet it would be an unpardonable fault, which would soon avenge itself, if men were to rest content with this. Scripture does not allow it. The church protests against this, and every child of God asks for more.

In Scripture the significance of the Name of the Lord is great and far-reaching, and the very Name calls us away from the current of feeling up to higher and clearer consciousness.

The feeling is a gift of God, but, as a feature of God's Image in us, the consciousness far excels the feeling. The feeling can do no more than furnish the material, which the consciousness thinks through, orders and transposes into clearness of form. Even the plant is sensitive, the feeling in an animal is sometimes exceedingly fine, but what neither animal nor plant received, is this glorious capacity of the higher consciousness, which enables man to take up the universe within himself, to see through it, to estimate things in their significance, to appreciate and to mirror them in his own thought.

This consciousness makes man a king, for in this consciousness he acts and rules.

The consciousness has all sorts of forms. A form for art, another form for the moral, and still another form for the religious life. But of all these forms it is always the consciousness first in which man finds himself back again, becomes capable of mighty action, and lifts himself up to the spheres of the eternal Word.

Therefore all onesided absorption in mysticism has always ended in degradation, and the sacred summons must ever and again go out from the Church of Christ, to exalt the sacred treasure of our religion to the height of our consciousness.

Mysticism, without more, is darkness, chaos, blackness of night. In our consciousness is the light.

In behalf of the knowledge of God this light is first lighted by the Name of the Lord.

This you perceive yourself at once, when on your knees before the Eternal, you first address Him with the universal term of God, and then proceed to call Him Abba, *Father*.

He who quietly, with emphasis and intention addresses God, calls Him by the Father-name, and whispers, "My dear Father," perceives at once, that in this Name a world of thought flows from his heart, and how thereby from His lofty height God comes nearer to the soul.

A name is that by means of which I address some one, and I can address only him whom I know. So the name is immediately connected with the knowledge of the person. The name is the brief summary in a single word of what presents itself to me in the person. And though our human names are impoverished, so that they no longer express anything, yet we look differently upon the man whom we hear addressed by name, than upon the stranger who passes us in the street.

And this can be applied to our God in a far higher sense, in so much as the Name of the Lord is the expression itself of His Being. Call Him by the covenant-name of Jehovah; as a child, call him: Our Father. Or address Him by the full name of Father, Son and Holy Ghost, and always in this Name the Being is expressed. You have not invented this Name. God has given it to Himself and has revealed it unto you. And in the Name a summary knowledge of God comes to you which brings God closer to you, carries Him into your consciousness, and explains him to you.

Without the Name of the Eternal Being, religion and idolatry merge into one another; then everything terminates in a dark religious perception; then the ocean of pantheism presents itself to you; and the personal knowledge of the personal God is ever more and more lost.

But with the Name of the Lord there comes distinction; the antithesis enters in between false and true religion; you come to stand personally before the personal God, and you know with whom you have to do.

Of course, provided you do not allow this Name to be lost in an empty sound. For this is what sin does. The Our Father may be said in a mechanical way, without any thought of the Father Himself, or of what this Father-name implies. It is the curse of habit which by continuous repetition, dulls the spiritual consciousness, so that there is hasty, thoughtless and senseless use of sacred sounds. And this goes on until, in a serious moment, you turn in upon yourself, and now with hushed reverence you repeat these selfsame holy names, putting your soul into them, and you become surprised at the riches that glisten in them.

And when you come to this, then the Name of the Lord is a torch ignited in your consciousness, and from the darkness of the emotions, gradually and of itself, the hidden Being of your God looms up before you with ever increasing clearness. Then you stand as a person before God, and His Name always explains as much of His being, as at that moment your heart needs.

But then our thinking consciousness can not and must not rest content with the mere stammering of that Name. Then the Name becomes the occasion for thinking out what that Name implies, and of clarifying God to our consciousness, as far as the scope of our consciousness allows.

Not every one can do this equally well. The capacity of the consciousness to absorb, is very limited with one, and with another wonderfully great. And, really, we never succeed farther than that each one enters into the knowledge of God, according to the measure of his consciousness.

But what must never be allowed, is, that as we enter according to the measure of our consciousness into the things of the world and into all the departments of science, we should neglect to do the same with respect to the Name of the Lord.

God's name must be *hallowed*.

And all indifference to the Name of the Lord is irreconcilably opposed to this hallowing of the Name of our God.

XLVII

THE NAME OF THE FATHER, AND OF THE SON, AND OF THE HOLY GHOST

Wondrous intimacy is at once imparted to social intercourse, when some one who was thus far a stranger to you, or whom you knew, but only addressed as "Sir," allows you to call him by name. And you feel that you have become more intimate still, when the family name drops away and gives place to the baptismal name.

Children do not know this transition. Only when the shoes of childhood have been outgrown, do the forms of politeness come into force which aim to elevate the conventionality of childlife, and to graduate it to those nobler forms which purposely create a certain distance between one person and another, in order that they can develop themselves more freely. But when in later years, either because closer acquaintance ripened into friendship, or because association in a common pursuit lessened the distance, and titles fall away again, and for the first time we address one another again by name, then we feel ourselves at once drawn closer together, and it seems that mutual confidence but waited the chance to reveal itself.

As a rule, the higher the station is of the person who allows us to call him by name, the greater the leap is from estrangement to the more confidential intercourse. It is indeed great when we call one by his family name; but greater when we address him by his personal name. Another difference is, that among women, even as with children, the personal, baptismal name is used, and almost never the family name, while, as a rule, among men the family name is in vogue, and the use of the personal name indicates a far higher degree of intimacy. In family life every more dignified title falls away, and the use of the family name would have no meaning, since everything hinges on the baptismal name, or passes over into an entirely different sort of name which expresses the relation one sustains to the other. So we come at length to the mother-name and the father-name. We speak of husband and wife, and parents say: "my child." These names commonly used in the family are more than sounds, and express something essential in the mutual relationships. They are somewhat on a line with the names we give to a physician, clergyman or sexton, which indicate that we do not mean their person but their office. But while with the latter, the person and the relation in which they stand to us, separate themselves, the father-name, the mother-name and the name of "my child" contain this excellent trait, that they express both the persons and the relation they sustain to us, and thus indicate the highest that a name can express.

If then, after these observations, we address God as "Our Father" or as "Abba, dear Father," we appreciate more fully than before the supreme privilege which this Father-name confers upon a child of God.

Not every name by which we seek to indicate the Eternal Being, is equally tender and intimate.

The vague name of "God" brings no approach. The mere word "God" indicates a highly-exalted Being, that far transcends mankind; but the word itself expresses nothing, it excludes, and reveals nothing, it points to no single relationship; and only when we put "my" before it, and speak of "my God," or of the "Covenant-God," does it become significant and vital.

The same applies to the name, "the *Most High*." In Scripture this name is used particularly in circles outside of Israel. It occurs in connection with Melchizedek, with Nebuchadnezzar (Is. xiv, 14), in the heathen world, where Daniel dwelt, and with good and fallen angels. In the sixth verse of the eighty-second Psalm angels are called "Children of the Most High." Gabriel speaks of "the power of the Highest" that shall overshadow Mary, and so likewise Demons call Jesus "Thou Son of God, Most High" (Luke viii. 28). This is but natural. This name of the Most High merely indicates that our God is exalted far above all created things, but it is not a name that brings Him closer to us or initiates one into His secret fellowship.

It becomes altogether different when God reveals Himself as the *Almighty*, as *Jehovah*, as *our Lord*.

The name of God Almighty, by which the patriarchs were permitted to call their God, speaks of protection, of a refuge in time of peril, of assurance regarding the given promise, of a fellow-member in a covenant, who will break every form of opposition in our behalf. Hence the rich development of this name exhibits itself in the manifold references to God as our *high tower*, or *refuge*, our *rock;* as of a God in Whose tent we may dwell, and Who is our hiding-place. It is all the unfolding of this one idea, *God Almighty* means an Almightiness that watches over us and works for our good.

The same applies to the name *Jehovah*.

This name also is not a mere sound, but an expression of being, and more particularly an expression of that in the Being of God, which we need for our comfort in the face of the anxiety with which the constant change, instability, unsettledness, and, at length, the finiteness, of human life fills us.

Everything about us comes but to pass away. We ourselves change continuously with every changing thing around us. Scarcely has the spring passed over into sum-

mer before autumn is at hand which in turn succumbs to
the winter sleep of death. This conflicts with our inner
being which calls for immortality, and which at the bar of
its own consciousness in old age, still maintains identity
with the self of the child. And still this change around us
and within us ceaselessly goes on. Nothing is sure. It is
all as the rocking of the waves on which we are rocked,
and on which we are irresistibly driven forward.

And now, in the midst of this restless ocean, this wondrous name of *Jehovah: "I am that I am,"* is the revelation of what endures, of what abides, of the eternal and of
the unchangeable, and merges with the name of Rock.
Thus the result of this revelation of the name is, that he
who has been apprehended by Jehovah, and who himself has laid hold on Him, has in God the fixed point from
whence he defies the restless tossings of the waters on the
sea of life, and in the God Whom he worships lays hold on
eternity itself. To know Jehovah is to have eternal life.

The same is the case with the name: "Lord."

He who only speaks of God, says nothing of the relation
in which he stands to him; but he who says, *"Lord, our
God,"* or *"God the Lord,"* bears witness to a relation which
he sustains to the Eternal Being. He is the property of
God and His servant; from God he expects orders and ap-
pointments; he recognizes that he must live for God, because He is his Lord, and that therefore he exists for the
sake of God.

But even this is not all.

The love of God, that sought and drew us, has made
still farther advances in the revelation of the name, and
has taught Israel already to know the *Father-name*, which
is by no means revealed in the New Testament for the first
time. When, by Malachai, God said, "If then I am a
Father, where is my honor?" this one saying already

shows, that in Israel the sense and meaning of this Father-name was clearly understood. Even the antithesis of the *child* was felt in it. Or was it not already said of David, "I shall be to him a *Father* and he shall be to me a *son?*"

Now every one feels that the Eternal Being comes close to us in this Father-name. It is as though all distance falls away, and as though by this name God Himself invites us to warm confidence, close fellowship, and intimate communion. The *mother-name* would have done this still more tenderly, but yet not so richly, because the mother-name is more closely associated with childhood and early youth, and the father-name embraces all of life. Moreover the Father-name of God includes both the tenderness of the mother-name and the energetic intimacy of the father-name. "Though a mother may forget her sucking child, yet will I not forget thee" (Isaiah xlix, 15).

Only, with the Father-name does inward religion unfold itself in all its richness and fullness. For now the family life originates, the continuous fellowship with God, the outpouring of the heart, the holding of oneself fast by God in confidence and love, and the fellowship of prayer, with a tenderness which no longer holds anything.

More yet, this Father-name includes the name of child, and with the "Abba Father" comes the surprising discovery that one is himself a child of God, and with it is disclosed the nobility of our race, the royal exaltation above everything in the unconscious creation that surrounds us, and the thought which transforms all of life, that our real life is not here, for that this is a life with and by and in our God.

And with this the last step is made possible, and, at length, comes the full revelation of *Father, Son and Holy Ghost*—of the one and threefold Being.

Hereby, at once, the relation in which we stand to God, is connected with the Being of God Himself.

By itself the Father-name might yet stand outside of the Divine Being, and simply have been borrowed from human family-life. So taken, it would merely imply that, as you are a child of your father in the home, so likewise God watches as a Father over you.

But now all this becomes different at once.

Now God is Father from all eternity in His own Being and in that Being of God is the Son, so that what is known in the family on earth, is merely the reflection of what was in the Being of God from all eternity. Thus there is no more comparison, but the reality lies expressed for us in that Father-name; and if we may be called God's child, this name does not come to us from comparison with the family, but directly from the Image of God.

He is not merely called our Father, but eternally He is our Father. And in like manner you are not merely called His child, but generated by Him, and born from Him, you *are* his child.

This now is salvation.

And therefore he who deems that the confession of the Trinity is merely a doctrinal question, does not fathom by a long way what lies in this revelation of *Father, Son and Holy Ghost.*

Only the Triune God is the wealth, the delight of our soul.

XLVIII

WHO DWELLETH ON HIGH AND BEHOLDETH THE THINGS IN THE EARTH

THERE is also sin when he who seeks to live near unto God does not know how to keep proper distance from Him.

This is sadly evident at times in prayer before and with others, and shows itself at once in the use of "you" in place of "thee" and "thou."

Let this not surprise one too greatly.

In countries where the language still has two forms of address, one more common and one more conventional, it has always been the fixed habit, in prayer to God to use the more familiar form. In French they say: "*Notre Pere qui est aux cieux, que ton Nom soit sanctifié;*" in English: "Our Father who art in heaven, hallowed be thy Name;" and in German: "*Unser Vater der du im Himmel bist, dein Name werde geheiliget.*"

In former times a Dutch child always said *you* and *your* to his father, but now it would be considered a breach on his part of the fifth commandment, if he were to address his father otherwise than by thee and thou; and when the healthy appreciation of language even in speaking to an earthly father avoids the use of the common term, it betokens a want of reverence before the Father Who is in heaven, when one shows a certain daring by familiarity of address to Him. It betrays the tendency to show how intimately the man who prays holds converse with his God. And when this is done at the expense of reverence towards God, it becomes *sin;* even though it must be granted, that with respect to the hidden walk with our God it is a loss that we lack the use of the former more intimate word.

Both what is lofty and what is ordinary have naturally a certain trait in common. A king on his throne is exalted; his butler is but ordinary; yet they have this in common, that their family name is seldom used, and that, as a rule, they are spoken of by their baptismal name. One speaks in England of King George, and almost no one thinks of his family name of Windsor; and, in the same way, every one knows the butler by his first name, but in case of a payment of taxes, his family name is frequently a subject of inquiry.

This has a more hidden cause.

What is lofty diverges from the ordinary measure of our life, and so likewise does that which falls below it.

When in Isaiah (lvii, 15) we read: "Thus saith the high and lofty One, that inhabiteth eternity, and whose name is Holy: I dwell in the *high* and holy place, with him also that is of a contrite and humble spirit," then here also the lofty and the lowly are mentioned in one breath.

Our ordinary life has a certain measure, a certain form, certain dimensions, certain well known figures and appearances. All these together form our human life. And it is the sin of everything that is called heathen, that it brings the Almighty down to the level of the human. Then an image is made of a man, or of an animal, and this is worshiped, and the profound difference between human life and the Divine life is brought to naught.

And in contrast with this, Holy Scripture discloses the holy sphere of the "lofty;" *i.e.*, of a life, that goes out far and high above our earthly, human life. Already nature gives us a type of it in the firmament that arches itself over us, in the vapors that hasten upward, and in the mighty thunder that rolls through the dark masses of clouds. With a heavy thunder storm, with a hurricane that rages upon the great waters, with an earthquake which makes the ground vibrate under our feet, with a volcano that vomits forth its lava, every one feels that we have to do with powers that exceed the limits of our human life. They are interpreters to us of the existence of a higher, mightier world than ours. And therefore all this takes its place in what we call "loftiness."

"Loftiness" ascends higher, when we lift up our soul and mind to the world of angels and of the blessed ones in everlasting light.

But higher still is the Most High, our God in His Majesty; and every portrayal which in prophecy God Himself gives of the Divine palace and of the Throne of His Almightiness above, lifts itself so far and high above every measure of our ordinary life, that quite of our own accord we honor therein the *Unsurpassed* in its completeness.

This must be so, in order that we should continue to be man, leave God to be God, and never forget the distance, at which the Creator stands high above the creature.

From the realization of this distance, reverence in worship takes its rise, the kneeling down in lowliness of spirit before His lofty Throne.

But this same God Who dwells in the High and lofty and Holy place, also dwells with him that is of a contrite and humble spirit. This same God Who dwells on high, is also the God Who humbleth Himself to behold things that are in heaven and on the earth (Ps. 113, 6).

Among men it frequently happens that the poor and the domestics are treated with far more consideration by those whose positions are assured, than by those of lower social standing. When a subject approaches his king, as a rule he is surprised that his king addresses him so kindly.

And since God the Lord is the High and Lofty One, Who is above every one of us, it is no contradiction, but belongs entirely to the same order, that when He turns Himself to His creature, He refreshes and comforts him by a holy, Divine familiarity.

And for this very reason, sacred reserve becomes every one of us.

Familiarity with the Eternal Being must always be *given* us of God, and may never be presumed upon by the creature. When man makes bold on his part to obliterate the boundary-line of reverence, then God repulses him. Then man exalts himself at the expense of the loftiness of his Lord, all secret walk with his God is then disturbed; and at length there is nothing left save a vain beating in the air after the Infinite, after a higher Being, a higher blessing, a name without content, a sound that volatilizes; and he has lost his God and his Father.

The Our Father puts us, therefore, under solemn restraint. By grace we are permitted to call upon God as "Our Father;" but, that reverence might be retained, there follows at once the "Who art in heaven," in order that, as a Catechism warns us, "we should not think of God in an earthly way."

That our God is the High, the Holy and the Lofty One who dwelleth on high, and that in the face of this there is a hidden walk with Him, since He humbleth Himself to behold the things in the earth, creates of itself a two-fold endeavor to overcome the distance that separates us from Him.

One is, that God comes down to us; the second is, that we lift up our souls to Him.

It begins with the first—the second follows.

In paradise after the fall, God comes down to Adam, and this bending down of Himself to us on the part of God, goes on throughout all Revelation. In the manger of Bethlehem this coming down consummates itself in behalf of our entire race. At the great Pentecost in Jerusalem, God the Holy Ghost descends into human hearts. Even now this descent of God continues with every soul that passes from death unto life. Then God comes to take up His abode in the heart. He prays for us, in us, with groanings that can not be uttered, and He Who dwelleth on high, dwells at the same time in the contrite heart.

And then, parallel with this, runs the lifting up of our soul to God. "Unto thee, O Lord, do I lift up my soul" (Ps. 25, 1). What we then seek is that we might dwell in the house of the Lord, to take refuge in Him as our High Tower, and to live outside of this life in order that we might dwell with the Holy One. "Seek the things that are above, where Christ is" (Col. iii, 1), and "to you will be given walks among those that are above" (Zech. iii, 7, Dutch Bible footnote).

When God comes down to you, the idol of your own self, like Dagon's image, must be thrown down; but when this is done, when your spirit is contrite, and you have come down from your imagined loftiness to a humbler estimate of yourself, then the wall of separation falls down, the distance lessens, and at length the moment comes that you feel God with you in your own heart, and that you can not be otherwise than *near unto Him*.

The result truly shows that reverence before the Almighty is most deeply vital and most richly evident with those who stand nearest to God. And that, on the other hand, with the many who have never yet taken part in the hidden walk with God, all salutary fear, all awe, all reverence before the Lord our God is more and more lost, even to this extent, that, recklessly and thoughtlessly, they continually abuse His holy Name by using it as an expletive in their ordinary conversation.

It is by *grace*, and nothing but *grace*, that the High and Lofty One incorporates his vain creature into His confidence, admits him to His hidden walk, permits him to enter His tent, and visits him in his heart; and they alone taste the joy of this wonderful privilege, who receive this grace with thankfulness and with adoring praise.

And theirs alone is the promise, that once they themselves will pass over from this earthly into the heavenly state, that they may dwell in the High and Lofty place, in the Father-house, with their God.

XLIX

BEFORE I WAS AFFLICTED, I WENT ASTRAY

THERE is also a knowledge of God which is altogether personal, and which comes to us through the ebb and flow of the tide of life's joys and of its sorrows.

This, however, should not be exaggerated.

The idea that disappointment and sorrow, as a rule, open the soul to God, and that suffering always makes perfect, is all too loudly contradicted by experience. Undoubtedly, a great disaster which strikes heavily and suddenly, a pestilence that breaks out, a storm that threatens shipwreck, a destructive earthquake, and, likewise, unexpected danger of death in personal sickness, make the thoughtless world, and those who have part therein, mindful for a moment of the fact that there is a God with Whom we have to do; but when the danger is past, it takes but a few days for the weak impression received to wear away, and it has not infrequently been seen, that after a deliverance from pestilence, for instance, unblushing worldliness showed itself more godless than before. Things were all right again. They were almost ashamed for a moment that at heart they had been afraid; and now they were themselves again the masters of their lot, and would improve their chance to enjoy life, before the possible return of similar ill luck. Or, where they did not take so wide a swing as this, and dissipation was carefully avoided, the return after disaster to former self-sufficiency was almost automatic, and life was lived again, if not directly *opposed* to, yet *without* God.

Not infrequently it did not stop with this. The cases are by no means rare, that a great adversity in life brought the soul, that formerly had shared a general belief, into positive Atheism. Thus far, one had lived under the conviction, that in the hour of need one had but to call upon God, and be certain of deliverance from trouble. At the sickbed of husband or child one prayed: "O, God, save them." But when it became evident that this prayer brought no relief, and inexorable death dragged the loved one into the grave, the whole soul rose up in rebellion. "When, in time of trouble, I pray, and it brings no help, then there is no God; or if there yet can be a God, He *can not* be a God of love," and the embittered soul curses God, and life is lived in rebellion *against* God.

Suffering makes perfect, very true, but only when there was previous knowledge of grace in the heart, and not with the unregenerate child of the world. It is true, suffering too can be a means in the hand of God to bring one who wandered away, to a halt and to conversion; but even then, this conversion is effected by God's work of grace in the soul, and suffering in connection with this is merely an auxiliary means.

As Job sat among the ashes, his wife did not hesitate to say to him: "Curse God and die;" and it is only a soul, which, like that of the Psalmist, is a subject of heavenly grace, that is able, after deliverance from trouble, to confess before God: "Before I was afflicted, I went astray, but now, being instructed, I keep thy word" (Ps. 119, 67).

In pleasure and prosperity matters are still worse.

Taken in general, the ranks of society which can live at ease, are farther estranged from God, than they who have to labor hard for daily sustenance.

The sharply drawn contrast between the rich Dives and the poor Lazarus, has been abroad in all ages and among all peoples. Radiant beauty, abounding health, unbroken prosperity in one's career or business, great happiness at home, and likewise abundance of material wealth, so that care and worry were unknown, have almost never seemed able to foster true piety. All this, rather, nerved a man in his self-sufficiency, in the exalted estimate of his own self, and, in so doing drew the soul away from God, rather than drew it to Him.

Such has been the case with individuals, such has been the case with families through many generations, and such has been the case with whole nations. When peace was permanent with a people, when its national power increased, when it could bathe itself in its wealth, almost always with equal pace it went spiritually backward. When the Dutch people had to fight hard and long for spiritual liberty, religion and public morals stood high; but how far they sank away in wantonness and propensity to sensual pleasure when, in the eighteenth century, gold streamed in from every side and wealth became the law of life. It went with us as once it did with the world-empire of mighty Rome, which by sobriety and self-restraint had become great and remained so until luxury and love of pleasure began that national decadence from within, which barbaric invasions from without brought to a finish.

Truly there are individuals, there are families and generations which, from warm gratitude for material blessings, have become more tenderly united to God; but this was purely because grace preceded, and because grace accompanied this prosperity in life.

Solomon remains the historic type of how even with God's children, prosperity can work a spiritual decline.

"They are strong legs," says the proverb, "that can carry wealth;" and the exception is rare, when Satan does not succeed in turning prosperity into a weapon to be used against Him from Whom it comes.

And yet the child of God is offered, both in joy and in

sorrow, a most helpful means, by which to enter more deeply into the knowledge of his God; negatively in joy, positively in sorrow.

When in examining his ways, the child of God discerns the danger he incurs in days of joy and plenty of becoming mechanical in prayer, of fostering pride, of trusting more in himself than in God, and of becoming less constant in his hidden walk with God, it will, if he is sincere, turn the trend of his mind and heart. As strongly as his heart inclined at times toward the good things of this world, he will now begin to be equally afraid of them. It now becomes clear to him, that God and this world's wealth do not harmonize, but rather antagonize each other. He feels that wealth itself is not at fault, for there was wealth in Paradise and there is nothing but wealth in the Father-house above, but that sin in our heart poisons wealth for us and turns it into a power that is hostile to God.

Thus God becomes to him ever more *spiritual;* and it is in God, Who is a Spirit, that he learns by contrast to understand better than before, the price, the significance and the worth of the treasures of the spiritual life.

And so there have indeed been men and women among God's saints, who in the midst of their wealth have become richer toward God, and have merely been stewards of the goods entrusted to them in His Name, for the good of His Church and of His poor. The impulse to do good sprang not infrequently from the fear that their wealth should draw them away from God.

More profound is the knowledge of God, which is learned in times of great sorrow, when one who, overwhelmed by grief, already had spiritual knowledge of his God.

Grievous affliction breaks down self-elation. It makes us realize that there are powers which we have not in our own hand which can violently attack us in our strength, in our state in life, in our family, in our prospects of the future, or in the affection of our heart. Call these powers death, sickness, slander, anger, hatred, or what you like, but when they come upon you and succeed in threatening or in breaking up the happiness of your life, then you feel that they stand as powers before you, that they are independent of you, and that they have more power over you, than you over them. And the revelation of these powers becomes to you a revelation of the real power which God has over you and over the world.

As long as life runs a smooth course, you truly know about God, you worship Him, and you discern His spiritual power in the inner life of your soul; but it is still something altogether different, when you observe the presence of the power of God in what you actually experience in your outward life.

In this life, affliction makes a breach; it breaks your life, and you see, taste and feel the power that comes into your life from without, working havoc and distress. You have no power that you can pit against this, and now it is in this powerlessness of yours that you discover, that in God alone is power, which alone is able to deliver you and to repulse the forces of evil that are arrayed against you.

Thus your life becomes an arena in which this destructive power fights against you and against your God, and the saving power of God enters into the combat on your side. First you continue to take part yourself, but when it becomes too fierce, all your strength fails you, at length you become altogether passive, and you feel and realize, that God alone with His angels fights for your salvation.

When they are snares of sin by which Satan seeks to foil you, this struggle is most exalted, most holy, so that at length you have a feeling, as though all angels and all devils stand by to watch with strained eyes what will gain the day in your soul, the power of sin or the power of God.

But also with outward sorrow this struggle can bear an exalted character when by means of this affliction Satan seeks to do you harm, but in the end, by God's appointment this very trial brings a psalm of victory to your lips. For then, through this outward struggle, the soul reaches the still richer knowledge, that in whatever Satan brings upon you, nothing is worked out save by the appointment of God's Love; that it is nothing but the purifying of yourself in the crucible, the separating process of the winnowing fan, the unfolding process of the power of your faith, the inspiring process of your spiritual heroism, a loosening of bands which you prized more highly than the tie that bound you to God, the fortifying process against still greater temptations to come, the anchoring of your soul to a higher world, the humbling of your own self within you, so that even in your heart God alone may be great.

And then the main question is no longer whether you shall be delivered from your trouble or whether you shall succumb to it. If God delivers you from it, then there is an outward triumph, which at times is necessary in order that the supreme power of your Lord over death and pestilence, over slander and anger, over Satan and fortune, may be gloriously exhibited.

But this deliverance is not the main thing.

It must suffice you, if this exhibition of God's supremacy is deferred to the life to come. The main interest at stake is, that the gold, which was darkened in you, may be brought to glisten again; that you emerge from your fiery trial richer in spiritual treasures than when you entered it; that Satan shall be the loser by you, and that God shall be the gainer; that God in His reality shall be revealed to your soul more clearly and more intimately; and that in the end, even as from David's soul, so likewise from your own, may arise the word of testimony: Before I was afflicted, I went astray, but now have I kept Thy word. To Thy Name alone be glory.

L

WITH THEE THERE IS FORGIVENESS, THAT THOU MAYEST BE FEARED

THERE is still another way that leads to knowledge of God, but it is one that should not be dealt with save with utmost delicacy and tenderness; we mean the awful way to the knowledge of God that leads through the depths of sin.

A single word of Jesus can explain at once what way we have here in mind. It is what Jesus said to Simon the Pharisee: "To whom little is forgiven, the same loveth little" (Luke vii, 47).

With this word, Jesus places two persons over against each other; on one side, a most honorable citizen of Nain, his host Simon; and on the other side, a woman who was known in the little town as a woman of ill repute, a public sinner, as was indeed the case. As she had sinned more, she had been forgiven more, and, as a result of this, she loved more. The virtuous Simon, on the other hand, who had sinned less, had been forgiven less, and consequently he loved less.

If, now, love for Christ is one of the richest sources from which the living knowledge of God flows out towards us, the way through the depths of sin became to this woman who was a public sinner, thanks to the larger forgiveness, the means by which to attain a deeper and a richer knowledge of God.

He who only strives after book-knowledge of God, can not enter into this, and will never be able to brook this vigorous word of Jesus. He, on the other hand, who knows from his own experience, that the warm, fostering knowledge of God is fed and carried most effectually by love for Him, gratefully accepts this word of Jesus, and yet—in the face of it, trembles.

The dark nature of sin stands in so sharp a contrast over against Holiness, that for a moment the soul must do violence to itself in order to understand how a deep way of sin can be one that leads to a richer knowledge of God.

And it behooves us to speak the more humbly of this way to a richer knowledge of God, which at first hearing repels, because even among us there are those who, abusing this word of Jesus in a satanic way, at times have shamelessly declared in private: "I had gloriously sinned again, and then had a blessed time of finding."

All such devilish sayings are nothing else than slanders on the mercies of our God. But even if this horrible abuse of Jesus' word compels us to use utmost carefulness, yet the heavenly gold that glitters in this word must not be darkened. It ever remains true, that more sin with more forgiveness can lead to more love and, thereby, to a richer knowledge of God.

It is this word alone that offers us the key to the beatitude of the murderer on the cross and the promise of Jesus that, presently with Jesus Himself he would be in Paradise.

It is fundamentally the same as what David wrote in Psalm 130, 4: "With thee there is forgiveness," not *if*, but "*in order that* thou mayest be feared."

It is from the forgiveness of sin, that the tender faithfulness in the service of the Lord is born.

Sin, forgiveness, love, and, from this love, knowledge of God, are the four beads on the one holy string.

In reality the whole Gospel rests upon this acknowledgment, and the exclamation of a former hero of the faith,

Felix culpa, that "There was something glorious in the fall" — can never be altogether ciphered away.

The angels of God have no knowledge of sin, hence also they have no knowledge of forgiveness, hence again they have no knowledge of that tender love that is born from forgiveness. Nor have they that richer knowledge of God, which springs from this tenderer affection. They stand as strangers in the face of it, and therefore says the Apostle that, with respect to this mystery, the angels are, as it were, jealously desirous "to look into it."

Undoubtedly, the revelation of the Being and Attributes of God, as it comes to us in the mighty work of the atonement, is far richer, more tender and more striking than the first revelation in Paradise.

The grace, the mercy, the compassion of our God for the sinner gives us a look into the Father-heart, such as never would have been possible apart from sin.

The knowledge of God, which we receive in and through Christ, far exceeds all other knowledge of Him; and yet in Scripture the sending of the Son to this world is caused by sin alone.

Every deeply moved utterance of love for God, on the part of any of the saints in both Old and New Testaments springs from the thrilling experience of the heart, that the servant and handmaiden of the Lord have been purged from sin and that they have been brought out of their misery. And neither this reconciliation and sanctification, nor this deliverance from misery would have been conceivable, had not sin engulfed the world.

Even now it is frequently observed that the indifferent sympathy for God, which you find with the unconverted, differs from the affectionate devotion to God on the part of the redeemed, in that the unconverted always leave sin out of their reckonings, and that the redeemed, on the other hand, always start out from the knowledge of their lost estate, in order from this knowledge of sin to ascend to the knowledge of God.

The love for God operates most purely, apart from sin, with the angels of God; and yet, however glorious their love for God may be, it is a different, it is a lesser love than that of the redeemed sinner for his God and Savior.

It will not do for us to say, how revelation would have unfolded itself, if Adam had *not* fallen and Christ had *not* come; but this much is certain, that the rich knowledge of God's boundless mercies is the highest for us, and that this highest knowledge of God is immediately connected with the undoing of Paradise in sin and misery.

And this applies to every individual case.

Especially in these times, the knowledge of sin is scarcely reckoned with on the part of many people who call themselves Christians. They have been religiously brought up, and they have not broken out in open sin. Therefore, sin is no burden to them. As a result of this, the sense of the need of reconciliation is largely lost from among them. The Cross affects them altogether differently. Their Christianity is rather one of high ideals and good works. The sad result of this is that they have less and less of that mystical, tender and cherishing love for God, and that "Blessed is the man whose sin is covered" (Ps. 32, 1), refers to a state of happiness to which they are utter strangers.

But there are those who have been led deeply into the knowledge of sin, either by a keen sense of the demands of God's law, or because God gave them a free rein to sin. But finally they came to a halt, and felt the rise within them of a burning thirst after reconciliation. And now that they have found this reconciliation in the Savior, their soul is aglow with praise and adoration of the compassions of the Lord. They feel their love for the God of unfathomable mercies burn ever more strongly within them. And according to the greater measure of their sin, they follow on to a far richer measure of fellowship with the Father Who is in heaven, and to the knowledge of His holy Name.

This needs by no means always the background of a more brutal outbreak in sin. A deeper insight into ordinary sin can create an equally burning desire after reconciliation. But still it remains a fact that of all the Apostles, S. Paul glories most enthusiastically in this love of the saved, just because, having persecuted the Church of God he felt himself to be the chief of sinners.

And likewise it still remains true that when, from a deep fall into sin, one has come to a full and genuine conversion, the thirst after reconciliation and the deep gratitude of love for this, reaches such a measure of intensity in him, as to affect others most wholesomely with its surprising warmth, even to the extent that at times you could envy him the warmth of his inner life.

Shall we then sin in order that grace, and with it the love and knowledge of God, may increase?

Far from it.

The very question itself is diabolical. He who propounds it, does not love God. He openly insults God's love.

But it does imply that it behooves each child of God to enter more deeply into the knowledge of the sinfulness of his own heart; not to let his secret sins escape notice; ever and anon to apply again the rich atonement to all the breadth and length of the sins of his own heart; and thus to become ever more deeply sensible how endlessly much there was for which he needed forgiveness, and is forgiven.

There is here a twofold way.

The one minimizes his sin; is offended when told of his guilt and does not want to hear it said that he is guilty of many offenses. He holds himself erect, and deems himself a saint.

This, now, is the way to cover up one's sins; *not* to thirst after reconciliation; not to give thanks for reconciliation and love; and consequently to remain far removed from the knowledge of God.

But there is also another way, even that of humbling oneself. In this way, God's child distrusts himself; gives thanks when some one points out his sin to him; examines ever more closely his own heart, his past, and the present state of his soul; and so there is, time and again new need of reconciliation, new joy in forgiveness received, more love for the Compassionate One, and thus an ever deeper entering into the knowledge of God his Savior.

And then, still this much more.

He who as Christian imitates Simon the Pharisee and deems himself just, can not bear that Jesus takes the part of one that is a sinner. For then there is an exalted sense of one's own righteousness, which has no place for the compassion that is shown the prodigal son on his return.

When, on the other hand, by a deeper knowledge of your own sin, you feel that you are small, but refresh yourself each day with new draughts from the cup of reconciliation, then there awakens in your heart something of that joy among God's angels over one sinner that repenteth, which is greater than the joy over the ninety and nine who have no need of repentance.

And, after all, this is the Gospel!

LI

I ACKNOWLEDGE MY SIN UNTO THEE

It is difficult for us, sinners, to recognize, what is an appointment of God for which to give Him thanks, that in the end sin is compelled to become the means to lead us to a deeper knowledge of God and to cause the Majesty of the Lord to shine with greater brightness for us.

The fact that Satan, and they who as his satellites tempt men to sin, abuse also this Divine appointment, in order in a heaven-defying way to mingle sin and religion, in no way darkens the glory of this appointment itself.

Also no one of us can say, whether, in case Satan first, and after him Adam, had *not* fallen, God the Lord would not have opened another way, now unknown to us, by which to lead us into an equally deep, if not a still more intimate knowledge of His Name and Being.

All such reflections as these, however, advance us no single step. The fact is that we have been born sinful in a sinful world. With this sinful world we have to reckon. And this being the case, it behooves us to thank God that from evil itself He causes good to come forth, and that He uses even sin to enrich the knowledge of His Name and Being in the inner perception of His child.

Grace, compassion, mercy constitute a deeper part of the love of God than His blessing in prosperity and His help in time of need; and yet, the knowledge of this grace and compassion can only be known by him who himself has tasted the sweetness of reconciliation, and may count himself not only among God's creatures, but also among His *redeemed.*

In Christ, a knowledge of God's Name and Being has come to us, such as never has been known outside of Him, and yet Bethlehem as well as Golgotha have found their explanation alone in the salvation of sinners.

But there is more.

Even the knowledge of the Almightiness of God has been greatly enriched by sin. For does not the Apostle say that the "exceeding greatness of his power, according to the mighty working of his strength was only revealed to us in the Resurrection of Christ and in the regeneration of believers?" (Ephes. i, 19).

In the re-creation there is a greater exhibition of Majesty and of Almightiness than in the creation; in causing Christ to rise from the dead, a mightier unfolding of Divine strength is shown than in the first calling of nothing into being. There would have been no resurrection without death, no re-creation without fall, and since fall and death both find their starting-point in sin alone, so likewise this higher revelation of the Almightiness of God, which is exhibited in resurrection and in re-creation, would never have come to us in this way, if we had not become sinners.

In order to exhaust what this implies, we must go down still one step more, and also come to recognize that, in God's hand sin becomes the means to make our sense of the *holiness* of the Lord more keen and clear.

Of course we leave for the moment out of account those who in their unconverted state still walk in the way of sin. In this connection we only deal with the redeemed, with those who in knowing God have found eternal life.

And how did the history of sin run in their case, how runs it now?

Two sorts of persons must here be kept apart. Those who in an offensive way broke out in sin, and those others who remained within the bounds of an ordinary sinful existence. Mary of Magdala and Salome do not stand in the same class. S. Peter, who denied his Master thrice, passed through an altogether different inward struggle than S. John, who remained faithful to his Redeemer.

The sinner who went far astray, in his conversion can sometimes rouse the jealousy of the sinner who remained within bounds. The first is far more deeply moved, his struggle in the transition is far more heroic. His jubilant delight in grace when at length the burden of his guilt glides from his shoulders, is far more abounding. The prodigal son, who returns, has something which the son who remained at home, lacks.

And yet he is mistaken, who deems that the calm, quiet sinner, if we may so express it, can not drain the cup of grace to the bottom. He who committed the heinous sin of drunkenness, immorality or dishonesty, runs the great risk of counting this extravagant dissipation his real, actual sin, and of not reckoning with his sinful nature that is back of it. Thus it frequently occurs that such sinners as have been signally converted from criminal practices actually get away from them without making any advances in sanctification of heart and life. And, on the other hand, you see very often that they who have lived unblamably before the eyes of men, after they have come to conversion, have a much keener eye for the less offensive, hidden sins of the heart, and, as a result of their faith, unfold a far richer Christian life. The convert from gross sins frequently continues all his life long to count with the weight of pounds alone, while the convert from less noticeable offenses weighs with the assay-balance.

This is not true of all. There are those, alas, and not a few, who, because they have continued free from great sins, deem themselves on this account alone to be possessors of a glorious record, and with their ordinary sins of pride and quiet selfishness go on to life's end, without ever putting up a serious fight against them.

Take, on the other hand, the redeemed in the narrower sense; in him the tenderness of conscience with respect to sin goes so far that he even mistrusts his own examination of his heart, and ever and again ends with the prayer that God will also make known to him his secret sins, and forgive them.

For when our own heart does not condemn us, God is greater than our heart, and knoweth all things, even those that hide in the innermost recesses of our soul.

But in whatever way and measure the inward struggle against sin awakens in us, it always begins with the accusation of our conscience; and that which troubles us in this restlessness of conscience, is always the voice of our God upbraiding us for our sin.

In part, this is the case even with the people of the world, who begin with a conscience that has not as yet been altogether extinguished. But with them the voice of God in the conscience is not recognized. They hear in it either nothing else than a troublesome resistance of their spiritual nature against that which their carnal nature craves, and sear their conscience, in order freely to go on in sin; or they see in it an impulse of their own better self, and imagine that they train themselves in virtuous living. This results in a good deal of social respectability and praiseworthy self-control, but it bears no fruit for eternal life, insomuch as they claim the honor of it for themselves, and withhold it from God with Whom they refuse to reckon.

But the conscience operates altogether differently with those who are redeemed.

With them the first effect of the troubled conscience is that they are startled; that they become angry with the sin they have committed; that for the sake of everything that is precious, they wish that they had never done it, and that now they stand embarrassed and ashamed before their God.

This gives rise to prayer.

Even in the midst of the cares and labors of the day they were aware that God opposed their sin; but in the general intercourse with people, and in work there is so much to divert their attention that they easily got away from the impression.

But this they have, in distinction from the people of the world, that *they still pray*. And when day is done, and they are at the point, before retiring, of bending their knees before God, they perceive a hindrance, they shrink from prayer, they feel that something wrong lies in between their heart and God, and they scarcely dare to appear before His Face.

And then comes the moment of decision.

If they refrain from prayer, their conscience takes the soporific drink, and unless God saves them, they are lost.

The third verse of Psalm 32 describes what follows: "When I kept silence, my bones waxed old through my roaring."

But David did not faint, he struggled on; however deeply ashamed he was of himself, he knelt down before his God. The fifth verse of this same Psalm contains the record: "I said I will confess my transgressions unto the Lord. So I acknowledged my sin unto thee. . . . . And thou forgavest the iniquity of my sin."

And then, when the soul does not give up but, in spite of everything, yet kneels down and cries unto God on account of its sin, then there comes blessedness: "For this shall every one that is godly pray unto thee, in a time when thou mayest be found. Floods of great waters may come, but they shall not come nigh unto him."

And in this contrition of soul there is a recognition of God's holiness, with an intensity such as has never been experienced before.

It was no longer a holiness of God such as was reasoned out and inferred from the commandment that is given; nor yet a holiness which lost itself in a vague admiration of its own purity; no, it was *the Holy God Himself* Who in our conscience pressed upon us, and by His holiness upbraiding us for our sin, made us test and taste that holiness in the bitterness of our self-reproach and penitence.

The holiness of God then presented itself to us in the light that of itself is formed by the deep contrast with the shadow of our sin. It revealed itself then to us as a power which, quick and quickening, antagonized the death of our sin.

This holiness then assumed a definite, concrete form for us in the inexorable condemnation of a definite, concrete sin. And after it was grasped by us in this definite form, it lighted up for us, as it were, an immeasurable realm of holinesses, that lay over against the dark background of our own soul's existence from which this definite sin had sprung.

This holiness did not merely hover over us, but it cleaved unto us, and so our sin-convicted soul came into direct contact, in immediate touch, with the holy God.

It brought us living, tangible knowledge of Him, with Whom we have to do.

The sin was dreadful; but through it God brought it to pass, that you obtained a better understanding of His holiness.

LII

WHEN GOD SHALL JUDGE
THE SECRETS OF MEN

I⊤ must be granted that the number of people who intentionally give a portion of their time to be busy with God and to press forward into the knowledge of God, is almost vanishingly small.

To pray, to attend church, to do good works, can all go on outside of this actual practice of holding tryst with God. A number of prayers are prayed, in all sorts of settings and on all sorts of occasions, in which the soul does not appear before God, nor God to the soul. Constantly, people go to church, and presently return home again, without having for one moment sought the face of God, or having been met by Him. Even though in the sacrament and during the preaching of the sermon the mind was engaged with Divine things, this by itself was not being busy with God. And as regards the good works, it needs scarcely be said that we can fill up an entire day with them without so much as devoting one thought to Him Who inspired us to do them.

Oh, there is so little of actually being busy with the living God.

And then we only had in mind confessing, believing Christians, who pray, live for their church and do good works; but now enter for once among those un-Churchly companies, which are not worldly in any bad sense, but rather cultivate seriousness of thought and honor virtue, and dote on higher ideals, but yet put religion to one side; and what do you find with even the noblest and best of them, of a being busy with God? And when you strike out still further, and come among the men and women who live merely for business and after business hours for pleasure, forsooth, are you not impressed yourself with the fact, that there is altogether no more such thing as a being busy with God? Of course the openly wicked and godless circles in society, and with these, those who are indifferent to all higher interests, are counted out altogether; so it is sufficiently demonstrated, that the number of those who give but a small part of their time to the practice of the presence of God is deplorably small.

And you also feel how painful, if we may so express it, this must be to God in His love for this world. "So God loved the world, that He gave it His only begotten Son." He imparted ability to the world to know Him, and to love Him in return. Of the world only a small part bears the Christian name. And in this small part, that lives under Baptism, there are day by day but few, very few, who turn their soul and mind to Him, and enter into His hidden walk. All the rest pass by on the other side; they are filled with other things, and the knowledge of His Name and Being is scorned by them.

But what according to the Scripture is certain, is this, that for every one, sooner or later, a moment comes in which God shall compel him to busy himself exclusively and with nothing else than with Himself.

He has appointed a day for this.

And for what man so ever this day breaks, in that day he shall have to appear before God, and God shall overtake him with His Majesty, and shall take entire possession of him, in such a way that he shall not be able to think of anything else than God.

And that day is the Day of Judgment.

In the representation of this Day of Judgment, art has done much harm.

As art, it could not do otherwise than give expression through visible form, and for this expression it borrowed its material and figures from an earthly court of justice, with all the millions and millions that have ever lived on earth, as defendants before God's holy tribunal.

It could not do otherwise, and more than one pencil or brush has done it in a masterly way.

But it should never be forgotten that here was represented outwardly what was of a radically spiritual significance, and that this spiritual action in the Judgment could not be represented in a picture.

When unbelief came in and also denied that there is a day set for Judgment, it took the outward representation, as an occasion for turning the matter itself into ridicule and for showing the impossibility of it. Where would there be room for these millions upon millions of people to stand? How much time would it not take, to try a single human life upon the particulars of every word and every thought? It is said to be one day; but for one single family it would require years.

The Confession of Faith struck a truer note, when in view of the spiritual character of the Judgment, it spoke of it as of an opening of the books of conscience.

So taken, the Judgment is nothing else than a review, in one clear vision, of every man's whole life; an immediate sight of totals; where before, we only reckoned with the unpaid accounts of each moment.

The Judgment is a settling of accounts. On this bill stands, side by side, what you owe God, and what God must recompense you for your deeds according as they are good or evil.

This is the teaching of *Scripture*.

"We must all appear," says the Apostle, "before the judgment seat of Christ, that every one may receive the things done in the body, according to that he hath done, whether it be good or bad" (2 Cor. v, 10).

And every accountant knows what accounting here means, and what it implies that, in the Judgment, God shall present us His bill in toto, together with explanations and proofs, so that we shall be convinced in our conscience, that the account is correct and just.

It shall be the total result, the whole résumé of our life, from childhood on, that will suddenly appear before us, with such overwhelming certainty as to exclude every suggestion of doubt.

On our automatic counting-machines, which are now in general use, the cipher of whatever is put in immediately appears in sight, and addition takes place of itself.

This is the image of your life. And he who throughout his entire life has refused to take due notice of the cipher that showed itself each day, will in the Day of Judgment suddenly see the total amount before him, in which nothing could be or was permitted to be forgotten, and against which nothing can be said. You will have the opportunity to examine it, but that will do you no good. A mistake in this account is unthinkable. And with the sudden clearing of the light of the conscience that will flash across your whole life, you will not be able to do anything else than acknowledge that God is just.

This now raises no apprehensions in those who believe and those who have fallen asleep in Jesus.

The end will show them also a terror-striking shortage, but, over against this, stands in their behalf the Atonement, which covers everything. Their judge is their Savior, and liberated from the curse, they enter into eternal blessedness.

But dreadful will be this opening of the book of the conscience for all such as have died outside of Christ.

For such a one it will then be too late for conversion; he can not hide in Christ; he can no more obtain a part in the Atonement; he has nothing to his credit in the face of his immeasurable guilt; and he must succumb under a sentence that is read to him in his own conscience.

This will constitute the eternal dreadfulness of it. This, in his inmost self, shall be the worm that restlessly gnaws, without ever dying; this shall be the heat in his conscience of the fire that can never be extinguished.

No outward torture needs to be added unto this. The fire itself within is the eternal punishment, and this inner self-consumption shall eat like a cancer throughout his whole being, and corrupt his whole life and his entire existence.

This shall be "the knowledge of God" on the part of those who here on earth have not *willed* to know God in His grace.

This knowledge of God is twofold.

On one hand, here on earth, through faith, it is a knowledge of God that saves. "This is *eternal life*, that they know thee, the only true God."

On the other hand, there is a knowledge of God, which only comes after death, in the Judgment, but for this very reason it is a knowledge of God which does not bring eternal life but eternal death.

On earth it was lightly asserted, that there was no God, or that God knew nothing about us, or that there was no need to concern oneself about Him. But after death, one stands at once before this disregarded God, feels the terror of His all-pervading Presence, and, try as he may, he can no longer rid himself of this God.

For this is not the end of the Judgment, that immediately afterward life can be continued again in the old forgetfulness, as though there were no God. No, the self-destroying impression which at the moment of the actual Judgment one receives of God, continues, and is never effaced again.

Of devils it is recorded, that they well know that God is—and that they tremble. And so likewise all those who in this life have evaded God, shall come, in the Judgment and after the Judgment, to the dreadful discovery that they have been mistaken; as before their own eyes they will see that God actually exists and they also — will tremble

Behind the veil of sensual things in this life, and back of the mists of our earthly limitations, one can shield himself with the pretense that he does not see God, one can even persuade himself that there is no God, because one wilfully does not see Him.

But all this ends, with death. Then this veil is rent from the top downward, then these mists lift themselves, then all semblance ceases, and then the Majesty of the Lord God appears and reveals itself in all its clearness.

The knowledge of God which was ignored for a whole lifetime, then comes of itself, it inundates the lost; but it is a repulsive knowledge, a knowledge which does not draw you toward God, but causes you to recoil from before His terribleness; and wherever you may look, there is nothing anywhere behind which you might hide yourself from the sight of the Majesty of God.

It then becomes the heat of a sun which does not cheer or cherish you but which sears you.

The Scriptures call this hell; and it is a hell, but it is only one which God makes by means of His holy Presence. If God could be brought to naught, or if withdrawal from God were possible, or if one could hide himself from God, hell would be ended.

But this is not possible.

God's holy Presence does not cease to deluge you, and that constitutes your eternal death.

And therefore it is well with him, who in this life has sought the knowledge of his God in Christ. After death this knowledge shall become to him the drinking in of Divine sympathy.

But woe to him, who first learns to know his God in the Judgment. To him this knowledge shall be torment.

LIII

DYING HE WORSHIPED

WITH respect to the knowledge of what lies beyond the grave, the moment of dying is deeply significant. Even the way in which we die, and see others die, contributes to our knowledge of God. So many things that in ordinary times stand between God and our soul, then fall away. Then one stands at the entrance of the invisible life, and the words of the Psalmist: "Our feet stand within thy gates, O Jerusalem," can also be applied to the entering in through the gates of the *new* Jerusalem.

But here, dying must be taken in its only real sense. Dying is an act. In being born, one is passive. Life then only begins. But when the end is come, and God has privileged us to reach the years of maturity, in taking departure from this and entering upon the coming life, the servants and handmaidens of the Lord must not be dragged out by death against their will, they must themselves *go out willingly*, and by the way in which they do this, reveal the fruit of the labors of their faith. The early Christians sang hymns of praise as they carried out their dead, and S. Paul exclaimed: "For me to die is gain, for to be with Christ is by far the best" (Phil. i, 21). Thus, dying was the last struggle, but not of one who defends his life against the waylayer, no, it was the struggle of the hero who bravely pushed ahead in order jubilantly to meet his God.

Truly, we may not court death. It is laid upon us as our bounden duty, to watch over our life until the very end. Suicide is no dying, but a doing away with oneself, a self-destruction. Dying is an exhibition of courage. Suicide is cowardice, it is surrender, a no longer daring to continue the struggle of life, a desertion from the ranks. But though until the very end, as long as there is hope and chance, nothing must be left untried, to extend our service of God here on earth until He issues forth the call—when He calls, the smile of holy joy is more in place than a mournful sigh. He who believes has always confessed that he does not belong here, but that his home is above. This is what dying must make real. In dying, the seal must be put upon all of our life of faith. Dying must be nothing else for the child of God than the entrance into an eternal life.

And this it can not be, unless it is an *act*. We must not be overtaken, arrested and carried off. We must hear Him who calls, and answer in reply: Behold, Lord, here am I, and then bravely enter the valley of the shadow of death and go through all its length, knowing that the Lord awaits our coming, and that at His hand He leads us through this darkness to the light.

Yet, let us add at once that such ideal dying is not frequent. The pains and sorrows of death often rob dying of its ideal, its exalted and holy character; and a state of coma not infrequently interferes, so that there is no possibility of a willing and conscious dying as *an act of the soul*. It even happens, alas, that a narcotic potion is administered, to turn dying into a sleeping of oneself away.

As long, however, as the person himself is irresponsible in this matter, let not such an impossibility of dying manfully on the part of a child of God be turned into a reproach. In this God is sovereign, and as a matter of fact, the Lord withholds such heroic dying in the full consciousness of faith from more than one.

Only there should not be too much acquiescence in this matter.

Scripture ever avoids the sentimental side, and therefore has extremely little to say about dying. Actually it only outlines the dying of Christ on Golgotha, and that of Jacob. But of Jacob we are told that when he felt the end draw near, "he strengthened himself, and sat up on his bed, and leaning upon the top of his staff, worshiped, and blessed his sons" (Heb. xi, 21).

Jacob *strengthened himself*, that is to say, he did not allow himself to be overcome by his weakness and distress. He struggled against it, took hold of himself, and gathered together the last of his waning strength, in order that in dying he might glorify God. He had no thought of care about himself, or of concern about his condition, or about breathing forth his latest breath; and even when he blesses his sons, it is no mere family scene, but a holy prophesying, how through his sons who together would be the tribal heads in Israel, the Kingdom of God would come, and how that Kingdom would flourish, and that one day the Messiah would come. "Until Shiloh come," this was the acme of his prophecy. He blesses his sons, but, in and through his sons, his prophecy points to the coming of the Kingdom of heaven.

Hence in the Epistle to the Hebrews this is described as his greatest *act of faith*. "By faith Jacob when he was dying blessed his sons and worshiped."

It can not be denied that in dying a darkness can envelop the soul. Satan can be let loose to harass us in our dying hour. But as a rule it must be said, that life is for the sake of making sure our faith, and that in our dying, the fruit of this assurance of faith must exhibit itself, to the glory of our God.

And therefore, it must not be conceded that on his death-bed a man is permitted to let himself passively be overcome by his distress and by his weakness. In dying, the will, the courage and the elasticity of faith must still struggle against the weakness of the flesh. In this holy moment the spirit, not the flesh, must conquer. And this is what Jacob did. He strengthened himself in order that he might die in a godly manner. Had he not done this, in all probability he, too, might have passed away in a semi-conscious state. But this he did not do. His mighty spirit shook itself awake. And so he glorified God in his dying.

A dying which even now is held up to every Christian as an example.

But then there is also in such dying a meeting with God, which before death enriches the knowledge of God, both for him who dies, and for those who watch at the bedside.

It is frequently told as the most desirable way of dying that one quietly and peaceably fell asleep, which, in fact, almost always means that without giving any intelligent sign of life he passed away in an unconscious state of mind.

Well, this is equally possible with unbelievers. And so you hear it said of those who died without Jesus, that they went away equally quietly and calmly; perhaps even less troubled in mind by care and doubt than many a child of God.

Nothing was said to them of any serious nature. They themselves spoke of nothing apprehensive. The physician continued to assure them that things were not serious. And so the dying passed from life in an ordinary way, without having known anything of the terror of death.

And others, seeing this, then got the impression that dying after all had nothing to it; it was all so quiet and gentle. Then came the flowers that were laid on the casket. As visits of condolence are no more in vogue, nothing connected with death is spoken of. And after the funeral every topic of conversation is resumed, except that which deals with things eternal.

And thus the mighty lesson of dying goes altogether for naught. Death ceases to be a preacher of deeper seriousness. And the Lord of life and of death is not remembered.

This is an evil which we Christians should not countenance. And yet, this is what we do, when in imitation of the way of the world we say of such dead that they have passed away "quietly and calmly."

Not quietly and calmly, but fighting and conquering in his Savior, such and not otherwise must be the death bed in the Christian family.

He who dares not face this, and is intent on nothing else than to spare the patient up to the last all serious and troublous thought, is not merciful, but cruel through unbelief.

In dying Jacob worshiped.

On his death-bed one can pray. Pray for help in the last struggle. Pray for those that are his and whom he leaves behind. Pray for the Kingdom of God. And already such prayer is glorious in that, on one's death-bed, one thus consciously appears before the face of God, every veil drops away, and one sends up his last supplication to the God Who awaits him in the courts of everlasting light! Such prayer teaches those who stand by to pray. Such prayer has overwhelming persuasive influence.

And yet Jacob did more.

Dying he worshiped. In dying he felt impelled to offer unto his God the sacrifice of worship and adoration; to give Him praise, thanksgiving and honor; to lose himself in the greatness and Majesty, in the grace and compassion of his God; and thus to offer Him the fruit of the lips, in a better fashion than he had ever been able to do in life.

Such a solemn worship on one's death-bed is a summary of the worship which we have offered unto God in our life; but now it is felt more intensely, more deeply than ever, as it immediately precedes the moment when among God's angels and saints above we shall bring Him the honor of his great and glorious Name.

In such a worship on one's death-bed all the knowledge of God that has been acquired before, concentrates itself, and in such a moment this knowledge is wonderfully illumined, enriched and deepened. Now God is known more clearly than He has ever been known before. It is almost seeing Him face to face.

And from this worship follow blessed results in behalf of those who watch and minister at the bedside.

At a death-bed, love is strongly aroused. The beginning of mourning already struggles in the heart, thereby, it is more receptive than ever; and the impression which it receives in such a moment, is overwhelming.

We know, we trust, that the loved ones believe on Jesus; but frequently one sees no evidence of it, and observes rather the contrary, in narrow-mindedness and sin.

But when the moment of dying has come, and children see it of their father, a husband of his beloved wife, that in this affecting moment the faith does not fail, but maintains itself; that at the gate of eternity the language of faith becomes more animated and strong; and it seems as though one overhears an utterance of soul from the dying one that goes out after God; then it is the dying one himself, who, through his worshipful prayer and supplication brings you, as it were, into the very Presence of God, and makes you feel that Divine Presence closer at hand than you ever felt it before.

Much dying could be far different from what it now is,

had the life been different. Then faith would awaken more effectually, and, in dying, God's child would understand that he still had a duty to fullfil towards God and towards his loved ones.

Then dying would be, far more than it is now, a preaching of sacred reality, and the fruit of it would be effective to the glory of God in the lives of those that are left behind.

LIV

GIVE YOURSELF TO FASTING AND PRAYER

It is inconsistent that, while among most Protestants fasting is not practised, willingness to live by the Bible as the only rule of faith and practice is readily professed.

Fasting is certainly a Scriptural rule of life not only in the Old but equally in the New Testament. Christ himself fasted forty days and forty nights. In I Corinthians (vii, 5) S. Paul exhorts the children of God, that they give themselves not only to prayer, but also to fasting. And what, if possible is stronger still, Christ has said that there is a kind of evil spirits, that goeth not out but "by prayer and fasting" (S. Matt. xvii, 21).

Over against this, it is true that in the days of Jesus' ministry on earth the question was raised: "Why do the disciples of the Pharisees fast, but *thy disciples fast not?*" And though on the ground of this it may be assumed that the disciples in those days did not observe the Jewish fasts, nevertheless, this is the reply that Jesus made: "When the bridegroom shall be taken away from them, then *shall* they fast" (S. Mark ii, 18-20).

History truly teaches that, from the beginning, fasting has been practised in the Church of Christ. At Antioch the followers of Jesus were first called Christians, and of this Church at Antioch The Acts (xiii, 2) relates, that the Christians there "fasted and prayed," and that while they were doing this, the Holy Ghost gave them a revelation. It is well known that in the Roman, Greek and Nestorian Churches fasting is practised; and it is also known that in Reformation days, days of prayer went hand in hand with fasting.

Is it not inconsistent, therefore, that with the significance which Scripture and history attach to fasting, the practice of it has almost altogether passed into disuse among us, and that neither they who know the Lord in particular, nor the Churches as a body practise fasting as a habit of their religious life?

It is ever our custom, as it was in Israel in the days of Hosea, to say: "My God, we Israel know thee" (Hos. viii, 2); but is there not something lacking, when Scripture shows us that the knowledge of God is mightily advanced by prayer, and prayer by fasting, if we, who say that we know God, nevertheless neglect to fast?

The answer to this question lies in Isaiah (lviii, 6).

In the days of Isaiah there was much fasting done in Judah, and yet Jehovah testified by his Prophet, that He did not accept such a fast, and then follows: "Is it such a fast that I have chosen, a day for a man to afflict his soul, to bow down his head as a bulrush and to spread sackcloth and ashes under him?" Upon which it further follows: "Is not this the fast that I have chosen, to loose the bands of wickedness, to deal thy bread to the hungry, when thou seest the naked that thou cover him, and that thou hide not thyself from thine own flesh? Then shall thy light break forth as the morning, and thine health shall spring forth speedily."

This striking protest against dead formalism, also in fasting, has justly aroused among us a sense of aversion to the formal practice of it. Fasting as a form, fasting as a purely bodily exercise, fasting as an exhibition before the world, does not sanctify; indeed, it can work profanation. Hence Jesus' warning in the sermon on the mount: "But *thou* when thou fastest, be not as the hypocrites, of a sad countenance, but anoint thine head, that thou appear not unto men to fast, but unto thy Father, which is in secret." Forsooth, this is an admonition, to which is added with equal emphasis: "And thy Father, which seeth in secret, shall reward thee openly."

As sharply as Jesus turns himself against formal, outward fasting, with equal emphasis He puts His seal upon godly fasting, and says that by grace it has its reward with God.

Hence we are safe only, when, on the one hand, we oppose dead formalism in fasting, and, on the other hand, bring into practice the real fasting, which has been appointed of God.

And when you examine your own past, and look abroad among the Churches, can you reach any other conclusion than that we have banished dead, formal fasting with scrupulous care, but that with it real, religious fasting, such as God has appointed, has almost utterly vanished?

This accounts for much spiritual loss.

We desire eternal life. "This *is* eternal life, that they might know thee, the only true God." This knowledge of the only true God is fed and nourished by nothing so much as by prayer. And it is especially by fasting that prayer becomes more intimate and profound. Is there, then, an escape from the reproachful conclusion, that by our neglect to fast our prayers lose fervency, and that in this way we suffer loss in this ever ripening knowledge of God, which is eternal life?

If this applies to you personally and to your family, must it not equally apply to the Churches? And when one observes, again and again, that in our Churches, too, a whole brood of evil spirits is abroad, which is not driven out except by fasting and prayer, is it too much to say, that the disuse of all fasting is one of many causes that such spirits continue to harass the life of the Church?

Must fasting, then, be introduced again as a rule on a given day of the week? By itself there would be nothing against this; but it is to be feared, that, whether we would or no, it would shortly decline again into formalism.

Fasting, taken spiritually, as appears from Isaiah (lviii) and I Corinthians, (v, 7) has a much broader basis than a temporary abstinence from food. It aims to deprive the body of its supremacy over the soul, and restore to the soul its dominion over the body.

You know, yourself, that everything that strengthens and cherishes the body, has a tendency to repress the clearness and the elasticity of the life of the soul. The side of our life that is turned toward the world, rarely operates in harmony with the side of our life that is turned toward God.

In solitude, as a rule, you feel yourself closer to your God than in company with society round about you. In the banqueting hall you are farther away from God than in your bedchamber. In the midst of exacting cares to increase wealth, you enjoy less of God's nearness than at the times when you give of your money to the poor. You are closer to your God when you feed the hungry than when with your family or with your guests you feast on choice foods and drinks. In brief, every one's experience confirms the truth that the thought of God comes closer to you the less enjoyment you seek in the world, and that the hidden walk with God becomes the more intimate the farther you get apart from the cares and distractions of the world.

Now, do not infer from this, that in order to know God, you must withdraw yourself altogether from the world.

This is what the stylists thought, the recluses and the contemplative monks. And this is wrong, for although

"fasting and prayer" is one of the means to find God, there
are a number of other means, which only present themselves in the midst of busy life.

Of these other means we have treated in former meditations. We need not refer to them again. But it must
be a permanent rule of our life that we leave no single
means unused to make our knowledge of the only true
God more intimate and profound, and that thus in the
midst of the world we should serve our God and enjoy
what He gives us to enjoy in our families and environ-
ments, as well as in the practice of "fasting and prayer."

And then it can not be denied, that it is a great help to
us, if, from time to time, we detach our soul temporarily
from the dominating power of the body and of the world,
and thereby make it more susceptible to influences from
above. In connection with this, one will feel more impressed with the need of fasting and retirement at set
times, and another will only come to it in moments of
anxiety and increasing seriousness. In this matter let
every one be assured in his own conscience. This depends
upon temperament and upon circumstances. Herein let
no one judge his brother.

But the matter itself has a right to be introduced into
our habit of life.

Your chief interest must be eternal life. This eternal
life can only be enjoyed in an ever more intimate knowledge of God. This more intimate knowledge of God, you
find more particularly in your hidden life of prayer. And
this hidden life of prayer has need, that, in the face of the
oppressive supremacy of the body and of your environment, the power of the soul be strengthened by fasting
rightly understood.

That sobriety in food and drink is an aid in this direction, is evident from the lack of inclination to pray which

you experience upon your return from a banquet hall. But this is merely the beginning of real fasting. It is by no means too rich food and drink alone, but also too great extravagance in ornaments and clothes, all sorts of recreation and gratification of the senses, and, very strongly also, your financial concerns, voluntarily or involuntarily, work the harmful effect that they make the mists between your God and your heart become thicker and darker.

Fasting which shall sanctify prayer and make it more fervent, consists by no means, therefore, alone in depriving the body of food or drink, but equally by generous giving to withdraw one's self from the dominion of one's money, in simplicity and sobriety, in freeing one's self from the supremacy of self-pleasing, and certainly also in seclusion and in releasing one's self from the domination of one's environment.

This is what the Lord testified by Isaiah, when He extended fasting to the loosening of the bands of wickedness and the feeding of the hungry.

From time to time the soul must make itself altogether free, cast away all bands, become altogether itself. Then the gates lift up their heads, then the door of eternity unlocks itself, then God draws near to us, and our soul draws near to God, and the knowledge of our God, which is eternal life, blossoms in the sanctuary of our heart.

LV

THAT OUR PRAYER SHOULD NOT PASS THROUGH

WHEN a child wants to ask his father for something, he first seeks him; and only when he has found his father, does he ask him for what he wants. To begin to speak, before his father has been found would be childish foolishness, an evidence of insistence without sense.

Is there no hint in this with regard to our prayer?

He who as child of God will pray to his Father in heaven, and in faith desires something from Him, must needs first go to Him, must first seek Him, and only when he has found Him, can he ask what he desires.

But in connection with prayer, this is oftentimes little thought of, and time and again one observes in his own prayer and in that of others that there is more talking in the air than there is prayer and address made to the living God. Nor can it be denied that, especially in extemporaneous prayer with others, and not least in church, there is sometimes more reasoning and arguing than actual speaking to the most high God, who is clothed with Majesty.

There is less to be said about prayer in secret. With this every one has only the observation of his own prayer at his disposal, or what others themselves may tell of it. But even if one confines himself to this, the complaints whispered in a brother's ear about the barrenness of prayer are sufficiently many to justify the fear that even, in secret prayer, sometimes, the muttering or speaking of words already begins before the soul is conscious that it has found its God back again.

Much prayer and long prayer encourage this habit. The eyes are closed, the hands are folded, and now one begins with certain formal prayers that have been learned by heart, not irreverently, but yet certainly not with that very profound reverence which becomes us before God. Even by the voice and by the tone of the prayer you sometimes feel that it is a mere form, and by no means a speaking to God.

Scripture repeatedly shows us, therefore, that not every prayer counts as such with God.

It speaks to us of times when our prayer is hindered, and makes us hear the word of the Lord: "When ye make many prayers, I will not hear" (Isaiah i, 15); and it records for us the complaint of the prophet Jeremiah (Lam. iii, 44), "Thou hast covered thyself with a cloud, that our prayer should not pass through."

Then the heaven is as brass; then there is no opening and no unlocking; then there is no access and no entrance; and there is no spirit of grace and of supplication.

In Zion there was an "oracle of God's holiness." And when the godly Jew wandered in the mountains or tarried at his homestead by the Jordan, he turned himself when he prayed toward this oracle (Ps. 28, 2). When Israel was in exile, they prayed likewise with their faces toward Zion.

As a relic of this, it is still the custom in many countries and in many communions that, for the purpose of earnest prayer, people do not stay at home but go into the churches. For this purpose, such church buildings are open all day long, and in the solemn seclusion of such a stately edifice, one kneels down unobserved and unknown in the expectation that in this impressive place the nearness of the Lord will more effectually reveal itself.

Especially to him who with a large family is confined to close quarters at home this undeniably offers an advantage. He who at home can always find an empty room at his disposal, where he can lock the door, and can spend some moments alone with God, has no need of this. But the great masses of people are not so fortunate. In those circles one is almost never alone, there is almost never quiet, and seclusion which is so greatly helpful to prayer can almost never be found. From the heights of spirituality one may condemn all such quiet prayer in an empty church as an evidence that one attaches too great significance to a so-called consecrated place; but he who so speaks, has presumably never known the painful lack of living in a home, where hardly ever a quiet moment for private prayer can be found.

But apart from this home difficulty, it must never be forgotten, that in Israel, God Himself had appointed such an oracle of His holiness, and had directed the souls of the faithful towards it.

There lay in this a measure of education by which from formal and outward muttering to attain real prayer, *i. e.*, a *speaking to God.*

Thus the pious Jew was reminded every time, that in order to be able to pray, he must first with the eye of the soul get sight of God, and that before he begins to pray, connection must have been made between his soul and God.

To pray without first having found God and knowing that now He can be addressed, is really only a caricature of prayer.

He who would pray must know that at that very moment God regards the voice of his prayer; that He inclines His ear to our prayer; that He listens to our supplication. And this spiritual sense can not be awake in your soul unless before you pray you have placed yourself with full consciousness before His Face.

God's child always prays in Jesus' Name. He must do this because, unreconciled and unredeemed, he would find no listening ear with God. But this prayer in Jesus' Name becomes a word without sense when one does not first place himself before the Face of the Holy One, and feel that of himself he has no right of approach, and that therefore he only appears before his God covered in Christ.

What presents the difficulty here, is the omnipresence of God.

It is the very perception of faith, that God is neither bound to time nor place, and that He is everywhere present, which accounts for the fact that one inclines to speak in the air without first concentrating his thoughts upon God, placing Him before our eyes, and seeking His Face until He has been found.

Yet God Himself in His Word teaches us otherwise.

Even though Scripture reveals the omnipresence of God to us in the most glorious terms, this has never any other meaning with respect to prayer than that we, wherever we are, always and everywhere can find our God. But equally strongly it reveals to us, that in whatever place we are, we have to do with the living God, Who besets us behind and before, Who compasseth our path and our lying down, and Who is acquainted with all our ways (Ps. 139, 5, 2).

And with all this, it always points us *upward*. In prayer we must *lift up* our soul. To the heavens our prayerful thoughts must direct themselves. There is a throne of grace, where God's Majesty shines out. It is the palace above, whither our prayers ascend. It is the living, the personal God Who inclines Himself to us, and toward Whom our praying soul must turn.

Truly, your imagination can not come to your help in

this, for God is a Spirit, and they that worship Him, must worship Him in spirit and in truth. But he who knows Him as his Father Who is in heaven, also knows, that he has not to do with a force that extends and spreads itself everywhere, but with his Covenant God, with his Lord and his King, and he can not rest until, in behalf of effectual prayer, he has restored the hidden walk with God and has obtained a new communion with Him.

In former days, when there was no telegraph nor telephone yet known, this seemed far more of an enigma than now. In these our times, on the other hand, we know by experience a communication among men at immeasurable distances, supported by nothing except a weak metal thread. And even this wire has fallen away. There is now a telegraphy without wire, which in its wondrous working has become a beautiful symbol for our prayer. Fellowship with God without any middle-means.

Also the so-called telepathy comes to our aid here. The authenticated facts that persons at far distances can have fellowship of soul with soul and disclosure of thought, is an illustration of how our soul can have fellowship with God and disclosure of thought, because, when even the human soul already is able to do this, with God the means of spiritual fellowship are so infinitely much greater.

The point in question is, that in and with our prayer we must attend to the indispensability of this fellowship, and not enter upon prayer, until we have obtained this connection with God, this communication with God, this access unto God.

When Jeremiah complains that his prayer did not "pass through," because God had covered Himself with a cloud, he shows thereby that he had sought this fellowship, and that he had perceived that he could get no connection.

As when one stands before the telephone and rings up central, and gets no reply because the wire is broken, so he who prays stands before heaven and calls after God for a hearing, seeks connection of fellowship—but there comes no sign of life in return.

This, then, shows that real prayer can not begin before you have obtained a hearing, before you have connection, and until you know that God's Face has discovered itself to you.

If, now, there is no connection, then your prayer is hindered; and the fault lies with you. It is either your sin, the wandering of your thoughts, the being engaged with worldly concerns, a wrong state of mind, or the superficiality and externality of the condition of your soul.

The man who prays from sheer habit pays no attention to this. He prays any way, even though every feeling and sense of connection is wanting, yea, even when he perceives that his prayer does not pass through. He has said his prayers, and that is the end of it.

But the genuine, godly man of prayer does not behave like this. If he feels that there is a hindrance, if he is aware that there is a cloud between himself and God, he turns in upon himself, he humbles himself before God, and seeks the sprinkling of the Blood of his Savior. And then the connection follows, the gates of heaven swing open to him, and in the end his prayer passes through and ascends before the Face of the Holy One.

This is the sanctifying power of the conscientious practice of prayer.

If at first there is no prayer, let no one rise from his knees until prayer comes and access to the throne of grace has been obtained.

And in this very struggle, the break with sin takes place and the grace in Christ is restored.

LVI

AND TO WHOMSOEVER THE SON WILL REVEAL HIM

WHEN, in The Epistle to the Romans (i, 20) we read that "The invisible things of Him from the creation of the world are clearly seen, being understood by the things that are made," and in S. Matthew (xi, 27) that "No one knoweth the Father, save the Son, and he to whomsoever the Son will reveal Him,'" these two do not contradict each other, only seemingly so.

There is knowledge of God that can be obtained in all sorts of ways by every man; and this was not only so in Paradise, but is still so in this fallen world, even in that part of the world which is darkened by the curse of heathendom. "The heavens declare the glory of God and the firmament sheweth his handiwork." Day unto day uttereth speech, and night unto night sheweth knowledge. There is no language nor country, there is no people, even unto the world's end, that do not hear the voice of the heavens. And not only does nature, which pulsates with life, pour forth speech for every one who does not purposely stop his ears; but there is also a speech of God, which goes forth to all peoples and nations, in the conscience. Not of the first created human pair in Paradise, but of the heathen in the corrupt ages of the Cæsars, S. Paul testifies that they "shew the work of God's law written in their hearts, their conscience also bearing witness, and their thoughts meanwhile accusing or else excusing one another" (Rom. ii, 15). The form in which the knowledge of God and the knowledge of God's will expresses itself among the heathen, may be idolatrous and oftentimes offensive, yet the impulse from which their idolatry and their offensive practices proceed, is never anything else than the wrong interpretation of the speech of God in nature and in the conscience. This is the seed of religion, the innate knowledge of God and the given knowledge of God, which was ever confessed by our fathers. And this was not confessed in order to glorify man who fell, but in order, on the contrary, to render the sinner inexcusable before God. Fallen humanity as such, and every individual sinner therein, stands so deeply guilty before God for the very reason that he whose eye is but fully open and whose conscience reacts in a pure way, perceives the eternal power and Divinity of the Lord Jehovah in his own inmost self and around him everywhere in nature and in history.

But how, then, is it to be explained that in the face of all this, Christ emphatically testified that "no one knoweth the Father save the Son, and he to whomsoever the Son will reveal him?"

It does not say that no one can have any knowledge of God save through the Son, but that no one knoweth the Father, save he to whom the Son has revealed Him.

Of Satan and his satellites it is clearly stated, that they know God and tremble. And this can not be otherwise. For Satan's fall was nothing else than rebellion against God, evil lust to dethrone God and to put himself in God's place; and how could this have been conceivable, if he had not known God's existence and God's omnipotence? But, with equal certainty, every one feels that Satan, though he knows God, has never known *the Father*.

He who knows the Father is comforted and reconciled; Satan, on the other hand, as often as he thinks of God, trembles. The knowledge of the Father maketh rich, gives peace and eternal rest; the knowledge which Satan has of God, makes him tremble. And yet, this is the difference between Satan and a great sinner on earth that, a criminal on earth can take a sleeping potion in order to quiet his conscience and to forget God, but this is the very thing that Satan can not do. For him this sleeping-draught of sin is inconceivable. His sense of God's Almighty Presence speaks loudly to him from moment to moment, and for this reason Satan trembles. The miserable estate of the lost in the place of outer darkness is explained by this same thing. Here on earth the ungodly can put his conscience to sleep and in the midst of sin live ordinarily without any anxiety. There are others whose conscience is so seared, that only now and then, in moments of intense emotion, they feel the anger of God, and for the rest of the time without God, and also without dread of God, they live on in their sin just because they close their eyes and stop their ears.

But when once this life is ended, and they enter upon eternity, this too will end; then their eyes also will fully open so that they will never be able to close them again, and their ears will be unstopped so that they will never be able to stop them again; and with open eye and ear to be eternally subject to the Almightiness of God, will be their miserable destiny.

If, then, it is written, that no one of us can know the Father, except the Son reveal the Father to us, it is evident, that this does not point to the general knowledge of God which is within reach of every man, but very definitely to that knowledge of God's eternal compassions which the sinner can not share until reconciled in Christ, and having become a child of God he has learned to know God as his Father and himself as this heavenly Father's child.

Hence there is no mention here of a doctrine which is

learned by rote, of a revelation in words which we make our own; no, there is mention here of a knowledge which the spiritual experience of being redeemed and reconciled brings us.

There certainly belongs to this also a revelation to our understanding. We know that the Son of God is come, and hath given us an understanding that we may know Him that is true (I John v, 20). All revelation begins with the Word. When Christ appeared, He went through the land preaching the Gospel of the Kingdom. The Gospel itself is the glad *tidings* of salvation that is to come and of redemption that is proclaimed.

But this preaching, these tidings, these words of the Gospel by themselves, do not suffice. These can be learned by heart and committed to memory without imparting to us any closer understanding of the knowledge of the Father.

This doctrine by itself, though it be embraced without reservation or resistance, never brings us further than to say, "*Lord, Lord.*" It is then as in the days of Hosea (viii, 2), when all the people said: "Lord, we thy Israel, know thee," even while the anger of the Lord was kindled against them just because they did *not* know Him.

Even if this doctrine, this message, this word of the Gospel has been carried into the world first by the Apostles and after that by the Church and the Bible, this by itself can never bring the knowledge of the Father.

This knowledge only comes, when the glorified Christ through the Holy Spirit brings the riches of His reconciliation to us, seeks us out as sinners and makes us children of God. And only then, when Christ has made us children of God, has the knowledge of the Father become our blessed and glorious possession.

And yet, even this does not say enough.

Christ does not come to us only in the work of redemption. He is the Eternal Word which before all things was with God and was God. All nature, together with the speech of God which it contains, has been created by Him. He is the *Word;* without Him no speech goes out from nature. Taken apart from the eternal Word, nature would be dead and dumb, and would have nothing to say to us.

More still.

Not only has nature been created by the Eternal Word of God and animated with a language, but we ourselves also, as a race, in the midst of nature, have not come into this world apart from Christ. Furthermore, the scope of our human nature is from Him. We, too, have been created by Him. And especially our whole spiritual disposition, and our ability to overhear and to understand nature, has been implanted in us by Him.

And the same is altogether true of our moral nature. Our conscience has come to us from Christ. He himself is the conscience of mankind. The fellowship, which our heart has with the moral world order, our perceptions of good and evil, of right and wrong, of what fills one with horror and enchants one through beauty, of selfishness and love, of light and darkness — have all come to us from the Eternal Word.

Hence it must not be taken to mean that we knew God apart from Christ, and that in and by Christ alone this God, Whom we already know from other sources, is revealed to us as our Father. No, the broad foundation of the knowledge of God on which is reared the knowledge of the Father, comes to us from the Eternal Word. The knowledge of the Father is not a flower wafted down to us from heavenly regions and fastened by Christ to the withered stem of our human nature; but the barrenness of our human nature has been animated by Him with new life, and so, the knowledge of the Father has been engrafted upon the knowledge of God which came to us through nature and upon the knowledge of God which came to us through the conscience by virtue of our creation from the Eternal Word.

Thus there are not two kinds of knowledge without an internal relation, externally standing side by side and linked together; but there is *one* knowledge of God, from the Eternal Word, that through nature and the conscience springs up within us, and now in and through the Messiah's work of Redemption is elevated and carried up to the knowledge of the Father.

Hence, it is a maiming of our faith which bitterly avenges itself when he who is converted contents himself with the work of Redemption as though this alone comprises the glory of the Christ, in order from now on to leave to the world the knowledge of God that comes from nature and from the conscience.

No, he who reconciled in Christ as child of God kneels before his Father in heaven, must let the light that has appeared to him in Christ operate reflexively upon the speech of God in nature round about him, and in the nature of his own human existence, both of which have their origin in Christ.

It is for this reason that the Gospel of S. John begins with centering our attention upon this tie with Christ that has been laid already in the creation of our world, in the creation of our own nature, and in the creation of our own person.

And then the result is that both this speech of God in nature and this speech of God in our conscience, thanks to our reconciliation in Christ, obtain for us an altogether different sound, increase in clearness and in meaning, and are now heard by the opened ear in a purity, which to our perception unites the life of grace with the life of nature in glorious harmony, and turns the whole world, and all of history, including our own life, into *one* mighty revelation of the Father, Whom we worship in the Face of His Son.

LVII

I SHALL THEN CONTINUALLY BE WITH THEE

You may sit close to some person in the same room without having any fellowship with him, without engaging in a word of conversation, or for one moment making approach with your spirit to his spirit. Especially on long railway journeys you may be enclosed within a comparatively narrow space, for a whole day and more, with others whose names you do not know, of whose lives you have no knowledge, and with whom you do not exchange a word.

But, on the other hand, you may be miles away from some one, so that you see nothing of him, observe nothing of him, can cause no sound to enter his ear or catch any sound from his lips, and yet, you are continually busy with him, think of almost nothing else than of him, and in your spirit enjoy closest fellowship with his spirit. It may sound strange but it is true that a mother who has lost her darling child may never have been so close with her soul to the soul of her child as in the first hours after its death, when that dear child went endlessly far away from her.

Local and physical presence can greatly aid the fellowship of soul with soul by the expression of the face, especially by the speaking of the eye and by the exchange of mutual thoughts; but our fellowship with some one's heart is not bound by this local presence. It is the very intimate fellowship of soul that makes us long for the presence of our friend. Our human nature is soul and body, and, therefore, only finds full satisfaction in a fellowship of soul, which at the same time enjoys the bodily presence.

Even in the realm of glory, our fellowship with God's saints will only find its blessed consummation in the seeing of one another in the glorified body. The fellowship of the blest in the Father-house above, until the resurrection of the dead, bears merely a provisional character and awaits the completion in Jesus' return. But however great the significance is which must be attached to the bodily presence and sight, the presence of our soul close by another's soul does not depend on it. God created us so that even when separated, we can have intimate fellowship one with another; fellowship by means of writing or of direct communication by telephone; but also, fellowship without the aid of any of these means, purely spiritual, purely in the feeling, in perceptions, in the thoughts and in the imagination.

Fellowship purely through bodily presence is no human fellowship. Fellowship of person with person must always be as from spirit to spirit, from soul to soul, from heart to heart. And the question whether we live near by a person or far away from him, or whether we are strangers to him, is one that is not decided by distance or presence, but exclusively by spiritual nearness or spiritual estrangement.

At a departure for long years, yea, at a last farewell before dying, one can say: "I shall continually be with you;" and more than one mother with respect to her deceased child, more than one widow with respect to the husband whom she lost, has literally fulfilled this.

That child and that husband, were gone from the earth, but the fellowship remained—awaiting the reunion.

Hence, when in Asaph's Psalm it reads: "I shall then continually be with thee" (73, 23), this must only be taken in the sense of this spiritual fellowship.

Of course locally we are never separated from God; we can never be anywhere where God is not near us. He besets us behind and before. Whither shall we go from His Spirit, whither shall we fly from His presence? We can not escape the Presence of God. "If I make my bed in hell," says David (Ps. 139), "behold, thou art there. If I take the wings of the morning, and dwell in the uttermost parts of the sea, even there shall thy hand lead me, and thy right hand shall hold me."

God is never away from us. He can not be away from us, and we can not be away from Him. For He is the omnipresent One. And, every moment, His Almighty power is operative in and with us; in every throb of the blood, in every quiver of our nerve, in every breath we draw.

But this omnipresence of God does not create, as yet, fellowship of our spirit with the Spirit of God.

Two things are required for this.

First, that God approaches our spirit, and in our soul and in our heart makes known the signs of His holy Presence; and, secondly, that our spirit opens itself to the Spirit of God, lets Him in, moves itself towards Him, and seeking Him, rests not till it finds Him.

This first part, this approach of God's Spirit to our spirit, can make nothing more than a superficial impression. And in this sense, there is scarcely any one who does not now and then, become aware in his soul of a certain impulse on the part of God, whether through the conscience or in connection with striking events in the life. Even in the midst of our sins we have been aware of this.

But this becomes something altogether different, when God discovers Himself to us, makes Himself known to us, takes up His abode in our soul, and announces Himself to us as the secret Friend of our heart.

Then only, the possibility is given for the hidden walk, and God remains sovereign Lord, either to grant His fellowship to our soul or to withhold it. Only let him who receives it, take thought that thereby a privilege is granted him above all privileges, a heavenly, a royal, a Divine grace of highest worth.

And that we appreciate this blessedness at this high estimate will be shown by whether we, too, from our side open our heart to God, and not merely once in a while, but as a steady grace of life *continuously* seek and enjoy this intimate, this hidden fellowship with Him.

In Asaph's song: "I shall then continually be with thee," the word "continually" must not be interpreted to mean "from time to time," "occasionally," "once in a while;" but "constantly," "all the time, " "unceasingly."

He had tasted and enjoyed the blessedness of God's fellowship, but only at intervals, now and then. Now he was near unto God, and then again he was away from God, and thereby his soul had erred. He felt that with his spirit he had wandered off, and that he had been at the point of becoming unfaithful to God's children; and from this maelstrom he had come back only after he went into the sanctuary of God and opened his soul again to fellowship with Him. And now, directed by this bitter experience of soul, he makes in his soul this high resolve, that he will do differently from before; not merely as heretofore, in the midst of all sorts of distractions once to seek God's fellowship, and then again to wander off from Him, but that from now on he would be with his God all the time, without break, without ceasing, for that is what "continually" means.

This declaration does not mean to say that from now on he would be absorbed in holy meditation, in order through the play of the imagination, deeply, mystically, to lose himself in fellowship with the Divine Being.

Provided it is indulged in with the utmost carefulness, such losing of one's self in the spiritual vision of the Infinite as result of private prayer, can have a value of its own. But this is not what to be continually near to God means.

It can not mean this, because with such holy mystical meditation all other working of our spirit is at rest. This would bring it about, that we would stand helpless before our task in the world and the fulfilling of God's will would henceforth be no longer possible.

No, the fellowship of being near unto God must become reality, in the full and vigorous prosecution of our life. It must permeate and give color to our feeling, our perceptions, our sensations, our thinking, our imagining, our willing, our acting, our speaking. It must not stand as a foreign factor in our life, but it must be the passion that breathes throughout our whole existence. This is not possible with the fellowship we have with any human person, but it is possible with the fellowship which we have with our God, because in God, from God, and through God are the issues of all holy and of all creaturely utterances of life.

Therefore inactive pondering is not what Asaph wanted, but a key-note, a fundamental temper of mind and heart, which, continually giving thanks, lifts itself up and worshipfully directs itself to God. An ejaculatory prayer is not enough. This proceeds only occasionally from the soul. What is required is that at all times and in all things our expectation be from God, and that continually we give Him thanks for everything. It is to let God inspire us. It is so to company with our faithful Father, that we never know a moment in which it would affect us strangely if He were to appear to us.

Even as we have our own *self* ever with us and bring it into every interest of life, so also to let the thought of God, the lifting up of the soul to God, the faith on God, the love for God continually operate in and with everything. That is what prevents estrangement, the straying away, and accustoms our soul to be continually near to God.

This is most strongly evident in this, that he who so lives, feels an aching void the moment he wanders away from God, and, therefore, takes no rest, till he has entered again into fellowship with Him.

LVIII

I HIDE ME WITH THEE

UNDER her eyes, and yet freely, the hen allows her chickens to run about *till danger threatens*.

But then, at once, with raised wings she clucks her brood toward herself and does not rest until the last chick has crowded itself under her wings, and animal mother-faithfulness covers all the young innocents.

But then the chick does not yet *hide* itself with the mother-hen.

It only *hides* when for itself it sees the danger approach, and of its own initiative runs to the mother-hen, in order to *seek* protection beneath her wings.

The "Jerusalem, Jerusalem," which Jesus declaimed against Zion, in its touching pathos was doubly upbraiding, because it reproached Israel both for having surmised no danger, and for having sought defence and cover only with men, and not with God.

In time of need, the people should have called upon God and should have poured out their prayer and supplication for help and deliverance to the God of their fathers, and without waiting for an answer to their cry, as soon as the waters in the flood of destruction that came upon them began to rise, with their whole soul they should have hidden themselves with God.

But this the people did not do. They trusted in their own strength, and underestimated the danger. And then, instead of the people calling upon God, God called to his people: "O Israel, flee to me and let me be your shield." So God called not once but many times. And Israel heard that call and those alluring words of her God, but hard-

ened her heart, and would not. And only then the aban-
donment became judgment: "How often would I have
gathered thee, as a hen doth gather her brood under her
wings, and ye would not; behold, *your house is left unto
you desolate!*" And at this judgment, Israel did not
weep with shame in self-reproach but planted the Cross
of Golgotha; and He Who wept over His people was the
Lord.

Here you stand before all sorts of spiritual conditions.

One will be in danger who neither knows God nor is
known of Him, and yet when the ship threatens to go
down calls out: "O God, help me," but with a cry that is
lost in the storm.

Another will be in danger, but he will bravely struggle
against it, and have no thought of God.

Still another in time of stress will hear the warning call
of God but will not heed it.

But there also will be those who, in the hour of grave
need, will of themselves flee to God, will call upon Him
and hear His call, and before the soul can be delivered, find
themselves hidden with their God, overshadowed by His
wings and covered by His faithfulness.

These last alone are they from whose soul in truth the
call of confidence goes forth: "I hide me, Lord, with thee."
(Ps. 143, 9 marg. reading).

Hiding with God is something else than dwelling in
His tent and knowing the secret grace of the hidden
walk.

Hiding never indicates a fixed condition, but is always
something transient. You hide from a thunderstorm, in
order, presently, when the sun shines again, to step out
from your hiding place, and continue on your way. The
chicks hide with the mother-hen, when the hawk is around;
but when it is gone, they run out again. And so, also, the

soul of him who knows God hides with his Father as long as trouble lasts; but when it is overpast there is no more need of hiding.

To hide with God is not the common, but tne special condition of a moment: "Until these calamities be overpast" (Ps. 57, 1), or as said in Isaiah (xxvi, 20): "Until the indignation be overpast."

Even he who fears God, does not hide with Him in every time of need.

Trouble and care follow us after all the days of our life; our cross must be taken up each day anew. But, as a rule, in every day life the child of God calmly pursues his way in the assured confidence of Divine protection. He knows that his God fights for him, that God is his Shade, that God, as his Good Shepherd, leads him, and that when too violent an assault threatens, God covers him with His shield.

He then truly dwells with his God, and God does not forsake him, but it is the daily, common activity of faith, the operation of God's faithfulness and of the trustful confidence of his child.

But *hiding* is something else, something more, something connected with the hour of terror. When the waters have risen to the lips. When dark dread has suddenly overtaken the soul. When there is no way of escape. When dark night settles on the heart. When faith has no more confidence in itself.

Then there is a heroic taking hold of oneself, and as in a moment of danger the child runs to mother and hides himself in her dress, so does the soul fly to God and draw close up to Him, concealing itself in His sanctuary, and hiding with Him.

In doing this, the soul has no thought of anything, nor time for making a plan, but seeks, solely and alone this one thing of being hid in God, of being safe with Him, and of finding deliverance with Him.

If there ever were such a thing possible as a despair of faith, then hiding with God would be defined most aptly as the act of despair.

And although there never is despair in faith, there is despair in that the child of God in his anxiety despairs of himself, despairs of all help and deliverance from without, despairs of the working of the ordinary powers and gifts, which at other times are at his disposal, and now gives up even planning means of defence or resistance, because he feels that he can not face anything like this, that it is too strong for him, that he must unquestionably suffer defeat, and, therefore, has no courage left to run another futile risk, but throws pike and shield aside, and, helpless and powerless, takes refuge with his God, uttering the suppliant cry: "O God, fight *thou* for me;" and now hides himself with God.

When the chicks have crept under the wings of the mother-hen, the hawk that drew near no longer sees the chicks, but only the angry mother-hen. When the child runs to his mother and hides himself in her dress, the assailant has no longer to do with that helpless child, but with the mother, who lioness-like takes the part of her child. And so, when the child of God hides with his God, then the battle is no longer between him and the world, but between this world and God.

He who hides with God, has committed his cause to God. He withdraws himself from it. All his support and hope stands in the justice of his Lord. And only when the fact that God has righted all has become evident to him, does he come out from his hiding place again, in order to finish his course.

And, therefore, this hiding with God is not an act of

the soul that is resorted to every time anything goes wrong. It is an act which only takes place amid circumstances of utmost perplexity and stress.

Only when David's spirit was overwhelmed within him, and he was forced to exclaim: "My heart within me is desolate" (Ps. 143, 4), so that he "dwelt in darkness as those that have long been dead," was this cry for help wrung from his heart, and he was able to strike the keynote and to find the word which in moments of like stress the soldiers of Christ have echoed from their overwhelmed heart.

There is, however, also a hiding with God in times of oppressive anxiety and need, which are occasioned by the common course of life. For though the call to fight the battle of the Lord, as in the case with David, is only exceptional with believers, something of the nature of this battle repeats itself in every family and in every course of life.

Instances of mortal anxieties, which in circles of the world lead to despair and suicide, are almost without number; and this is the noteworthy point in faith, that that which through despair brings a man of the world to suicide, impels the believer to hide with his God.

They both give up, the man of the world and the child of God, but while the man of the world seeks surcease in self-destruction, just merely to get away from his troubles, the hope of eternal life dawns on the soul of the believer, and he also seeks to do away with himself, but only by not expecting anything more from his own capacities and powers, and by resigning everything to the hand of his God.

Thus one may be incurably ill and suffer agonies, and be no longer able to endure them and expect no more help from medicine, and yet he may hold out unto death, because he can hide with his God. So there can be despair in the family, through consuming sorrow, through bitter sin, through never-ending adversity, through lack of bread. So there can likewise be a grievance, through scorn and slander, so deep, so cruel, that there is no more restoration of honor possible, and life becomes a burden.

In all this, the cause of the Lord may be involved, but, for the most part, such is not the case, and all this dreadful darkness comes looming up from the common course of life. But even though the matter itself has nothing to do with the battle for God, yet of itself this battle enters in, just because these grievous troubles spend their wave-beat against the faith in the heart of God's child.

And then it can do no other than become a battle of faith, a combat between the authority of the world and the power which the faith will reveal. Anxiety would strike faith dumb, and faith will yet persist in crying for help against this mortal dread.

And in all such cases faith begins with resisting it, then tries to conjure the storm, then fights as long as strength holds out; and when at length it can do nothing more, and feels that it is ready to faint, then it puts forth the last heroic effort, by which it triumphs; for then it lets go, it gives up, in order now to leave it all with the Lord, and then the tempest-tossed and distressed one hides himself with his God, and his God binds up his wounds.

LIX

THOU DOST NOT ANSWER ME

A REAL prayer calls for an answer, for an answer from above, an answer from the side of God.

By no means every kind of prayer; the difference is very great between a purely formal muttering and an earnest outpouring of the soul in supplication.

You make a grave mistake, when you say that formal prayer is devoid of all merit. In formal prayer there is a prayer-preserving power. And this goes on until suddenly a spark from above enters this lifeless prayer, and at once true prayer bursts into flame from it.

But though it is altogether untrue, to say that he who prays in this purely formal way had better not pray at all, it must be maintained with equal emphasis that a lifeless prayer is an infected prayer, with respect to which the man of ardent prayer will presently invoke the cleansing power of the Atonement.

If you would examine the true character of prayer, you must first of all dismiss all thought of formal prayer; and center your attention solely and alone upon true supplication of the soul; and to all such supplication applies the fixed rule that he who prays awaits an *answer;* such as in olden time was given in a revelation, in a word spoken in the soul, through a vision, or by the appearance of an angel; or as is common now, through a direct answer to our prayer, through a meeting with some one, which comes as a glad surprise, or through an impression in the soul, which the Holy Spirit produces in us.

But it is always he who prays in a godly manner, who awaits an answer.

An answer, not only when in his prayer he asks for something, but also when he offers worship, ascribes praise or returns thanks. For he, too, who worships and offers praise or thanksgivings, by no means intends by these words merely to glorify the Name and Majesty of God, but desires very earnestly that his God, Whom he worships will accept this worship and thanksgiving from his lips and from his soul. Also this adoration, praise and worship are called offerings in Scripture. In Hosea (xiv, 2) they are called: "the calves of the lips," and in Isaiah (lvii, 19) "the fruit of the lips," in order to indicate the plain significance of an offering which such worship implies. And the historic record of the first fratricide tells us that there is an offering which God accepts, but also an offering which He rejects; and nowhere is it shown more clearly than in Cain's anger and wrath that, with every offering, the human heart awaits an *answer from God.*

But this answer does not always come. Sometimes it is deferred. And amid the sorrow of the heart and the distress of the soul, nothing is so painful nor yet so grievously hard to bear as that delay of an answer from the Lord.

See it in the complaint of Job (xxx, 20): "I cry unto thee, and thou dost not answer me; I stand up, and thou regardest me not." This is yet more strikingly evident in the twenty-second Psalm, where the Messiah complains: "My God, my God, why hast thou forsaken me! O my God, I cry in the daytime, but thou *answerest* me not, and in the night season also I take no rest." Or as it reads in Micah (iii, 7), "Then shall the seers be ashamed . . . for there is no answer of God."

The failure of obtaining an answer from God is, therefore, by no means always the fault of him who prays. With the Messiah, at least, this is unthinkable. Every one knows from his own prayer-life, that sometimes he has obtained an answer even with an accusing conscience, and that, on the other hand, not infrequently there came no answer from God, when his prayer had been most earnest and real.

In many instances no answer comes from God, because our prayer was sin in our lips. Giving no answer on the part of God certainly finds its cause and occasion, many times, in the sinful disposition of the heart of the worshiper during prayer.

But it is not true, that sin on the part of him who prays should be the only reason why God withholds His answer to prayer.

The most devout saints in Israel complained again and again that God did not answer their prayer, and this was ever a source of deep grief to their hearts; and this very grief was proof that their prayers had been earnest and sincere.

The *Lama Sabachthani* on the Cross shows the highest point which this sorrow of the human soul can reach; and on Golgotha it was more strikingly evident than it could be in any other case that withholding an answer on the part of God can be *intentional*.

On mount Carmel the question in dispute was an answer from Above.

Elijah and the priests of Baal both acknowledged that if God lives and man prays unto Him, a sign of life must proceed from the side of God as an answer to prayer.

The priests sought this answer with their Baal, and Elijah sought it with Jehovah. And all day long the cry went forth from a thousand mouths: "O Baal, answer us, answer us!" and they cut themselves with knives and lancets, because no answer came. Then Elijah prayed, and God answered by fire.

The question here at stake was, whether the God who was invoked *could* answer. A God who is not, and has no life, can not answer. Jehovah, Who lives in glory, could answer, and the dreadful answer came down from heaven by fire.

But ability to answer is not enough. God must also be *willing* to answer; and the *Sabachthani* is the very highest expression of the awful truth, that at times God is *intentionally* unwilling, and then not by chance or mistake, but, in accordance with His counsel and plan, He withholds His answer.

He withholds it even when His child continues to cry; withholds it even when the most earnest worshiper pours out his soul before Him; withholds it even when His own dear Son cries unto Him from the Cross.

And, therefore, in that very cry from the Cross, every soul that cries and gets no answer finds comfort. Otherwise the silence of God might readily bring the soul to despair. But when, as now, it appears, that even the prayer of God's own Son remained unanswered, why should a sinful suppliant complain or be driven to despair, when he too is numbered with the Son of God?

Is, then, this non-compliance, arbitrariness on the part of God?

Far from it. Such an idea is altogether unthinkable in regard to God. This withholding on the part of God from answering our prayer is an outflow of the love-life wherewith God encompasses the soul of His child.

The danger lies at hand, that in our prayer-life we seek the gifts of God and not God Himself. Our prayer is almost always the invocation of God's help, of His assistance, of His saving and blessing power; and our prayer so seldom reaches that stage where, entirely looking away from ourselves, from our own interest and from our own condition of need, we aim first of all at having dealings with God Himself.

The Our Father gives us instruction in this. It teaches us to pray first for the hallowing of God's Name, for the coming of His Kingdom, for the doing of His will, and then only it goes on to the prayer for our daily bread, for the forgiveness of our sins and for our deliverance from evil.

But this is the misery of our soul's estate, that even in our prayer, we so seldom stand at the sacred height of the Our Father.

This impairs the tender love-life between God and our soul.

Prayer for help in time of need is truly natural, but yet it always springs from the love which we bear to ourselves. In that case it is God Who must help us, assist us, save us, and so it comes to appear at times as though God merely exists for our sakes, for our benefit, to deliver us from trouble.

Love is different.

Love for God in prayer is that, first and most of all, we are concerned with that which glorifies God's Name, God's honor and God's Almighty Power.

If it be true, that love alone maketh rich and exalteth the soul, it is grace and nothing but seeking grace, when God the Lord by withholding for a time an answer to our prayer, initiates us more deeply into the life of love, represses our egoism in prayer, and comes to quicken love also in our life of prayer.

And therefore let not your soul become faint, when answer to your prayer tarries. Apart from the fact that the answer does not need to come at once, and that so often it has appeared later on, that in His own time God did send His answer, there is yet no single reason why, when God does not answer you, you should be discouraged.

Why should *you* be spared, what overtook the saints of

God in both the Old and New Testament times; yea, what your Savior suffered in the dark hour of His death upon the Cross?

This very withholding of an answer on the part of your God when your soul cries out to Him, may be the token that your God loves your soul better than you love it yourself. A token that He wants to raise the life of your soul and the life of your prayer to a higher vantage ground, that He wills to initiate you into the deeper ways of love, and that, by *not* answering your prayer, He prepares a more glorious future for you in which you shall pray better, supplicate more earnestly, and then receive a far more glorious answer.

Even among us you frequently see that a temporal withdrawal on the part of one who loves you is the means to quicken tenderer love.

And how much the more, then, is this true of Him Who Himself is Love, and Who by this very act of causing a cloud to draw between you and His Majesty, leads you up to higher and richer enjoyments of love.

LX

THE COURSES OF THE AGE
ARE HIS

WITH the completion of the year another limit is set upon your life and upon the number of your days.

A new year is brought into the allotted span of your life. It was 1903, and so it remained throughout all those months, all those weeks, all those days. But now it is ended. It is gone and will never return. Now you pass into 1904, and involuntarily you ask what this year will bring you and yours. Whether this year will outlive you, or whether you will outlive it. And this of itself prompts you, at the threshold of this year, to look up to your Father in heaven, to ask little but to trust much, to lay the hand upon the mouth, and, quietly as the weaned child, to await what God will bring upon you, and upon your dear ones.

"The courses of the age are his," declares the prophet (Hab. iii, 6, Dutch Ver.). God counts and reckons with centuries, as the dial of your clock, with hours and minutes. You are the little one in need of help, who counts with tenths of a second; your God bathes Himself in eternity with millions of time-periods at once. There is no comparison conceivable between your reckoning of time and the time-reckoning of God. With God it is the ever welling, the always bubbling up, the perennially bountiful, overflowing fountain of the eternal; with you it is the dripping of the moments, audible to you in the tick of the seconds. How unbearably long sometimes, when you must wait, five single minutes seem.

Never must this more than gigantic difference between

you and your God be lost from sight; a difference that stretches so far that it is absolutely impossible for us to make plain to our understanding the relation between our time and the eternity of our God, though we know that this relation must be there, and is.   Surely, if you die happily in Christ, you, too, shall one day enter upon this eternity, in order to enjoy therein great things eternally; but yet, even this shall never be to you the eternity of your God.   Though presently you live eternally, you have had a beginning, but your God never.   "Before the mountains were brought forth, yea, from eternity to eternity, thou art God" (Ps. 90).   And this never applies to man.

But however inconceivably great this difference is between you who live by hours, and your God to Whom the courses of the age belong, such is the grace of your Lord, that He breaks the period of your life-time, from the cradle to the grave, into parts of years, and into parts of days, and into parts of hours and minutes, and thereby imparts to your otherwise so short life, a breadth, a lengthening of duration and a richness of scope, which makes you bathe yourself in the little pond of the brief years of your life as in an ocean.

Time and its division into years and days has not been invented by you; it has been ordained for you by your God.   "And the evening and the morning were the first day" is the creation word, whereby this entire order and division of time was appointed in your behalf, before man had yet appeared on this earth.   Sun and moon and the rotation of the earth and the pulsation of the blood in your veins, have been disposed with the view of dissolving your life into minutes and seconds.   And it is through this wondrous means, wonderful in its simple design, that the grace and the loving kindness of your God has created, in behalf of you and because of you, a wealth of life in the past, now in the present, and before long in the future, whereby your life, which by itself is so short, becomes almost immeasurably long and great, both in retrospect and prospect.

Even that one year that now again lies behind you seemed so long to you that only a few of its more significant days are clearly remembered, and the new year that begins makes an impression as though it could never end.

Yea, and what is more, not only has your God Whose ways are everlasting, richly divided your life and thereby mightily enlarged it in your idea, but He entered and continually enters into this your minutely divided life with His faithfulness and Fatherly care.

From week to week, and from day to day, His compassion and His love are over you, new every morning and glistening with new brightness every evening. From hour to hour He goes before you on the way. And all along to the very subdivisions of your hours into minutes and seconds, the pulsation of your blood in your heart is His work. He takes notice of every sigh that from your heart goes up toward Him.

He is the Father of the everlasting ages, Who from sheer grace, for the sake of enrichment, divides the life of His child even to its minutest parts, and enters into every one of these parts and subdivisions with His grace to protect you.

But if God Himself thus divides your life, and enters into every part of it with His grace, it is incumbent upon you, on the other hand, from this temporarily divided life to reach out after the courses of the age, and lift up yourself to the eternal.

In Revelation (x, 6) we read, that the angel, who stood by the sea, lifted up his hand to heaven, and "sware by him, who liveth for ever and ever, *that there should be time no longer.*"

Time is a form of existence that is given us by grace, but it is unreal; eternity alone is real. In eternity alone our destiny lies, and from the viewpoint of eternity alone can your existence, your future, your destiny be understood.

Whatever year of your life you may consider, it is never understood by itself. Before God, your whole life, with all its years, is one plan, one design, one whole. This plan, this design did not begin just with your birth but traces its lines backwards to the life of your parents and grandparents. And, likewise, in looking forward, this plan does not end with your death but extends across death and the grave into the everlasting ages of eternity. Even though you live here seventy or eighty years, this part of your life which you live on earth shrinks almost into nothing, when you put it alongside of the thousands and tens of thousands of years that await you in eternity. Your whole life on earth is nothing but the starting of the line to the first station in order after that to begin the real journey through your field of eternal life.

And not to understand this plainly and clearly, is the great cause of the discouragement that overtakes so many people, time and again, as they journey through this short earthly life.

A year of your life can never be understood by itself. Every year of your life must be viewed in connection with your whole life here, and with your whole life in the hereafter, because it stands so, and not otherwise, before God, and is so, and not otherwise, to be explained.

He Who fashions, forms and prepares you for eternity is the Lord. In His fashioning of your heart, in the forming of your person, in His preparation of your spirit within you for eternity, the courses of the age are His. Not what would provide you pleasure and love for the moment is the standard here; but what, in the course of the ages, you are to become, governs His plan of your life and existence.

On this long way, He leads you now through darkness and depth, then again through sunshine on the mountains of His holiness, but His plan, His design regarding you always goes through. And not what would smile on you this year, but what must happen to you in order to carry out His eternal plan concerning you, determines and decides what this year shall bring you. And why it must be so and not otherwise you can not understand now, but will hereafter.

He who forgets this, has no peace; but he who with his whole soul enters into this doing of his God, rests, whatever comes, in his Father's faithfulness.

If, now, caught within the narrow bounds of time, you continue to reckon by the day, by the week, and your heart becomes bitter every time that that day things go wrong or bring nothing but disappointment, then you become the prey of irresolution and gloom. Then it becomes one unbroken recital of complaint, a steady wail and lament; and the habit of seeing all things black overmasters you. Then there is no courage of faith, no inspiration to work out your destiny, no uplifting joy in God. Thence it comes that thousands upon thousands become either coldly indifferent, or continue the weary struggle with dejection and disheartenment till the end of their days. And he who so lives, what is he other than a playball before the wind of the day, and how far he sinks below his dignity as man! For does not the Prophet say (Eccles. iii, 11) that "God hath set eternity in the heart?" And "eternity in the heart," what else can it mean, than that God created in us the capacity to lift ourselves up from this whirling of the flakes of time around us, to the fixedness of the eternal?

With this "eternity in the heart," let every child of God, therefore, bravely face the newly-opening year. He knows that he worships a God Whose are the everlasting ages, and that therefore God designs and also directs his life only in keeping with what eternity shall one day demand. He prays that it may be peace and joy, for after happiness his heart thirsts. But if this year he must go through a period when God puts him in the smelting furnace, or makes finer cuttings on the diamond of his soul, then, though tears make his eyes glisten, he will nobly bear up in exaltation of faith; for then it is certain that he is in need of this, that it can not be otherwise, and that, if it did go otherwise, his life would be a failure forever.

To have to undergo a painful operation is hard, and yet the sick one willingly submits, and in the end pays large sums of money to the operator, because he knows, that this drastic treatment alone could save him.

And just like this, God's child stands before his Father in heaven. Not he, but God alone, must know what is indispensable and necessary for him this year, and what, in view of his *permanent* fashioning, this year must bring him. And should it be the case that this year such a Divine operation proves to be necessary, he will not murmur and complain, but willingly submit himself to God, yea, though the waves of sorrow should go over him, he will nevertheless rejoice in his God, knowing that what He doeth, *must* be done, both for the sake of His honor and for his own highest good.

LXI

PRAISE HIM UPON THE STRINGS AND PIPES

In urging and driving the soul to God, Scripture is altogether irrepressible.

What presses itself upon you in God's Word—the exalted command to sobriety and purity, the great stress not to pursue your way with a proud look, but with humility—is no less the very sharp admonition to be on your guard in every possible way against the deadening power of money and to consecrate your goods by generous giving. But nothing of all this can be compared to the impelling force wherewith in God's Word the Holy Ghost, sparing nothing, restlessly urges and drives you to worship, to seek fellowship with the Lord, to cultivate nearness of the soul to God.

The Scripture even places itself at a still higher viewpoint.

In its estimation, it is not enough that the saints magnify Him, Whose is, in the most absolute sense, the Majesty and the Power. *Every* child of man must glorify God's Name. But even so, the circle is not fully drawn of what must render praise to God. In this circle the Scripture includes, together with everything that is called man, the hosts of angels. "Praise the Lord, all ye his hosts, ye ministers of his, that do his pleasure" (Ps. 103, 21)— All Cherubim, Archangels and Seraphim.

And then this circle descends again from heaven, in order also to include the inanimate creation. Not only must everything that hath breath praise the Lord. All His works, in all places of His dominion, must glorify His renown. "Praise ye him, sun and moon!" "Praise him, all

374

ye stars of light." "Praise the Lord, ye snow and vapors, stormy wind, fulfilling his word" (Ps. 148). Mountains and hills, cedar trees on Lebanon, and likewise beasts and all cattle, creeping things and the hosts of birds that sing among the branches, all must make God great, all must pour forth abundant speech. There must be no people and no language, where their voice of praise and laudation is not heard. "O Lord, our Lord, how excellent is thy name in all the earth" (Ps. 8, 9).

Thus you, as man, are called to praise the Lord, in the midst of a creation, which is vocal with rhythmic melody. This music of nature itself entices you to chant the praises of your God, and presently returns an echo to your hymnody of praise and adoration, that resounds among the spheres.

This is not a dead creation stricken with dumbness, but a creation that lives, that utters speech. And he who has an ear to understand this language and this music of creation overhears in it a purling stream of worship which is in perfect accord with the music and the language of adoration in his own heart.

And between these two, these impulses of your own heart and these undulations of sound in creation, Scripture has laid a tie in the emotional sphere of the world of sounds, in the wealth of musical art, in life's treasure of sanctified song.

Psalm upon Psalm calls you, not alone to overhear the voice of the Lord in creation, and you yourself, with your human voice, to glorify your God, but also to praise Him with pipes and strings (Ps. 150, 4), with lute and harp, with high sounding cymbals and joyful noise.

Playing upon instruments, therefore, is no secondary, but an indispensable constituent part of worship; a means that God has placed at your disposal by which to enjoy yourself more richly in His praise and adoration; and through the world of music also to come closer to Him with your soul.

Grant that praise in the house of prayer with only human voices can be solemn and deeply impressive, even then, this human singing is musical art, and improves in merit and gains in effect, when it is artistically trained and developed.

Joyful sound from the throat and joyful sound from the harp, both take hold of the harmony which God hath included in a wondrous world about you, and which, at one time through your throat and at another time by playing on the organ, or on the harp, you quicken, and set in harmonious motion with the world of your heart.

And whether to this end you strike metal, or cause taut strings to vibrate, or by your own breath drive out sound from flute or trumpet, it is always again a motion, an impulse in your soul, which interprets itself in a vocal utterance of the world of sound, which in all spheres surrounds you.

Not the singer, not the harpist creates this world of sounds. God created it. It was there before the first man for the first time heard the joyful noise from between the branches of the trees in the garden. It lies enfolded in the air, which is susceptible to vibration and undulation, all around you. And to you, as man, it is given, by your voice or by your hand, to set this wondrous world in motion through vibration.

And when your throat, or your hand through the instrument, sets these sounds in motion, then it is as though the undulation, the motion, the inner song of your heart flows out in it, catches an echo from it, is carried along with it, is relaxed by it and wonderfully enriched. Enriched in no small part by the fact, that, at the same moment, others together with yourself undergo like emotions, experience like sensations in the soul, and that thus your praise and adoration through song and organ-play flow together with theirs into one mighty stream of adoring love and praise.

Yea, more still, because these vibrations and these undulations of sounds react upon you as a power from without and lose themselves in the infinite, it is as though this glory "when the voice may mate itself with the sound of strings," brings you into fellowship with God Himself, even as this praise and adoration ascends from out this earth and passes through the heavens till it reaches the spheres where angels finger the golden cithern and everything merges into one grand chorus of praise and adoration around God's Throne.

Altogether wondrously the human throat and voice have been adapted by God to this world of harmonious sounds, and there is no joyful sound of earth that excels the loveliness of the human voice.

It is a gift unequally divided. In countries of southern climate, people are endowed with more mellowness of voice than people in northern lands; and even in the same regions, the difference is very marked between the discordant street-singing, and the rhythmical, developed voice of the artist singer.

But whatever difference may present itself, the human voice remains in its wondrous ranges a joyful sound of heavenly origin; and only in the realm of glory that is to come will it be heard in all its purity, in all its wealth of expression and cadence, before the Throne of the Lord.

And yet, by itself, the human voice does not suffice and therefore God has endowed it with an equally wondrous complement in the musical instrument.

A piece of brass, a tightly-stretched hide, presently

strings, a horn from an animal's head, even down to a reed cut by the riverside, such are the seemingly futile, and yet, in their effect, the glorious means, which God himself has ordained for man as supports for the human voice, to unite human voices in grand chorus, and to bring the human heart into co-operation and into harmony with the world of sounds that surrounds it.

Herein, also sin works, and has worked. A musical art has developed itself which aims to exist for the sake of man and not for the sake of God. An art which strives after no higher calling than to please the ear, to make the emotions experience unholy sensations, to provide a wealth of pleasure without higher aim.

A sin, less in evidence with the great masters of music, than with a public estranged from God, which abuses the products of art purely for their own pleasure, even where these aimed to glorify God and to inspire what is holy.

This accounts for the distaste for this secular music, which is in evidence among a more godly generation.

And this is beneficial, for music is never without influence for good or evil, and vitiated music is a power that degrades. It counts its victims by the thousands.

But what should not be countenanced is that, because of this abuse, God's children should leave out vocal and instrumental music from the services of the sanctuary.

Rather offset this abuse by the sanctified use, in godly circles, of voice and of stringed instruments.

And therefore the revival of sacred music is always a sign of a higher inspiration of life.

A Christian nation that does not sing and play upon musical instruments for the glory of God, enfeebles itself.

LXII

IN SALEM IS HIS TABERNACLE

Salem is the shortened form for Jerusalem. "In Salem is his tabernacle," means in its first, literal sense, that the Tabernacle which first was carried about from place to place in the wilderness, and since had tarried now here, now there, had finally been removed to the top of Mount Zion, and that thus the dwelling place of the Lord God was within Jerusalem's walls.

There is something strange in this to us, and the question arises of itself: How can our God be *omnipresent*, and at the same time dwell in one particular city, on one particular mountain-top, in one tent or temple? And then, no less this other question: If in the old dispensation God in the earth had His tabernacle in Salem and His dwelling place in Zion, was not Israel under the old dispensation richer than we are now? Have we, then, not gone backward, instead of forward? Is the Gospel that has no more knowledge of Jerusalem on earth not poorer in that case, than the ritual of shadows, that could point to the place of God's Presence on earth?

Especially, when in the Psalms we read of "praise" that waiteth in Zion, and of a "doorkeeper" in the house of the Lord, clearness of insight on the part of every child of God is here greatly to be desired. Though one begins in early youth to learn these sentences and recite them half thoughtlessly, with the advance of our years the consciousness demands increasing clearness.

This clearness is not furnished by the study of history. Here everything depends upon your personal, your intentional communion and fellowship with the living God;

upon the heart of all religion, upon the urgent effort of the soul to be more and more in continuous touch with God.

And here you always face an antithesis which you never can or shall solve with your understanding, and before which all science stands helpless, to wit: the all-dominating antithesis between the *Infinity* of the Lord and the *finiteness* of every creature.

In two ways it has been tried to put a bridge across this gap.

It has been tried *by man* in vain, but it has been brought about by God.

In vain it has been tried by the heathen, in that they have confined the infinity of the Almighty to the finite forms of an image; and the result was spirit-deadening, and, at length, petrifying idolatry.

But it has been brought about by God in that He has reversed all polytheism and idolatry by centralizing His worship originally in one place, by barring from His Temple on Zion every image of Himself, and by maintaining the spiritual character of His worship. It has been performed by God in that, in the end, after the dispensation of shadows had fulfilled its calling, He gave us His temple in the Incarnated Word, and, on the day of Pentecost, extended this Temple to His whole congregation, even the Israel of the New Covenant.

Along this wondrous way of our Lord the end has been reached, that now, without in the leastwise weakening the sense of God's Infinity or Omnipresence, God's children know full well that in Christ they must seek to have contact with their God; that in the Communion of the saints they can enjoy His fellowship; and that through the Holy Ghost they see their own heart fashioned more and more into a dwelling place of God in the Spirit.

The clear idea to which this leads is that in no single

place, in whatever darkness and amid whatever trouble, is the child of God ever grieved by the vexing thought that his God is far distant from him, and is not to be found in his immediate presence by prayer.

Wherever God's child kneels down, he knows that God is there, that He is close by, and listens to his prayer, that He sees and searches him, knows his way in every particular; and that no heart-string can vibrate with sorrow or with joy but God knows in advance what sound it will emit. "There is not a word in my tongue, but lo, O Lord, thou knowest it altogether. Thou compassest my path and my lying down, and art acquainted with all my ways (Ps. 139, 3).

But also, on the other hand, the child of God is constantly under the sense of the Lord's Majesty and loftiness. The glory and the holiness of the Lord must not be lost from our idea by His descent to us. And to this end He has so appointed it, that we realize that this selfsame God Who is ever close to every one of us is enthroned in the heavens, that there alone He unveils His Majesty, and for no single moment is lost in the smallness, insignificance and finiteness of our human life.

The life above and the life here on earth, are to our perception distinctly separated, and not here, but only when we shall have passed through the gate of death, shall our eye see Him in the fullness of His glory in the Jerusalem, that is above.

But between these two lies the transition. The transition in Christ, the transition in the congregation of saints, the transition through the indwelling of the Spirit in our heart; and this is now the Tabernacle in Salem, this is His dwelling place on Zion, this is His Presence amidst His Israel.

This operates back and forth.

In Christ our flesh enthroned in heaven, and the Spirit descending into our heart, and, as well as in Christ as in the Holy Ghost, God Himself worshiped by us.

Here is the mystery.

The Son of man, one of us, our Brother, near to us, and in our nature entered into heaven, not standing outside of God, but Himself being God, and thereby realizing the most intimate fellowship, which is conceivable between God and the children of men.

And, on the other hand, as Christ is for all, the Holy Spirit descending and taking up His abode in the heart of every child of God, separately, and thus founding a Salem in the hidden parts of our own soul, where God Himself indwells, where His Divine life inspires us, the Source of all our holier and higher emotions, sensations and impulses.

And these two continually operate upon one another and mutually complement each other.

So that there is no fellowship with Christ without the indwelling of the Holy Ghost, and, conversely there is no indwelling of the Holy Ghost without the foundation of our fellowship with God in Christ.

Our nature in Christ in heaven, and the Holy Ghost indwelling in our heart on earth.

Thus the bridge of the holy life is laid by God Himself, with one terminal anchored in the heavens, the other resting in the center of our own human heart.

But even these two points of support need in turn a point of union, and this they find in the congregation of the saints.

Every one feels for himself that when he is in touch with the saints on earth, the fellowship with God becomes of itself more real, and how this fellowship loses in clearness and serenity, when he has no other human contact than with the people of the world.

The deep joy of the sacrament of Holy Communion comes to him from the focus of this fellowship. This sacrament testifies to him the glory of the Christ, but in the congregation of believers, not outside of it. And, therefore, no higher and holier institution could have been given to man, than when in the night in which He was betrayed, Christ brake the bread and poured the wine, and called His holy Supper into being.

Here is the center, here is the confluence of all the lines along which fellowship is established between our soul and God.

Nothing, therefore, is more heinous than the sinful doing of those, who by dissension and by passionate contention for the right of their own particular views, cause this fellowship of God's saints in and outside of the Church to weaken and to grow faint.

A new commandment our Savior gave us, that we should *love* one another. This new love which He recommended to us, is the most tender love imaginable on earth, since it is in the stream of this new love that our God will draw near unto us, and will lift us up to Himself.

And he who fails of understanding this new love, and uses the Church and the holy fellowship of love to propagate his own particular views, achieves no other end than the breaking down of Salem. He puts to naught the tabernacle of God, and, as far as he is able, impedes the fellowship with Him.

LXIII

THE NIGHT IS FAR SPENT

AFTER our conversion, after we are brought to our Redeemer, we are here on earth in a middle state until our death.

"The night is far spent, the day is at hand," but as yet, it is not noon. That only comes when the glory of Christ shall break in upon all spheres. Until that hour we are ever approaching the day in its fullness, even though in fact we still walk in twilight. We truly walk in the light, but that light is still dim.

Even after conversion we continue, therefore, provisionally in a certain kind of sleep, and can only gradually shake ourselves free from its after effects.

So it is now, and so it was in the days of S. Paul when the change of conversion, especially with respect to outward conditions, was so much more overwhelming than now. Speaking for himself and for the converts at Rome, the Apostle emphatically declares: "It is now (*i.e.*, so and so many years after their conversion) high time to awake out of this sleep (which is still upon us), *for now is our salvation nearer than when we believed.*" And then he adds: "The night is far spent, the day is at hand" (Rom. xiii, 11).

This, of course, detracts nothing from the incontrovertible truth, that he who came to conversion today, and tomorrow falls asleep in his Savior, is sure of his everlasting blessedness. But it does say, that he who after conversion is given yet many years of life upon earth, gradually passes from the twilight into ever clearer light, gets ever farther away from the shades of night, and continually feels the closer approach of the light of day.

In nature there is no sudden departure of the night, in order with equal suddenness to give place to the day with the noontide sun. In nature there are transitions from darkness into glimmering light and from dawn into broad daylight. Transitions which are of longer duration in some parts of the world than in others, but which occur everywhere.

And so it is in the spiritual life. One does not become altogether holy in his deliberations, in his tendencies, in his actions and daily manner of life all at once. From being alienated from the life of God, he does not with a single bound come into full fellowship with Him. Where it was night in the soul, the sun, after conversion does not immediately stand at the zenith. Here also are transitions. Even in this way, that it begins with a first ray of light; for the first time the clouds part; for the first time the mists break, and higher brightness strikes the eye of the soul. And then it goes on farther and farther—from grace to grace. With one, more quickly than with another. First a waking out of the sleep of error and sin. Then a shaking of oneself loose from this sleep. After that, a waking up. And presently, a going out into the light.

And in this very transition hides the restlessly moving power of the Christian life. It is not a standing still and remaining where we are, but a going on and a reaching forward to make advance.

It is first a star that rises out of Jacob. Presently it is the sun of salvation which stands at the horizon. And finally the sun spreads effulgent light on those who first wandered about in darkness.

It is all one procession of triumph and victory for those to whom the lack of such light would mean an endless night. And it is a waxing light, a light that rises ever higher, and gradually becomes more clear. And your life as a Christian would have no worth in this world, if the eye of your soul, in its gradual accommodation to the stronger light of grace, did not acquire by this light an ever clearer insight into the richness of God's compassion.

Herein is a threefold increase.

Increase in inner strength; increase in an ever more effective exhibition of the powers of the kingdom; and increase in your fellowship with your God; *i.e.*, in the heart of all religion.

There is increase in inner strength, insomuch as more abundant strength flows out to you from the heavenly Kingdom. The night is far spent and already clearer light shines down into your soul. This is the favor of God, which He shows you in your personal life. A brighter glow in your personal sky. Less night, more day, and in that day more and clearer light reflected on your pathway.

But this increase in inner strength leads necessarily to an increase in the exhibition of your power. He who is obliged to travel before dawn makes little headway, but when brighter daylight falls on his path, he quickens his pace. Hence the admonition of the Apostle: "Let us therefore cast off the works of darkness, and let us put on the whole armour of light. Let us walk honestly as in the day."

As long as light and darkness struggle with each other in the soul, we constantly hesitate and our foot slips. But when a fuller light dawns on our pathway, we gain in moral courage. We become more animated. There enters into us a spirit of sacred daring. More light shines out from us on our loved ones and companions. Instead of tottering, the step becomes more firm. Instead of daring to venture half-way, there is completion and consummation.

But it does not end here.

However high a level our *moral* development may reach, our development of *Christian* character is more richly significant, and the richest gains which the clearer shining of heavenly light within brings us is the increase of intimacy and tenderness in our fellowship with God.

A dark and anxious night weighs on the heart of mankind through the stress of error and sin.

God is, and God is close by, but although mankind feels its way in seeking after God, it is not aware of Him, it does not see Him, it discovers nothing of His holy Presence.

What compasses it about and distresses it is fearful darkness, and in that darkness the sense of uncertainty, and of anxiety, and of suspicion, like a serpent steals into the heart.

In this dreadful darkness lies the explanation of all idolatry and of all heathen anguish. And therefore Simeon makes his boast in Christ as "a light," so great, so wondrously beautiful, which having come down from heaven's throne, lightens the darkened vision of the Gentiles.

The most dreadful darkness of the peoples is that they know not God, that an eternal night shuts them off from God, that no ray of light from above illumines their pathway, and that without God in the world they walk out from this world to the Judgment of God.

Therefore, every one who is converted is called a *child of light*.

The redeemed not merely walk in the light, but from that light they are born as children of God.

Light from above in the soul, even though that soul caught but a single ray, is inward wealth. It is peace for fear; rest for anxiety; confidence for despair; courage for inward faintness.

This light shines on his way. It makes him know his own heart and the heart of his fellowmen. It brings wisdom for self-conceit. It enriches his entire human existence.

But highest and holiest of all is the fact that this light gradually discloses to him the way of access to his God. It lifts the ban that separated and excluded him from God. And now by degrees, begins the tender, blessed life which enters upon the hidden walk with God and makes him discover God at every step of his life's way—as his Father Who loves him, as his Shepherd Who leads him.

And this fellowship, this walk with God, this dwelling in the tent of the Lord, does not continue to be what it provisionally was, but it advances, it makes progress, it gains, it increases in tenderness, warmth and clearness.

It is not only that the night, which to the eye of his soul hung also over God, is far spent, but from that night he gets ever farther away. It is continually the moving away of oneself from that night to ever clearer day. Until at length, there comes a fellowship with God, which the world does not know nor understand but which to him is the highest reality, the ever more abounding flowing fountain of the strength of his life.

Now, there are too many Christians, alas! who even after their conversion, continue to love to slumber, and therefore enjoy nothing of this more intimate fellowship with their God.

These are the sick ones among the brethren, from whom no virtue can go out.

But there are those, God be praised, who know nothing of standing still; who enter ever more deeply into the secrecies of the infinite, and now waken every morning with their God, and with their God labor all day long, and with their God retire to their rest by night.

And these are the salt of the earth, the salt even of God's Church among the saints, who preserve His church from desecration, and the congregation of the Lord, from dissolution.

LXIV

WITHOUT GOD IN THE WORLD

DENIAL of God is on the increase. It steps out into the open and lays aside every mask. It does this not merely with single individuals but in broad and influential circles.

Twenty and more years ago this was different. An individual atheist, here and there would openly proclaim his denial of God and thereby arouse aversion, which with many people turned into abhorrence. And although, even then, the ranks were broad of those who in fact had broken with all religion, yet any one of them would have resented the implication of being called an atheist. This they certainly were not. They had broken with your views regarding Divine things to be sure. But, as they said, the eye of their soul was ever open to the eternal, and the desire of their heart still went out after the Unknown, the Infinite.

Now, however, a further step is taken. Even the semblance of being religious can be laid aside without fear of singularity. Atheists have discovered that they are far more numerous, especially among the cultivated classes, than they had dared to surmise. They see that, when they come out openly with a denial of God, public opinion takes it calmly, and sometimes even hails it as an evidence of honesty. Even among the faithful, we have gradually become so accustomed to the increase in numbers of those who deny God, that we scarcely any more remember the shudder which this open denial occasioned in better days.

This is significant.

When for the first time a child hears his father or mother evilly spoken of, his feeling reacts against it. And when, in the course of years, he has grown accustomed to such talk about his parents, and can listen to it calmly, he has suffered moral loss.

The same holds true of a people with respect to their king or government.

When infraction of the royal majesty first begins, expressions of unbounded indignation will be heard among the people. But when one constantly moves in circles in which this infringement is common, in the end he ceases to be affected by it. Respect for what is high disappears.

And in the same way, people have lost something of the golden dust of their wings, when they have become so accustomed to the idea of the denial of God that no more protest is raised against the disavowal.

Especially with respect to this do "evil communications corrupt good manners."

Here, all unobservedly, a poison works that extinguishes higher aspirations and unnerves the elasticity of the confession of one's faith.

"Without God in the world" is not yet the most dangerous form in which this denial of God presents itself. Many are atheists from sheer indifference. They care for nothing. Others deny God because in their pursuit after sinful pleasures, they will not brook a troubled conscience. Others, again, are atheistic because in their own wisdom they are too proud to bow before God. But each of these three groups rather maintain silence regarding God, than, from enmity, drive propaganda against the faith. They live without God in the world, but they are not fanatics to the extent that they try to banish God from the world.

When it comes to this, spiritual infatuation reaches its highest degree and every prospect of recovery is cut off.

That this God-denying fanaticism now and then obtains public hearing, and that some people purposely circulate tracts bearing the most shameful titles, in order to slander the faith in God, and make it appear ridiculous, is a most serious menace to the life of a nation.

It betrays the presence in the national life of a poison that insidiously works harm and breaks national elasticity.

It was among the heathen that such slander of the gods was first made punishable. And almost every nation that first was great and afterward went down, shows in history this sad process, that it began by becoming wealthy; that from the wealth proceeded moral decay; that moral decay led to religious indifference; that then, in the more cultivated circles, people lived "without God in the world;" and that at length a fanaticism broke out against all religion, whereby in the end the people became altogether degenerate and were overtaken by ignominious ruin.

In the days of S. Paul, like conditions of ungodliness prevailed in Ephesus, and of those who there had been converted to Christ, S. Paul, who knew them, wrote that even they in former times had been without hope and without God in the world (Eph. ii, 12).

And this expresses in a painful way what we see on a broad scale all around us.

Though here we find a difference in degree.

There are those who, year after year, live without any more thought of God and have nothing to say of Him. No single religious book ever comes into their home. They have no family altar and they let their children grow up without any religion. They have no regard for baptism. They marry outside of the Church. They bury their dead as we bury a dog. Their lives are consummated without God in the world.

But most people have not as yet gone to such lengths. Especially at marriage, they cannot yet dispense with the solemnity of the church service. Many have their children baptized. When sickness, with danger of death, climbs in through their windows, they still call at times upon God. There are some among them who, in behalf of their growing children, do not consider religion a superfluity, and give their servants time to attend church. But apart from these minor exceptions, they live altogether "without God in the world."

And the worst of it is that they can live on in this way, year in and year out, and not feel unhappy about it. The need of fellowship with a higher life has almost altogether been taken out of their heart, so that they do not miss the life with God. A life without God has become to them second nature. When it is over, all is done. There is no home-sickness within them after higher things. From one pleasure they go to another. However small a measure of religion you would hand out to them, it would give them no satisfaction, but prove a burden.

The very same tenor of mind and heart which was abroad for two thousand years in the declining heathen world of the Roman Empire, has made itself master of these present-day out-and-out people of the world.

This does not estrange them from higher endeavor. They are lovers of art. They take part in works of philanthropy. With respect to the development of the people at large, as they understand it, they are enthusiasts. Sometimes they dote on ideals which awaken poetic talent in them.

But rather than being trained thereby *to worship*, this higher, more ideal life becomes to them an occasion to interpret all religion as superfluous.

Religion may be good for the lesser man in the *lower*

walks of life. The upper classes have outgrown it. To "live without God in the world" is in their eye the very means by which to secure high places in the life of the world.

Love alone can here work salvation.

At Ephesus people who had lived "without God in the world" were, nevertheless, converted unto Christ by the hundreds, not through reproach and harsh judgments, but through the love wherewith the Apostles approached them.

In that Apostolic love shone the reality of a life in the world *with God*. And it is this reality of a life in the world with God that has thawed out hearts and captured them.

Of course this "reality" is not divorced from the Creed. There is no greater witness for the truth and the facts of the Gospel than S. Paul. Neither is this reality of a life with God without forms. Preaching, Baptism and Holy Communion have ever stood in the foreground. But (and this accounts for the power) back of the Creed and that ministry of forms, was the work of the Holy Spirit, the indwelling of the Holy Ghost in the heart, a life in constant fellowship with God.

If, then, in these times the Church of the Lord would raise a barrier again in the way of this wide-spreading godlessness, let her maintain her stand by the Articles of the Faith, let her continue faithful in the sacred ministries of the sanctuary, but, before all things else, let her see to it that back of these forms the essence be not lost, and let her cultivate with young and old the high, spiritual reality of the life with God.

This demands effort.

For you must live in the world. Only at your death does God call you away. And in the world almost everything draws you away from God. Not only wealth and temptation, but also the incessant activity of life, labor that is strenuous and exacting, a multiplicity of interests, much trouble and sorrow.

This accounts for the fact that among confessing Christians there are all too many who, while they count themselves Christians, can live for hours, some times whole days without thinking of God. Even in their prayer the mind wanders. They perceive scarcely anything of being near unto God and of living with their God in constant fellowship of the Spirit.

And this lack can not be made good by faithful confession of the faith, neither by bearing constant witness.

Much activity and good works can not take the place of the reality of a life with God in the world.

The lamp can not burn unless it is continually replenished with oil.

Not in us, but in God alone, is the power and might that can stem unbelief in the world. And in this conflict you can only be an instrument in the hand of your Lord, when His might inwardly inspires you, when His Spirit inwardly drives you, and when to be near unto God, and to live with God in the midst of the world has become to you your second, your regenerated nature.

LXV

I WILL WALK AMONG YOU

Not only personally, but also *collectively* you must stand in living fellowship with your God.

The personal is that which touches only the world of our own heart. *The collective* is everything that we go through together, go through with others with whom we are connected by fixed ties. You have a collective life in your family, in your church, in your nation and in your trade or profession. And it is not enough that you have living fellowship with your family, in the hidden places of your soul. No, also in your family, in your church and in your social life this fellowship with your God must be your strength. And this fellowship with God must find its expression in this, viz., that *God walks with you* and that *you walk with Him.*

Not only the first, but also the second.

It is not enough, by any means, that both personally and collectively you have blessed experiences of a steady outgoing of your soul after God. This can always be the practice of communion with God *from afar.* The walking together on the highway of life demands, on the contrary, that you go to God, that God comes to you, that the holy meeting be mutual, and that henceforth, at the hand of God, you continue the journey of your life.

If it has come to this with you personally, you are a Christian soul. If it has come to this with your family, you live in a Christian home. If such is the case with your .church, you enjoy a church life which is not merely in name, but in reality Christian. And when in social or political circles you have the same experience with those with whom you are in contact by reason of like calling or conviction, then here too, not merely has the Christian banner been uplifted, but it is a truly Christian movement in which you, together with others, suffer and strive.

To Moses and Israel the Lord expressed this as follows: "I will walk among you" (Lev. xxvi, 12). Of Abraham it is said personally that he walked with God. But with Moses there is mention of the *collective* fellowship of God with His people. Hence it does not say: "I will walk with thee, who art the shepherd of my people," but quite differently: "I will walk in the midst of you" (Dutch version). The Lord going forth with His people, and the people at every step of the way being conscious of the nearness of God and of fellowship with Him.

Thus there can be a mutual fellowship, a walking together in the way of holy love. There can also be a walking together *in sin* on the part of man, and *in anger* on the part of God.

"If ye will walk *contrary unto me*, said the Lord, then will I also walk *contrary unto you*, and will punish you yet seven times for your sins" (Lev. xxvi, 23, 24).

"Contrariness" is what we call *antipathy*.

You can walk by the way with some one who is antipathetic to you, whose presence disturbs you and whose company you wish were away. He who feels and observes that God walks with him by the way, and still inclines unto sin, feels himself constrained by the presence of the Lord. Just as a child who is bent upon mischief, does not dare to do wrong as long as his father or mother is close by, but takes his chance the moment his father or mother has gone, so a Christian does not dare to carry his sinful design into execution as long as he feels that God is close by.

If only he could outrun God. But this is impossible. He

can close his eye so as not to see God, but even then the Lord continues to reveal His Presence in the conscience.

This gives rise to the unholy struggle of *willingness* to sin, and of *not being able* to do it because God stands in the way. And then it comes to pass, when you do not let go your sin, that contrariness against your God springs up in your heart, the deeply sinful antipathy against God's nearness. And since nothing so angers God as the inclination, the tendency of your heart not to seek Him, but to be rid of Him, His favor towards you turns likewise into holy antipathy. And so you walk with your God on the pathway of your life in enmity and in bitternesses, grieving the Holy Spirit.

This does not happen with a child of the world.

The child of the world does not walk with God. He travels his pathway of life *alone*. He perceives nothing, feels nothing, sees nothing of the nearness of God. And therefore the child of the world *can not* fall into sin in this way. *His* sin bears an altogether different character.

But if you belong to the redeemed of the Lord, if you walk with the people in whose midst the Lord walks, then either that which is sinful in your life must be resisted, or, if you yet continue in it, the dreadful sin of *contrariness*, of antipathy against God, germinates, you injure your own inner life and presently your very lot in life.

And that which here misleads with so great menace is, that this contrariness, this antipathy only shows itself at the point of your particular sin. Thus arise these distorted conditions, that in all other ways you seek your God, that you are zealous in his service, and devoutly practise the habit of prayer, but as often as this particular sin wakes up again in you, the balance at once is lost, and you, perceiving that God continues to walk with you, find no more comfort in that blessed nearness, but merely a hindrance to your sin. And if then you still persist in your sin the most dreadful *contrariness* follows, even the ominous *contrariness* of your God.

Such is not the case with sin that is committed because your strength fails. For then, when sin crouches at the door of your heart, the heart will take refuge with God. Then you feel that Satan aims to undo you, and you hold yourself the more fast to God that He may protect you against Satan.

And though you may fall even then, in the very act of it you will take refuge with the unseen Companion Who walks by your side. You will call upon Him for forgiveness and help. And He Who knoweth whereof you are made will take compassion on you and will keep you from self-destruction.

But, then, on your part must be the earnest endeavor, when you walk the way with your God, to follow Him, and not choose a path of your own in the expectation that God will follow you.

The goings of God, both in history and now, are altogether such as lead to the kingdom of heaven and result in making great His Name.

What now is the "way" of your life? What is your purpose in life? Whither does your path lead?

A child of God prays every day: "Hallowed be thy Name. Thy Kingdom come. Thy will be done." And if this threefold prayer is not a mere form of words, but the compass of his life, the way of his life will coincide with the way of God. Then you walk with God in the selfsame direction, with the same end in view. Your God in His infinite greatness, and you in the vain littleness of your quickly-passing life. But nevertheless as one of the drops you move along in the wave-beat of the ocean of God.

Your whole life and existence then moves itself in the

direction of God's mighty plan, and so you can walk with Him, the whiles He walks with you, in the bond of a mutually holy love.

But this is usually only possible when it takes place in collective fellowship. There is only One who has trodden the wine-press alone. All other wrestlers have been carried by the example, by the sympathy, by the companionship, by the fellowship of what is called the people of the Lord. This is a holy appellation which no single group may arbitrarily appropriate to itself, and which is only real where God Himself walks in the midst of those who share His favor.

You feel, therefore, at once, in your family, in your church, in your social intercourse, whether the purposes and endeavors coincide with the goings of God, or whether they are mere exhibits of outward forms of piety.

This semblance does not satisfy you, it gives you no support, it does not bear you up. You are at rest only when you perceive that the Presence of the Lord in your family, in your church, in your social circle, is a spiritual reality, and that God Himself walks in the midst of them.

Then it does not suffice you that God walks with you, and you with Him, but then you feel this in equal measure of your wife, of your husband, of your children, of your pastor, of your church officials, of your societies and associations. You know it then one of another. Then you make the nearness of your God clearer and more vital to one another. You are not silent about it. You enjoy it together. And together you receive from Him the sacred impulse with united forces to go forward in His way, and to hold up the honor of His Name.

The Lord is then not only close to your heart, but He is in the midst of you. He is the common center of all your interests and the tie that binds you together.

There is then not merely a pious frame of mind, but a godly life, a consecrated purpose, a godly co-operation, and from this, that holy activity is born which in every department of life overcomes the world and makes virtues shine out which are not of us, but which flame out in us from Him Who walks in our midst, because He is the Source of our light, of our strength, and of the inspiration of our life.

LXVI

CLEAVING UNTO HIM

Sin propagates itself nowhere more rapidly than in Religion.

Religion, as the service of the Triune God, is the highest, the best that enriches our human heart. But the best is always the first that is exposed to corruption.

The Almighty created and supports in this world, outside of Europe and America, a thousand million people who continually die and are replaced, but who in this coming and going are and remain utterly estranged from the secret of salvation. Missions have done *something*, but what is this compared with the thousand millions of Asia and Africa and the united forces of Islam and heathendom?

These millions and millions, especially in Asia, are by nature *very* susceptible to religious impressions, much more so in fact than most of the nations of Europe. But they choose their own way and are dead to all true knowledge of the way of the Lord. And every morning and every evening that God from His Throne looks down upon those millions in Asia and Africa, there is always wanting among them the echo to the chorus of praise and adoration on the part of the heavenly hosts. They kneel before all sorts of things, but never before the Triune God.

It is very true that compared with this nightly darkness in Asia and Africa, in Europe and America it is light. You will scarcely find in these parts of the world a single village where the Sacraments of Baptism and Holy Communion are not administered, where, large or small, there is no church of Christ, and where there are not found some deeply spiritual souls who live very near unto God.

But does this make it a secret that in the thickly populated cities and even in larger villages the great majority of people are either utterly estranged from the service of the Lord, or merely outwardly adhere to it without attaching to it a spark of spiritual reality?

When this degeneration and corruption of religion took on proportions of too serious a character, a gigantic effort was put forth to purify the service of the Lord, to reform and to transform it, and this at first worked admirably. But look at the conditions that prevail in the religious world today and confess whether we do not face a new disappointment, and whether the half of the population in these so-called Christian countries is not estranged again from all inward, spiritual religion.

It is true that by the *Reveille* and by the spread of infidelity a Christian revival ensued, which fortunately is still in progress; but how unpleasantly you are affected, again and again, in these very circles that have been revived, by the coldness, formalism and lack of sacred fire.

And when at length you look at the narrowest circle of the families which still hold themselves in touch with the service of the Lord, and examine with some care what degree of warmth the spiritual life there attained and maintained, how constant is the disappointment that awaits you, and the question forces itself upon you, again and again, whether this is all that these people feel, and can spare, for their faithful God and Father.

Yea, when finally you look at your own family, and, closer still examine your own heart, and ask yourself what in home and heart the spiritual life is that you live with and for your God, and what it ought to be in view of His Fatherly faithfulness—who is not conscious, again and again, of the cry of despair which forces the question to the lips whether constant, inward, devoutly tender, increasing Godliness has become impossible for us?

And this question can in part only be answered in the affirmative.

Sin is so enervating and so weakening, that even in the most godly circles, real inward religion is at a low level, and only in moments of unusual tension does it rise a few degrees higher.

And the sad result of it all is, that God truly still looks down upon this world every morning and every evening, and faithfully continues to care and to provide for His fourteen hundred millions of human children, but that only here and there from a devout heart the psalm of worship and of pure love ascends to Him.

And yet, in everlasting love God continues, age upon age, to entice us by His Word, to call us and to draw us to this full, inwardly true and all-sufficient religion, which finds its terse expression in the supreme commandment that "thou shalt *cleave* unto the Lord thy God" (Deut. xxx, 20).

It is the image of the child at the mother's breast, who literally cleaves to her and hangs on her, cherishes itself in the warmth of the mother-life, feeds and satisfies itself at the fountain of her breast and cries the moment it feels itself apart from her.

And this supreme commandment that you must depend on God and cleave unto Him enters a protest against all merely outward religion and against every endeavor to reduce religion to mere form.

It does not exclude *thinking* on God, but it does say that to be busy with your God *intellectually* is not in itself religion. It demands that you shall *confess* the Name of your God before the world, but it denies you the right to imply that this confession of God's Name is the whole of religion. It demands a holy life and the abounding in good works, but it takes away from you the illusion that real piety can ever satisfy itself with this. It is very solicitous that you should hold in honor the outward forms of religion, but it opposes the idea that you should ever mistake these forms for the essence of religion itself. Apart from zealous activity in the cause of God religion is inconceivable, but it continually impresses it upon you that though you were to devote all of your life to Him, yet, had no love, you would remain "as sounding brass, or a tinkling cymbal."

It does not tolerate and will not allow you ever to make your boast of having real religion, as long as you have not come to a personal fellowship in the secret walk and communion of soul with your God.

And even though you may thank God for the grace that at times, in earnest, passionate prayer, personal fellowship with Him in Christ is heavenly food for your soul, it still continues to tell you that such occasional seeking after Him is not the true, not the full religion, because real religion demands that without cessation you shall cleave unto Him and uninterruptedly hang, as it were, on Him.

And such hanging upon God means that from moment to moment you shall feel that He is with you in your heart, that you shall ever be expecting Him, and that with all the powers of your soul you shall *hold yourself fast* by Him.

As a matter of fact, however, even they whose lives are most saintly here on earth will confess that such a state and condition of soul is impossible on this side of the grave. Our heart is not attuned to it, and life round about us is not in the spirit of it. Far from it. And to acknowledge this openly and candidly is simple honesty, provided that this confession goes hand in hand with self-accusation and shamefacedness.

There have indeed been those who have tried to attain this highest good. For the sake of thus cleaving solely unto God, men and women in every age have renounced the world and have secluded themselves in cell or hermitage. But even though they were able to shut out the world from their retreat, their heart they took with them, and it was the heart itself that continually stood in the way of the more intimate fellowship with their God.

This was possible in Paradise, and it has become so again in the congregation of the saints made perfect above.

But it is not within reach here on earth. To withdraw ourselves from life in the world lies not in our province. We have rather therein to fulfill a calling and render a service to God. It is equally impossible to separate ourselves from our heart. The heart goes always with us.

But God knows us. He knows that of which we are made. He ever remembereth that we are but dust. And our guilty lack of ability to attain this highest good, which our sin has rendered unattainable, He covers with gracious forgiveness.

Only you are not to rest content with this. Neither should you resign yourself to it. You should place the imperfection of your religion ever more clearly before your eyes. You must make accusation against yourself. And this very self-accusation will become a stimulus to you the more earnestly to seek from day to day and from week to week to make real this more intimate fellowship with your God.

And herein the difference between superficial and real religion shows itself.

The superficial worshiper understands that he can never attain unto such an unbroken cleaving to God. So he simply pursues the even tenor of his way calmly and unconcernedly, and never comes to know the hidden walk with Him.

On the part of all deeper and truer piety, on the other hand, it is a matter of genuine grief, that this fellowship of soul with the faithful, loving Father is interrupted with such frequency. It trembles every time it perceives that it has lost again its hold on Him. It rebukes itself and takes hold of itself to resume again this interrupted communion. And the end of it is, that the moments that are spent with and near unto God increase, and that, on the other hand, the moments of the breach with Him become less.

To cleave unto the Lord, with all the heart and soul and consciousness—is, then at first a heavenly joy which perhaps may be tasted only once a month. Gradually it becomes the communion of soul without which no week passes. By degrees it becomes an elevation of soul which repeats itself almost daily. And with progress like this there is joy in God many times a day, and even by night upon waking, the nearness of the Lord is consciously felt.

And although, even so, the highest still remains beyond our reach, this cleaving unto God begins to occupy ever wider room in our life.

And not only intimacy with God in solitude, but, much more, intimacy with God in *the midst of our busy life* becomes the booty of the soul.

It is then no longer a singing *after* Asaph: "As for me, it is good to be near unto God," but it becomes a singing *like* Asaph from the blessed experience of one's own heart.

LXVII

SAMUEL DID NOT YET KNOW THE LORD

When some one asks you about a certain person whether you *know* him, the meaning can be twofold. It may mean, just casually, whether you would know him if you met him. If the inquiry concerns his character, it means, whether you *understand* him.

He who on the eve of your departure abroad entrusts an important document to your care for some one living there, merely intends by the question whether you know who he is, to prevent your handing it to the wrong person. If, on the other hand, some one were to consult his father about engaging in some business with this or that man, the father's question in reply: "Do you know him?" would mean: "Are you sure that he is honorable, reliable and in his department an able man?"

This twofold, very different meaning in this matter of *knowing* any one personally must be reckoned with in the uses of the term in Scripture, in religion and in the knowledge of God.

To "know" is fundamentally always to observe a *difference*. He who is not conversant with Botany, sees, as he goes out of doors, nothing but trees and shrubs. He, on the other hand, who has learned the difference between an oak and a beech, oleander and rhododendron, jasmine and snowball, begonia and heliotrope, *knows* what he sees and has learned to enjoy the riches of this knowledge. The same is true among people. If you walk through a crowded street in a foreign city you see nothing but people before and on all sides of you, who do not speak to you in passing. On the other hand, when you walk the street of your own home town almost every one is familiar to you, and sometimes you can call even the smallest child by name.

But this goes no further than the *difference* between one person and another. As you pass them you make no mistake. Their outward appearance is familiar to you. The moment you see them you know them.

If, on the other hand, you mean that closer and more intimate knowledge which enables you to judge of a person's character, of his inner life, endeavors and aims, you come to an entirely different *distinction*. Not the difference in facial features and outward appearance, but the knowledge of his utterances and feelings. Knowledge then becomes *examination*, the entering into the inner existence of a person.

When, in I Samuel (iii, 7) we read that Samuel did not yet "know" the Lord, it means exclusively this first outward knowledge. It by no means indicates that deeper, truer knowledge of the Divine Being which only springs from secret fellowship with Him.

In one of the watches of the night Samuel heard himself called by name. He heard it as clearly and distinctly as though Eli had called him. But he knew not yet the *difference* between the call that comes from God and the call given by a man. Three times therefore, he went to Eli saying: "Thou didst call me." And only when Eli repeatedly assured him that he had *not* called him, and finally suggested to him that this might be a call from God, a new light arose upon Samuel and in that voice he himself now recognized the voice of his God.

The voice is a wondrous mystery. Each man has a voice of his own. It is because of this that you at once recognize a voice in the dark as that of your father, your husband,

your brother. The wonder is equally great that each man
and each child should have a voice of his own, as that we
should have the ability to recognize that difference between
voice and voice.

And the Lord also has a voice of His own, and it is for
us to distinguish that voice of God from the voices of men.
He who does not understand this difference does not know
the Lord as yet. He who understands it knows the Lord.
And it is this provisionally still outward knowledge of God
which precedes the more intimate fellowship with the Lord,
and so, by degrees, attains unto the rich full knowledge of
His attributes, which is eternal life.

In this knowledge of God there is a *twofold* dispensation.

The first in the Old and the New Testaments was the
portion of the patriarchs, Prophets and Apostles. They
received a special revelation from God. God spake with
them through dreams, visions and appearances, and also
through internal address, in their heart, or through external address, to their ear. And, of course, this might
have gone on in this way, so that we, every one personally
for himself, might have heard the voice of God.

But it has not pleased God so to do. It has seemed good
to Him first to give His Revelation personally to Prophets
and to Apostles, with audible voice or through visible
appearance, and finally in the Incarnated Word.

Later, however, this changed. The revelation given up
to that time has been collected in Scripture, and this
revelation gathered together in full has since become the
common good of all believers, the permanent durable
treasure of the whole Church of Christ.

This does not mean to say that now there is no more
secret fellowship with God, nor that now God can not give
any one personal leading and direction. But nothing more
is added to Revelation. To the truth as it has been revealed

there is no augmentation. And sickly mysticism that imagines that this is still possible has not been able these nineteen centuries to add a line to the Scriptures.

The way of knowing the Lord has thereby become different for us from what it was for Samuel.

For us the *Word* is the voice of God. And we no longer hear ourselves called by our name. We receive no more *by audible voices* new light from above.

But the selfsame difference nevertheless goes on.

Scripture speaks to every man. But with this difference. One will read the Bible and not hear the voice of God in it, because he does not know Him. Another will read this selfsame Scripture and hear God's voice in it, because grace has brought him to the knowledge of God.

This is hard to understand. You, who have been permitted to grasp the mystery of the Word, and day by day to undergo its blessed, mystical operation within you, and have come thereby to a fixed, unshakable faith, stand amazed that in so many families the Bible has been laid aside; that he who still reads it finds nothing in it worthy of special note and that you find yourself bitterly opposed when you maintain that every one is in duty bound to subject himself to that Word.

And yet nothing is more simple. The many who have broken with Scripture, do not know the Lord. They do not distinguish nor recognize His voice. They do not perceive nor feel that in the Scripture Almighty God calls them and speaks to them.

And this makes the separation. This digs the abyss. This makes division in the same land between one part of the population and the other. And this is something that breeds bitterness, because these very people, who do not know the Lord and in Scripture do not hear His words nor His voice, are baptized members of the Church of Christ.

Not only do they insist on calling themselves Christians, but they pride themselves on the fact that they honor Christianity as a purely moral power, and with this understanding of it stand on higher vantage ground and are more enlightened than those who narrowly adhere to barren Creeds.

This leads to an ever more sharply defined difference between people and people.

They who do not know the Lord, who do not hear His voice, and who reject His Word are not able to put themselves in the place of their fellow-countrymen who delight themselves in the knowledge of the Lord, who refresh themselves in the hearing of His voice, and who in His Word have firm ground for their faith.

And, on the other hand, they who know the Lord can bear witness to it. They can openly confess it. They can come to the defense of the ordinances of the Lord. But they are not able to impart their faith to others. They can not open the inner ear of their fellow-men to that holy mysticism of our God.

And yet there is a difference here.

Among those who do not know the Lord there are enemies of God, who have stopped their ears to every utterance of His voice. But there are also seeking, wandering souls who envy you because you have faith, and who would thank you, if you might be the means, in God's hand, of bringing them to it.

Of the former, Jesus said: "Give not that which is holy unto the dogs, neither cast ye your pearls before swine" (S. Matt. vii, 6). With them nothing can be done except to bear with them, to suffer whatever injury they might inflict upon you, and to show them the power of your faith.

But of the latter, Jesus said: "He that is not against me is for me" (S. Matt. xii, 30). On these the service of seeking love must be expended. These are the spiritually sick who are waiting for spiritual treatment.

A treatment of a twofold kind.

First, that you shall treat every one according to the nature of his spiritual malady. S. John the Baptist had a particular message for every man that came to him. And more striking still is the example of Jesus who dispensed a special medicine to every spiritual invalid. Herein lies the admonition to those who deal with all unbelievers in the same way, and who thereby show their lack of spiritual discernment.

And secondly, this treatment includes the no less urgent claim, that you who do believe shall spare them offense.

Nothing is more repulsive and more steadily offensive to those who do not as yet believe than the *unspirituality* of those who believe; their formal profession without moral and spiritual fruit, their zeal without the background of consecration and holiness, their bold assertions without corresponding seriousness of life.

They feel inclined to accept your sacred mysteries provided they can but discover that sacred power goes out from you. And when they see that there is no such power, that the good works which they expect from you are not forthcoming, that this higher seriousness of life is not in evidence; when on the contrary they constantly hear of hypocrites who present themselves in good form, and then prove themselves inferior in character and ·in their inner life to those who make no profession of the faith, they are offended by it and this holds them back from Christ.

So it was in the days of Samuel, when Hophni and Phineas abused things that were sacred, and Eli showed himself lacking in moral courage to enter righteous protests against them.

The conflict becomes so fierce!

Oh, that the children of God might understand their sacred calling, with manly courage to confess their faith; but above all else, by their family example, in their business and social activities, by their seriousness of purpose —in brief, by their whole life to be preachers of the Christ.

LXVIII

THEY MAKE HIM A WELL

In a country such as ours, with its plentiful provisions of water, it is difficult to form any idea of what thirst is.

This accounts for the fact that what Scripture says about *"thirsting* after righteousness" or *"thirsting* after the living God" is commonly interpreted among us in far too weak a sense. Of course it frequently happens now that on a hot day after a long walk, or at a time of feverish emotion, you reach out eagerly after a cup of cold water. But this stronger desire for water is by no means yet that *thirst* which one suffers in mountainous regions when the tongue cleaves, not metaphorically but literally, to the roof of the mouth, when the last moisture in the mouth is dried up and the swollen throat with difficulty lets the breath pass through. With such a thirst the pressing and ever increasing craving for water becomes a real *passion;* and he alone who so understands it, fathoms the depth of the longing for the nearness of God, which is so frequently expressed in singing by the worshiping congregation, even though he has no idea that there is anything real in that panting of the hart (Ps. 42, 1), which under the exhaustion occasioned by thirst sinks to the ground and cries out for the water-brooks.

And who in our days knows anything of the "thirsting after righteousness" such as the Old and the New Testament saints have known? Even when the cup of righteousness full to the brim is set before us, on the part of more than one it is considered much if he stretches out a heavy hand for it and slightly moistens his lips with it. But to thirst for it, to cry out for it, not to be able any longer to

414

go without it, with weeping to supplicate for it unto God—
where do we see anything of it? Oh, there are still some
thirsting ones, but has not their number diminished? And
is not the very infrequency of this strong burning of the
real *thirst* after God, and of the real *thirst* after righteousness the common danger of our times?

Sin works this.

Sin is the cause that, unless God shows mercy, the stimulus of this thirst scarcely operates.

It requires special grace in certain periods to revive
the vigorous activity of this stimulus again.

Such grace was operative in the days of the Apostles,
and in every season of revival that has been known in
the Church since.

And at the present time this *thirst* operates, oh, so weakly! The circle within which it operates is so small! And
even in this narrow circle its operation is so faint.

Be grateful to God if in your own heart you may perceive sometimes something of this real *thirsting* after the
living God.

Thousands upon thousands live on and die without ever
having felt anything of this thirst.

How great then is the grace that has been shown to you!

The Prophets and Psalmists, Jesus and the Apostles,
lived in mountainous regions. From thence it is that
water and the thirst after water occupies so broad a place
in Scripture.

"With thee is the fountain of life" (Ps. 36, 9). "All
my springs are in thee" (Ps. 87, 7). "Ho, every one that
thirsteth, come ye to the waters" (Isa. lv, 1). "Whosoever
drinketh of the water that I shall give him shall never
thirst" (S. John iv, 14).

And such is also the striking saying regarding the valley
of mulberries in Psalm 84.

The mulberry ripens most lusciously in hot, sunny spots. So the valley of mulberries is the image of those conditions in life when everything within us languishes, occasions anxiety, and almost chokes us with grief. When the heat of day and the heat of battle makes us pant for air and for relief. When we are no more able to go on. When fear overtakes us that unless God help us we shall drop by the way.

Now in these mountainous districts, there is, of course, abundance of water, which flows from the snow fields and leaps down in murmuring brooks. But in the mountains themselves the water is unequally divided. In one place it threatens to drag you along in its wild course. In other parts you will travel a barren path for hours and hours, where no drop of water can be found. And then there is only one hope of relief, that somewhere a tiny spring will trickle from the mountain side, wherewith the traveler may refresh himself and quench his burning thirst.

And for this reason, in connection with the valley of mulberries, the Psalmist speaks of two forms of relief. The first is, that in the midst of scorching heat, all unexpectedly, such a tiny spring is discovered. And the second is that rainclouds gather overhead, and beneath their broad shadow protect the traveler from the heat of the sun.

So it is in the valley in the midst of mountains, and so it is, metaphorically speaking, for God's children in the midst of troubles. When they are no more able to do anything of themselves, when they are breathless and hard pressed, then *God is their spring*, and then it is God Who stretches out broadly the rainclouds over them and covers them with their shade.

"When they pass through the valley of mulberry trees they make Him a well; yea, the raincloud shall cover them with blessings" (Ps. 84, 6, Dutch Ver.: *vide* R. V.).

To worship *the Fountain of life* in the living God and in His Christ has thus become our comforting imagery.

And now you must have seen for yourself in mountain villages what the village well, the village spring there, is, in order to grasp the rich significance of this imagery.

In those small villages, there is, as a rule, only one well, one fountain located in the midst of the public square.

From this one fountain, from this single well, the whole village drinks. Every one goes from his house to this well to fill his pitchers, and morning and evening to carry the provision of precious water to his home. Horse and cattle are led thither to drink from this same spring. And, likewise, soiled clothes are carried there, in order when washed white to be taken home again.

So this one village-well is the center of the whole village life. Everything gathers around it. At the well, people meet one another. At the well, conversation is held. At the well, the common life is lived. And so the whole village community feels that this well is in very deed the fountain of life for the entire village.

If, now, in such a place you should sing the Psalm that God is the Fountain of life, every one will understand you. The delightful imagery of it will appeal to all, and the pregnant thought will enter into every soul, that without God we would perish from thirst in our miseries, and that God, and God alone, is the center in Whom all they that fear His Name realize that they are one, and that together they lead one life.

In Christ this is brought closer yet.

In Christ the Fountain of life has been brought into our human life and into our human nature.

There are not *two* fountains of life, one in God and one in Christ, but it is the one Fountain of the Divine life which springs up in the Father, has come near to us in the Son, and through the Holy Ghost flows into our heart.

Therefore your Christianity is gone when you do not surely worship Christ as God and kneel down to Him as such.

This *one* Christ is the Fountain of life for the whole village, if we may so express ourselves, of the congregation of the Lord in the earth.

No one has the water of life for himself in his own house. Every morning and every evening each child of God is duty bound to go out to this one Fountain which is in Christ, to fill the small pitcher of his soul against the long day and the long night. And this Fountain never disappoints. It always flows. The water of life is there to be found flowing fresh every moment. There is no shortage for any one. There is abundance for all. And though our eye does not see it, invisibly throughout the whole world every true believer is given water at this one Fountain.

And thereby this one Fountain of life in Christ is and remains the center of life for us all, and the center of fellowship for the heart of us all. All sorts of distances and all sorts of separations, in the social world and in the churches hold you apart. Spiritually and unseen, however, all that are born of God come together day by day at this one Fountain of life, and it is this one Christ who from His abundance gives water to all.

And it is from this being one in Christ, and from this real life which is refreshed and sustained by water from this one Fountain, that believers on earth, in spite of difference and dispute, derive each day anew the strength of unity by which to realize and to work out the kingdom of heaven on earth.

But faith must be put in action.

It says: "*They make Him a well.*"

It does not act of itself. And thousands upon thousands, alas, come and go, without ever having known this Fountain, without ever having admired it or taken a drink from it.

The act of faith alone brings one into fellowship of soul with this Fountain.

Christ wants to be accepted. By faith you must *make* Him your Fountain.

With this also it is as in the mountain village.

Sometimes in such a mountain village there is a rich man who has dug a well in his own grounds for his own use. He has no more need therefore every morning and every evening to go to the village well.

But the rest, the poorer ones have no such well of their own.

And so it also applies here: Blessed are the poor in spirit, because they go to the Fountain of life, and therefore theirs is the kingdom of God.

LXIX

BY MY GOD I LEAP OVER A WALL

WHEN God created our first parents, He gave them paradise for their home, where they were not exposed to dangers of any sort. Neither the elements of nature, nor wild animals, nor the climate nor any sickness made them run any risks. All paradise was with them. It was, altogether, pleasure without drawback. At one point only, danger threatened. That one point was their *soul's condition*. Therein they were vulnerable. And if they were injured in the soul, they were overcome. And if God did not save them they were *vanquished forever*.

The curse which came upon the earth immediately after their fall showed that at once pandemonium—the power of hell—had been let loose against them, that the whole creation on all sides had entered, as it were, in conclave to destroy them.

If, now, you think how absolutely helpless these two people stood, almost without clothing and altogether unfortified, in the face of these unloosed and raving forces of the world and of nature, then you understand at once that nothing, absolutely nothing, would have remained of them, and that in less than twenty-four hours they would have perished as the prey of wild beasts, if in no other way, if from the side of God no hidden wondrous grace had watched over them.

You need not ask how our human life now saves itself. Now, in the face of the evil and destructive powers of nature, we stand strongly fortified in all sorts of ways. It is the exception when a flood surprises, a hurricane destroys, an epidemic works havoc, or wild animals carry off human victims. But Adam and Eve had *none* of the means of resistance at hand which are now at our disposal, and they were but by themselves.

It is therefore most remarkable that our race was not at once destroyed, that it maintained itself, that it increased and obtained the upper hand. Even for centuries together, after paradise had disappeared, man, in need of help, was forced to wage war to the death with the wild forces of destruction. To this day the name of a Nimrod, or of a Hercules, is alive in the memory of nations, as of heroes who were able to restrain the monster of destruction.

Most people live by their ordinary strength. Weaklings do not use such as they have. There have always been a few *who have excelled themselves.* And these heroes have been honored by after generations as men who have achieved the *superhuman*, and who, by labors which required an almost superhuman inspiration, have left a blessing behind them for the entire human race.

At times difficulties stood before them like a *wall.* And while others stood before that wall in utter helplessness *these* knew how to scale it, and to clear a way for those who followed after.

When the fight against the monster of the elements and the forces of nature had so far led to victory that with much caution and watchfulness human life to a certain extent became possible, Satan set up *man against man*, and an entirely new conflict arose, the conflict of human beings against human beings—the evil game of Cain and Abel.

To despoil the other of his goods, to aim at one another's life, to subject the other as slave to oneself. No longer now the pandemonium of nature, but of human wickedness, broke loose in the bosom of humanity itself. And the

misery that has come upon our race by this second conflict is untold. First lust of robbery and of murder, of
man against man, of house against house. And then from
this, war of nation against nation, of people against
people.

And then heroes have arisen. Men, again, who have excelled others and themselves. A Samson and a David, a
William the Silent and a Washington. Heroes who under
the inspiration of a lofty idealism have broken the ag-
gression of the tyrant and have worked deliverance for
their people.

It was again the *wall* against which every other man
dashed his head, but over which *they* leaped. And thus the
deliverance of the people came about. And the names of
these heroes are held in lasting honor. Not by our whole
race, but by the people whose deliverance they have
wrought.

In between these two, a third conflict has then ensued.
Not against nature now, and not against the lust of robbery and of murder, but the struggle of the kingdom of
the world against the kingdom of *heaven*.

The grace of God descending, the light of God shining
within, in order to bring the children of men into the inheritance of the children of God. And in opposition to
this, the power of Satan, sin and the world to bring to
naught the cause of God in the earth.

And then, again, there have been heroes who, excelling
others, themselves have stood their ground where others
fainted. It was again *a wall* which inexorably foiled the
many, but over which in high exaltation of spirit they
leaped. A Noah, an Abraham, an Isaiah, presently the
martyrs and the Apostles and after them the saints of the
Christian centuries. It is always the high exaltation of
soul—and the wall at length thrown down, and their

name held in grateful remembrance, not by one people now, nor by our whole race, but by the generation of all the children of God.

The center of this conflict was the Lion of Judah's tribe, the supreme Leader and the Finisher of the Faith, the Son of God and the Son of man, the vanquisher of death in His glorious Resurrection.

He Himself God, and, therefore, by Him the wall of sin and death demolished forever and the way opened to everlasting peace.

And now your conflict.

It is a conflict in threefold form. Against the *forces of nature*, in sickness, and dangers that threaten your ruin; the struggle for a living and for comfort of existence. Against your *fellowmen*, when they do you wrong, slander you or threaten your rights and liberties. And, in the third place, against the power of *Satan, sin and the world*, in behalf of God's honor, the cause of the Lord and of your own soul's salvation.

From the combination of these three powers that array themselves against you, spring all your woes and miseries, all your sorrows of soul and carping anxieties. Man has a battle to fight here on earth. This conflict is not equally fierce and sharp in every case. But it frequently appears that on the part of some it is a struggle against hellish powers.

And in this conflict one stands cowardly and helpless. The larger numbers struggle with little more than ordinary effort. But there are always a few that take up the fight with uncommon heroic courage and triumph through the faith. It is again the wall. Others falter before it, but they know how to leap over it. They do it with their God and in the name of their God. And they leave a blessing behind them to the good of their kindred and their whole circle of life.

Wherein now lies the secret of the courage and the vanquishing power of these heroes and heroines?

Of course in that they *excelled themselves*, that is to say, in that they were able to apply a power of will which really far outreached their own strength. And this great power does not come from without, but from within. From their fixed heart, from their soul that takes hold of itself, from the spirit that is within them.

By comparison one perceives something of this high tension in the man who runs *amuck*, in the drunkard, in the insane, in the man who is carried away by his passion.

Every one runs out of the way of him who runs amuck, because every one knows that no one can face him. So he is thrown by a shot from a gun. Sometimes three police officers are unable to overpower a subject of delirium tremens. The insane must be rendered harmless sometimes by a straight-jacket, which shows what gigantic strength they can develop. And in a fit of passion many an excited person has withstood three men and thrown them.

These are altogether exhibitions of human misery, but in them all a gigantic development of strength shows itself because an inward something was able to cause this tension of spirit and muscle, such as passes all measure.

But even as such a tension of the muscles can spring from evil excitement and over-exertion of spirit, so by an inner tension of the Holy Spirit our soul can double its strength, yea, increase it threefold. Not in this instance by reason of human misery, but by reason of a holy exaltation of spirit which is bent upon resisting human woe.

Then there is again a wall: The wall of injustice that is committed against us. The wall of trouble that overwhelms us. The wall of a wrong that can not be tolerated. The wall of opposition that threatens to undo us. The wall of sin that aims at our descent into hell. A wall which must be demolished, which must be broken through, or we are vanquished and lost.

And then heroic courage must show itself. Not the heroic courage of wild, ungovernable excitement, but the pure, calm, persevering courage of the hero who never gives up and in the strength of God overcomes.

Then it is the making true for ourselves of what the Psalmist sang (Ps. 18, 29): "By my God have I leaped over a wall."

"By my God;" this does not mean to say with the help of God, or through a miracle which God wrought, but it means: With God in my heart, with this highest inspiration which the working within of the Holy Ghost alone can bring about in my soul, so that I know that God *wills it,* and that, therefore, it *must* be done.

Then it is, if you like, a miracle, for what you do and endure goes far beyond your own strength.

But the wall yields, the wall breaks down and you leap over.

And on the other side of it you kneel down to ascribe praise and honor, and to make great the Name of Him Who has enabled you to do the superhuman.

LXX

MINE EYES ARE EVER TOWARD THE LORD

In the *Te Deum* the Church of God sings: "To thee all angels cry aloud. . . . To thee Cherubim and Seraphim *continually* do cry: Holy, Holy, Holy Lord God of Sabeoth. Heaven and earth are full of the majesty of thy glory."

Continually, without ceasing, without pauses in between, always the never ending ascent of the hymn of praise from the angelic choirs unto God.

This unbroken, this constant unchanging and fixed permanency of things, is the peculiar characteristic of the mode of existence of the world before God's Throne. In the Father's house above there is no time, but there is eternity, and, therefore, there is no waste of life in a night, there is no transition of the morning into midday, but it remains an eternal morning. There is no standing still and beginning again. No stopping and then again a resuming. There is no intermezzo there of rest or of relaxation. It is all one life, forever springing up and returning unto itself, without the wasting of power and, therefore, without need of change. There is no development any more; and, therefore, transition from condition into condition is unthinkable.

There is no diminution, neither discontinuance, in the fullness of that blessedness which eternally flows and streams forth; and, therefore, the word *continually* in the *Te Deum* expresses so admirably and tangibly the characteristic of the super-earthly, of what is consecrated to God, of the Kingdom of heaven.

And now it may indeed sound paradoxical to us, when the Apostle admonishes us to: "Pray without ceasing," or to, "rejoice evermore," and when the Psalmist declares: "I set the Lord *always* before me" (Ps. 16, 8); "Nevertheless I am *continually* with thee" (Ps. 73, 23); or again, "Mine eyes are *ever* toward the Lord" (Ps. 25, 15). In connection with this "continuous" note of the higher life, he who is no stranger to the hidden walk with God feels the holy significance of this continuousness, this going on without ceasing at all times.

For consider well, that sometimes "continually" means: "now and then!" A nurse in the hospital *continually* makes the round of her patients. But this is not the meaning here. When the Psalmist sings, "Mine eyes are continually toward the Lord," the meaning in Hebrew is not "now and then" but "always and without ceasing."

It means to say: the eye of my soul is never directed away from my God but is always toward my Father Who is in heaven.

It means that in your hidden walk with God you do not draw God down *into the temporal,* but you let God draw you up *into the eternal.*

Hidden fellowship with God is enjoyment in advance of what is heavenly in its essence.

It is no musical instrument from which you entice the music for a moment in order presently to shut off the combinations again, but an organ that plays of itself, and which merely waits for your ear to catch the sound of its heavenly harmonies.

And now do not say that prayer without ceasing, that to feel always blessed in God, always to hold him before your eyes, always to look toward Him, and continually to fix your eye upon Him, is simply impossible, because from the nature of the case your human life, your environment, your professional or business cares plainly forbid it.

Taken in this sense, both David and S. Paul well knew that our life is no endless devotion and the world no monastic cell.

But neither the Apostle nor the Psalmist meant it in this way.

Surely there are moments when in some secluded spot, alone with God, we fall on our knees and do nothing but pray. There are moments when we purposely seek solitude and meditatively, or in perplexity, sit down, that we might lose ourselves in thinking on God. There are moments when we shake ourselves free from everything that belongs to this life in order to busy ourselves solely with the things of the hidden life.

And it must be acknowledged that for him who first begins, this is, mostly, the only form in which he can imagine prayer, his fellowship with God and his looking unto God, to be possible.

The life of such a one is, then, still divided in two parts. One life broadly extending itself *without* God *in* the world and by the side of this, an exceedingly limited life *with* God and *outside* of the world.

He then has truly grasped something of the kingdom of heaven, but the life of the world is still his real life, and as an oasis in the desert of this worldly life, off and on, come moments which he devotes to God.

And so long as this state of things continues, there is of course no mention yet of praying without ceasing, of rejoicing at all times, and of a continuous abiding with God.

There is, then, as yet no indwelling with God, but a dwelling in the world, in order, now and then, to go out from this world and for a brief moment to seek God. He then prays briefly. Momentarily he thinks on God. Presently it is over. Then the closed eyes open again to the world, and in the life of this world, he spends the rest of the day.

Such is the existence of one who, of the four and twenty hours of each day and night, spends perhaps eight in bed, more than fifteen in the world, and, taken altogether, no half hour yet with God.

And by such as he, it has frequently been tried to withdraw themselves, now and then, a half hour longer in solitude, and lose themselves in holy meditation, but life is so busy, it rushes on and on so restlessly, and all too often, in these moments of self-isolation, the distraction of their thoughts is too great for them to be able, through the power of their will, to pull themselves back to what is holy.

And, disappointed, they are then so easily inclined to give it up.

No, this steady, this uninterrupted, this ceaseless continuance of fellowship with God, does not depend upon our thinking, and can not be reached by our will, but must of itself spring up from the inner motion of the heart.

You believe that you are a temple of the Holy Ghost, hence that God dwells in you, and that thus God's being near to you and your being near to God takes place of itself, independently of the fact whether you think of it or forget it.

God the Holy Ghost does not come into your heart to stay but a moment, and presently to leave it again.

There is an indwelling. There is a coming once for all in order to abide with you forever. And even when you do not pray, or know not how to pray as you ought, this God prays in you with groanings that are unutterable. Even as the mother continues to keep watch by the bedside of her newborn babe, though the babe has no sense of it whatever.

The only question, therefore, is whether the inner disposition of your heart gradually attains that sanctification, that opening up to Divine things, whereby you begin to feel and to become aware of what takes place in your own heart within.

First you live outside of your heart, and your heart floats in isolation, as a drop of oil on the waters of your life. But gradually there comes an awakening. You begin to live somewhat more with and in your own heart. And when you enter sufficiently deeply into your own heart, then you there find God the Holy Ghost who takes compassion on you.

This now of itself brings you to a life in two phases. On one side a life toward what is without, and on the other side a life toward what is within. Though at first these two are strange to one another, gradually there is a mutual approach until they mingle themselves and permeate each other through and through. And finally you reach the point where the life from within glows and shines through the whole of your outward existence, and where inwardly, we do not say the clearly conscious fellowship, but yet that which is felt with the tentacles of your soul, goes on more and more uninterruptedly.

First this is holy mysticism. Nothing more.

But it does not stop with this.

Of itself the eye of your soul begins to discover more and more clearly the reality that your God not only dwells within your heart, but that also, in the outward life around you He is the everywhere present, the all-directing, the Almighty and the all-providing Worker.

So you begin to discover a God Who in everything, by everything and through everything presses upon you.

The note which rises from the depth of your heart receives its echo from the entire life in which you fulfill your calling. That which formerly distracted you in life and threw you back upon yourself, now begins with wondrous enticement to draw you ever more toward your God. And not by the process of reasoning, not with outspoken thought, but, in the immediate perception of the life of the soul itself, God begins both inwardly and outwardly, almost endlessly, to unveil your eye to His Majesty.

Sin interrupts this again. That is true. But also hatred of your own sin never wakes up in your heart more strongly than when it throws its discord again into the accord of the psalm of your life.

And to break with sin, in order to lose yourself in worship and blessed fellowship, then becomes of itself the rising impulse of your heart.

LXXI

THY OVERSIGHT HATH PRESERVED MY SPIRIT

YOUR spirit within you is that by which you live. It is likewise your breath of life and your spiritual inner self. Your spirit is what you are, above and aside from your body. It is that which was breathed into your "unformed substance" to make you *man*, as man to make you *live* and to make you a *person* among the children of men.

To give up the ghost is ordinarily nothing else than to die, to breathe out the breath of life. When, on the other hand, the Apostle says that "no man knoweth the things of a man save the spirit of man which is in him" (I. Cor. ii, 11), the word "spirit" means our conscious self, our spiritual existence as man, our inner personality.

Although this seems to be something entirely different, in Holy Writ the breath of life, which we breathe out in dying, can never be separated from our spiritual existence. Our life and our person within us are expressed by the word *spirit*, and both together are called *our soul*.

When the Psalmist cried: "O Lord, deliver my soul," or when he sang: "Thou, Lord, hast delivered *my soul* from death," it refers, in Psalm 116, 8, to the saving of life, to deliverance from danger, and not to *spiritual* redemption.

But our inner spiritual existence is equally well called our soul. As in the forty-second Psalm the cry comes up out of the depths: "As the hart panteth after the water brooks, so panteth my soul after thee, O God. *My soul* thirsteth for God, for the living God," in verse 4: "I remember these things and *pour out my soul in me;*" and again: "Why art thou cast down, O *my soul*, and why art thou disquieted within me."

The Scripture makes no distinction between our life and our spirit. In God's Word our physical and our spiritual existence are one. In paradise God forms man from the dust of the earth. But the material form is not yet man. Man only comes into existence when God breathes life into it. But when life enters in, then it is a human life. And there is no human life save as utterance of a soul's life. Neither is there any soul's life apart from a self, a person, a spiritual being that is hidden in our heart.

Any one that is human can sully this spiritual existence within himself, he can sin it away, he can corrupt it. But he can not shake it off, neither can he lay it aside. Death does not annihilate it. It abides, it continues to exist, even with the lost in the place of perdition.

Man's *spirit* is his real self. Everything else about him is but the dwelling-house, the tabernacle, as the Apostle calls it. But the real, the actual man, is the spirit that dwells in this tabernacle.

This spirit within you is yourself, your person. This includes your disposition, your nature, your consciousness, your will, powers, gifts and talents. In brief, all this together which forms your inner existence constitutes an individual being, bears its own stamp, expressing itself in its own character.

In Scripture it is always the same antithesis.

In paradise it is the form fashioned from the dust, and the spirit which God breathes into it. In Psalm 139 it is the "unformed substance" which is wrought as an embroidery, and to this, the self that was made in secret is added. The same occurs in Job (x, 9-12): "Thou hast made me as the clay. Thou hast poured me out as milk, and curdled me like cheese. Thou hast clothed me with skin and flesh, and hast fenced (crocheted) me with bones and sinews." But aside from all this: "Thou hast granted me life," *i.e.*, my *spirit*.

What is before our eyes, what is visible, what is tangible comes first. And afterward there enters into this what is invisible, what exists in the secrecy of your heart, and that is your spirit.

And God does not leave this spirit that is within you to itself. No, this spirit remains in His hand. It continues under His care. He watches over it. More yet. Over this spirit that is within you, God holds supervision. And of this supervision of God Job testifies: "Thy oversight, O my God, hath preserved my spirit" (x, 12, Dutch Ver. See Marg. read. R. V.).

At first man knows nothing about this supervision which God has over the spirit. Even as the little child that slumbers in the cradle knows nothing of the oversight which the eye of the mother keeps, or as the sick man in his sleep perceives nothing of the person who watches at his bedside.

Of this supervision of God over your spirit you only begin to notice something in later years, when the eye of your soul has been opened to the leadings, the care and the faithfulness of God.

But even then this is of slow progress.

It is provisionally a discovery of God's oversight, of the care of your Father Who is in heaven, in behalf of your outward existence. And even this occurs only in special cases of deliverance in times of special need. We are then under an impression that the course of our ordinary life runs of itself, and that only at particular times the Lord our God looks after and cares for us. It is for this reason that thanksgiving and prayer for years together assume a more fervid character only in moments of special danger or anxiety. And the years must be far advanced before this restful, blessed feeling of assurance takes hold of us, that every day and every night, in ordinary and in extraordinary circumstances we are continuously watched over, cared for and looked after by our God.

But then alongside of this there gradually dawns on us an entirely different consciousness: even the growing conviction that likewise our inward, our hidden soul's existence is in God's hand, that He likewise notices this, that therein also His continuous care is at work, and that He constantly practises an *oversight* over our spiritual nature within us.

The discovery of this is first made in the conscience.

He who has oversight not merely makes provision for things, but he also looks after them. He examines things, he classifies them, exercises authority and power over them and bestows praise or administers reproof. And it is this side of God's supervision over us with which we first became acquainted. In most instances it happens for the first time after a wrong has been committed, by as much as we feel the judgment of the omniscient, holy God enter painfully into our inner being.

Then we feel that God the Lord has an oversight over us which extends to the smallest deeds for which we incur responsibility. That He has the superintendence and supervision over our entire inner person, in everything.

Over what we do, over what we leave undone, over our inclinations, over our desires and wishes, over our thoughts and words, yea, even over the ebullitions of our imagination.

And when it has come to this, we are certain of two things:

First, that God's supervision extends over our lot in life, over our prosperity and adversity, over everything that happens to us, and that one line is drawn through the whole of our life which binds our present to our past and merges this present into the future. We then know that we are creatures of God, that He owns us, that we are His property. That He disposes of us and not we of ourselves. That the whole plan of our life has been determined by God for us, and that the course of our life shall run according to this plan.

In the second place, we then observe that in our inner life we are not lord and master ourselves, but that this selfsame God keeps His holy eye unceasingly upon our moral existence as man, and judges us at the bar of our own conscience as often as we go contrary to His holy will.

And from these two there arises gradually the still higher appreciation that God's oversight over our spirit bears not only an admonishing and a judicial character, but that it also possesses that selfsame character of faithful care which we have learned to adore in our lot in life.

We then perceive that God not only has his eye upon our inner being in order to estimate its worth, but also that He is continually busy in this inner substance of our soul, that He constantly cultivates it and ceaselessly devotes His care to it.

The Apostle describes this in the metaphor of a husbandman who cares for the crop that germinates in the field which he has cultivated and sown.

So is our soul a garden of the Lord, in which His planting germinates and blooms, which He waters with his dew, which He weeds and shields and in which He causes fruit to ripen.

We also cultivate our soul ourselves. And good and evil influences affect us equally from the world of men and spirits.

But the constant activity of God in our soul bears a far more serious character. Even though we do not notice it, God has at all times free access to our hearts. Even in our sleep He comes to us in order to cultivate our inner existence. He prepares in us the powers which we presently shall need. He disposes and directs in us the powers which must be applied to a given end. What only after ten or more years shall come to be expressed by you, He is even now already busily preparing in you. Nothing in your inner soul's existence escapes Him. Your sensations, your inclinations, your rising feelings, everything stands under His holy oversight. He feeds in you what otherwise would languish and die. He bends and turns what otherwise would wrongfully grow up in you. And as a mother cares for her babe in outward things, so your faithful Father provides against every difficulty, against every need of your soul.

This is a work of God which began in His counsel, which was reckoned with in your ancestors, which, from the cradle on, has been accomplished in you, which has never ceased all the days and all the nights of your life. A work of God on your soul which goes on when you are alone and when you mingle in the crowds, which does not desist while you are at work, and which is directed with a firm hand to what God has intended by Himself to make of you now and eternally.

Your own plan with respect to your development and formation of character does not extend for the most part farther than this brief life. But God's oversight over your spirit stretches itself out into the everlasting ages of eternity. And *here* preparation is made in you by the painstaking care of God of what shall only unfold itself on the other side of the grave.

This oversight of your God is simultaneously a fostering

care and an educational training. It is the labor of the supreme artist, who is busy in preparing for himself from the life of your soul an ornament for his Father-house above.

And this work of God on and in your soul, this oversight of God over your spirit, you can oppose, and thereby you can grieve the Holy Spirit. But you also, as co-worker with God, can do your part. And the latter is the aim of the holy impulse of childship, which is ever seeking strength in the humble prayer of Psalm 138: "Forsake not what thy hand began, O, Source of Life, Grant thy assistance."

LXXII

EVERY ONE WHICH SEETH THE SON

Of all things among men the chief thing is to believe on Christ.

In every note of the musical scale it is proclaimed to us in Scripture that God hath given "his only begotten Son, that whosoever believeth on him should not perish but have everlasting life." And there is added to this with equal emphasis that, "He **that** believeth not the Son shall not see life, but the wrath of God abideth on him" (S. John iii, 16, 36).

When asked what the great work is which in obedience to God we have to do, Jesus answered: "The work of God which ye have to do is, that ye believe on me." (S. John vi, 29).

It is faith in Christ that shall one day bring about the division of mankind in eternity, and it is this same faith that already here on earth leads to this result.

Not a general religiousness, not personal pious inclination, and not, again, a general faith in God, but, solely and very positively, the faith in Jesus — according to its presence or its absence—denotes eternal destiny, and answers the question whether one already here belongs to the flock of the Good Shepherd or whether he stands outside of it.

Upon this faith is based the entire Gospel.

It is this faith in Christ towards which the whole Revelation of God — read it in the epistle to the Hebrews (xi) — was directed.

The *sola fide*, by faith alone, is still in another sense

than that in which Luther proclaimed it, the ground thesis for all higher human life.

There are among men at large all sorts of other marks and badges and rules and relationships which indicate other movements in our life, or which impart other tendencies to it. And all these can be worthy causes, and have significance of their own.

Only, all these other movements in life can interest but limited circles, for a limited period of time, in limited measures. Sympathy, inclination, predilection, affection — all blossoms with a silvery blossom, but all together never dominate the whole human existence, do not transpose the ground of existence, have no results that make final decisions and eternally abide.

And, for this reason, faith on the Son of God stands so highly exalted above all else that flourishes among men and unites and inspires.

All these other interests are only in part, they all lack the deep fullness of life, they are all as grass that flourishes in order, presently, when the wind passes over it, to wither.

What alone remains as foundation of the inner life, and decides as to what the tone of life must be, and guarantees this life in endless unfolding, is the faith in the only-begotten Son of the Father, or as was said in the prison at Philippi: "Believe on the Lord Jesus Christ and thou shalt be saved."

Saved; this is in itself the all-embracing, the all-permeating, the complete and perfect happiness; the happiness that endures until and throughout the eternal morning.

What this faith is, how it operates, wherein it consists, needs no consideration here. It is a mystery which the Church of Christ has repeatedly endeavored to express in terms of speech, but she has never been able to express the fullness thereof in words, and to exclude all misunderstanding.

When the Church defined the faith too zealously it led to cold and barren intellectualism without spiritual glow. When she entered more deeply into the mystery of the hidden life of the heart, she crowned too frequently a feverish mysticism which presently evaporated in excitement.

Only this is, and always was, the heart of the matter, that a lost world, a human heart in its self-inflicted insolvency cried out for deliverance; and that age upon age, all human genius, all human heroism, all human compassion had ineffectually endeavored to bring this deliverance about, until at length God wrought it for us.

He imparted it to us not in the form of a gift but in a most holy Person. And this person was not one taken from among us, but One Who came down to us from heaven. He came down not as an angel who as God's servant and our helper stands outside of both the Divine and human natures, but as One Who was sent down from heaven and Who came to us as the only begotten Son of the Father, Who having entered into our nature brought God Himself to our view. "Philip, he that hath seen me hath seen the Father; and how sayest thou then, show us the Father?" (S. John xiv, 9).

And therefore the faith in Christ can not be otherwise than the highest, the *one* and the only thing that counts.

Where God in Christ gives Himself to the world and enters so deeply into our human life, that this Son assumes our nature, that the Word becomes Flesh, on the ground of which angels proclaim the *Immanuel*, God with us — there the absolute, the infallible, the in itself perfect revelation of Divine compassion has come to us.

There it can not go higher, it can not go farther. There the boundary has been reached of what is eternally complete in itself.

And, therefore, nothing transcends the faith in Christ. There is nothing that can be placed by the side of it. There is nothing that you can compare with it. It far excels all human invention. Nothing can be substituted for it, it can be surpassed by nothing.

The faith in the Son of God brings deliverance, or there is no deliverance.

No deliverance for the lost world, and no deliverance for your self-lost heart.

For the rise of this star of faith in the life of your soul, Jesus Himself demands an *activity* on the part of your soul.

Not, as is self-evident, that any activity whatever on the part of your soul would be able to create the faith in Christ, produce it, imprint and implant it. The seed of faith is a Divine kind of seed. The faith in Jesus itself is a *gift*, even as the Christ Himself is a gift. Faith is a product of Divine compassion wrought by the Holy Ghost.

But all faith in Christ is peculiar and necessary in this particular, that it must be taken up into our consciousness, and that to this end it enters into our consciousness with irresistible power. It makes entrance for itself as a sensation, as a driving power, as an inspiring principle, as a power that rules and transfigures our whole life.

And, therefore, this faith must obtain for our consciousness a content, a form, a figure. Truly it brings emotions with it, unspeakable emotions of extraordinary power. But, above and beyond all this, it has an intellectual content, which wills that it be understood, a content which fills itself with what we know from the Sacred Revelation of the Person of the Son of God, of His life on earth, of

His works, of His words, of His sitting at the right hand of God, and of His continued activity from heaven, after His Ascension.

And herein consists what is learned by rote. There is memory-work in it, memory of names, facts, conversations; memory of words and deeds, mortal sufferings and glorious Resurrection.

But the memory does not nurse the faith. Conceptions are not one in essence with your faith. In your faith, learning does not ignite the glow.

And, therefore, says Jesus, that your faith, in order to become ever clearer, stronger and more inspiring, needs this *one* thing, viz., that you *see the Son of God*.

"Every one which seeth the Son and believeth on Him, he hath everlasting life" (S. John vi, 40).

This seeing of the Son of God, this alone supplies such enchantment to the soul as keeps the glow of faith alive and causes it to burn brightly.

All the content of your memory, therefore, must be reduced to the unity of the Image of the Son of God. It must all be united and epitomized in order to bring this Image in its sacred purity before the eye of your soul. And when this Image perfects itself in you, every inner impulse and sensation, every holy emotion in you must merge in this Image, in order that you too may enjoy it. And this living Image of the Son of God must impress you, must interest you, must not loosen its hold on you, must keep you engaged, must transport you in holy ecstacy.

Not as a knowing after the flesh. No, it must be a spiritual vision, but always in such a way that the name of Jesus passes over into the Person of Christ, and that from this Person of the Christ the inner Divine Being takes hold of you and draws you with magnetic power.

No Jesus-glorification which fathers the vain wish that

He were still on earth, so we could hasten to Him. That would be to descend from the high to the low. The spiritual vision, the seeing of the Son of God with the eye of the soul, stands incomparably higher than the experience vouchsafed to the disciples, who saw and handled the Person of Jesus on earth.

The *Apostle* knows the Savior in a far richer way than the *disciple* has ever known Him. The Ascension has not impoverished but enriched us. And the seeing of the only-begotten Son of the Father, which cultivates the faith, feeds it, and continually refreshes it, is such a conscious fellowship of the soul with the Lord of glory, that, in and through Him, you make approach to the Eternal Being Himself, and seeing the Son spiritually with the soul, you as child of God, know and feel yourself one with the Father, the Son and the Holy Ghost.

Listen to the petition in the high priestly prayer:

Holy Father, I pray thee, that they all may be one, as thou Father art in me and I in thee, that they also may be one in us: that the world may believe that thou hast sent me (S. John xvii, 21).

LXXIII

MY FOOT STANDETH IN AN EVEN PLACE

THIS saying: "My foot standeth in an even place" has a threefold significance.

It is the exclamation of satisfaction on the part of the prosperous man of the world; it is the cry of relaxation on the part of him with whom the struggle for success has been hard and bitter; and it is the calm utterance of higher peace on the part of him who believes.

The imagery of the Psalmist is clear.

A road by which you must travel can bear a twofold character.

It can be as smooth and level as a bowling alley, as many streets are in cities and in towns; or it can be a way, as in mountainous districts, at one time down a steep decline and at another up to giddy heights, while the unevenness of the path taxes your strength to the utmost.

With us, a stretch of sandy or muddy road may make the going difficult, but, as a rule, our roads are smooth and easy-going, and no figure can be borrowed from them by which to describe the pathway of our life. A road may seem long to us, it may be lonely, or it may repel us by its uncleanliness, but all this presents no contrast such as we find between a road through *level country* and a *mountain path*.

Scripture on the other hand had its origin in a mountainous country. The Psalmists have roamed and wandered in the mountains. And their fertile minds would naturally borrow images from life in the mountains by which to express the contrasts of life.

Thus easy travel, with light step, on a smooth, straight and even road, of itself suggested to them the image of a life in which, in the language of a sailor, we would say that everything went before the wind. On the other hand the strong exertion which makes it even difficult to breathe, on a mountain path along which sometimes for hours together you go down a steep decline and then for hours you must climb a steep ascent, presented of itself the image of the wrestler of whom, again, in terms of the sea, we would say that he can scarcely keep his head above water.

And, therefore, the saying: "*My foot standeth in an even place*," may well state the self-sufficiency of the man who in everything has been successful, who has never known adversity, and who, devoid of carking care has never seen anything else than sunshine on the pathway of his life.

On the other hand there is much more in this exclamation, "My foot standeth in an even place," when it becomes the expression of what goes on in the soul of him who has been thrown, time upon time, and with keen disappointment has seen all his efforts fail, but who nevertheless kept on, did not give up; who when he fell, got up, and climbed the steep path again, until at last the point was reached where the straight way through the highland extended itself before his feet, and prosperous life began, and happy existence under the fulfillment of his ideals.

But the fullness of meaning in this saying, "My foot standeth in an even place," is highest when it is the joyous cry of the conviction of faith which with spiritual buoyancy knows that it can overcome the depression of this earthly life, and now bears witness with Habakkuk (iii, 17): "Although the fig tree shall not blossom, neither shall fruit be in the vines; and there shall be no herd in the stalls, yet I will rejoice in the Lord, I will joy in the God of my salvation."

Let the child of fortune, as the man is called who has never known reverses, be on his guard.

A life without care, without anxiety, without sorrow, without disappointment, enervates one so easily.

Undoubtedly optimism cultivates a happy frame of mind, but it lacks the power to steel character, to practice buoyancy and make it taut, and to enrich oneself with the noble treasures of the mind.

Yet this is not the worst of it.

Far worse it is that the prosperous man inclines so readily to attribute his good fortune to himself, and to cherish the notion that the others whom he sees toil and plod so painfully must lay this to the door of their own inefficiency. He is the man who always had good insight, he the man who had the correct view of everything. Others allowed the right moment to go by unimproved; he always knew enough to act at the proper time. And so there rises in his mind an opinion of his own excellence, which nurses the sense of pride in his heart, and, in his inmost self, chokes the sense of sympathy with the sorrows and reverses of others.

Or, in case such a fortunate individual is still somewhat inclined to be religious, his heart so easily tempts him to look upon himself as a particular favorite of God, by reason of which preference his way was ever smooth. And now he lives along in sure confidence that his lot in life will be disposed by God in wealth and prosperity until the end.

And this goes on with the increasing opinion of his own excellence and privilege, until there comes a turn in life and the sun goes hiding behind the clouds.

Then everything collapses at once. Then there is no power of resistance. Then there is no disciplined strength. There is nothing to hold him up and to enable him to struggle against misfortune.

And the end is a sinking away in self-perplexity, without courage to live and without hope for the future.

How altogether different this is with the wrestler.

To such a one every new year of his life disclosed a new struggle to keep himself standing.

With one, it was a struggle to keep himself and his family alive with honor; to succeed in his calling and to do well in what he undertook. With another, a struggle against slander and envy. With a third, a struggle to obtain an opening for his conviction, for his insights, for his ideas. With still another, an endless struggle with broken health. And then again, vexation, sorrow of soul on account of a child that brought disappointment; or grievous mourning for a child, for a beloved wife that one lost by death.

And although there are many with whom such going through the depths are interspersed with sunnier days, there are also those who have fought for many years of their life literally in continuous tension, in never-ending disappointment, an endless fight without outlook.

Frequently this brought the bitter result that gloomy melancholy subdued the heart; that irascible thoughts began to predominate; and that, taking it for granted that their chance in life was lost, they at length gave up the fight, and without will and without hope pined away in ever deepening gloom.

But there have always been others who have persevered, who have not given up, who have not extinguished hope, and who, nerved by great will-power, in spite of everything have reached the point where they could breathe freely, and the opposition seemed broken.

Thanks to the practice acquired in their struggle they then put forth one last, gigantic effort. And, yes, now they succeeded. Now it was done. Now better days began. And with a feeling of delight such as can not be told in words, but as great as this earthly life can bring, they exclaimed in an altogether different way: "God be praised, now my foot standeth in an even place."

Does this already seem glorious? There is yet a still higher standpoint.

Against the current of life it is sometimes impossible to row. Sometimes adversity can darken your life so deeply that it follows you to the grave.

Even he who is most grievously afflicted has no single guarantee that better days will come. An outcome such as Job obtained is assured to no one.

It can be the good pleasure of God to glorify the majesty of the grace of faith in a life on which the sun of happiness has never shone. To poor Lazarus the hour of gladness only struck when by angels he was carried into Abraham's bosom.

We have no *right* to anything. And he, who is no stranger to the knowledge of his sin, will never face his God with the demand for happiness or for deliverance from misery. He may pray for it and supplicate for it, but yet it always remains: "Father, if this cup can not pass from me, not my will, but thy will be done."

And the glory of this is, that a wondrous faith reveals its strength, not only when the suffering is turned into joy; but also, and still more wondrously, *in* the suffering itself; and even most of all when the suffering follows us to the grave, and the cross casts its shadow on the pathway of our life until the very end.

For this is the glory of the faith, that it discloses to us another, a higher way, a way on the top of the mountain of God's holiness, which excels the way of our earthly life and dissolves for us all sorrow and all misery and all agony of soul in a higher vision.

This way of faith does not run under the cloud which prevents the sun from shining on the pathway of our life. He who walks by this path has the clouds underneath himself. He enjoys the unhindered shining of the sun of grace.

And whether, then, in his life things go with him or against him, whether he must begin the struggle anew, or whether, finally, he is above the struggle against what the world calls fate—in pleasure and in distress, in grief and in gladness, in prosperity and in adversity, his soul remains in balance, his heart remains undaunted and fixed, and, glorying in the faith, he jubilantly bears witness: "Whatever comes, my foot standeth in the even place which my God has disclosed unto me through faith."

LXXIV

AN ABUNDANT REFRESHING

In the world above, an entirely different stamp is imprinted upon life from that here on earth. In that realm of glory is no sin and, therefore, no redemption; no misery and hence also no deliverance. Neither can there be any transition there from doubt into faith, from weakness into strength, from sorrow into joy, from mourning into being comforted. In brief, everything that, by the single fact of sin and misery, brings into our life on earth continual breaks, disturbance, transition, restoration and higher exaltation, is excluded from the life eternal.

This continuous change was likewise foreign to the life in paradise. But when sin entered there, paradise was lost and the curse came upon our earthly existence.

Not as though in paradise the deadly tediousness of monotony prevailed, or that in heaven about God's throne the absence of all change throws a somber pall upon the life of the blessed. Without endless variation no higher life is conceivable. And that richer development of life before God's Throne shall once exceed and excel anything we have known on earth in the way of higher life-development or have dreamed in poetic imagination.

But the life hereafter can not be measured after the standard of this life. It is different in kind. It bears an entirely different character. It obeys a wholly different law. It interests and charms by an entirely different beauty, wealth and enjoyment. But for this very reason it remains to us an object of faith and hope, and does not lend itself to a forecasting in this life. And though figures of speech borrowed from this life may be used in Scripture in order to give us an impression of it, every one feels that the marrow full of fat and the unmixed wine of the marriage-feast of the Lamb serve exclusively to quicken the impression of festal joy, and not in the least to indicate wherein it shall consist.

It is not yet revealed what we shall be. Enough that we know that it shall be a life in endless happiness and glory. But how this happiness shall once disclose itself, and in what form it will present itself to us, faith leaves with God. And upon that Father Who is in heaven and upon His Son Jesus Christ, all the longing of the soul on the part of God's children centers itself in expectation of that glory.

Here on earth, on the other hand, sin characterizes our entire life and our whole human existence. And this by no means merely in the sense that continuously every day and night sin is committed, and that these sins bring ruin; but more in this sense, that sin breaks up our human life, that it removes its supports and makes them alternate, and causes the way along which life moves forward not to stretch out straight before you, but restlessly to go up and down; now through the depths, then across heights, now through the light, then through the dark, now marked by laughter, now by the weeping of those that mourn.

That there is pleasure and pain; that there is joy and sorrow; that there is health and sickness; that there is birth and death; a carrying in to baptism and a carrying out to the grave; that there is exhaustion and revival of strength; that there is corruption of soul and conversion; that there is temptation and then allurement after Christ; in brief, that our whole human life reaches upward and breaks into endless contrasts, all springs from the one all-dominating fact of the existence of sin.

If you are once convinced that without sin there would

be no misery, no sickness and no death in the earth, then it is sin which puts its stamp of rupture and of healing upon our entire earthly life, and it would be most interesting for once to picture your entire human existence from the viewpoint of this rupture.

Without sin there would be no judges to pronounce justice, no physicians to heal the sick, no ministers of the Word to preach the Word of God, no work of mercy nor of compassion, no Church of God on earth.

From this, of course, it may not be inferred that this *broken* life which has burst into all sorts of differences and contrasts is our *real* life. Life in holy harmony and unbroken unity stands infinitely higher and shall one day show itself to be our real, truly human existence, as it now is for God's angels.

But it does follow from this that our life here on earth must be one that is continually disturbed and shaken, continually harassed; and that our life here on earth becomes ever richer, more interesting and more significant in the measure in which we are exposed to stronger tempest-tossings and the height and depth experiences of our existence assume stronger proportions.

These vicissitudes in our life are unequal. With one they are far more difficult and striking than with another. There are those who are scarcely touched and consequently know but very little exaltation in life. But there are others who are hurled into the deepest abyss, and who are afterwards able to take most blessed walks on the mountains of God's holiness.

Of the latter, one is continually the speaker in the Psalms.

Hence, on one side, that call from the depths of misery, and complaint that the bands of death and hell strike terror to his soul, and on the other side, that jubilant exultation that tells of deliverance and redemption, and gives birth to the grateful acknowledgment that God has led him forth into a *"very abundant refreshing"* (Ps. 66, 12, Dutch Ver.).

This refreshing means renewal of strength. A fresh team before the wagon means one that comes from pasture in the fullness of strength. A fresh corps of troops means a battle-array which has taken no part as yet at the front, but marches forward with unimpaired vigor.

And so there is a refreshing when you come out from a period of deadly exhaustion of soul, of utter loss of strength, of inner undermining, and now rejuvenated and renewed in vitality you feel yourself given back by God's grace to yourself, in order that with renewed courage and in the full realization of God's grace you may take up the battle of life again, as though nothing had ever been the matter with you.

This refreshing can therefore bear a twofold character. It can be a refreshing from spiritual declension, but it can also be a refreshing from reverses in your lot in life.

You may have come to the valley of the shadow of death, and now walk again in the lovely light of the sun which illumines your entire life.

The depression and distress which trouble, adversity, bereavement and suffering bring can come down upon your heart with the weight of a ton, and almost crush it. By far the greater number remain strangers to this. They, indeed, likewise drink their cup of sorrow and mourning, but it is handed to them by measure. They would have no strength of soul to endure more. But there have always been a few against whose breast the waves of the bitter lot in life have beaten pitilessly and without sparing. Only their innate heroic nature, through God's grace, kept them from fainting.

Such a period can continue long, in spite of the fact that this persistence of depression and suffering is unspeakably exhausting and prostrating.

But when, at last, there comes an end to this suffering, and sunny days arrive, and the oil of gladness is given for mourning, then, not infrequently, God the Lord is pleased to bless such a bearer of the Job-image with a super-abundance of the joy of life. And then it is from his lips that, with a cry in which his whole soul participates, the song of rejoicing proceeds: "O, my God, thou hast brought me out into an abundant refreshing."

More quiet, but still more blessed, it is when this super-abundant refreshing comes upon us spiritually.

Of course this only comes to the man who lives spiritually, who inwardly leads a spiritual life and who can thirst after God as the hart thirsts after the water-brooks.

The thousands upon thousands who live along unconcernedly, without ever missing the fellowship with God, have no part in this.

But if you are aware of a spiritual life in your soul; if you know what it is to have been initiated in the secret walk with God; and if you have learned every morning and every evening to draw your real strength from the seeking and finding of your God; then life divides itself for you into two sharply contrasted sorts of days: days when you are rich in your God, and living near unto Him you feel your soul within you leap for joy; but alongside and over against these the other days when heaven seems like brass, and when, thrown back upon yourself, you perceive nothing but shadows and darkness within yourself, and you feel that you have wandered away from God like a lost sheep.

This can be a result of committed sins, but it can also be that God purposely leads you through the darkness in order to try your faith, and inwardly to operate the more deeply upon you with unseen grace.

So there may be days and weeks, yea, sometimes months, that God's Face is hidden from you; that no star breaks through in the dark sky of your soul; and that, feeling yourself forsaken of God, you mourn within yourself with a sorrow which the world does not know and does not understand, but which cuts you sorely through the heart.

But this suffering is only for a time.

In the feeling of forsakenness you were not forsaken, but God was operating on you with a grace, the blessed result of which you would only presently know and understand.

And when, finally, these days of spiritual darkness have come to their end, and the light breaks through again, and God comes back to reveal Himself to you in the fullness of His grace, Oh, then for you there is a superabundant refreshing.

And then you perceive it, you acknowledge it, that if God had not led you through this depth of forsakenness, you would never have experienced such a thoroughgoing joy as has now become your portion.

Only after having led you through this depth of darkness was God able to lead you out to so abundant a refreshing of your entire inner existence.

LXXV

FROM STRENGTH TO STRENGTH

To go from strength to strength is to grow, to wax strong, to increase. Not to remain what we are, and for the most part go backward, but, on the contrary, to make advance, to progress, to become richer, fuller, more abundant in faith, and, thanks to this more abundant faith, to become richer in Godliness and in fruits meet for repentance.

This going from strength. to strength, God the Lord shows us in the plant. When the oak first began to grow, you could bend it over with your hand. But when the oak, slender at first, obtains its trunk and becomes a full-grown tree, its strength resists even the hurricance.

God shows you the same in the animal. That same young colt, which at first was scarcely able to stand up has in a few years become the strong horse, after whose strength man measures the power of steam, which laughs at the heavy load and, with his rider in the saddle, leaps over wall and hedge.

In a still more telling way God shows us this going from strength to strength in our own child. First the helpless babe which is fondled on the lap and has to be carried on the arm. Then the creeping with the difficult lesson of learning to walk, until, finally, the first successful venture is made when the ankles have become stronger. And so the growth goes on until full maturity is reached. And then there is strength for a strenuous run, for the bold leap, for climbing of steepest rocks, for a defying of all weariness and fatigue.

All this is but material, the growth of oak and horse, and the growth of the child.

But this growth in strength is not limited to the material. From the visible it passes over into the invisible. There is, likewise, development in the human spirit.

Development by exercise of the artistic talent, which was latent at first, then made itself known, and gradually became capable of more vigorous expression. But also development through training, education, through independent exertion on the part of the thinking spirit to furnish the galleries of the memory with ever richer treasures, to clarify more and more the insight into the world about us, to grasp the unity in the multiplicity, to feel the relation between dull reality and the high ideal, and thus to stand ever more strongly in power and in spirit.

Always growing, always going forward, with the *excelsior* flag wrapped around the breast, climbing the mountain steeps.

And this development, this growth, this going from strength to strength becomes different again when you pass from the unseen of art and the unseen of the understanding to the sphere where character unfolds and the moral stature is formed and nerved. To acquire power in the will and gradually to nerve this will-power. To feel the waking up of the sense of honor and to see it come to an ever finer point. To watch the bud of fidelity and honesty unfold and to see it blossom ever more beautifully. Over against the sense and love for truth to see the rise of hatred against falsehood. To feel the sense of justice cut in ever more deeply; to see the seriousness of life expand. It all presents the beautiful image in the inward personality of a going from strength to strength.

In the body the man grows; in the understanding, the scholar; in the character, the person.

And yet all this does not explain what is meant by the "going from strength to strength" in the song of the Psalmist.

There is in the child of God still another life, the life of Divine grace.

And in this life also, there must be progress, there must be growth and development.

Here, too, the law must be effective. Not to remain what we are, but to go on further and further.

A going from strength to strength.

In the material sphere growth knows its measure, its limit.

Already in the acorn it is determined how high the oak, which springs from it, shall be able to lift itself up. First it sprouts, then grows and expands, but finally the limit, the measure is reached. And then the oak may enlarge in thickness of trunk and breadth of foliage, but there is no more increase in height.

So it is, likewise, with the growth of the animal. From small it becomes large, it broadens itself and becomes full grown. After not many years, sometimes after only a few months or even after a few weeks the measure of the animal is exhausted, and it remains in size what it now is.

And no different is the growth of our body. Far slower than with the animal, man reaches gradually his limit in height. Sometimes this growth takes twenty and more years. But at last here, too, the measure is complete. And then there still is change, increase in strength and expansion, but he gains no more in height, and in old age there is not infrequently even shrinking and diminution.

With the artist there is a moment in his life when he has reached his zenith, when the fullness, the wealth of artistic utterance rather decreases than gains. And in the intellectual domain there may be a few whose brain at seventy or eighty years of age is still green and fresh, when it even still increases in depth and wealth of scope; but for most people here, too, a line is drawn beyond which there is no more advance, and which indicates the limit of development.

Only in the sphere of morals and in the development of character this limit by itself can not be shown. Love and devotion can always increase. Solidity of character can increase in strength even unto death.

And this same thing is put as a claim before every child of God.

Never here on earth to arrive at a goal, but always to go on farther and farther.

Until the day of our death a *going from strength unto strength*.

But here our lost estate appears, which, alas, inexorably shows itself even in the work of grace.

Consider it in your own case, watch it in the case of others. See it in a child of God, whom, after an absence of ten or twenty years, you meet again.

Then, indeed, he should see in you, and you in him, as with eyes, and be able to handle, as it were, with hands, the ripe fruit of this ten or twenty years old work of grace.

And is such the case?

Can you truly say that a child of God who was converted in early life, is ten years farther advanced in grace at sixty years of age than he was at fifty? Do you feel and realize a doubling of power in grace, when at forty years of age you meet again him whom you lost from sight at thirty? Do parents, in the measure of their years, as a rule, stand so much higher? Is the oldest among the children in the same family always farthest advanced in grace?

Notice particularly certain defects in character, certain (to you) well known weaknesses and little sins, which

ten or twenty years ago you found offensive in a child of
God. And is it a rule, that in meeting such a brother or
sister again after the lapse of ten or twenty years, you at
once observe the change, and perceive with delight that
all those obtruding sins and defects of the long ago have
tracklessly disappeared?

Is it not rather true that after twenty and more years
you find your acquaintances and friends, your own children and your own parents, all too frequently beset with
the same limitations of grace which you mourned in them
before, and the gift of grace as intricately bound up with
the same thorns and thistles as then?

And more yet. When you consider yourself, and examine your own life in the presence of God, are you then
not bound to confess with shame that sometimes ten long
years have advanced you almost no step further in spiritual increase, and that the old weeds still flourish with old-
time luxuriance in the field of the heart within?

What is the ordinary course?

Is it not this, that one becomes converted; that after
conversion one sets his mind and soul on holy things; and
in all sorts of ways acts differently from before, and that
thus he feels within himself that the past is broken with
and a new life has begun. At first it is even too ideally
strung, so that after a few years a calmer state ensues.

And then this stadium in the life of grace in most cases
becomes fixed. It remains what it is, but growth there
is none. One feeds on what spiritual capital was acquired
during this first period of grace. One increases fairly well in
knowledge, also in spiritual experience and in spiritual wisdom, but it does not come to higher strength. Sometimes
there is even backsliding, from which one does not recover
save with difficulty. So one is satisfied. Strives after nothing
higher. And remains what he became until his death.

We do not say that this is the case with all.

Thank God, there are those who as shining lights shed luster upon the life of the congregation, and who until they die, do not cease to take full draughts, again and again, from the cup of grace.

And yet how wholly different would be the revelation of the Kingdom of heaven among our people, if all believers, if all they who are conscious of the fact that they are the children of God, from the hour of conversion until the day of death, would continually cause the call of *onward and forward* to find its echo in their soul.

Who can say what it would be in your heart, in your home, in the Congregation of the Lord, if with all of us it were, and continued to be, an ever constant and unceasing going from *strength to strength*.

LXXVI

BLESSED ARE THE PURE IN HEART

A REALLY sinless, pure heart is in the eyes of a child of God as the pearl of great price, for which he constantly implores God. Yet here on earth it never becomes his portion.

They who stand outside of the faith can have no mention here. We readily grant that among them also purity of heart is highly esteemed. We do not deny that among them there are strivings after it. But what they aim at is something different. To the child of God, purity of heart is the means by which *to see God*. To them it is rather the means by which not to fall short of high moral character. And these two can not be mentioned in one breath.

It is a saying of Jesus: "Blessed are the pure in heart." It was addressed by Jesus directly to the children of God, as S. Matthew (v, 8) distinctly shows. For is not this "pure in heart" followed immediately by the: "Blessed are the peacemakers, for they shall be called the *children of God*." And it truly speaks for itself that the seven beatitudes together treat of the same persons. "The peacemakers," "the pure in heart," "they who hunger and thirst after righteousness," they who are "poor in spirit," and so on. Each points to those alone, who place themselves under the guardianship of Jesus, and will to enter into the kingdom of heaven that has come nigh.

Virtuous people, as the world counts virtue, moral idealists, are not considered here. Undoubtedly there is a great deal in them, that with respect to this earthly life must be highly prized. But all this is of no account here.

The reference here is to those who have been initiated into the secret of Salvation, those who have passed from the world into the kingdom of the Son of God's love. This purity of heart which leads one *to see God* is not conceivable otherwise than in a child of God.

With trembling this is said.

To know who is a child of God and who is not, is so extremely difficult. There are those who are children of God, and yet scarcely dare to confess it of themselves. There are others who appropriate it to themselves, yet so little exhibit the marks of it. And there are more still who obtrude themselves in a way which makes you seriously doubt whether their confessed "childship" is not stolen goods.

But apart from all this, this much is certain, that the children of God who are most devout and most truly consecrated are continually in the midst of bitter combat just because there is still so much impurity in their heart which continually sullies their life.

Sometimes this sullying goes very far, and the fifty-first Psalm is still being prayed, after David, from the sense of bitter guilt which forces the painful cry to the lips "cleanse me of my sins of impurity."

And even this does not say enough.

It must be confessed that not seldom in life two men or two women stand side by side, one of whom zealously labors for Christ and the other rejects the Christ, and that upon applying the test of purity of heart and of behavior the confessor of Jesus is shamed by the denier of the Christ.

This is grievous for the faith. It is to be mourned over with tears. And yet you may not conceal it. David did not do so, and S. Paul was his follower in this. "The good that I would, I do not; but the evil which I would not, that

I do" (Rom. vii, 19). And through all ages, this painful struggle has been carried on in Christ's church. The hypocrites, the false brethren stand outside of this. They have no part in this. No, it is among the sincere followers of God that, age upon age, this selfsame complaint has been heard. Sometimes it has even been worked out into a sinful system of the old and the new Adam, as from his viewpoint of unbelief Maeterlinck is doing now. But however experienced, interpreted or explained, the phenomenon exhibits itself again and again: confession was honestly meant, faith is of the right stamp, and yet, hand in hand with this, the hopeless struggle goes on with the impurity of one's own heart.

To be pure in heart is in such instances for the most part still misunderstood, as though it referred exclusively to purity from sensual sins.

Impure is then said to be the voluptuary, the man who drinks to excess, the epicure, the miser, the effeminate. And surely these gross sins should be the first to be denounced.

But yet, he who is free from these is, therefore, by no means yet pure in *heart*. Purity of heart embraces the whole life of our soul. Pride, arrogance, dishonest practice, anger, hate, falsehood and the many other vices, including ordinary vanity and satisfaction with oneself, which make the waters of the human heart muddy and unclean.

Impure your heart becomes by everything that does not belong to it. As a pond becomes unclean by everything that the passerby throws into it, so is the human heart defiled by everything that God did not create in it, and by everything that creeps into it from Satan or from the world.

And this, now, is the dreadful part of it, that already

at our birth so many germs of impurity were present in it, which, until our death, will never entirely be eradicated. That we live in a world which encourages so strongly the germination of these impurities. And that we associate with people, who, inwardly as impure as ourselves, accustom us, provided it does not come to gross excess, to make light of this impurity in ourselves, and to make equally light of impurity in them.

This weakens, then, our moral sense, our moral judgment, and makes us dream of a pure heart, the whiles in many points we remain impure of heart.

If, now, Jesus had meant that only they went out free who had never caught their own heart in any impure thought, inclination or sensation, then this beatitude would fill the soul with despair.

For so no one is.

Until our death we continue to struggle with the impure germs in our heart.

We make progress, but never in any other way than by the application of ever finer tests in order to begin to see impurity now in what before never so much as roused the thought of sin in us.

The more advance we make in faith, the more keen the eye of the soul becomes in the discovery of sin, and just because of this, the sense of guilt does not grow less, but rather more in the measure in which we get away from sin.

The world does not understand this when it hears a saintly soul, a very angel of love and mercy, plead touchingly for forgiveness of guilt. But by itself there is nothing strange in it. These very ones who are far advanced now discover *sin* in what perhaps before even seemed *virtue* to them.

Jesus knew this, and so this can not have been meant.

And, therefore, He does not say: Blessed are they who have a pure heart, a heart without sin, but: "Blessed are they who *are* pure in heart."

In your heart your ego dwells, your person acts, the child of God thinks, ponders, forms judgments and makes choices.

There is a difference, therefore, between what your self finds in your heart and your own self that rules in your heart.

And since no one of us dwells anywhere else than in a heart that is inwardly sullied, and from which all sorts of poisonous vapors arise, the question whether you are pure or impure in heart is only answered by the other question, whether your attitude toward these poisonous inclinations of your heart is one of hatred and fiery indignation, or whether you sympathize with these evil inclinations, and make concessions to them with your will and mind.

That you frequently succumb is no proof yet that you are impure in heart. It is but the question whether you have struggled against it, whether you have battled against it with all the spiritual power at your command, whether, with the invocation of the help of God and of His Christ and of His angels, you have avoided everything that prophesied your defeat, and are continuously imploring: "Lead me not into temptation, but deliver me from evil."

On this, and on this alone, it all depends. You yourself must be pure as you stand in your own heart opposed to the impurities that well up from your heart.

When this distinction between your self that believes and the evils that stir in your heart is lost, you are undone. Then you identify yourself with these impurities. Then you sink away in the evil waters of your own heart, and are drowned in your own sinful inclinations.

If, on the other hand, you are courageously and firmly determined in the inner chambers of your heart, yea, armed with bitter hatred against your own sinful inclinations, as against your mortal enemy, then your heart may remain full of impurity as long as you live, but you, your own *self*, are pure in heart, and by God's grace you triumph every time over the sin that waylays you in your own heart.

Then Satan can not tempt you, for God is your ally. Then this very struggle which is never given up makes you crowd yourself the closer to your God, and here you will know certain moments, even in the very heat of strife, when with the vision of the eye of your soul you, as it were, *see* your God.

LXXVII

IN THE NIGHT I COMMUNE WITH MINE OWN HEART

Our sleep and our prayers have this in common, that, both he who sleeps and he who prays, closes his eyes and withdraws himself from the light into the darkness.

And yet this is not the same.

He who would pray shuts his eyes in order not to be distracted by what is seen around him. If it were possible, he would prefer to stop his ears as well, in order not to be disturbed by any noise from his surrounding.

There is prayer in company with others to which a wholly different consideration applies. But one who prays by himself seeks his strength in isolation.

This is no less strongly expressed in what Jesus said to his disciples: "But thou when thou prayest, enter into thy closet and shut the door behind thee" (S. Matt. vi, 6). And by His own example, Jesus expressed the very same idea, as often as He withdrew Himself for prayer into the solitude of the wilderness or into the loneliness of the mountains. Yea, even in Gethsemane the Lord seeks the lonely spot for His last conflict of prayer, and He leaves His disciples to remain behind at a distance, in order that He might be *alone* during His prayer.

In so far as this expresses a seeking after rest and quiet for the sake of our prayer, it agrees with what we seek after in sleep.

But with this the similarity ends.

For in *prayer* we withdraw ourselves from the world, in order that in our fellowship with Almighty God we may be the more fully awake to the order of higher things.

In sleep, on the other hand, we isolate ourselves from the world in order to sink back into unconsciousness and into forgetfulness of self.

At least so it is when conditions are normal. In the state of paradise it would always have been so. But in the hard reality of things as they are now, prayer and sleep are constantly confused in a twofold way. So that in prayer sometimes, we are overtaken by what belongs to sleep; and contrariwise when we lie down to sleep, the soul passes over into the attitude of prayer.

Not as though so many actually fall asleep in prayer. We grant that this does happen when the prayer of another is too lengthy. But this, of course, is very exceptional. But what does frequently happen is, that he who joins in prayer under the devotional leadership of some one else, allows his mind to be diverted or unconsciously lets it rest.

And, on the other hand, that the night, which was intended for sleep, not infrequently ends in prayer, is seen in the case of Asaph, who in Psalm 77 (R. V.) mourns: "My hand was stretched out in the night to my God in prayer. Thou, Lord, holdest mine eyes watching. In the night I communed with mine own heart, and my spirit made diligent search."

When we close our eyes, whether for sleep or for prayer, we go out from the light, by excluding it, into the desired *darkness and obscurity.*

With sleep we do this in order that our spirit may sink back into the darkness of the unconscious life; with prayer we do this in order that, shut out from the light of day, we may seek with *clearer consciousness* the higher light which glows about God's Throne.

By nature it is not darkness that comes to disturb the light. Darkness is there of itself. And it is only by the dawning light that darkness is overcome.

It was not light that existed first but darkness. The earth was without form and void, and darkness was upon the face of the deep. And in that darkness, light broke forth by the creative Word of God.

And when afterwards the darkness yet covers the earth again, this darkness does not come from without into the light, but it is there of itself, as soon as the light withdraws itself.

This is so in the world of matter, and it is not otherwise spiritually.

There was darkness in nature, and this continued until God created the light. And this comes back again as soon as God withdraws the light of sun, moon and stars. Then there is deep night again.

And even so there is in the spirit of a newborn child, first perfect unconsciousness and ignorance. This lasts until the light of the consciousness awakens in his soul, and gradually increases in clearness. Here, likewise, this clarity of the self-consciousness can set again in darkness. This takes place with one in a fit of faintness, with one who becomes hypnotized, in part with the insane and with the dotage of old age. Moreover, this selfsame thing happens commonly every twenty-four hours.

For sleep is nothing else than that the light of our consciousness passes over again into the twilight of slumber, and finally into deep, sound sleep.

In the night, the light of day around us and the light of the self-consciousness within us have set in darkness and unconsciousness.

It may even be said that the more perfectly the light of the self-consciousness went out in our sleep, the better and the more healthy the sleep was.

On waking up in the morning, not to know anything

of the seven hours which we slept away in the night is the most normal operation of nature.

So the first man slept, before he fell, in paradise. So sleeps the young babe at its mother's breast. So sleeps the weary day-laborer whose mental activity is limited. But such a sleep is no longer the rule. And our sleep becomes restless all too frequently, either because of physical disturbance, sickness or excess, or because the spirit within us is too deeply stirred to permit perfect forgetfulness to settle down upon our self-consciousness.

And so there comes both the dream-life and the half, or entire, sleeplessness.

The dream-life is still a realm which has been but little investigated. Enough that we know that it can occasion fear and anxiety; that in sinful imagination it can sully our consciousness; that sometimes prophecies and premonitions loom up in it; and that, more than once, God has made use of the dream-life by which to execute His holy Counsel.

But next to this sort of dream-life, and still more painful, stands the misery of the sleepless night, when care keeps the heart waking; when the spirit within us is overwrought; when a task that awaits us in the morning begrudges us our sleep, or when sickness holds back the passionately longed-for sleep from our eyes.

This sleeplessness is a part of our human misery, a part of human suffering still foreign to those of younger years, but which with advancing years is spared to few.

As in all true prayer the spirit shuts itself off from this world only to wake up the more fully in a higher world of thought, so it can be the case in this dream-life and in this sleepless slumber.

For in sleep the spirit ought to sink away into forgetfulness, but instead of this it is the more fully alive in terrifying or in holy dreams. And so in that sleepless slumber our spirit finds in place of rest only a higher tension and a far more busy and wearying activity.

And God the Lord is in this also.

Asaph expresses it with fervent piety: "Thou holdest mine eyes waking."

But this very acknowledgment on the part of the saint, that it is no chance, but that it is the Lord Who holds our eyes waking, shows, that this dream-life too, as well as this sleepless slumber serves a *purpose*.

The Lord has an intention with respect to them. And when in the night our heart communes with itself and our spirit makes diligent search, this, too, is a part of our life for which we are responsible.

Sin lies not merely in words and works, but also in thoughts, in what goes on in our spirit. Even for our dreams we are responsible. Not for what happens to us in those dreams, but for what we do in them. Not every one has the same dreams. Every one dreams according to the content of his imagination. And however little we may be lord and master over our dreams, every one feels that if our Savior has known a dream-life, it can not have been otherwise than one that was perfectly holy.

In the night itself we can not make a dream different from what it is, but the purifying of our imagination and the cleansing of our thoughts can in the long run guide our dreams into sinless realms.

But, from the nature of the case, our responsibility is far greater for what our spirit does in the sleepless hours of night. Then our spirit can either bring thoughts of the world into the dark of night or it can think and ponder upon holy things. Or it can vex itself within us to no purpose and for no good.

But what our spirit then *should* do in the darkness is to

unlock the gate of the realm of what is holy and commune with a higher world.

In the case that in the midst of sleep you are awake but a few minutes, you can and should engage your spirit with your God. And upon awaking, your very first thought should again be of Him. "O God, Thou art my God; early in the morning will I seek thee" (Ps. 63, 1, Dutch Ver).

To him who so understands it, sleepless hours are a spiritual gold mine.

There are not a few who in just such sleepless nights, or in hours without sleep, have spiritually been wondrously enriched.

This, too, is an instance of the loving kindness of the Lord.

Sleeplessness is one form of our misery, but this, too, God by His grace turns to our good.

Yea, there are those who in such nights have been remembered spiritually by God so generously and so richly that a night of deep sleep has sometimes seemed to them a lost night.

The work of God upon the souls of His elect goes on in the hours of night in a way ever glorifying to His Name.

LXXVIII

I WAIT FOR THEE ALL THE DAY LONG

NOT only in the forest and in the desert upon earth, but also in sun, moon and stars it is the Spirit, Who with the Father and the Son maintains all power and causes it to operate. Wherever a creature exists it is the Spirit Who operates therein. Without the working of that Spirit no force of nature is even conceivable. And this Spirit Who operates in every creature is none other than the Holy Spirit Himself Who in the Triune Being is to be worshiped as the third most holy Person.

But this is the distinction: this Spirit is neither known nor worshiped in His holiness as *Holy Spirit*, save among the creatures which are themselves spiritual of nature, and which have themselves become *conscious* of their spiritual character. Above, the angels of God; here on earth, the children of men.

A star in the firmament is brute matter and knows of no holiness. A plant is devoid of holy sense. And although in Scripture an animal is conceded to have a soul, and though it exhibits sometimes certain wit and power of will, the animal stands outside of the sphere in which the holiness of the Lord is acknowledged.

A connective sense of the holinesses of the Lord, here on earth is found in man alone.

But not immediately upon birth. The babe in the cradle exists merely physically; it knows no holy emotions as yet. Only with its further development does this sense gradually awaken. And then it often takes many long years before the higher moral sense of the holinesses of

God awakens far enough for the conscience to react vigorously against the unholinesses of this world.

But, even so, all this still lies outside the domain of our
Pentecost.

Pentecostal grace is something which only the Church
knows. It is the high and holy privilege of the ransomed
of the Lord. The world does not know this grace and does
not see it. It has not even a faint perception of what this
grace might be.

But for this very reason it requires great carefulness
lest on the ground of this privilege the church should take
for granted that the Spirit does *not* operate in this, as yet,
unsaved world; and at any rate is foreign to the forces of
nature in the material unconscious creation.

They who are too mystical and hyper-spiritual lean all
too often upon this error. And, therefore, it must every
time be confessed again and remembered that the Spirit
is in every creature, the Holy Spirit operates in every
creature that has a rational life; but the fellowship of the
Holy Spirit, which the Pentecost-miracle brought, is only
known and tasted in the Church of the Lord.

In this mutual relation, the working of the Holy Spirit,
the prompting of the Holy Spirit and the communion of
that Holy Spirit must be bound together as in one bundle.

Otherwise the child of God leaves without compassion
the unconverted world to itself and enters into direct conflict with the prayer of the Lord: "I pray not that thou
shouldest take them out of the world, but that in the world
thou shouldest keep them from the evil" (S. John xvii,
15).

And now the second point, which should be carefully
considered is this.

The Holy Spirit was poured out at first and once for all
on the day of Pentecost, and from that hour on, He has

continued to dwell in the Church, will never leave her, and will dwell in and with her forevermore.

But—and this is all too frequently forgotten—what is present in the *Church* is by no means, therefore, always present in every one who is *connected* with the Church.

The real Church of the living God is the Body of Christ, the mystical Body of which He is the Head. And in this mystical Body dwells the Holy Ghost, first in the Head, and from thence along all articulations and tissues and veins animates every one that as a living member has been incorporated in this Body and lives his life in connection with this Body.

It is not one here and another there, who each by himself received the Holy Ghost, and who by uniting together now form the Body of Christ. A body does not originate in such a way that first you have members, which are afterwards put together to form a body. The body is conceived and born with the crusts and beginnings in it of every member that at a later period shall come out of it. Even the beard, which only in later years covers the chin, is not brought to it from without, but comes out from a germ which the infant at birth brought with it.

And in this body is the *life*. Not in a member by itself. An amputated leg is dead. Even an arm that is still joined to the body, by an accident or illness can be rendered as good as dead, and this arm only becomes alive when the blood from the body circulates through it again.

And so it is with the Body of the Lord, which is the Congregation of the Saints. The Head of that Body can not be touched. Christ is in glory. From Him the Holy Spirit never departs. And while, as the Head, Christ is inseparable from that Body, the Holy Spirit, the life of the Church, is always insured and guaranteed in that sacred Head.

However nearly extinct at a given moment life may be in the members of the Body, it streams with irresistible pressure from the Head to the members again, and presently practises again that wondrously assimilating power which shows itself so gloriously in every reveille.

Of course this Congregation is not identical with the visible Church. But yet the visible Church, also, does not live otherwise than by the Holy Ghost, Who, overflowing from the Head of the invisible Body of the Lord, keeps this Church alive as long as the vital relation with this invisible Body is not abandoned by her.

And this is the effect of this indwelling of the Holy Ghost in the Church, that he who in an organic, spiritual way as a living member is united to this Church, knows and tastes a fellowship with the Eternal Being such as does not exist outside of it.

Outside of it, too, among the unconverted there is truly found a certain sense of the existence of God. Also a certain feeling of dependence upon a higher power. The voice of conscience, too, may be overheard in their heart, and, especially with advancing years, they often think upon what shall follow after death.

But not all. Far from it. It may not even be denied that the number steadily increases of those who do not concern themselves either about God, or their sin, or their lot after death.

But this does not take away the fact that in Christian, as well as in heathen, lands there are always many people who still maintain a certain general religiousness.

But what these people lack is not the operation of the Holy Ghost in the conscience, but *fellowship* with Him. And, of course, fellowship with the Holy Ghost is nothing else than fellowship with God Himself.

Fellowship with God, not taken now as the fellowship

of the flock with the Shepherd, not as the outward compliance with God's appointment in our lot of life, nor as a conscious dependence upon God—no, but taken as the immediate meeting between the *Ego* of God and the *Ego* of our heart, in the mysticism of grace.

You have heard of the Holy Apostle, and you have certain fellowship with the man of Tarsus as you read his epistles. But it would be something altogether different if you could spend a year in S. Paul's company.

This same difference applies here.

You may have heard of God, of His miracles, of His virtues, of His powers and mightinesses, and yet this God may still be a stranger to you.

But this is what fellowship of the Spirit imparts: It allows your soul to meet this God in Person, to learn to *know* this God personally, to have personal dealing with this Eternal Being, and thus as a child with his father to hold converse with this Triune God.

And this is what *waiting on the Lord* brings you.

A friend meets friend in order presently to part again. But the child expects his father because he belongs to his father and misses him when he is away. And so it is, likewise, in this fellowship with God through the Holy Ghost.

He who has once come to this, that he personally has learned to know God as his Father and has been initiated into secret communion with Him, can not on this account always remain there. The multiplicity of our labors does not permit this. The distractions of the world oppose this. We ourselves cut this off continually by sinful suggestions from our impure heart. And not infrequently the Lord Himself withdraws this fellowship from us in order to stimulate our desire after this fellowship anew and to strengthen it.

But—and this is its trait—a child of God, a believer,

who has once enjoyed this fellowship, and then has lost it, *misses it*, he feels an emptiness within, he has no rest until it is restored. And on his waking in the morning, the first impulse of his soul is to obtain this fellowship back again.

There must be one of two things: either the child of God has this fellowship, or he longs for it, prays for it, *"waits for it all day long"* (Ps. 25, 5, Dutch Ver).

In the hour of conversion it is a seeking after what one did not as yet possess. Afterward it is a seeking to regain what was lost.

And here, too, this applies: "He that seeks shall find; he that knocks, it shall be opened unto him."

LXXIX

O GOD, MY GOD!

THE flower-bud of prayer unfolds in the soul of the child very slowly. Not as though the little child does not already have a certain early inclination to pray. But though the bud sets itself early, it is another question when this bud shall be developed.

For many months the little one was present when mother prayed, but he did not perceive anything of it, yea, not infrequently he disturbed her prayer by his crying. But at length a moment comes when through the prayer of mother, or of some other member of the family, he undergoes a peculiar sensation and comes under the impression of what is holy. Tender mother-piety then endeavors to confirm this impression. And soon the little one kneels when mother kneels, and when he is put to bed the first effort is made to teach him to pray himself. Then mother folds the little hands together, closes the little eyes and dictates a simple little prayer. And the precious one mumbles with his infant lips what mother says before him.

But in this the form is already ahead of the reality. The impression of reverence and awe before the Majesty of the Eternal Being is there. A young child even loves these first attempts at prayer. But the Eternal Being has not yet discovered Himself in a clearly conscious form to the infant soul. For this reason a young child learns prayer to Jesus more readily than direct prayer to the Most High God. What the young child says in his infant prayer is not yet *his own* speaking to God. He only repeats what he hears, and when he first weaves something himself in his prayer, it is not worship, but an asking for something which engages his mind in his infant world. All this remains a speaking into an unknown Holy sphere which is around or above his little bed. It all follows a steady but slow development. Extremely little shows itself, as a rule, before the tenth year of age, of prayer from an inward impulse of the soul to a God Who is to be addressed personally, and who is, at least in some measure, personally known. There are exceptions with children of five, six or seven years of age, especially when they die young. But, as a rule, the fuller unfolding of the flower-bud into personal and conscious prayer of one's own does not come much before the twelfth year.

Particularly is this true when back of that tenth or twelfth year there were some unfavorable years when the child was obliged to sit still during long drawn-out devotions, and the motherly tenderness of the teaching to pray turned involuntarily into a purely formal compulsion to keep eyes closed and hands folded.

What God Himself accomplishes during these early years in the infant soul, His holy angels know, but we do not. Only later on does the result of it become evident to us. And this begins to show itself somewhere about the twelfth year. At that age it is already noticed whether a spiritual sense has been quickened in the heart, or whether indifference to, if not aversion against, what is Holy, predominates. But if a spiritual disposition of heart shows itself, then it is about at this age that God Himself takes the mother's task in hand, and lures the lad or the young girl by an inward impulse to a first personal prayer.

But from this time, to the moment when the soul pours itself out in the words, "*O God, my God!*" the way is long.

In many cases the kindly, tender glow of childhood prayer is not a little darkened by the time maturity is reached. By then, an entirely different world of thoughts, from all sorts of books and experiences, has entered into the consciousness. And this new world of thought appears bitterly prosaic by the side of the poetry of the life of prayer. Or if it should dazzle the mind by a choice collection of ideals, which may indeed promote an enthusiasm for rich plans and purposes and expectations, nevertheless it is no more centered in the worship of a glorious Eternal Being.

And these two currents, the current of the practical and ideal life in its multiplicity, and the current of the unity of our life as it lies recapitulated in prayer, struggle with one another for the upper hand; and sometimes in this combat, prayer is forever lost. There are those, alas, who, though pious as children, have as men altogether lost the habit of prayer.

It also happens that prayer is maintained, and that it gains in seriousness and depth, but with repulsion of the world, so that the life of the world stands unreconciled by the side of it, until ofttimes a sickly mysticism or overwrought spiritualism more and more makes itself master of the soul.

But in the ordinary way of piety, this period of struggle gives place to a period of spiritual stability. One has now settled the relation between the life of his soul and his life in the world. The bark no longer drifts with the caprice of wind and wave-beat. A rudder has been put aboard, a compass put in place, the lee-boards can be let down sideways. So the soul can direct its own course as it cuts through the waters of the sea of life. And so, heroic devotion to one's task in life goes hand in hand with a life of prayer that ever more richly develops itself.

Even these two, the sphere of the prayer-life and the sphere of one's daily occupation, begin more and more to cover one another.

The moments of real prayer multiply themselves, because in the midst of one's work the lifting up of the heart unto God becomes more frequent and the ejaculatory prayer occurs more often, until, at length, a prayerful disposition of soul becomes more and more habitual. And, on the other hand, the whole of one's life's task is more and more brought into the secret prayer, and one begins to realize that prayer is not bound to single holy utterances, but that our whole existence, together with all its needs, may be committed to God and in God be sanctified.

So prayer grows in significance, so it begins to cast a benign shade over our entire life, so it becomes in increasing measure the strength of our life.

The saying "Fervent prayer is half the work" which is at first repeated after others now becomes blessed experience.

And so the moment approaches in which, at last, the words "O God, my God!" can become the clear, pure expression of what the inner life of the soul experiences and enjoys in its most intimate and holy impulses.

Coming to the lips too readily these words from Psalm 43, "O God, my God!" would be guilty egotism, covetous selfishness. An appropriating of the Great God to oneself. "My" God, without a thought of others. A sin of prayer so strikingly overcome in the "*Our* Father." Always a praying: not give *me*, but give *us* our daily bread; not forgive *me*, but forgive *us* our debts; not deliver *me*, but deliver *us* from evil. Never to stand before God alone, but in the fellowship of love with all God's saints. To pray, as a member in the body of Christ — which you are — not as though you stood by yourself all alone.

But the "O God, my God" does not exclude this in any respect. It has something altogether different in view. It springs from the altogether different meaning that God

the Lord not merely cares for all His children, as a king
watches over his millions of subjects, but that the King of
kings has this advantage over all the princes of the earth,
that He knows all His children personally, that He understands them personally through and through, that He
sustains a personal relation to every one of them, that to
each of them He has given a special calling, that He has
reserved a particular task for each one of them, that He
continuously trains each one of them for a unique destiny
in eternity, and that therefore He not merely sustains
one general relation to all of them together, but that over
and above this He stands in a particular relation to every
one of them. This relation is so peculiar that it can not be
exactly the same with any one of the others.

"*Our* Father!" but as a father who has seven children
is the father of them all, and yet distinguishes between
them, and companies with each of his children differently
according to the difference of nature, disposition and
character; so is the Lord our God Father of us all, and yet
to each of us our Father in a special sense, in a distinctive
manner, coming down to us in a mystical way, and revealing Himself to us in mystical sensations, which bear
their own character and carry their own stamp. He
knows us, and we are known of Him in a way that can be
the case with no other person who is differently consti-
tuted.

He is the *one* Sun, but glistens in every dew-drop differently.

Only this: the dew-drop does not *know* it; God's child
can know it. And when this knowledge dawns on him,
he kneels down before God, *his* God.

Now distinguish carefully.

On the side of God, this particular relation, which with
each one of His children is a different one, existed from the

moment of conception and of birth; yea, already before the conception, in the call of the elect from eternity.

The difference lies alone on our side.

Years of our life go by in which we know God and have a prayer-life before His Face, but in the general sense, as distinguished from the particular. We pray as others pray. We are one of God's children, but we are not yet discovered to our self as such a one in whom something special of the Father comes to expression.

But from the general, the particular by degrees separates itself. What lends us a character of our own, gives us a calling of our own, causes us to be an individual person, and to begin to enter into particular fellowship with the Lord our God. And now it is the unsearchable richness of our God that He, Who created and elected all these His children with their particular dispositions and with their proper callings, wills and is able to be God to each of them, in the way that best suits their nature and condition.

Not a general fullfilment for all alike, but for each of them that particular supply which he needs.

Not only His most particular Providence, but also the most special self-discovery of His Divine Majesty in the mirror of the life of each soul.

And when it comes to this, but only then, there springs of itself, artlessly from the heart, the jubilant cry of adoration: "O God, my God!"

LXXX

THE LORD IS THY SHADE

NOT only the child but also he who is older would rather look at pictures and prints, than read; or at least likes them for the assistance which they lend to his imagination. Hence the predilection of our fathers for the illustrated Bible, and the strongly revived demand among us for illustrated books and periodicals.

For a time there was no love for the illustrated book. This was partly because the plates were poor, and partly because readers were over-wise. But since nature has been somewhat restored in us; and photography, together with photo-engraving, in less than a quarter of a century have brought the illustration up to a degree of excellence and perfection unknown before, the old love to *see* things has come to the fore again, and by this seeing of pictures our imagination has been uncommonly enriched. Everything is now embellished with portraits and pictures. In a good sense and in a sinful sense, the power of letting things be seen is again recognized. Even newspapers begin to seek their strength therein. At first it is still the picture that accompanies the reading matter. Gradually it becomes more pictures and ever less reading matter, until exaggeration in the end avenges itself, and the more normal proportion returns.

The main point in hand with respect to all this is, that our nature has been so created, so disposed, that by predilection it best loves immediate sight, and that it extends this love into the realm of the spiritual.

This will to see, rather than by the effort of our thinking to arrive at *insight* is therefore no defect in us, and much less is it a result of sin—it is Divine instinct.

It is not prophesied of the glory above that the redeemed shall be dialectic thinkers, but that in this particular also they will show themselves to be *children* of God in that they shall desire to *see* the Eternal Being; and that, in fact, they shall enjoy this clear vision.

Philip's request: "Lord, show us the Father and it sufficeth us!" was for this life the all too naïve expression of this deep desire, and Jesus' answer to this question shows that the whole Christian religion can be recapitulated under this viewpoint of *sight*. The Apostles gloried in the fact that they were the first who had seen and beheld the Word of Life. Already in prophecy the vision had prepared the way for this seeing. And when the Apostles describe the glory that is to come they prophesy that now we see as in a glass darkly, but that then we shall see face to face, and in this seeing we shall know as we are known. Not reading, not reasoning; no, the seeing, the clear beholding shall be salvation. And to this S. John adds: "Beloved, it is not yet made manifest what we shall be, but this we know that we shall be like him, for we shall see him as he is" (I John iii, 2).

This ability to see is cultivated by picture and print, and ability to see spiritual things is trained by the emblem. The Cross, the All-seeing eye, the emblems of faith, hope and love—the catacombs of early Christians are still full of such emblems.

And what says still more, nature, life itself, is full of imagery, and more than any other book the Bible makes use of it in order to exhibit the spiritual to us. Besides picture and print, and besides emblem, it is this *imagery* which does not stand *alongside* of the word, but enters into the word, and through the word itself shows the realities. The true Vine, the good Shepherd, the Lamb of God, the Sower that sows the seed, and more, are all images borrowed from nature and from life, which God uses in His Word in order to bring the spiritual nearer to us.

Scripture does the same thing with respect to the Highest, in its effort to bring the Eternal Being closer to us.

That Eternal Being then makes His approach to us in such imagery as The Lord is our "Rock," the Lord is our "High Tower," He is our "Shield," He is our "Keeper," He is the "Father" in the "Father-house." He is our "King" seated upon the "Throne of His Glory." And among this number of figures there is this beautiful one: "*The Lord is thy shade*" (Ps. 121, 5). Isaiah uses this imagery when on his knees in worship he exclaims: "O Lord, thou art my God . . . Thou hast been a strength to the poor . . . a refuge from the storm, a shadow from the heat . . . as the heat by a thick cloud, so shall the noise of tyrants be brought down by thee" (Isa. xxv, 1, 4, 5, Dutch Ver.). And in the same way, the song of Hamaaloth repeats it: "The Lord is thy Keeper; the Lord is thy Shade upon thy right hand."

This figure of speech is beautiful because it is so gentle and tender.

Here is no exhibition of power. Here no strong arm bares itself. A scorching heat prevails, such as in the desert of the East beats down all life. And behold! a thick cloud travels quietly and majestically across the desert level, and the sunlight no longer blinds, and the sun-heat no longer singes, and man freely breathes again, refreshed and brought to himself by the Divine shade from above.

Shade! Oh, we sons of the West do not know the glory which lies embedded in this short word to the man of the East.

Dog-days excepted, the sun is never the fierce tyrant to us that makes life a burden. The sun is to us a lovely something which we seek. The sun refreshes and cherishes us. We love his radiancy.

But in the land where the Prophets prophesied and the Psalmists sang, where Jesus walked about and the disciples dwelt, all powers of invention are on the alert, and by means of thick walls, heavy hangings, high trees, and long white garments try to modify the fierce tyranny of the sun. In the hot season everything there burns, everything glows, everything singes, and on the table-lands of the desert, man and beast are helpless victims of the scorching sand below, and of the burning sky above.

Everything calls, everything prays for shade.

And all this, applied by imagery to the struggle of God's people and to life's battle on the part of His servants, inspires both Prophet and Psalmist to refresh Israel with the glorious word of comfort: "The Lord thy God is thy Shade."

Thy Shade against what?

Against the heat of the day, metaphorically used with respect to the distress of your lot in life, of the heat, the fierceness wherewith the provocation of opposition, of adversity and persecution goes against you.

The Lord is thy Shade! is allied to this other figure of speech: the Lord is thy Shield! but has yet another tendency.

You have to do with an enemy, a persecutor, whom you know, whom you see before you, and whose blows come down upon you, and you are in need of a *shield*. And whosoever in such threatening moments has sought his shield with God has always found it with Him.

But it is wholly different when trouble, like heat from the desert, comes upon you, which you can not withstand, and which from the mysterious background of your lot in life, or from covered opposition, as an elementary

force presses upon you from all sides, and against which
you have no means of resistance at your command. So it
is for the Arab in the desert when the heat of the sun
makes the sand under his feet burn, and causes the
roof of his mouth to be parched. And so it is for God's
people when opposition presents itself on every hand,
when here it is water that threatens inundation, and there
it is the whirlwind that carries everything before it. Yea,
so it is in your personal life when, for the sake of God's
will and of His cause, you are driven from one difficulty
to another, from trial to trial, and the heat of battle
steadily increases in intensity and at length you threaten
to succumb.

And in such an hour as this, when, as we would say, the
water reaches up to the lips, while the Scripture—which
comes from the East—speaks of so scorching a heat of
the sun that its fierceness threatens utter prostration,
then is the Lord your soul's intimate Comforter, because
He is then your Shade Who covers you and makes you
breathe again.

This can be done, according to the sacred metaphor, by
means of a cloud which intercepts the heat of the glowing
sun, but it can be effected in a still more tender way.

A father in the desert can himself take the side of the
sun, and so be a shade for his child that walks with him.

And this is the picture the Psalmist brings to mind
when he sings: "The Lord is thy Shade *upon thy right
hand.*"

So the Divine tenderness of highest love mingles itself
in the comforting.

Your God does not leave you to yourself. The way
through the wilderness cannot be spared you. The heat
must singe. But the Lord follows after you. He comes
to you. He draws very near to you. He places Himself

between this heat of the sun and yourself. He takes you by the hand. He covers you with the shade which His Majestic greatness casts upon you. And so you go on upon your way with gladness, refreshed by the love of God and covered by His holy Shade.

All this is poetry. We know it well. But though poetry is that "fine art which addresses itself to the feelings and the imagination by the instrumentality of musical and moving words," it is nevertheless no *fiction*.

There is that which no eye sees and no ear hears, and which would not enter into the heart of man, but which already in this life, God gives to be understood, to be seen and to be enjoyed by those who have been initiated into His secret walk.

God can be very far distant from you, but He can also be very near to you. This depends upon His grace. This depends upon the inner disposition of your soul.

But this is certain, when He is near to you, when the heat of day threatens to cause you to succumb, then is He your Shade and you feel His cool Shadow come over you at your right hand.

The cooling which the Shade of your God brings, you must feel, feel in your soul, and if you do not feel it, is it then, perchance, because you are *not* near unto Him?

LXXXI

HE INCLINES HIS EAR UNTO ME

You incline your ear to some one either when you yourself are hard of hearing, or when he to whom you listen has a weak voice, or, finally, when too great a distance separates you from him.

Now the first can not apply to God. How should "He who has planted the ear not hear?" How should He who has created sound and the hearing of it not overhear every creaturely sound?

Hence, when it is said of the Great God that He inclines His ear to our prayer, it always means a grace to us-ward, an act of Divine compassion whereby the Majesty in heaven adapts Himself to us, bends down to us, and, seeking us, comes to meet us.

Real prayer is always clothed with deep humility. There are all sorts of prayers. Prayer that is said; words thoughtlessly muttered; prayer because the hour of prayer has struck; prayer from sense of duty; prayer from necessity; prayer from home-sickness after God; prayer in order to drink in higher heavenly strength; prayer from joy in happy thankfulness; prayer for oneself; prayer for others; prayer alone; prayer with others; prayer spoken aloud; silent prayer; the form changes endlessly, and every form has value of its own. But whatever the form, in the prayer that enters more deeply into the spiritual, the soul feels small, your ego becomes conscious of its powerlessness, in your own estimation your own self feels as nothing, and less than nothing, before the Triune God; there is even a feeling of sinking away, so that God Himself must draw us up to Him, if the heart is to be lifted up and liberty of utterance be granted.

What is this whole world in comparison with the firmament, and what are you who pray compared with this world upon which you are only one of more than a thousand million living souls? Now there are a few mighty ones in the world, who feel, and must feel, that after the standard of the world they are great. Think of a Napoleon, think of a Bismarck. But there is nothing of all this greatness in the ordinary worshiper whose name is scarcely known outside of his village or city. Truly, the mighty ones on earth have their own account with God. This lies outside of what we deal with here. Here we are concerned with the plain but devout man who is scarcely known outside of his limited circle. And what is such a one, when he bends his knees before the High and Lofty One, the omnipotent Creator, Keeper and Governor of this small world and of those thousands of suns and stars that sparkle and shine in the sky which endlessly spreads itself over us.

In true prayer, in a prayer in which the soul at least in some measure forms a conception of God's Majesty and greatness, the worshiper can therefore never in his own feeling be anything.

He can but realize very profoundly that his prayer is but a passing breath, if it does not please the Lord *to incline his ear unto it.*

This need springs from the weakness of the human voice, from the immeasurable distance, and more yet from the indispensability of a personal turning on the part of God toward the suppliant.

Our voice in prayer is so much the acme of weakness when we want our prayer to pierce the heavens, that it makes no difference whether a leader in the house of prayer raises his voice and makes it resound through the arches or whether a sick man on his bed breathlessly whispers his low prayer to God. Even where no sound of voice is heard at all, the low and silent prayer need be none the less real in the soul. Our voice here avails nothing. Among people we can compel a hearing by speaking louder and by raising the voice. But when we would speak to "our Father who is in heaven" the significance of our voice falls altogether away. Then the stentorian voice of the mighty orator avails nothing more than the weakest voice of the child; and whether the shipwrecked man in his last extremity cries out his "O God, help me" in the face of the howling storm—it is all one and the same. Our voice loud or weak, affects nothing. The bleating of the lost sheep can make the shepherd hear. Our mere voice can never move our God to listen.

In prayer the voice serves and aids us and those who pray with us. Even upon our knees in solitude we feel impelled to express our prayer in words. Only through these words clearness enters into our prayer. It releases, it unburdens the soul. The undulations of the emotions within come to rest in the whispered or spoken word of prayer. A prayer without words may well cry out from the soul to God; but that takes place instinctively, we do not even call it prayer.

Real prayer goes through our consciousness. He who prays must know what to pray for. His memory must revive itself. He must think of the several needs in behalf of which he offers prayer. He must know the blessings, the benefits, for which he gives thanks. He must have a clear vision before him of the task in behalf of which he implores Divine help. Before him he must place the Majesty which he magnifies and adores. From the mysticism of the heart the praying soul must come to clear consciousness. And that comes out in the word, that is established by the voice, *that* consummates prayer.

In praying with others this is still more strongly evident. Then the voice is the instrument which brings the prayer of him who leads, to the soul of those who pray with him. With him who leads, prayer rises from the soul and finds expression in the word. With the others, prayer enters into the soul through the word. He who leads in prayer must be as one who plays the keys of an organ. His soul plays. The soul of the others must be attuned to his. And thus originates *common prayer;* a special grace given us by God.

Then comes distance.

When we want to ask something from some one who is on the other side of a pond or stream, we naturally raise our voice, and it is a help when he on the other side turns his ear toward us and by putting his hand behind his ear shows that he listens and tries to understand our call.

What broad waters undulate between us and God, when we undertake to call upon Him.

The whole world lies between, all the absorbing interests of daily life, and, then, there is that immeasurable distance to the heaven of heavens, where the Lord is enthroned in everlasting Light.

Our Savior admonishes us not to begin our prayer by speaking to the Holy Ghost within us, not by invoking the Omnipresent One Who compasses our going about and our lying down and Whose hand is upon us; but with a reverent invocation of *"our Father who art in heaven,"* and the Catechism puts it so cogently that we should do this in order not to think of the High God in an *earthly* way.

Naturally this is not all. In the course of progress, prayer becomes more intimate; which is to say, that, as we pray, God gradually discovers His holy Presence to us, and draws near unto us; yea, at length enters our own heart, and the Holy Spirit prays *with* us and prays *for* us,

and then tells us how we should pray.   But to begin with
this is sickly mysticism.

First we stand before the distance.   The soul must
lift itself up to higher things.   Not here below, but above,
is the altar of the prayers of the saints, which as incense
rises up before His Face.   No longer here below, but in
heaven our Savior sits enthroned on God's right hand praying for us, and by His intercession supporting our prayer.

First, "Lift up your hearts"—the *sursum corda;* and
then, as we pray, God in His Majesty descends graciously
down to us, sometimes into our very heart.

And this real urgency of prayer expresses itself with
us in this, that praying can sometimes become, as the
Psalmist says, a crying, a weeping, an impetuous demand-
ing; and only when we observe that God turns His ear
to us, that He takes notice of us and listens to our prayer,
does the praying soul find rest.

When during prayer we feel that the listening ear of our
God inclines itself to us, then the distance has been
bridged, and we know that He has come near to us and
that we are near unto Him.

And so prayer reaches, at length, its highest blessedness, in what in the third place we called the personal
turning of God to the suppliant.

There are so many thousands and thousands who every
morning and every evening call upon God for help and
deliverance.   It is true the numbers are on the increase
of those who no more pray.   But yet, how incalculably
great the number still is of those who in distress and in
danger of death call upon Him for help.

And now to feel that among those thousands and thousands we, too, come to be noticed, to realize that God
looks also upon us and that He knows that we too call
upon Him.   Among these crossing and mutually jarring

voices to have our voice also pierce through to the Almighty. If we may put it in a very human way: to know, to observe, to feel, that we, too, come to our turn, and that for us, also, there comes a moment of hearing—this is what we suppliants mean, when we jubilantly give thanks, that God also inclines His ear to our prayer.

Naturally this is not so with God. He does nothing by turn. He hears every suppliant *immediately* and all at the same time. But to our human sense there is always in our prayer, when it enters through, a feeling that God now also turns Himself to us, and inclines His ear to our personal prayer.

He inclines differently to you than to another, because this Most High God knows your particular life, fathoms your personal existence, sees through and through your particular need of soul, and, therefore, has laid up for you an altogether particular hearing of your prayer.

And this is the glory of prayer. You call upon your God and He knows you. He distinguishes you as one individual among those many thousands. And however insignificant you are, and with whatever burden of sin you come to Him, He does not pass you by, He despises not the voice of your supplication, He turns Himself to you, and inclines to you His listening ear.

So prayer becomes to you a seal of your election, when you become aware of this turning of God unto yourself.

To earthly kings, the mighty and the great alone have access. To Him Who is King of kings, the most humble and despised are admitted.

So you pray, and God inclines His ear unto your prayer. So are you near unto your God, and your Father who is in heaven seals to you the fact that not only are you now enriched with His Presence, but that eternally you belong near to where He is.

LXXXII

TAKE NOT THY HOLY SPIRIT FROM ME

THE Holy Scripture makes mention of a seeking of God's Face. "Blessed is the people that know the joyful sound: they shall walk, O Lord, in the light of thy countenance" (Ps. 89, 15).

There is mention in Scripture of a something yet more intimate, namely, that there is a *mutual* fellowship, so that not only the light of God's Countenance shines on us, but that our soul likewise lifts itself up to God. "The secret of the Lord is with them that fear him; and he will show them his covenant" (Ps. 25, 14).

But Holy Writ mentions a stage that is yet higher, and that is when God Almighty not only makes His Face shine on us, and admits us into His secret walk, but when He enters into our heart, transforms our heart into His temple, and as the Holy Ghost takes up His abode within us. "The Spirit Himself maketh intercession for us with groanings which can not be uttered, and He that searcheth the hearts knoweth what is the mind of the Spirit, because He maketh intercession for the saints" (Rom. viii, 26-27).

These three stages of fellowship should be carefully distinguished.

He who is in the first stage has indeed turned his back upon the vanities of this world and has accustomed himself to the light that shines upon us from above. He trusts himself no longer to his own light but walks in the light of God's Countenance. The darkness is past. He knows in whom he believes. And the people who not merely at times enjoy the light of God's Countenance, but who walk in it continually, Scripture pronounces blessed.

Then of itself the second stage of fellowship is reached, which is an entering into God's hidden walk. And here it is not merely that the light of God's Countenance shines upon us all, but that, with it also, the soul has become a mirror from which this light is reflected. Even in this way, that God shines on us and that our soul shines out toward God. This is the secret of Salvation that is inwardly disclosed to us.

Even this is not the end.

The inward preciousness of being near to God extends still farther, penetrates still more deeply, until it comes to that unspeakable, indescribable, unfathomable reality, that the Lord God Himself in the Holy Ghost unites Himself so closely with our spirit, that He is not only above and around us, but that He is also in us, that He takes up His abode with us, makes our heart His dwelling place, and that conversational communion between God and our soul takes place in our own inmost self.

This highest blessedness is not reached at once. There is progression here, a blessed development and a deepening, which not every one obtains, and in which they who have obtained it provisionally continue only now and then.

To them these are moments of highest blessedness, even as the peace of God which comes and goes, and which when lost is sought again anew.

This breach can be occasioned by lack of spiritual discipline. It can come about by an invasion from without. It comes mostly through our sin.

The latter was the case with David, and so from his desolate (because God-forsaken) heart arose at once the prayer: *"Take not thy Holy Spirit from me"* (Ps. 51, 11).

When mention is made of the Holy Spirit, we feel that we walk among mysteries. Our language has no words for it. Our understanding here stops all analysis. We can believe, we are susceptible to impressions, we have the capacity of enjoyment, but at least not here on earth and in our sinful state can the mystery of God's Triune Being be unveiled to us.

We worship.

We worship God Almighty as our Father Who is in heaven. We worship the God of all grace in the Only-begotten Son, Whom He gave unto us and sent and sacrificed for us.

And still more ardently we worship the thrice Holy in the Holy Ghost Whom as Comforter we have in our own heart.

Wherever our thinking and pondering turns itself, whether to the world round about us, whether in the world of our own heart, it is always God Whom we meet, in God that our searching look finds its point of rest, to God that our worship and holy admiration uplifts itself.

It is always God Who overshadows us, God Who inwardly penetrates us with His holy love.

One and the same God, *one* glorious and most blessed Being; Almightiness that carries us, quickens us.

But it remains a mystery. A mystery, tender for our heart, rich in blessed enjoyment, ever more intimately revealing itself to the seeking soul, but it stands high above all our thinking, all our understanding, all our musing and pondering.

It is the most real of all realities. It is the one thing that will stay by you, when once the world shall sink away from you and your consciousness shall darken itself in the haziness of death.

It is the secret of the Lord, which the scorner laughs

at, which leaves the world cold, which awes and terrifies the sinner, but which according to the covenant of peace is shown to God's child in the stillness of solitude.

It is the Holy Ghost Himself Who, entering into the heart of God's child, sets the seal of this Triune mystery upon it.

But for this very reason, fellowship with this Spirit within us is so extremely sensitive and tender.

There must nothing come in between, or it will vanish.

It can bear no resistance without being lost.

It can suffer no disturbance, for then it will flee away.

Not that the Holy Spirit therefore took His departure and left you to yourself. On the contrary, He remains in the heart that He has chosen for His dwelling place. Neither Satan nor the world can expel Him from His temple.

And herein is His Divine love, that He continues to dwell in you, while He allows *Himself to be grieved*, allows Himself to be affronted, to be wounded and spitefully entreated by you in your sin.

But to your dull sense this is not so.

In your feeling, in your inner perception, the moment you have sinned the Holy Spirit has become a stranger to you. He has removed Himself far from you. He is scarcely reachable any more by your earnest supplication.

He maintained His dwelling place in your heart, but in that heart itself a wall of separation was reared between your spirit and the Holy Spirit dwelling within you. The door of the temple within you was locked by your own self. You went down in your own being to the deeper underground above which this temple raises itself. In this temple the Holy Spirit was still enthroned, but you had no more access to it. All fellowship is then broken off. All secret communion is then cut off. Your sin has enveloped you as a spider the fly. And while the Holy Spirit Whom you have grieved, in tender compassion turns Himself toward you again, you draw yourself back within your sense of guilt.

And yet, even in such moments, the faith, though not understood, continues to shine through.

David after his deep fall felt the anxious estrangement. He felt that as long as God looked upon his sin no restoration of fellowship was possible, and therefore he prayed: "Hide thy face from my sins, and blot out all mine iniquities" (Ps. 51, 9). He became inwardly aware that his sullied heart was bound to estrange him from his God, and that is why he pleaded in such touching and beautiful terms: "Create in me a clean heart, O God, and renew a right spirit within me." He walked in deep darknesses, and so he prayed that the light of God's Countenance might again pour down its beams upon him. But though he beat his guilty head against the wall of separation, yet in that striking moment the sense of faith glimmered through the dark, that, from the other side of this wall of separation the Holy Spirit still reached out with deep yearnings towards him to comfort him. And so he did not pray: "Give me thy Holy Spirit again," but altogether differently: "Take not thy Holy Spirit from me."

This is the holding fast of self to faith on the part of the soul that is troubled and in itself is lost.

The soul does not understand this, it does not fathom this, but it feels that grace does not let go, that grace is in God, that God with His grace still operates within. And the one anxious fear that now takes hold of it, is that this grace which is present in God alone may depart from it.

And against this fear the soul prays, supplicates, cries: "O God, abide with me, abide in me. Let not go Thy hold on me forever."

And this supplication keeps on, this crying deepens in fervency and in sincerity, until finally the door of the temple in infinite mercy unlocks itself again.

And then comes the joy of salvation again. The meeting again between the soul which had so deeply grieved the Holy Spirit, and the Holy Spirit, Who, rather than let go the soul of God's child, suffered Himself to be grieved.

Blessed is he who in his sin has experienced this for himself.

He understands what it is to know the Holy Spirit as his *Comforter*.

LXXXIII

KNOW YE NOT THAT YE ARE THE TEMPLE OF GOD?

In Jeremiah (xiv, 8) it is said: "God turneth aside to tarry for a night." This is the figure that is borrowed from the wayfaring man who at sundown turns in to spend the night, and when in the early morning the sun stands again on the horizon, leaves the hospitable inn in order to pursue his way. Applied to the Holy One of Israel this means that the Prophets knew times and moments when they were conscious of an indwelling of the Spirit in their soul. But this was not permanent. It was transient, and, soon after, the God close by had become again a God afar off.

By the side of this experience of a God Who turns in to tarry for a night and then leaves the soul again, Jesus places His promise that on the day of Pentecost God the Holy Ghost shall come to the people of the Lord, and not go away again, but shall abide with them forever.

S. John expresses this strongly in his Gospel (vii, 39) when he says: "The Holy Ghost was not yet given because that Jesus was not yet glorified." Of course this can not mean that the Holy Ghost did not yet exist, but signified that the Holy Ghost had not yet permanently taken up His abode in the Church, inasmuch as only after His Ascension, Jesus would send the Comforter from the Father to His Congregation.

And so it must be understood when the Apostles constantly speak of the Church as of a "Temple of God" and of a "Dwelling place of God in the Spirit." "Know ye not that ye are the temple of God, and that the Spirit of God dwelleth in you?" (I Cor. iii, 16) by no means signifies only that the Holy Spirit enters into the heart of saints, but much more and much more strongly that He, having entered the heart of God's saints, abides there *permanently*, *remains* there, and never deserts again the heart that has once been enriched by His indwelling, but, according to the promise of Jesus, He remains with God's children for ever.

This points to a changed condition, to an entirely different dispensation of the Spirit.

What took place transiently under the old dispensation, what was a temporary descent into the heart of a few, is under the new dispensation an age upon age indwelling in the whole Church.

Under the Old Covenant, that which made separation was maintained. The only permanent dwelling was then the dwelling of God upon Zion. But under the New Covenant by the expiatory sacrifice of Golgotha the wall of separation has fallen down for good. What made separation has been brought to naught for ever. God has not merely come *to* His people, but He has come *into* His people. The temple of Mount Zion has ceased to exist, and in the place of it has come the Church of the living God. She is now the temple of God. God dwells in her.

Thus, humanity is divided.

On one side, the still unholy world, because of which the separation continues, and which has now no more temple on Zion. On the other side, the people of the Lord, that now live no more carnally, but only spiritually. And in that people, in that Congregation of the Lord, all separation has fallen away. It is now more closely related to heaven than to the world. It has become the permanent, the abiding, the never-ending dwelling-place of God in the Spirit.

Yet we should be cautious here.

It should not be taken, as though the Spirit of God reveals His operations *alone* in the saints of God.

He who says this would deny the omnipresence of God the Holy Ghost, and limit the sphere of His working.

The Holy Ghost is Himself God, and, therefore, there is nothing in the whole creation of God conceivable to which the working of this Spirit would not apply.

Not alone in everything that is human, but in every creature there is the working of the Holy Ghost, like as there is the working of the Son and of the Father. With any other representation the unity of the Threefold Divine Being would be lost.

In the creation itself the Omnipotence of God is evident; that is to say; the Omnipotence of the Father as well as the Omnipotence of the Son, and the Omnipotence of the Holy Ghost.

From the Father is the fullness of power, from the Son the fullness of thought, from the Holy Spirit the fullness of all energy.

There is no natural force, there is no organic working, there is no Divinity evident in the richness and in the beauty of nature, but the Holy Spirit glorifies Himself in it.

And if this is already so in the inanimate creation, it comes out far more strongly in the *conscious* creature. To think that in angels every talent and gift should operate apart from the Holy Ghost, is absurd.

The same applies to *man*. No general has ever excelled, no poet has ever been brilliant, no thinker has ever astonished the world, no artist has ever enriched us with his creations, but it was the Holy Spirit Who made the spark of genius glow in him.

So and not otherwise Scripture teaches.

Yea, it even comes to this, that no gift of the Spirit, no talent among men has ever turned itself against God, but that it was the Holy Ghost Who not only apportioned this gift and this talent, but also maintained it and caused it to work.

And this, therefore, is the dreadful judgment that shall be pronounced upon every man who has abused his talent in opposition to God, that once he shall himself be bound to experience what it is, with a gift of the Holy Ghost as a weapon, to have turned himself against God.

But something altogether different from these gifts is the *indwelling* of the Holy Spirit in the soul.

Entirely apart from our talents and gifts we have a personal life. This personal life enables us to company with the three Divine persons *personally*. Even as among men we company with one another, so that their self enters into conscious fellowship with our self to the extent that we undergo their influence, receive their love and give love in return, enter into their thought and let our thought enter into them, recognize their superiority, enter into covenant and relation with them, devote ourselves to them and make sacrifices for them—so it is given man to company, likewise, with the Holy One in personal intimacy, in secret fellowship, in holy communion.

And now the indwelling of the Holy Spirit in us signifies that God not only allows Himself to be sought by us, but has come to us; by regenerating us He has enabled us to attain unto such a personal fellowship with Himself; and has not waited until we found Him, but has made His approach to us; not from without but from within. He has touched us, and in the deepest hiddenness of the life of our soul He has established the bond which, in the heart of our very being, in the deepest ground of our sensations, in the immediacy of our first perceptions and feelings, has made us taste His Presence.

This does not depend upon gifts and talents, for those

who are most richly endowed with genius can be deprived of it, and the lowliest among the lowly can enjoy it to the full.

In our humanity itself God has imparted to us the disposition for this. Sin alone has disturbed this disposition. And what God works in regeneration is the restoration of this disposition.

Then this is capable of action again. Then this comes to itself again. Then man in the deepest parts of his soul is *one* again with God.

That is the work of the *Comforter*.

It is not yet the heavenly state which will be all pure enjoyment, when even the memory not only of our sin, but of our ever having been sinners shall for ever be removed from us and shall be cast into the depth of the sea.

Here we still feel that we undergo a Divine operation. The contrast between this glorious indwelling of the Holy Ghost, and the being born in sin, is constantly brought to mind by our ignorance and blindness and unworthiness.

With us the Holy Spirit still reacts every morning and every evening against our merely human manner of existence.

And therefore here on earth He is and remains our Comforter.

For this is the blessed comfort of a child of the dust, that while on one side he still sinks away continually in his misery, underneath it all and with it all he remains conscious of the blessed presence of the Holy Ghost.

That the Holy Spirit does not go away, that He does not let Himself be sent away, that He does not give us up, but continues to dwell with us, and to take us as we are—that is His infinite, that is His Divine Love.

That He not merely "turneth aside to tarry for a night," but that He abides with us forever—this on earth is our joyous bliss and the glorious richness of our Comfort.

LXXXIV

ACCUSTOM NOW THYSELF TO HIM

In the exhortation that we should *accustom* ourselves to our God, lies a reproach that shames. It is as though one should say to a child: "Accustom yourself to your mother!" This may be said of a stepmother, or of a stepfather or stepbrother, but we do not *accustom* ourselves to our own mother who has carried us under her heart. We love her with all the fidelity and affection of the heart of a child.

You can only accustom yourself to what was strange to you, or by estrangement has become strange. And therefore when you are exhorted that your soul, that your self, that your inner being shall accustom itself to your God, then it means that your Father Who is in heaven has become a stranger to you; that this estrangement still stands in the way of your fellowship, your converse with Him, and that, therefore, you should take pains, the sooner the better, to accustom yourself again to Him, that so this obstacle might be removed out of your way.

Now this becoming accustomed to the Lord our God has naturally not the same meaning as when among ourselves we speak of getting used to some one.

When for the first time you meet a man who acts somewhat strangely, who is strongly given to peculiarity of manner and is uninteresting socially, it is then required of us not to let ourselves be repelled by this, but by the happy faculty of making allowances, to cultivate acquaintance with him and adapt ourselves to his peculiarities. Or we may speak of accustoming ourselves to some one who either by a difference of education or social refinement stands far above us, or who by a wholly different position in life has a wholly different outlook upon life. There is then a difference in inclination and sympathies, a difference in activity of the mind and chosen purpose in life. He is interested in what does not interest you. And in the great drama of life you play in quite another act than he.

With all such meetings and occasions of contact, this accustoming of oneself to another, means that we should restrain ourselves to some degree, that we must smooth down the sharp edges of our own character, and that, constrained by the obligation of love and by the necessity of social intercourse, we should enter into his life, in order to understand him, to sympathize with him, and thus gradually give him a place in the circle of our good will.

But with the Lord our God this is of itself entirely different.

With Him, we have to do with our God and our Creator, with our Lord and our King, with our Father Who is in heaven.

Here, everything in Him that is strange to us is our fault, our sin, and is the sign and token that we are in the wrong, that we have become untrue in our sensations and feelings, and that we have gone astray in the deliberations of our heart.

Were we what we should be, there could be no mention of estrangement from Him, nor of our accustoming ourselves again to Him.

"Accustom now thyself to Him!" (Job xxii, 21) is a judgment that is pronounced upon us, a complaint against our inner manner of existence, and at the same time a holy admonition to become a child again in fellowship with our Father.

What in our days is unbelief? From what cause, even

in believing circles, begins the wavering, with more than one, of the quiet restful confidence in what God has revealed to us?

In reply to this, one speaks first of impenetrable mysteries; then of problems which defy the understanding; gradually one comes to doubt whether what is revealed to us is accurate, and ends, at last by boldly assigning the human interpretation of life, as the only valid basis of truth, over against Scripture and experience.

And what does this come to except that as one feels himself a stranger to God and His Word he refuses to accustom himself to God, His doings and His Word, and on the contrary, demands that God shall change Himself, and shall show Himself to be conformed to our thought.

"Accustom yourself to Him" means that you should so change and reform yourself that at length you will be meet for Him; and what doubt and unbelief demand is, that our Creed about God shall so modify itself, that at length a God shall spring from it Who shall be meet for us.

Now this conflict was not so fierce and bitter even as much as a century ago, for the reason that the Scriptural interpretation of life, at least in its main lines, was also considered valid in science, valid in public opinion, and, therefore, valid in education and in the better forms of social intercourse. It was almost alone in the circles of scorners and of the godless that unbelief brutally present-ed itself.

He who believed was thus carried in those better days by the common tenor of life, and his heart was not chal-lenged to resist. This was true, likewise, of the younger generation.

But now all this has become different. Every funda-mental conception about God, the Creation, the Fall, the work of Atonement, the life after death and the Last Judgment, once common property, has been abandoned by science, has been brought to waver in public opinion, is banished from education, and tabooed as topics of conversation among the more serious-minded folk.

And not only this, but gradually an entirely different system of fundamental conceptions has been put in place of it. A wholly different creed has come forward, a wholly different catechism has found entrance. Broadly ramified, the interpretation of life on the part of unbelief now stands in public opinion over against the Creeds of Christendom.

Thereby in addition to the estrangement from God that is occasioned by our sin, a second estrangement has now come, which entices us to accept an interpretation of life which is in open conflict with the counsel, the doing and the wisdom of God, as these are revealed to us in His Word.

Thereby to many everything, yea, everything in their God has become strange to them. They feel themselves in no single respect any more at home with Him or in His Word. The child no longer recognizes his Father.

And for this reason the exhortation: "Accustom thyself to Him!" has now obtained a doubly serious significance.

"Accustom thyself to Him!" now means: Loosen the tie that binds you to the wisdom of the world, and enter again with all your senses and your ponderings into the counsel, into the most holy thoughts of your God.

Do not understand this in a philosophical sense, but take it practically with respect to life, especially with respect to the mystery of suffering, to which Eliphaz also applied it in argument with Job, even though he did it mistakenly.

Suffering amid the trouble of this world would be no mystery to us if constantly, with true balance, it were weighed out to every individual on earth, in accordance with his misdeeds against God or men. There would then become evident in suffering nothing else than righteous retribution measured out according to strict justice, and then everyone's lot in life would be alike.

And in this thought there certainly lies this unchangeable truth that there shall be an eternal retribution, and that this retribution shall be in accordance with every man's deeds, whether they be good or evil.

But the mistake, the fault here is that this punishment and this retribution of the eternal justice are confused with the mystery of suffering here on earth. This suffering thus taken individually and tested by each personal character and walk in life, stumbles on the hard fact that we are constantly offended at the godless man who prospers, and that we are even more sore at heart when we see a devoted child of God, a noble character, a faithful servant in Christ who, as we would say, did nothing wrong, swallowed up by the waves of affliction.

That men can do so, we can understand. When a tyrant honors the godless and oppresses devout children of God, we think it dreadful, but it is always God Who allows it; and we can submit to this. But that God Himself does this with sickness, in His disposition of our lot in life, and by cruel death, that is a stone of offense which one can not get over, and one that has killed already so much rootless faith.

What accounts for this, save that God's thoughts are so altogether different from our thoughts, and that we, instead of accustoming ourselves to His counsels, stubbornly maintain our interpretation of suffering in contradiction to His?

In the mind of God, individual retribution has its accounting in the Last Judgment and not in the sentence imposed by an earthly judge, and far less yet in the suffering which He brings upon us.

According to the teaching of Scripture, sin is not an evil that cleaves to a few individuals, but a poison that has infected the whole human race. The creation of man was not individual either, for we are created a race. All mankind, therefore, through all ages and among all nations form one whole. We are not a great number of people, who only afterwards by laws and other means are counted as one whole, but we are *a human race* from which individuals spring, and to which they belong as twigs and leaves to a tree.

In order to save this race of men which He created, God brought suffering into our world to counteract this poison of sin. He regards this suffering as a cup of holy medicine, which He administers not to the individual person but to our race, in order to counteract the working of the poison of sin. And now He Himself elects the priests and priestesses, who are called for His sake, to administer the sacrament of suffering to the world.

If to this end He chose only the godless, they would harden themselves against suffering, and the godly would pride themselves on being spared. The medicine would do no good. Spiritually it would cause petrifaction. Bring loss for gain.

No, to bear that suffering, He calls first of all the best, the most godly, the most noble—His Prophets and His martyrs. Thereby the medicine produces its holy effects and accomplishes that whereunto it has been appointed.

The Cross provides the explanation.

So God loved the world that He gave it His only begotten Son. Personally Jesus stands altogether outside of sin. He is not only the most godly, the most noble, the best among all the children of men, but He is the Son of

Man, and the woe of suffering comes down upon Him as never any man has borne it. And never has there gone forth from any suffering among the children of men a power unto salvation as from His Cross.

And therefore in that Cross lies expressed the thought of God, the counsel of God and the wisdom of God.

Every one who would understand his own sorrow and the suffering of the world must accustom himself to this counsel, to this thought and to this wisdom of God.

And he who does this has heavenly comforting, yea, he can give thanks that the cup of suffering has not passed him by.

He feels that he himself is a priest, in order that following after the One High Priest, in the name of the Lord, he may be a server at the sacrament of suffering.

LXXXV

THE SPIRIT OF MAN IS A CANDLE OF THE LORD

To be near unto God is a luxury of soul, which by Grace can be our portion even in an unconscious state.

When a child of God, who has enjoyed the hidden walk, is put under an anesthetic in order to be operated upon, the fellowship between his heart and his God is not thereby broken. The same holds true of fainting, during which consciousness is lost. In high fever, when the heated blood over-stimulates the brain, and the patient becomes wild with delirium, the tie that binds him to God remains equally intact. Even of sleep, which deprives us for many hours of "our own knowledge of ourselves," no other idea should be entertained, and this quite apart from our consciousness by night in dreams.

Only, in each of these conditions in life the being near unto God has become inoperative as regards your conscious life. The consciousness of the fellowship with God has not gone out from you. Being gently touched, and having become awake, you feel it again and resume it. It was only *inoperative* in you. It is with this as it is with your capacity of sight. This too in your sleep is not gone, but is at rest. The electric light illustrates this to us so clearly. Turn the button or even slightly touch it with your finger, and everything is light, turn it once more and everything is dark. But equally quickly and immediately you have the light again. The electricity itself was still present; it only withdrew its radiancy.

And to this must be added the fact that from God's side, fellowship with the life of the soul of His child operates uninterruptedly; even when His child is under anesthesia, in a swoon or asleep, it maintains itself and continues its activity. To know this imparts that sense of rest wherewith one undergoes an anesthetic, and, no less, that peaceful feeling wherewith by night we sink away in sleep. "In my sleep let me wait for thee, O Lord, then shall my sleep be peaceful," as reads the Moravian hymn. And who can doubt but that in our very sleep the bracing and strength-renewing ministries whereby our Father Who is in heaven favors His children, are still more manifold and effective than by day. The third part of our life which binds us to our couch serves by no means the needs of the body alone. It has a higher import. Especially by night God builds His temple in our heart.

Yet this does not do away with the fact that to be near unto God obtains its highest significance for us only when our clear day-consciousness permeates the blessed fellowship with Him, when we become aware of it, when we feel and know that our soul is near to God, and that God is close to our heart. When, humanly speaking, there is an exchange of heartfelt response between our God and ourselves. When, speaking reverently, with the telephone of prayer we call up our God and far from on high the answer comes.

But impress it well upon yourself that this calling and this answering are not exhausted by the words that you stammer nor by the thoughts that thereby become active in you. A mother has tender, inward fellowship with the babe at her breast apart from any word and outside of any intellectual understanding. What operates in this communion and what maintains it is the life itself, the drawing of the blood, the fervency of the feeling. And though this fellowship, when the infant has become a youth, will express itself in words and ideas, yet the root of this communion, in later years, will be far deeper seated than on the lips that speak the word. What does not the look of the eye convey, the expression of the face, a tear, a smile, and how sweetly in and underneath all this operates the fellowship of the same blood, the tenderness of sheltering love.

And all this is not unconscious, but is part of consciousness. It is as the fragrant exhalation of a flower, the distillation of love which we breathe in. It is the perfume and spray of the heart which we drink in with full draughts. And what the scent of a rose or of a hyacinth is you know full well, you are fully conscious of it, though the ablest botanist can not analyze this scent, nor describe it in words.

To be near unto God with your *consciousness* goes far deeper, therefore, than your understanding or your stammering. It is a becoming aware, a perceiving, a feeling, which you should not attribute to your emotions. That would be false mysticism. But a perceiving and an expressing of yourself in a spiritual way in the immediacy of the linking of your inner sense to the life of your God.

To make this plain, Scripture makes a difference between our soul and our inner being.

It speaks on one side of our heart and of our soul, and on the other side of something that lies far back and deep underneath these two. Plastically this is expressed in several ways, mostly by placing our *reins* in contrast with our heart, and by contrasting the soul with the "innermost parts" (Prov. 20, 27). Translating this into our way of speech, *the soul of man* here means our *consciousness*, and the innermost parts, what we call, our hidden inner being.

And in this sense it is said that our consciousness is a candle of the Lord that searches our inner being. Our consciousness is a searchlight which God Himself causes to illuminate our whole inner being, in order that by the glow and the clearness of this searchlight we should know our own inner self.

Thus only are these words intelligible to us. Thus only do they unveil before us a deep, far-reaching thought, with respect to which we feel how it enters into us and addresses us.

Our consciousness is not our handiwork. Our becoming conscious is not our deed. But all consciousness in us is a working, quickened in us by God, and from moment to moment it is maintained in us by God.

It is to be compared with the sun.

The sun is the light in the world of nature, by which God enables us to see nature, to observe and to investigate it.

And just so is the consciousness a light ignited by God in our personal ego; or rather a light which God lets shine in the world of our inner being, in order that in this spiritual light we should examine our spirit and appraise it.

This light of our consciousness is called a *candle*, because when we look into ourselves we begin to sink away into darkness, and in this darkness of our inner being God meets us with the candle of our consciousness.

Of course our consciousness is no candle which the Lord uses in order to search our inner being.

God has no need of the light of the sun by which to see His whole creation. In the deepest parts of the earth, where no ray of sunlight ever enters, before God it is light as the day. As David expresses it in Psalm 139: "Yea, the darkness darkens not for thee, but the night shineth as the day; the darkness and the light are both alike to thee."

What here applies to the world of nature applies equally to the world of our inner being. In neither region has God

need of a candle whereby to give light. In the darkness of
our inner world also, the darkness shineth as the clear day.

But we have need of this candle, and it is by grace that
God lightens the darkness of our inner being with the
light of this candle of our consciousness.

We ourselves make artificial light. We do this by our
thinking. We do this by our reasoning. We do this by our
imaginations. And this too can have its use. But this
artificial light ofttimes shines falsely. It misleads. And it
never enters deeper than the surface. Into what Solomon
plastically describes as "the innermost parts" this artificial light of our inventive and imaginative thought
never enters. And all too frequently it blinds our eye,
so that we can not see the light of the candle of the
Lord with the eye of our soul. Thereby the so-called
civilized world of our time is for the most part blind to the
light of God's candle within us.

The light of this candle of the Lord within us does not
argue, does not analyse, but lays bare whatever there is
in us. It places our own being before the eye of our soul,
gives us self-knowledge and cuts off all self-deception.

And now it is the light of this candle of the Lord which
makes us see clearly, in the deepest underground of our
being, the fibers by which the undermost parts of our
being have fellowship with God. Fellowship by reason
of our creation after the Image of God. Fellowship
through the blessed, glorious regeneration of our sin-cor-
rupted nature. Fellowship through the Divine indwelling
of the Holy Ghost. Fellowship through the glorious
working within of ever-increasing grace. Fellowship above
all through the tie that binds us to Christ, causing us to
be a member of His Body.

The brightness of this light is always the same in degree,
but the effect of it gradually increases in strength.

At first there is still so much wrong in our heart, the dust of sin, which covers so much in it and renders brightest light invisible to us. But gradually the unclean dust flies away before the breath of the Lord, and then our eye comes to see what lay hidden underneath this dust. And so it can not be otherwise but that the deeper the light can shine in, the more gloriously it becomes manifest to the eye of our own soul how with all the ties of our life we are bound to our God, and how our fellowship with Him embraces the whole of our life.

LXXXVI

I IN THEM AND THOU IN ME

THE soul's nearness unto God and the mystical union with Christ belong together. All the Apostles put emphasis on this; and in their writings the greatest leaders in the life of the Church every time come back to this mystical union with Christ as indispensable to deeper devotion in religion.

The temptation to which, alas, so many succumb, to continue one's stay at the Cross, and on Golgotha to close up their account with Christ, is fatal to the faith.

The way it happens is as follows: The conscience wakes up for a moment; the weight of sin burdens the soul; fear of the coming Judgment strikes terror to the heart. In such a moment, the comforting thought of the Cross arises invitingly in the soul. For if the Atoning Sacrifice is but accepted, one is saved. Nothing needs to be done for it save only to believe. One lets himself be persuaded to do this. And to say it as sharply as the case deserves, one closes the bargain. And now one deems himself saved. Now he accepts the fact that he is assured of eternal life. He finds the Atoning Sacrifice to be glorious. It brings perfect salvation. Thus to such a one, Christ has become the Savior. But of a more intimate, tenderer tie that binds his soul to Christ, nothing is learned from his conversation, nothing suggests it in the utterances of his religious life. He is now saved and that is the end of it.

Yet this is nothing but self-deceit. Nothing stirs in it save spiritual egoism. Escape is sought from eternal punishment. One wants to insure himself for eternal salvation. But nothing in this suggests thirst after the living God; nothing of the child's home-sickness after the Father's house; nothing of holy jealousy for the honor of God's Name.

From this no spiritual power can go out. No religion can operate in it, nor come out from it. And what is more, it can not be true that in this wise Golgotha can bring propitiation for the life of the soul.

So the Gospel does not speak like this. It does not interpret the Atoning Sacrifice in this way. Never in Scripture is the power of redemption attributed to Golgotha, except as the mystical union binds our inner life to the life of Christ.

It must be a being buried with Christ in His death in order to rise with Him unto life. They alone who have become one planting with Christ share in the grace which He has obtained.

They alone who have become sheep of His flock can follow the great Shepherd of souls.

It is not the Cross that saves us, but He Who saves us is the Christ who died on the Cross.

You must be *one* with Christ, member of His Body, accepted and incorporated under Him as your Head before one single drop of His grace can be sprinkled upon you.

You must have been given in the Father to the Christ in order that His glory may become manifest in you.

The mystical union must have laid the tie of love forever between Christ and your soul.

Yea, it must become Christ in you, in order that, through this middle link, your life near unto your God may become a reality.

For so prayed your Savior Himself in His High Priestly prayer: *"Holy Father, I in them, and Thou in Me!"* (S. John xvii, 23).

Yet, if our mystical union with Christ shall preserve

its truly religious character, and not degenerate into sentimental Christolatry, this tie that binds us to Christ must never find its final end in itself.

The Christ is your Mediator, and there can be no Mediator save for the one purpose of causing you to approach God.

To be near to God, with a child's confidence; to feel yourself close by God; here on earth to abide in the nearness of God through faith, and once, after your death, to serve God eternally in the Father-house above—that is and remains the final end; and all that the Scriptures reveal unto us regarding the Mediatorship of Christ must result in this, and can never rest within itself.

Once the Christ Himself shall deliver up the kingdom to God and the Father, that God may be all in all.

He who confines himself to the interests of his own soul, or has no further desire than that he may be numbered with God's people, arrests the spiritual progress in his soul.

The ideal final end at which we aim may and can be nothing less than that, in the ages of eternity, we may enjoy our God, and exist for nothing else than the glorifying of His Name.   And just because this is the ideal final end, every religion here on earth remains imperfect which does not even here bring us nearer to God, makes us abide in the nearness of our God, and impels us to spend all our strength and all our talent in His service.

Piety that spends itself in self-soothing emotionalism, and in an inward spiritual enjoying oneself, lacks power and animation. Only when we love God with absolute devotion does energy enter into our piety so that we know no higher enjoyment than to drink the cup of His peace, no higher purpose in life than to dwell near unto Him, and no holier ambition than to fight and to suffer for His holy Name.

And from this, not even your service of Christ may detract anything. Never has your Savior Himself willed or purposed anything else than to bring you to the Father; and whosoever transposes this into a sort of Christ-cult which keeps you standing with the Christ, and loses from sight your pressing forward toward your Father Who is in heaven, honors not Christ, but goes against Him, and does not confirm the mystical union with his Savior, but tears loose the fibers thereof.

For this reason this union is mystical, that is to say, it does not consist in feelings, in receiving impressions, and in meditations, but rests in the essential substance of your soul.

Truly indeed, the feelings which you cherish for the Christ, the impressions which the Person of your Savior and His Grace convey to you, and also the thoughts of Him on which you meditate, on which your Creeds are based, are highly meritorious. They are absolutely necessary. Your entire conscious life must be saturated with Christ.

But without more, you have no setting yet in the mystical union. What in a holy sense is counted mystical lies deeper than your consciousness, and strikes root in your essential self.

Hence the teaching of Scripture regarding regeneration, renewal of life, the new creature, the new man. There is not merely Atonement and forgiveness on the part of God, and on your part confession, believing and singing praises.

No, the Christ has entered into our nature. This was possible because our nature has been created after the Image of God, and for this reason that which shall snatch you away from yourself and from sin, and shall bring you back to God must grip you in your own being, even in your very manner of existence, must bring about the change

in your person, in your outward life, and thus be a holy
and a Divine work, which takes place not upon your lips,
not in your mind, but in the mystical underground of
your being.

And this wondrous work is not accomplished by the
Father directly, and in every one individually, but it goes
through Christ, it is bound to Him as the Mediator of
all, and finds in this very Mediator its indestructible
guarantee.

For the tie with which Christ binds Himself to you in
your own self is of so holy a nature that He Himself com-
pares it to the tie that binds Him in his Divine nature to
the Father.

"I in them and thou in me, O holy Father, keep through
thine own name those whom thou hast given me, that they
may be one, as we are" (S. John xvii, 11).

Of the "Body of Christ" you should make no external,
no mechanical representation. It is true that among ourselves we speak of the body, of the corps, of the corporation, of those who are like-minded, who co-operate for
the same end. They who belong to it are then called
members of such a body, and the management is the head.

But with the Body of Christ all this has a far deeper
meaning and a far more serious significance.

Here you do not become a member of the Body of
Christ by application, or by signing your name to your
creed. Here you are not incorporated in this Body by
a military oath. Here you do not appear as a member,
in order presently from choice to resign your membership.
No, the Body of Christ lies anchored in the nature of the
soul. It is an organism invisible to the eye, but known
to God, which forms one indissoluble whole, to which
a child can belong as an integral member before it has
ever lisped the name of Christ.

You do not fit yourself into this Body, but God Himself takes you up into it, incorporates you with your own nature into it, and appoints you, as a member of Christ, with a fixed place of your own in it, whereby at the same time your calling and your destiny is forever determined.

In this Body you are a fellow-member with other members, not after your choice, or after their choice; but according to the Divine disposal, you with all the others form a union which can never be broken. And with all these you are under Christ as your living, life-quickening and animating Head from Whom alone the glow of love can come to you. And your existence, as a member in this Body and under this Head, has no other aim than to cause you through the Mediator to be near unto God again, to assure you of an eternity in His holy Presence, and so to guarantee the highest end of your existence, an existence throughout the everlasting ages, for the honor of the thrice holy God.

This is the mystical end in behalf of which the mystical union with Christ serves as means, and for this reason Christ interweaves the tie that binds Himself to His own with the tie that binds Himself to the Father: *"I in them and Thou in me!"* A union sealed of God Himself.

LXXXVII

FOR THE SPIRIT OF GOD RESTETH UPON YOU

It was a glorious word that Jesus spake—a word that still pours balm into many a wound, and revives the courage of faith that has grown faint; a word that has made martyrs, and has strengthened and comforted them—when, at the end of the beatitudes He said with so great emphasis: "Blessed are ye, when men shall revile you, and persecute you, and shall say all manner of evil against you for My sake" (S. Matt. v, 11).

It is a word that reaches farther than the prophecy that prison and martyrdom awaited the disciples. This took place in only certain periods in the struggle of Jesus' church. But what is not bound to any one period of time, what always continues, and ever repeats itself, is this very personal grieving and annoying, this mockery, scorn and disdain from which the world can not wean itself whenever it meets a real manifestation of strength on the part of the Lord's people that opposes it and has courage to resist it.

Persecution unto blood is exceptional. This other persecution which strikes at the heart with the lancet of scorn and abuse goes on in all ages. And, therefore, this beatitude of the Lord enters so deeply into our human life. It betrays to us that tender fellow-feeling of Jesus for what awaited His own. It is a word that every day finds its application, now here and now there. No day passes but it practises its ministry of encouragement and comfort. It does not tend, daringly and defiantly to meet the world that is offended at the cause of the Lord, but the effect of it is this, that it makes the disciples of the Lord, when they would retract, stand their ground, and, in the face of injury and slander, remain unmoved.

But do not forget that this word has also its dangerous side, because it has so frequently been quoted and applied where the application was not permissible.

This depends upon the question of what it is in your actions and omissions, in your words and manner, that incites people to do you injury and to persecute you and falsely to say all manner of evil against you.

This may be your earnest endeavor to advance the cause of your Lord, but it can also be your over-zealousness, your eccentricity, your loveless enthusiasm, or, worse yet, the gap that yawns between your profession and your practice, the hypocrisy that to some extent disfigures your life.

And though in this latter case the strength of your resistance against the world may lie in your zeal for the cause of Christ, actually you put into this zeal so much of your own self and act in behalf of your own interest to such an extent that the "for my sake," which Jesus put as the condition for His beatitude applies to you but in part.

Yea, it can be, and does happen, that the scorn, the abuse and the slander of the world are so almost exclusively invited by this your own sinful alloy that even not a few among your fellow-believers are bound to take the part of the world against you, and, far from calling you blessed in Jesus' name, feel as by instinct that your example hurts more than it helps the cause of your Lord.

Understand this well. This implies by no means that you are in the right only when the world honors your lovableness of character, your honesty and uprightness, and pays homage to what is called your philanthropic and ethical nature.

This the world has shown differently to Jesus himself. If we do nothing else in the name of Jesus than what the world can approve and laud in us, the distinctive characteristic itself is gone from our profession and from our practice.

On ethical grounds nothing could be laid to the charge of the Apostles of the Lord, and yet the world has done them shame, and has not rested till it had hounded them to the death.

In our profession, and practice, and zeal the essential factor must always be that which the world can not tolerate, what offends it and impels it to offer resistance.

Only, what may never be wanting, if the beatitude of the Lord shall be applicable to us, is what S. Peter (I. iv, 14) expresses thus: "If ye be reproached for the name of Christ, happy are ye, for the spirit of glory and the *Spirit of God resteth upon you.*"

This must be the case.

The Spirit of the Lord must rest upon you. The Spirit of the Lord must speak from what you do and do not do. It must not be against you but against that Spirit of the Lord, that the fierce anger of the world turns itself.

Then you are reviled for Christ's sake, and then from this abuse there germinates in your behalf the blessedness after which your heart thirsts.

Here too it depends again upon your being near to God, for when you are near unto God, God is near unto you, and then it is not against you but against God that the world turns itself, and against you only because you are found to be near unto God and God near unto you.

Proof of this is, that the world is instantly ready to turn its scorn into praise and its abuse into applause, the moment you cut loose from God.

Undoubtedly, in the sin of the world there is also hatred

against the neighbor. This began with Cain. But in so far alone as the personal hatred of egoism operates against the neighbor, the fire of this hatred is brought to bursting out into flame by the passion for personal gain, by material interest, by the struggle for position, by slavery to passion and jealousy. And this hatred of the world does not turn itself in particular against the Christian people, but is astir in the world itself, as one rises up against the other.

But in the deepest bottom of what is sinful in the human heart lies the hatred not against the neighbor but against God. So it began with Satan, and so Satan has transplanted it in the human heart.

This hatred against God may largely express itself in covered form, and only occasionally turn into open denial of God and blasphemy, yet it is this hatred that propels the current of the life of the nations. The never satisfied passion for emancipation. The will to be one's own lord and master, and to recognize no God as Lord and Master above one's self. To be as God, and to be God oneself, and the determination not to bend the knee, is the evil germ from which all sin unfolds.

And because the people of the Lord enter protest against this, and openly plead for the Majesty of God, the world turns itself against that people, in order to stop their mouth, in order to rob them of influence, and to doom them to inaction.

But fiercely and bitterly the fire of this hatred bursts forth only when the world discerns that it is no more you who speak of God and bear witness for Him, but that the living God Himself is with you, that He dwelleth in you, that you are near God and God is near to you, and that for this reason, in you it can strike at God Himself and at His Christ.

When it perceives that the Spirit of the Lord rests upon you, then it can not tolerate you, and forces the choice upon you of letting go of this God, or of incurring its deadly hatred which shall not rest till it has actually or morally ruined you.

To be near unto God, *so* near that He has formed your heart for His temple, and with Christ has come to you, in order in the Holy Ghost to tabernacle with you, is glorious, blessed sweet mysticism of soul; but there is more.

Your heart can be no cover to hide the light that shines in you. When the Spirit of God really rests upon you, it becomes evident, the glow of that light radiates to the region without, and he who hardens himself against that light comes not at once, but gradually, to the discovery that you are a person who stands in contact with the living God, and that whoever has to do with you has also to do with that holy Power which is God's.

And then comes the opposition, not because of anything of secondary importance, not because of accidentals, but because of that highest and most glorious reality that is in you.

When Asaph sang of the blessedness of being near unto God, his mind was absorbed in thought of this antithesis between the world and its God.

This antithesis can not be separated, therefore, from the nearness unto God.

The nearer you are to the world, the farther you are from God. But then, too, the nearer you are unto your God, the greater the distance that must mark itself between you and this world.

If, having come near unto God, you could go out from the world, no conflict would kindle in your heart, and no hatred in the world against you.

But this you may not do.

"I pray thee O Father, not that thou shouldest take them out of the world, but that in the world thou shouldest keep them from the evil" (S. John xvii, 15).

The high seriousness of your position is just this, that you, with God in your heart, must yet live in the midst of a world which at heart and in its life is opposed to this God.

And now it has indeed been tried, as Christian *so* to behave oneself in this world that the world hands you out a passport and grants you an honorary diploma as one who "though Christian, is yet a tolerable person;" but such a seductive exhibition of favor on the part of the world is never bought otherwise than at the price of dulling the sharp edges of your creedal profession.

If, now, the world could only make such a separation between you and the God Whom you profess and for Whom you zealously labor, that it would be able to continue its opposition against Him without affecting you, it would be ready to do so. To you as man it still feels ties.

But just this it can not do with the real followers of Christ. They are *so* near God that the eye of the world discovers no more distance.

And therefore it attacks you personally. It magnifies as broadly as possible whatever wrong it discovers in you. It makes sport of every unsanctified utterance that is observed in you. And then falsely and slanderously it says all manner of evil against you.

To be near unto God and to bear this grief belong together. In such a way, however, that you may never court it, that from desire after the martyr crown, you may never incite the world to it.

That alone which is wholly natural and springs up of itself is here also inwardly true and has value with God.

And then the blessedness does not come only later on, but is already tasted in the midst of the oppression, and then God's angels see, and then God's children perceive, that already here, in the midst of tribulation, the spirit of glory, the Spirit of God rests upon you.

LXXXVIII

ONE AFTER THIS MANNER AND ANOTHER AFTER THAT

THERE is an evil abroad among the devout friends of the Lord which should be corrected.

This wrong consists in this, that in things spiritual one tries to impose a law of his own upon another.

They limit piety to one given form. In the way in which they practise piety every one else must practise it. Small divergencies may be tolerated, but, in the main, one and the same sort of piety must show itself in all God's children. And then in the nature of the case, the piety which they practise is set up as the standard for all spiritual order and spiritual criticism.

That pride has a part here can not be doubted, yet pride, at least at first, is not the motive.

It rather proceeds like this. That one began with an earnest desire of soul to belong to the people of God, partly to assure oneself of his own salvation, but, very really as well, to be able to take a zealous part in the work of hallowing the Name of the Lord and in the advancement of His kingdom.

Both at home and elsewhere one had met certain persons who made a deeply devotional impression, and of whom it was said in general that they were esteemed as very godly people. Such persons were to be envied. Oh, if one could only be like them. And so he sought the company of these godly folk. He watched their ways. He took notice both of what they did and of what they avoided. And as he listened to their conversations, gradually an idea was formed of what one himself should be, in order with equal assurance to be introduced as one of God's dear children into His hidden walk.

Thus a given type of piety was set before the mind. After this fixed type one sought to reform his life in the world, his life with believers, and his life before God. And when finally he had reached this standard, he rejoiced as one who had won the prize; and when he was received by the "pious" as one of their own, he was supremely happy. From now on he pursued his way under the positive impression that every one else should come along exactly the selfsame way, should correspond entirely to the selfsame type, should go through the entirely selfsame experiences, yea, show in their very language and stereotyped phrases the very same thing, which as an ideal had long escaped the censor himself, and which now at length he had obtained.

Our fathers used to say that this is putting oneself in the place of the Word of God. The standard by which to test the genuineness of childship, as well as the genuineness of the gold of our godliness, should not be borrowed from ourselves, nor from any saint whatever, but exclusively from the Word of God.

These critics did not deny this; only they took pains to show you that God's Word makes the same demands and requires the same marks of true grace which they themselves advocated, and which with severity they applied among themselves.

But the one thing they forgot was the thing that gave rise to much harmful spiritual unnaturalness; they failed to see that as in everything else, so also in the spiritual life, the Word of God allows room for very great diversity, and that in this very diversity it seeks strength.

This does not mean that Scripture recognizes two kinds of children of God. Of course not. There is but one kind,

and yet, among this one true kind Scripture recognizes
an almost endless diversity, an always new variety, an
ever surprising individuality, difference and alternation
in every way; not only in the groups but also in the individual child of God.

It is in this as it is in the world of flowers. The rose
among flowers is in a class by itself. No one will confuse
a lily and a rose, or take a field violet for a rose. The rose,
in order to be a rose, and to be a real rose must correspond to certain fixed marks, or else it is no rose. But,
what endless diversity there is between the Belgan rose
and the swamp rose, the tea-rose and the Alpine rose.
What varieties again in each of these groups. What difference in growth, leaf, color and fragrance. Yea, does
not every richly unfolded rose address us as a something
by itself, with its own peculiar charm and beauty?

So it is in the whole creation of God. God calls every
star in the firmament by its name, and in this name lies
the expression of an individual nature. And on the earth
every mountain line is different, different is every animal,
even every insect, and different, likewise, every vegetable
and every food that springs from the ground.

And in like sense, among the children of men every one
is "after his kind," every race, every tribe, every nation,
every family, and every person in the family is different.
No mother is ever mistaken in her children.

And just so it is in the spiritual. "The Holy Spirit
divideth to every man severally as He will" (I Cor. xii, 11),
or to express it yet more strongly with the Apostolic word:
the one can be no standard for the other. S. Paul himself
as Apostle refuses to be this. And he states with utmost
emphasis: "*Every man* (*i. e.*, each individual, head for
head) hath his proper gift of God, the one after this manner and the other after that" (I Cor. vii, 7).

So it is, and so it must be, just because our spiritual life, if genuine, is not our work, but a work of God.

It is a difference as between writing and printing. What the printing-press throws off is in all the copies of the same work precisely alike; in the writing of each man's hand a particular character comes out. It is the difference between what nature, and what the factory, produces. A factory produces things after a fixed model, all alike; in nature, wherein God works, everything differs and everything exhibits something of its own.

If, now, the spiritual life of piety is pressed and forced violently into one and the selfsame form, then the work of man chokes the work of God; then one obtains spiritual unnaturalness—painted flowers, not real flowers; then no virtue goes out from it, and this sort of imprinted piety does not bring one nearer to God, but rather puts up a wall of separation between God and our soul.

Then follows spiritual depression, dullness and morbidity, whereas God's children should glory in their liberty, and by reason of this free, glorious feeling of the breaking of bands, should rejoice with an angel-song in the heart.

The lark that flies upward to meet the sun with a song; not the snail that on the hard clay marks his slimy track, is the Image of the redeemed in Christ.

Only, confuse not here liberty with license. Every bird sings its own sort of song, but it received this sort from God. And so has God, Who created you, inlaid and increated in the hidden parts of your being that individuality of yours from which must spring your character, your person and so likewise your own form of childship.

Everything in you hangs organically together. Your ancestry, the sensitiveness of your nerve life, the connection between your understanding and your imagination, the stringing of your heart, your disposition, the embroidery of your inclinations and sympathies, the range of your conscience, your susceptibility to emotions and sensations, your education, your environment your business—all this together puts a peculiar stamp upon your whole spiritual being.

The one is after this manner, and the other after that. And in connection herewith the Holy Spirit divides His spiritual gifts, without ever making a mistake, and not as you imagine it to yourself, or as some one else demands it of you, but *as He wills*.

Spiritual uniformity of a selfsame cut is thereby unimaginable. As God clothes the lilies of the field diversely, so He also weaves for each one of His children its own spiritual robe. The uniformity must be dropped, and this your own spiritual garment must unfold itself in the sight of God and of men.

As every precious stone has its own lustre, and the jasper can not become an emerald, so in your heart the diamond of your childship must sparkle with its own brightness.

Then only, the hidden walk with your God becomes free and spirited, and full of meaning. For so only can you appear before your God and Father in the form, clothed with the spiritual robe, and adorned with the spiritual ornaments, which your Father has presented to His child.

To be near unto God is not a going with the crowd, but an approach unto God in this unique, particular, personal and peculiar way, which God has appointed for you.

A mother knows each of her children by his own voice, even though she does not see him. So does your Father Which is in heaven know you by that particular child voice, which He Himself elicits from your soul.

A SOUND OF GENTLE STILLNESS

To be near unto God is by no means always the same in every case, but like everything else that touches the deepest intimacies of life, it is with "one after this manner and with another after that." They who have drifted off in the stream of what they call practical religion, do not feel, or at least do not recognize this, and hence the barrenness in spiritual things, that attends their zeal for works. They are always interested in outside things. They toil and labor zealously for Jesus, but there is so little about them of the gentle stillness in which the hidden walk is enjoyed.

On account of our sin, there is always this fatal one-sidedness, even in holiest things. On one hand mysticism holding itself back in quiet reserve, unable to create a current in the stagnant waters of existence, and on the other hand, the busy worker who is never at rest, and who, in over-zealousness, has at length no more eye nor ear for the ardent intimacy of a saved soul with its God. And therefore the mystic has something to learn from the zealot, and the zealot from the mystic. Only from the impulse of both can soul-satisfying harmony flourish.

By itself, a mystical seeking of the Divine is by no means necessarily Christian. The heathen in Asia practise such mystical seeking even on a broad scale. And though Islam has largely lost it yet Islamism has practised it, and among the Sufi in Persia and the Dervishes in Asia Minor it is still known.

To bear the Christian stamp, nearness to God must be through the Atonement and relationship to the Mediator.

"*I and the Father* will come and make our abode with him" (S. John xiv, 23).

This excludes ever deadening uniformity from the method of seeking after God, and of being near unto Him. In this holy domain imitation leads to nothing but self-deception. All mysticism of soul that seeks after God and finds Him, truly rests content in the fixedness and sameness of the unchangeableness of God, but the reflection of this Uniqueness in God, as it casts itself in the human soul, is never just the same, and never can be just the same in every case, because soul differs from soul in nature, disposition and utterance. And, as the very result of this, each soul has its own history from which its own needs and its own talents arise.

It is not correct therefore when from Elijah's experience at the cave you would infer that the Lord reveals Himself only in: "A sound of gentle stillness" (I Kings xix, 12; R. V. Marg. Reading). The commission which Elijah received shows this. It was the commission to anoint Jehu, but to that commission was added these words: "Him that escapeth the sword of Hazael shall Jehu slay, and him that escapeth from the sword of Jehu shall Elisha slay." There has been no bolder fanatic than Jehu.

"Not in the fire and not in the storm, but in a sound of gentle stillness" by no means says that Moses did not find God in the fire at Horeb, nor David in the storm of persecution by Saul. It merely says that for Elijah, at that moment, and in that state of mind and heart in which he then was, the glow must first pale, and the storm in his heart must first spend itself, before he would be able to meet his God, and to receive his prophetic commission, in a sound of gentle stillness. On Carmel was fire and storm; and if ever and anywhere it was on Carmel that Elijah beheld the Majesty of the Lord.

The impossibility of making *one* rule with regard to being near unto God, which must be valid for all, extends so far, that a selfsame rule for the whole of life, even with one and the selfsame child of God is unthinkable.

He who is old and full of days has known the years of his manly strength, and back of these the years of his youth, and again, preceding these, the days of his childhood.

Now let him speak who during these four periods of his life has known something of the holy, hidden walk with his God, and he is bound to confess that in each one of these four periods of time it was altogether different. In general there was progress; even so; and yet in such a way, that now as man he can sometimes long again for the days when he was a child, and understand what it means that Jesus blessed the children and said: "Of such is the Kingdom of heaven."

It is, therefore, a profanation of what is holy when we who are older have no eye for the peculiar character of the soul-life of a child, and trample down this simplicity, this brightness, this enthusiasm of the child, under the weight of our heavy, insufferable forms. To train a child in spiritual things is first of all to start out from the faith that God also works in this child, at least can work, and that the Holy Spirit doeth this "as he wills" (I. Cor. xii, 11).

In the right sense one can not possibly be father, mother, older sister or brother, yea, even nurse-maid, and especially a teacher of children apart from this spiritual insight. Wrongly understood love for the child singes so much in the child heart that otherwise would bloom luxuriously.

And if it is so with the child, it is not otherwise with the lad and the young maiden. For every period in life there is a particular form of the soul-life, with its own needs.

He who understands this educates, trains, supports and strengthens, leads and wins, souls for God. But he who insists on applying the model of his own soul's condition, checks and chokes the growth of other souls.

It is not otherwise with respect to the mighty difference which God has put between man and woman.

Surely, there are men who make you think of women, and there are women who make you think of men, and, especially among women in our times, an ambition gains ground not merely to develop oneself more independently, which is right, but also to obtain this development for oneself in a form like that of the man; which goes against the Divine ordinance.

But apart from these odd characters, every one feels that the soul-life of the woman bears another stamp, and is strung differently by God from that of the man. Perceptions, powers, feelings and talents differ.

The lily is not less than the palm tree, but it has *another* beauty, *another* glory received of God. The one sun of God's heaven works differently upon one than upon another plant.

And so it is with respect to being near to God, on the part of the man, and the being near unto God, on the part of the woman. It is the *one* Sun of righteousness. But it works differently in each case.

The mother, the father, who looks upon son and daughter alike, and does not deal with them differently, spoils, yea sometimes perverts so much in the child that, with more intelligent insight, could flourish gloriously.

Only father and mother together can suffice for the mixed family, and where father or mother falls away, the task of causing the difference in nature and disposition of son and daughter to come to its own is for the remaining one extremely difficult.

In the case of husband and wife, also, this applies, especially when one is farther advanced in the way of salvation than the other.

The godly wife who longs to win the still hesitating husband for God defeats her own purpose when she tries to graft her feminine soul-life upon her husband; and so, likewise, the husband who in order to win his wife for God drives her under the spiritual yoke of his own masculine life, is himself the cause of his bitter disappointment.

Surely, the husband should strengthen the wife spiritually, and accustom her to the storm and the fire, and the wife should chasten the husband spiritually, and accustom him to a sound of gentle stillness, but the main feature of the particular soul-life of each must remain inviolate.

The wife lives in nearness to God differently from the husband.

A similar difference presents itself with respect to the several different conditions in which we find ourselves.

Take the ecclesiastical conflict.

In this conflict there is now a period of necessary, unsparing, strong resistance against what aims to desecrate God's covenant. But afterwards, when victory has been gained, there is a time of rest and peace, and of quiet work for God's kingdom amid the struggle against sin and distress and misery. And how often it is seen that men who in this first period nobly persevered and were full of the Holy Ghost, in a succeeding period of rest and peace lost spirit, visibly weakened, and abandoned their former spiritual viewpoint.

And as it is in the struggle of the Church, so it is in the struggle of our own life, in the backward and forward movement of a mighty rise above our sin and the yielding in the face of too great temptation.

All this creates a difference of condition, of circumstances, of feelings, of experiences of soul; and woe to him who amidst all this has but one string to the harp of his soul.

Our heart has been strung by God with such wondrous richness, that for every turn in life our heart should be able to play another string to the glory of God and for the comforting of our inner man.

Elijah's example shows how God Himself reckons with this, and how, according to the nature of our condition, He approaches our heart from a different angle.

He alone who has a listening ear for this, who adapts and disposes himself to it, and who is inwardly so richly equipped that he seeks God at any gate which in such circumstances his Lord may open to him for holy approach, will feel that "to be near unto God" is not only continuous amid all circumstances, but will in every circumstance also most richly enjoy it.

Now in quiet meditation, now in bitter conflict; now going out, now coming in; but always vital, animating and vigorous.

The seeking on God's part to draw our soul unto Himself and to make it open itself before Him is alternative like the seasons of the year in which nature undergoes the workings of the sun.

And therefore he who spiritually knows but *one* season of year, becomes impoverished.

He who adjusts himself to the changes which God brings upon him is the wealthy child of the wealthy Father in heaven.

XC

THOU DIDST MAKE ME HOPE WHEN I WAS UPON MY MOTHER'S BREASTS

God's hidden walk is not alone different on the part of one child of God from that of another, but this difference is also inwardly connected with every one's disposition, character, nature and temperament.

Where there are two persons that live close to God, the one practises this not only differently from the other, but the way and the manner of it on the part of each is connected with each one's disposition and nature of soul and even of body.

Therefore, you are never able to watch the nearness unto God of another and imitate it. It is no lesson that you can learn by heart. Every one must herein seek his own way until God the Lord makes him find it.

The being near unto, the holding converse with, God can never be anything else than the result, the product of our own personal spiritual life. With you, therefore, if it is not imitated but real, it will of itself assume its own form which wholly corresponds to your nature, and which would not at all do for another.

This tends, in the first place, to comfort you and to put you at ease.

Frequently, indeed, it happens that a dear, godly, but extremely simple child of God hears the story told by others of a fellowship with God which he can not grasp; or reads of an intimacy on the part of S. Augustine and others with the Eternal Being in a measure and form which far, very far, exceeds his own experience. This makes him doubt whether he himself will ever come near unto Him. "This can never be the case with me," he thinks, and yet *so* the hidden walk must be.

Thus Satan annoys the souls of the simple.

For this is not so. With S. Augustine, that great spirit, it was bound to be so and could not have been otherwise, but for this very reason, it can not and never shall be so with the humble and the plain. What it was with great saints would not suit your particular case.

But next to this comforting thought, there is also in this a strong stimulus and spur for you.

It imposes upon you the obligation, from your own nature and in connection with your own spiritual existence, to produce from your own soul's life your own form of hidden fellowship with your God. It will not do to say: "To the height of a S. Augustine, I can never come!" No, just because you are no S. Augustine renders it impossible for you mechanically to do what he did. But you are called of God, and held responsible by Him to seek from yourself and for yourself that individual and only path, along which you, and no one else, can come to this hidden walk and persevere therein.

This does not mean that there is not a blessing in hearing others tell how they sought and found the Lord. Or that the reading of what certain great spirits have written about their nearness to God can not edify us inwardly. It surely can. The humblest poet can learn from Bilderdyk and Shakespeare. The humblest artist can profit by the works of Rubens and Rembrandt.

All this can be productive of great good.

Only, as the one and the selfsame bread forms in each individual's system its own blood and maintains its own life of the nerves, thanks to the inner processes of digestion; so likewise there can be one holy material on which many subsist, but always with every individual the inner spiritual feeding has a process of its own, and leads to an individual result.

Not alone in the case of S. Paul, but also of Jeremiah and David the Holy Scriptures explain to us the cause of this particular character in every one's hidden walk with the Eternal Being.

The twenty-second Psalm bears a strongly marked Messianic character, and only in its application to the Man of Sorrows does this song of bitterest grief of soul come to its own. But yet it would utterly lead us away from the right path of exegesis, if we should not let this psalm start out from David's own experience of soul, and if we should not begin with applying it to the Psalmist himself.

As S. Paul declares (Gal. i, 15), "that it hath pleased God *to separate him from his mother's womb,* and to call him by his grace," and as we read in Jeremiah (i, 5):

"*Before I formed thee in the belly, I knew thee:* and *before thou camest forth out of the womb* I sanctified thee," so also David confesses that the Lord's concern about him began already before he was born.

For, thou, so he sang in the twenty-second Psalm: "*Thou indeed art he that took me out of the womb, thou didst make me hope when I was upon my mother's breasts. I was cast upon thee from the womb, thou art my God since my mother bare me.*"

Entirely apart from the deeper significance of all this as applied to the Messiah, it was yet from David's own inner life that this conviction was born concerning his own walk with God, and it should not be lost from sight that in the hundred and thirty-ninth Psalm apart from his calling as a chosen Servant of the Lord, he applies it altogether generally to the forming and creation of the human being.

"Thou hast covered me in my mother's womb. I will praise thee, for I am fearfully and wonderfully made. Marvelous are thy works, and that my soul knoweth right well. My substance was not hid from thee, when I was made in secret and curiously wrought in the lowest part of the earth. Thine eyes did see my substance, yet being imperfect, and in thy book all my members were written, which in continuance were fashioned, when as yet there was none of them."

This is spoken outside of David's special calling in an altogether general human way, and in singing this psalm the Church has never hesitated to apply this to herself.

Thus to form a right estimate of the beginning and the development of our hidden walk with God, we should go back not merely to our conversion, but back of our conversion to our conception and birth

The way in which every one of us shall find his own, personal walk with his God, was written in God's Book in days before we were formed.

If you say that Jeremiah and S. Paul did not state this fact in connection with their personal initiation into fellowship with God, but very definitely in connection with their calling, as Prophet the one, and as Apostle the other, it is readily granted.

But conversely, it is equally certain that in behalf of their calling as Prophet and Apostle, the personal spiritual development of each was of highest significance. In their prophetic and apostolic calling they have had to fight and to wage spiritual battle. Their official life was not lived apart from their soul-life. In the fact that already before their conception God the Lord had preordained in them everything they should need in behalf of their calling, there was included that at the same time their spiritual quickening, training and development had equally been provided for on God's part before their birth, and that in their conception and birth such a human person was called into being, as the case required, in order that he should be able to enter upon such a spiritual condition and fulfill such a spiritual calling.

In whatever way, therefore, we take it, the three strong statements of David, Jeremiah and S. Paul, always contain this positive teaching that already *before* and in their conception and birth, the Lord their God has *so* ordained and created them as man, both as regards soul and body, that, both in their spiritual and bodily creation, everything was found that was necessary in order later on to discipline them in this particular way and insure their spiritual development.

If now we apply this to ourselves, we should not doubt but that, likewise, our conception and birth, entirely apart from our own yet unconscious condition, was a work of God, after His counsel and compass, and under His holy working.

As concerns the unique character of our disposition of soul, our gifts and talents, our form of existence, and even of our body, there is here no accident at play, no caprice, no fate, but the counsel and the working of our God.

Thus we have not been made as we are, in order that God subsequently might consider what He might make of us. No, everything here has been thought out. Here everything forms *one* whole. Here from the beginning everything is directed to a final end, by an omniscient, fore-seeing and Almighty God and directed at the same time to what is required at every point of the way, in order to attain this final end.

If now this final end is your everlasting salvation, and if your spiritual inner life, including your hidden walk with God, leads to this end, then it can not be otherwise than that the whole appointment, regarding the form in which after soul and body you should be born, was from the first immediately connected with what once as child of God you were to be, and with the particular way in which God would be willing to receive you, you yourself, in distinction from others, into His holy, hidden walk.

If experience with people daily teaches you that sometimes you meet people who have much in common with yourself, and you with them, but that yet you never meet with any one of whom you can say in every respect: *"Such am I, this person is precisely my double,"* then there must be in your disposition of soul and in your bodily existence something that is different from others. And this not by chance, but after God's will and counsel. And all this individuality that constitutes your person is in turn no play of natural wealth, but is thus and not otherwise disposed, because you had to seek your hidden walk with your God *in your way* and *along your way*, and because, in order to find this way and to be able to walk it, you were in need of such a disposition of soul and of such a manner of existence.

This sets you free from people, even from godly people who press *their* piety upon you, but you are bound thereby to your God, personally, in everything, from your conception and birth.

For consider, and forget not, that the twenty-second Psalm also says: "Thou didst *make me hope,* when I was upon my mother's breasts."

And to cause to hope *so* that the soul itself hopes, is to evoke an inner working from the soul itself.

David reckons his spiritual life from the moment when as infant he cradled at his mother's breast.

XCI

AND WORSHIP HIM THAT LIVETH FOR EVER AND EVER

PRAYER and *worship* are not the same.

You feel this at once when you consider the distinction between religion in heaven and religion on earth.

On earth we are in the midst of all sorts of trouble and misery, we endure a thousand anxieties, we contend against disappointment and adversity, and our life each day is an endless chain of wants that call for supplies.

This is a condition which of itself impels us to prayer, to ask, to supplicate, to invoke, and implore help and deliverance, relief and the fulfillment of our desires.

In religion on earth prayer, supplication, the invocation of higher help is altogether appropriate.

But this is wholly different in heaven.

Undoubtedly there is prayer in heaven, even much prayer. Christ Himself lives to pray for us.

But prayer in heaven, both on the part of Christ, and of the angels, and of the blest, bears another character than that of our prayer on earth.

"Our Father who art in heaven, hallowed be Thy name, Thy kingdom come, Thy will be done on earth as it is in heaven," can also be prayed above. The kingdom of glory tarries. The conflict between Christ and the power that sets itself against God goes on. The end has not come yet. And therefore it is natural that everything that is in heaven invokes this end and implores the fruition of the kingdom of glory.

It can also be understood that prayer in heaven is in behalf of God's people on earth. The Scriptures teach this plainly with respect to Christ. That angels remember us in their supplication is quite certain. And that the blessed ones themselves, though they have no immediate knowledge of our needs, unite with Christ and the angels in prayer for the triumph of God's kingdom in the earth can scarcely be thought otherwise.

But though you go into this as far as Scripture will permit, yet it speaks for itself that neither the angels nor the blessed can pray with us: "Give us this day our daily bread, forgive us our debts and lead us not into temptation, but deliver us from the Evil."

The blessed may pray that they might be clothed with the body of the resurrection, but their condition is not one of need, of misery, of lack and want. They are happy and drink with full draughts from the Fountain of bliss.

Where we are permitted a look upon the life in heaven, as in Revelation, you find almost no mention of anything regarding angels, seraphs and cherubim and of the blessed, than that they *worship*.

"Holy, holy, holy is the Lord of hosts. The whole earth is full of his glory."

If, then, there is this difference between religion above and religion on earth, that among us prayer, and in heaven worship appears in the foreground, it is of utmost importance that we carefully consider the character of this worship.

Prayer is the seeking of God's nearness, in our behalf, that He might be gracious unto us. *Worship* is the seeking of God's nearness, from our side in order that we may offer laud, praise, thanksgiving and honor unto God.

In principle, therefore, the *one* is the direct opposite of the other.

He who prays asks that God may give Himself to us; he who worships demands that his soul and all that is within him shall offer itself unto God.

He who prays desires something that might come to us from God, he who worships desires something that might come unto God from us.

That in worship, also, grace operates, speaks of itself, but it is another kind of grace. It is grace, that the Infinite, Almighty and self-sufficient God will accept the magnifying of His Name from the creature.

He is so infinitely exalted that the creature can not bring Him anything, and though every angel-voice and human tongue were silent forevermore, the Eternal One would need nothing, and remain all-sufficient in Himself.

And herein is grace, that the most High God, Who needs nothing, will take pleasure in the songs of praise of His angels and of men, and allow them the sacred joy of showing forth His praise.

All worship, all thanksgiving, all songs of praise, all ascription of honor, rests upon the foundation of this, to us, impenetrable grace.

Thus worship and ascription of honor can truly likewise serve to magnify God's Name before our fellow-creatures, but at least in worship this is not the aim.

He who sings Divine praise can do so for the sake of witnessing for his God in the face of unbelieving multitudes, and of winning them for God, but worship is a holy utterance of soul, which goes on between our soul and God, and at the most can only adapt itself to the worship of fellow-believers.

Worship in its highest utterance can not be mechanical. It only becomes worship when the soul loses itself in God, in admiration becomes astonished at His virtues and His acts, and of itself breaks forth into praise even as the Aeolian harp emits its dulcet strains when the wind plays upon its strings.

Examine now your own inner life, not whether you pray more than you worship, but whether in your outpouring of soul, next to prayer, worship, likewise, has its own, sufficient place.

And then, alas, it must be an honest avowal on the part of many that in the prayer-life this worship forms all too moderate a part. We do not say that most people do not worship as well as pray, but we dare express the surmise that the blessed delight of worship is, by all too many, too little known and sought.

And this should not be so.

He who seeks the hidden walk, who wills to be near unto God, should not in his prayer-life be too exclusively engaged about himself nor about those who are his, and when he is on his knees before God he should not defer to concern himself about God's glory until the end of his prayer.

The knowledge of God lies in worship, far more than in prayer.

He who prays for something thinks, first of all, of his own need and want and embarrassment, and loses himself in the Being of his God no further than that with Him there is power and might wherewith He can come to the help of his suppliant's need.

On the other hand, he who worships loses himself in God, forgets himself, in order to think of God alone, to let the lustrous beams of God's virtues shine upon him, and to cause to radiate forth from his own soul the reflex of the greatness of God as it mirrors itself in his deeply moved and wonder-wrapped soul.

Only when the kingdom of Glory shall have been ushered in on the new earth under the new heaven together with all God's angels, shall we not do otherwise than worship. At present, need presses prayer continuously to the lips. And yet, woe to him, woe to her, who does not already here know something of that real life which finds its blessedness in worship.

Let thanksgiving be here your training school.

One of the formularies of the Church makes the whole life of God's child consist of a testimony of gratitude, for thanksgiving is the beginning and the continuance of all worship.

Who would not daily pray for the forgiveness of his sins? But it is deplorable when ardent thanksgiving for forgiveness obtained at the Cross remains lacking, or at least does not fill our soul.

So it is with all of life.

There is always need and want, and the pressure of soul from the depths, to call upon God that He might be gracious unto us.

But is there ever a moment of prayer when there is no occasion as well to give thanks for grace obtained and to honor Him Who gave it?

Thanksgiving is not yet the full worship. Giving thanks is only just worship with an eye to what God was to us. But he who has learned to give thanks, real, ardent thanks, comes of himself to this still far richer worship, which wills nothing else than to glorify God's Majesty.

With the heathen, at times, there is more worship before their idols than one finds with us before the Holy One. The Mohammedan, indeed, daily recites the virtues of Allah from the Koran.

Is, then, the admonition superfluous, that from the very first we shall accustom our children not only to prayer but also to giving of thanks and to *worship?*

Nothing brings our soul near unto God so effectively as worship.

THE BODY IS NOT ONE MEMBER, BUT MANY

CHRIST is your King.

Not merely King anointed over Zion, the mountain of His holiness. Nor yet, after the earthly Zion had been profaned, King merely over God's kingdom on earth. No, Christ is also King over the persons who are His subjects.

Your relation, your personal connection with Christ can not be expressed in one word. It is a many-sided relation.

When you think of the guilt of sin which threatened you with doom, then Christ is your Reconciler. When you seek protection with Christ from the power of sin and of temptation, then this same Christ is not your Reconciler but your Redeemer. Or, when you look to Christ for direction and guidance on your course through the labyrinth of life, then, again, this selfsame Savior is not your Reconciler, and not your Redeemer, but your Shepherd Who goes before you in the way and leaves you His example.

But your many-sided relation to your Savior is by no means exhausted even with this, for this selfsame Christ is also with the Father your glorified Head, the Lord before Whom your knee must bend, Whom your tongue must confess; and therefore your King Who has incorporated you with His people; Whose subject you have become; and in Whose palace you shall one day be expected.

So little is this honor-title of "King" here accidental, that the great vindication on Golgotha is at length fought out under this title, and before the judgment-seat of

Pilate the conflict between the Emperor of Rome and the Anointed of God centered itself in the struggle for the honor of Kingship.

The Lamb, so it is proclaimed unto you in Revelation (xvii, 14), is not merely your Reconciliation and your Surety, not alone your Redeemer and Savior, nor yet alone your Shepherd and your Guide. No, the Lamb of God—and in this antithesis you feel what amazes and inspires—the Lamb of God is at the same time Lord of lords and King of kings.

The Lamb with the crown, the high, the holy union of self-effacement and dominion.

Your King!

But how, in what sense?

Is the king here on earth the real, the actual; and is the kingly image of the earthly prince applied to your Savior purely by way of comparison by which to express His power and honor?

Christ also your King! Tends this title of honor merely to have you think of Christ as in a distant hamlet the man behind the plow thinks of his Sovereign in the Royal residence?

One who is to him a hidden and a mysterious power, expressed in the image on the coin, but, for the rest, a power which remains foreign to him, a power from afar, of whose splendor and luster, of whose glory and pomp, he can form no faint idea, but which he honors from afar. A Sovereign in the glorious palace, but who as far as this farm-hand is concerned is unapproachable, to whom he pays taxes because he is subject unto him, and for whom, if he is godly, he intercedes in his daily prayer.

And surely there is a likeness here. Christ, too, is enthroned in a palace of glory, even in such a one, that compared with the splendor of His greatness all royal splendor on earth pales. He who is Jesus' subject also places his child at the service of his King. His money he sacrifices in the ministry of love, his strength he spends in behalf of what must be done for His kingdom. And this King too is enthroned afar off. And here on earth His subject shall not see the King of God's Kingdom.

But herewith the likeness ends.

For, that Christ is your King, is so little an imagery borrowed from earthly princes, that rather the kings on earth are merely image-bearers of His glory, and that true, real, actual Kingship has never been realized in a prince on earth, but is known alone in Christ.

Head, Lord, and King are but three rays of the same glory.

Head points to the inner relationship and solidarity of your life, of your existence, of your inner being, with the life, the existence and the being of your Savior.

"Lord" expresses the fact that Christ owns you, that you are His property, that you belong to Him, that He has bought you free from the dominion of Satan and has obtained possession of you by His Blood.

And only in this twofold relation, because He is your Head and your Lord, therefore, is He also *your King*, Who has taken you up into His kingdom, has incorporated you with His people, made you a sharer in a common lot with Himself, and now rules you with His Royal law of life.

You are His subject, but this alone because, and in consideration of, the fact that you are a member of that selfsame Body of which He is the Head.

This is surely, at first hearing, an enigmatical relationship. But it gloriously explains itself, when you clearly understand the significance of that Body, and, in that Body, of the Head, and, under that Head, of each member.

Imagine to yourself man, as in paradise he came forth from the hand of God. The pure, perfect beautiful body; in that body all the members in which it manifested itself; and with that body the noble head, with all the fullness of facial expression, with the fine expressive features, with the animation that outpours itself from it; and thus only can you have the Image before you of the Body of Christ, and in that Body the members, and over all these members the glorious Head.

And yet the *human* body by itself here is not the perfect Image. "Body" in this connection indicates rather in a broader sense what we are more accustomed to call an *organism*, in which sense also the animal is an organism, and the plant an organism, and as we also apply the image of a body or of an organism to all sorts of associations of man and man.

Thus we speak of a corporation which is nothing else than a body, signifying thereby all sorts of associations, societies and confederations that are formed. So we say that the family has an organic existence. And so we speak of the body of the State and of the body of the people. And for this reason, and in this connection, we call him among the people who directs such a corporation the head of such an association or the head of the body of the State. And it is even the rule to call those who belong to such a society or body, the members of the association, or the members of the Church. To become a member of a nation is to become incorporated in that nation.

And this is an image which the holy Apostle applies to Christ and to those that are His.

Also the organism of the plant renders service in behalf of this. Did not Jesus Himself say: "I am the true vine, and ye are the branches?" And does not S. Paul speak of having become one planting with Jesus?

Thus it is always again that one effort to make it tangible to you, to make it clear to you, that Jesus' Kingship is to you no external dominion coming upon you from without, but that before you become a subject of Jesus, you have been linked into His life, that with the strand of life itself, if we may say so, you have been bound to Him; so that it is *one* life-blood that courses through you and Him; and that it is *one* spirit of life that animates you both unto life. Yea, as little as you can move your head from one place to another, but that your foot, your hand, your eye, your ear goes with it, so, likewise, every movement of life on the part of your King of itself stirs also in you, and puts you into motion with Him.

Christ is your King because of itself the member necessarily follows the body, and the body goes wherever the the head directs.

XCIII

LORD, TEACH US TO PRAY

IF the temper of your soul were pure you would never feel yourself nearer unto God than in your prayer; and while at prayer you would never be able to be far away from God.

To pray, and not be near unto God, rightly interpreted, exclude one another.

And yet, how much prayer is not made every day in every city and in every village, yes, one might say in every home, time and again, during which the soul for not so much as a single moment comes under the overwhelming impression of standing before the Face of God.

Sin weakens our inner life in all sorts of ways. Hence the spring of the life of our soul can not force itself upward, as we ourselves so ardently would wish. In fact, at times, we can not pray. Yet we would not neglect it. And so we fold our hands, and stammer our prayer; but when the "amen" has been said we feel discouraged by the lack of elevation and animation that marred our prayer.

Apart from leading others in prayer, every one *must* and every one can pray. And yet to pray well is an exceedingly difficult art, or rather it is a holy exercise which demands the utmost clearness, urgency and readiness of soul, and which may never become mere art, else it ceases to be prayer.

Even the disciples felt this, and when they had been witnesses again of that holy act, when Jesus, having gone a short distance from them, had separated Himself in prayer to the Father, it so quickened the sense of their own inability to pray aright, that, when Jesus came back to them one of them said: "Lord, teach us to pray, as John also taught his disciples" (S. Luke xi, 1).

Now a hyper-spiritual child of God, in our days, would readily have turned off such a request with a rebuke. Every one, indeed, must pray of himself. What merit can a memorized prayer have before God?

But Jesus was not so hyper-spiritual. He, indeed, always prayed of Himself. But He understood, nevertheless, how difficult real prayer must be to us who have sinned, and though His disciples were one day to become the teachers and leaders of the Church of all ages, He appreciated their request that He should teach them how they should pray, and so in His heavenly language He gave them the Our Father to pray.

He did not say: "Pray after this manner." He gave them the *Our Father*, not as an example of how to pray. No, the Lord expressly said "When ye pray, *say*."

John, too, had evidently given his disciples such a form of prayer. And so Jesus, too, gave His disciples a prayer in a fixed form, a prayer evidently intended and appointed to be prayed by them in unison. For the form is in the plural: *Our* Father, *our* daily bread, *our* trespasses.

In all ages, the church of Christ, in all her forms, has remained true to the *Our Father*. And our forefathers have not only adopted written prayers in our Liturgy, but have ordered again and again the use of the *Our Father* in public worship by the congregation of believers.

But since the eighteenth century, this has been discarded. Especially from Scotland the influence came that pushed everything aside that favored a fixed form, and in public worship permitted nothing but extemporary prayer by the leader.

The aim was high; but was it not too high, and has not the overspiritual all too grievously injured the spiritual?

Undoubtedly it is highest perfection when, superior to every sort of support, from the free urgency of spirit, the soul may lift itself up to God, and, upon the wings of the Spirit, in holy consecrated language spread itself before Him. There are such glorious moments in the prayer-life. And it is plain that in such moments even the *Our Father* is not sufficiently concrete to lead the soul in its utterance before God.

But ask yourself once seriously, how many among the great and the small in the congregation have risen to this sacred height, and if there are such, how many are the moments of a long day, when they are in such a pure and holy mood?

Count with reality. Think not only of yourself, but have compassion upon the poor sheep in the congregation and in your own home, whose spiritual standing is still low and who yet must needs pray, and to whom it is no less glorious than it is to you, if in prayer they can come a little nearer to their God, and may experience something of His holy Presence.

How much higher the Apostles of Jesus stood above us, and yet, even for them, Jesus deemed such a form of prayer *so* little aimless or superfluous that He Himself gave them such a one.

It is true that even written prayer leads to abuse. But would you suppose that Jesus has neither foreseen nor known to what abuse the *Our Father* would lead? And yet He gave it to His disciples.

Nothing is so holy that our infirmity and our sin will not turn it to abuse. Baptism is abused, and the Holy Communion is abused, and the Scripture is abused. Shall, therefore, all this be condemned?

And so with respect to prayer we here stand before such a painful choice.

Say that the Spirit's prayer from one's own soul alone is acceptable to God, and forsooth, there is no more abuse, but then you will also have thousands of families wherein prayer is no more said at all and remembrance of it is gradually lost.

But, on the other hand, restore the use in the written form, and then of necessity you get the muttering with the lips, from which the soul is absent. Not with all, thank God, but with many. And thus many a prayer is profaned.

Standing before this choice many incline to say: "Let the others not pray, provided there are a few who pray aright, and, in any case, prevent the work of the lips in which there is no heart."

And yet we *may not* speak thus. What Jesus spake to His disciples excludes this. Let us be more humble. Let us confess that even the congregation of the Lord stands at too low a level to appreciate so highly spiritual a standpoint; and that, if prayer shall continue, if it shall be a power in the whole Church, in every home, in behalf of every member in that home, great and small alike, *both* must be maintained, the Spirit's prayer from one's own soul as well as the written prayer which all can pray, because all have been instructed in its use.

Our offering of praise in hymn and psalm would likewise be of a far higher order, if every one of us were a born poet, and if we never sang a hymn from any book, but always a song from our own inspiration and spiritual urge.

Yet this we do not do. It is impossible. We are no poets. And public worship would be impossible if the same hymn could not be sung together.

This too leads to abuse. Hymn upon hymn is sung in the congregation which more than one sings with his lips, while in its words his soul has no part.

But who would for this reason banish the worship of song from God's house?

This would be a reaching out after hyper-spirituality of life which would bring death into our public worship.

But there is a still more deeply significant reason.

Do you not know from experience, that when your soul wills to be near unto God, nothing at times is more helpful in this behalf than to repeat by yourself some favorite verse from the Psalter that you have always remembered, and which by its consecrated language of itself loosens you from your ordinary world of thought and lifts your soul up to God? At times when you would pray, and prayer would not come, has not the saying of the *Our Father* frequently been the grateful means of bringing you into the mood for prayer? Scripture, too, is a formula, and ever remains the same, and yet, has not the very reading of Scripture, before you entered upon prayer, constantly been the means by which you have been enabled not only to pray, but to pray in that consecrated language which carries the soul with it?

A twofold cause operates here.

First *the language*. There is a distinct language also for our prayer and singing of praise. That language does not spring up of itself from every individual soul. There have been those who have received the gift for this particular purpose. And is it not natural that they who may sing after David, or pray in the words of S. Paul, should feel that this helps and elevates them and brings them further than of themselves they ever could have come?

But there is still something else. Words of prayer and uplifts of praise, which from youth on have gone with us through life, impart to the utterance of our inner life a steadiness which inwardly strengthens and hallows us. And when, in addition to this, we have the glorious sense that these words of prayer and these uplifts of praise are not alone familiar to us, but now and in earlier ages were the language of God's children, then it is as though some portion of the precious ointment of Aaron has been poured out upon it all, the sweet odor of which refreshes the heart.

The seeking and urging still remains underneath all this to experience the blessed nearness of God. Thus the *Our Father*, quietly, reverently and seriously repeated opens the gate of heaven to our soul. Psalm language of itself carries the soul upward. Everything that lends to our wandering, oftentimes so impotent soul the support of the consecrated word, tunes us to higher harmony. And, likewise, everything that causes us, in and during prayer and singing praises, to experience the communion of all God's saints and the fellowship with our own more godly past, establishes a protecting power over against the power of the world that aims to keep us far distant from our God.

The benediction at the close of public worship, every preacher can likewise compose for himself; but yet, as a rule, this is not done; that in this benediction a fixed form has been retained, is a gain for which we may well give thanks.

Now the preacher may put nothing into it of himself so that you can forget him; but just because thereby he steps into the background and does not come to the fore, the benediction affects you as a gentle dew of grace which comes to you from God.

AS IN HEAVEN

THE being near of our soul unto God implies that with our inner sense we lift up ourselves from our every day surroundings into the sphere of God's Majesty. It is this that in Scriptural language has become the *Sursum corda*, the urge to lift up soul and senses to God and to appear in the audience chamber of His Holiness.

It is true, God the Lord in infinite compassion comes down to us to make tabernacle with us, and with His rod and staff to comfort us; but though this by itself brings God near unto us, it by no means always brings our soul near unto God. God's seeking love can for long times be near, around and in our heart, and our soul's perception fail to discover it with any clearness. An infant can be carried by God's nearness and have itself no clear perception whatever of God's Majesty. In conditions of sickness, which deprive us of our self-consciousness, God's nearness departs not from His child. And when in dying our consciousness fails us, the nearness of God continues to support the soul which he has called unto Himself.

You should always distinguish, therefore, between these two, however closely they may be allied. It is something different whether our God is close to us and whether we are close to our God. And not in behalf of the former, but of the latter, it is highly advantageous that our sense be not too greatly entangled with the world of visible things, and that we understand the sacred art of transposing our soul's perception from this world into that which is around God's Throne.

At first the soul learns this in prayer, and it is note-worthy how in the short form of the *Our Father*, again and again, Jesus leads our thoughts to the invisible world.

At once in the address: "Our Father who art in heav-en." This means, in the words of the Heidelberg Cate-chism, that we should not think of God in an earthly way. This is correct, provided it is taken in the deeper sense. Not as a sound, a word, a term whereby to express some-thing supermundane, but as an effort of the soul, at the very beginning of the prayer, to loosen itself from the earthly imaginations which immesh it, and to enter into those high and holy spheres that surround the Throne of God.

This same result is effected by the prayer: "Thy King-dom come," since that kingdom can not be anything else than the kingdom of heaven, and the prayer, for this rea-son, intends that the powers of this kingdom from heaven should enter ever more mightily into our life.

But sharpest and most clearly expressed is the commun-ion with the life around God's Throne in the third prayer: "Thy will be done on earth among us, *as in heaven* among thy angels."

Here the reference to heaven is immediate. Here it is clearly and plainly expressed. Here are delineated simul-taneously both the similarity and the dissimilarity of the life on earth and the life in heaven. Here Jesus Himself urges us, in the prayer which He gave us for our pilgrim journey, that in our prayer and in the seeking after God's nearness we acquaint ourselves with the world of angels and of the redeemed, and by our fellowship with their world strength-en our approach to God.

Yea, so strong is this urge on the part of Jesus, to bring our soul by prayer into touch with the invisible world, that in the last petition He conversely makes tangible to us the working that goes out upon us from the head of the fallen angels. "Deliver us from the Evil One" is the prayer that makes us mindful how the evil, how the sin that springs up in our heart, is fed and impelled by a higher power from the invisible world, and how our God alone can deliver us from this deadly influence.

Is it then too boldly spoken when we say that in this short prayer of six petitions Jesus causes us to go out every time from the earthly sphere of visible things; and that He unveils to the sense of our soul, clearly and mightily, the reality of the invisible world; and all this in order that by this very thing itself we should enjoy the being near unto God the more deeply and the more intimately.

This fellowship with the spirits of the invisible world appears in Scripture, more than once, to be inseparable from the being near unto God. Only think of the vision of Isaiah and of the Revelation on Patmos.

Isaiah saw not only the Lord upon His Throne, but also the Seraphim who surrounded His Throne, and he heard the: "Holy, holy, holy is the Lord of hosts," that rang and reverberated with glorious harmony among the arches of heaven. And it was not otherwise on Patmos. There too the seer's eye does not penetrate to the Holy One without the simultaneous sight of the Cherubim that reveal God's Majesty, and he hears, what says still more, also from the elders, from the circles of the blessed, the anthem of praise: "Thou, Lord, art worthy to receive honor and glory and power."

And so runs through the whole of Scripture a golden line of heavenly light that brings the prayer and the anthem of praise on the part of God's people into fellowship with the anthem of praise on the part of the angels and of the blessed.

It is not only the angels and blessed in unapproachable light, and we who on earth in our twilight sing praises unto the Father, the Son, and the Holy Ghost; but between angel-voice and human tongue there is a connection. Sometimes it seems as though we give but an echo to what is jubilantly sung around God's Throne, and our heart finds rest only when there is holy accord, when there is blissful harmony between created spirits above and the creature that on earth thirsts after the nearness of his God.

But this of itself presses the question upon us, whether this necessary fellowship with God's angels and with the saints before God's Throne has not passed too greatly into disuse among our circles.

That we must be on our guard against abuse is clear as sunlight. Not improbably even idolatry has sprung from this seeking after fellowship with the world of spirits. And even within the boundaries of Christ's Church the search after this fellowship has all too frequently drawn souls away from the nearness of God, instead of leading them into His holy Presence.

The soul's concern, if we may so express ourselves, with angels and with saints, has but too often tempted it in its anxious carefulness to create middle agencies between itself and God, whose help rendered recourse to the help of our God needless.

It is plain, therefore, that in order to correct this abuse safety was sought in sobriety, and that from a holy impulse the endeavor was made not to allow oneself in one's prayer to be diverted by anything, not even by angels, from God Himself and from His immediate fellowship. But can it be denied that this carefulness, by exaggeration, has led to the other extreme; and is it not true, that in prayer at public worship, in prayer at the family altar, and in personal supplication, the spirit world was almost altogether lost from view, and that thereby all such prayer came into conflict with the note which Jesus himself struck in the *Our Father*?

In the *Our Father* Jesus brings our soul, again and again, in touch with this higher spirit world, while from our prayer this fellowship has almost altogether vanished.

So, in order to avoid the abuse of one extreme, one can unconsciously and naturally, fall into the other, and it can not be otherwise but that this must work injury to the life of the soul.

He who dies knows that he will not find his God and Savior singly and alone, but surrounded by a world of saints. There awaits him not alone a Father, but also a Father-house, and in that Father-house the many mansions, and in those mansions, with God's angels, the saints that have gone before.

And though we now speak of that world of glory as of the world *above* because we can not think of it otherwise than as being far above this guilty earth, we know equally well, that this distinction is no separation, and that already, here on earth, we can enter into communion with that world. When the Psalmist would praise God, he calls upon the angels to extol His praise (Ps. 103, 20). There is a host of the Lord that encampeth round about them that fear God. Not alone Satan, the head of the fallen angels, but the good angels also stand in communication with our soul. In moments of blessed exaltation of spirit it has been to your soul, too, as though it actually felt the nearness of God's good spirits, and as though they made you feel more tenderly and blessedly the nearness of God.

From people we undergo the same influence for good or for evil.

Sometimes one wicked person in your environment can draw your whole soul away from God, estrange in you every utterance of soul from God, and throw you back into your earthly, sinful shallowness.

On the other hand, one devoted child of God among your associates can effect the result that every unholy thing drops out from your conversation, that your soul responds to holy thoughts, and that association with him brings you nearer to God.

And so too it is here.

He who accustoms himself to have part in the holy world of God's angels, and already, here on earth, admits the company of the saints into the world of his inner life, will thereby not alone banish what is evil, but will himself attain a holier mood. In his devotions of praise and prayer he will feel himself upborne, and will find it less difficult to lift himself up from his earthly life into the nearness of God.

We have not been created for solitariness. The moment in which, deserted of all, you discover that you have to fight your battle alone, you feel that something unnatural has come upon you.

Not alone, but "with all saints" we shall come to the knowledge of God.

And if in eternity it will be the wonderful exaltation of your life, that with all the angels and saints you will eternally glorify your God, why, then should you forsake and neglect this glorious power, which already here on earth can unfold itself in your prayer, if already here by anticipation you live in the blessed fellowship which awaits you above?

We are with all God's saints *one* Body in Christ as our Head, but on earth we taste so little of this fellowship with the whole Body of the Lord.

On the other hand, fellowship with saints and with God's angels is always open to you.

Blessed, then, is he who revels herein not alone in behalf of his own soul, but who also understands how to deepen thereby his delight in the nearness of God.

STRIVING AGAINST SIN

ONE who in mature years and in his right mind does not at times fight against this or that sin is almost unimaginable. The human heart is such an unfathomable riddle, even with highway robbers and drunkards we have been surprised sometimes by a shy tenderness, which manifested itself in an aversion to more than one sin which in better circles is given all too frequently free passage.

But this does not make every resistance that is offered to some striking sin, whether in oneself or in others, by any means always what the Apostle calls *striving against sin* (Heb. xii, 4).

Everything here hinges upon the question of what it is that moves you to oppose this or that sin. One will avoid a sin from concern for his health. Especially with sensual sin this motive is often preponderant. Another is on his guard, lest, if his sin became known, it would injure his good name. A third resists a temptation because yielding to it would ruin him financially. A fourth puts a mark against a particular sin because in his narrow circle of life it is sharply condemned. Just call to mind Sabbath desecration. And in this way and by all sorts of persons this or that sin is put under the ban from reasons that have nothing to do with the real striving against sin. With not a few there is even no mention of a conscious motive, and all their opposition to this or that sin springs from a certain moral instinct, from the judgment of public opinion, or from a certain impulse to be decent. So in our civilized circles profanity has noticeably decreased, but far more because it is now looked upon as coarse and impolite than from fear of the Holy God.

Now you should not look down from your own heights upon all this opposition to all sorts of sin and count it indifferent.

Because of its great contagiousness, every sin that comes into prominence is so dangerous. Sin, apart from its guilt before God, is by itself a moral disease, and everything that reacts against the outbreak or the progress of this disease is gain.

Only this opposition to any sin whatever *without higher motive* brings no *spiritual* gain.

What David exclaimed: "Against thee, thee only have I sinned" remains the maxim here. And only when you strive against sin because sin opposes God, does your striving obtain the holy, higher character.

Striving against sin, because sin resists God and God resists sin, brings you close to Him. Your struggle then remains no merely moral conflict, but it becomes *religious,* it becomes an expression of godliness, and at the same time a precious means of extending your being near unto God into your whole life.

See it in the life of nations and of societies, how the waging of a common war creates alliances, makes close affiliations and knits ties for the present and the future.

The same is seen in church and public life. When some great political issue awaits decision by ballot the preliminary campaign will create fellowships between temporary fellow-members of clubs which affects their whole future. Yea, in every department of life it is evident, again and again that nothing unites so closely and brings people so near together as a fight against a common foe.

The same applies to the striving against sin, if in all honesty you wage this war *because sin is inimical to God.*

For then God and you fight one and the self same battle. Then this conflict of itself impels you to join forces with Him.   Then you do not fight alone but with God, and with the weapons which He furnishes you for this battle, under Christ as your Captain.   There is nothing that makes you come so near unto God, and remain there, as this life-long continuance of the bitter fight against the enemy of God, and of your own soul, and of the souls of your loved ones.

But, then, let it be a lifelong striving not against one particular sin, but against *sin*, against all the sinful influences, instigations and workings that go out from Satan upon yourself and upon all your surroundings.

Surely, there are bosom sins, and it is no minor fault when you know your heart so little that you should not be able to confess before God what sin most assaults and vanquishes you.   It can not be otherwise, therefore, but that every one who takes his inner life seriously is more specially on his guard against certain besetting sins, and is more exercised in his thoughts and in his prayers with these than with other sins.   His effort directs itself most strongly against that evil which overcame him most frequently and worked him most harm.   And in the remembrance, the shame and the sorrow at having been vanquished in the battle against this particular sin will obtrude themselves most strongly upon him.   It was this sin that inflicted upon him the most cruel wound and left the blackest mark.

But do not overlook the danger that lurks in this.

For is it not heart-breaking to see to what a number of lesser sins in their character-life even seriously-minded Christians are almost stone blind?

And for this, one-sided striving against some special sin is largely responsible.

Where a greater danger threatens, all lesser dangers that might harm us are almost of themselves lost from sight.

When one of your loved ones lies at the point of death, no one inquires after the concerns of cellar and kitchen. When a runaway horse races through the streets no one looks out to avoid muddy places but scurries out of the way. When fire breaks out in your house no one is troubled about the draught from an open window. When someone in the water is in danger of drowning, the rescuer does not ask whether in doing it he might tear his clothes. When war breaks out, all sorts of other quarrels however important are silenced. And thus a more serious wrong will always cause the fight against a lesser wrong to weaken.

And such, likewise, is the course of things, in your soul.

As long as you continue to struggle to resist and to avert the one sin which tempts you the strongest, many other sins have almost free play and their progress is unnoticed. He who continues to wage the main fight against his arrogance and pride, against his sensual propensity or against his thirst for gold, thereby actually exposes himself to the danger that little untruths, dishonesties, infidelities, bitter animosities, vanities, selfishnesses, and so on, become almost a second nature to him, strike root ever more deeply in his heart and sully his inner life.

This, then, is only noticed when the worst enemy has at last been as good as worsted. Then the tenderness of conscience concerns itself at once with these erstwhile neglected sins, and it frightens one to see the luxurious growth of weeds in the garden of his heart.

And to what cause is this disheartening result to be attributed save to this fact, that one indeed strove to undo himself of his worst foe, but had no consideration for the fight against sin on the ground that *God* fights against it.

Thereby it remained an effort on his part to liberate

his person, to measure his strength of spirit and of will against the strength of this particular sin. A being dissatisfied with oneself every time defeat was suffered, and the will not to rest until victory was achieved. But it went on outside of the hidden walk with God. There was invocation of God's help to overcome the enemy of your soul, but there was no awakening on the part of your soul to beat off as a poisonous adder *the enemy of your God.* And, therefore, such a battle could not bring you nearer to God, but threw you every time again back upon yourself.

Should you, therefore, give up the fight against the sin that tempts you most and only give your attention to your numerous lesser sins?

Of course not. He who would leave the main entrance to the fortress unprotected in order to resist the assault at the side entrances, would soon find himself attacked in the rear and be forced to abandon all resistance.

No, what you should do is, with an eye open to the moral danger that threatens you, by a far more serious exercise of your powers, to fight to the finish, the sooner the better, the battle against your special sin, not by giving it free play but by breaking with it once and for all.

Thus only will you obtain free hands, in the Lord's strength, to bring spiritual harmony into the further discords of your soul.

And that this is possible is evident from the witness on the part of many a disciplined child of God who finally girded on the whole armor of God and triumphed gloriously.

For this is the wrong in question, that one makes his besetting sin his bosom sin, and so comes to regard this particular sin as an evil that by a certain fatality he is doomed to fight till his death.

The enigma of our human heart is, that we fight our besetting sin and at the same time cozen it. A duality within whereby, through lack of heroic action, we accustom ourselves to it as to a necessity of life.

It is, then, not the spirit in us, which, united with the Spirit of God, fights in our soul God's battle against sin for God's sake, but a dual which we fight within ourselves for reasons of our own.

But this evil must be overcome.

It must become a lifelong fight against every sin, against our evil nature for the sake of the holiness of God.

The child of God, for the sake of coming closer to his *holy* God, must take service under Christ in the warfare which God himself wages against Satan and his workings; and thus simultaneously reach the twofold result: that he overcomes where thus far he suffered defeat, and whereas he wandered away from his God, now he knows himself to be *near* to Him.

LIVE IN PEACE

WHEN Asaph wrote: "But it is good for me to be near unto God," and thus expressed in words a deep avowal of his soul, which age after age has found an echo in thousands of hearts, he who sought God had more help from life than we do now.

Even now it is still the custom in the East where Asaph lived, to relate everything that happens to God; in everything to remember God, and to pronounce the name of God. There is so much that draws us away from Him, and therefore religious usage demanded that the child from earliest infancy should be trained to the habit of purposely bringing to mind God's Name with every occurrence of life. Under the Islam this is still so. It is even so much overdone that it must give rise to abuse.

But in the matter itself there is something that attracts. The call to prayer from the pinnacle of the minarets has the same tendency. Where so unspeakably much draws us away from God, a counterpoise was sought in life by which to bind the soul to God.

The Christian Church did the same in the Middle Ages. The ringing of bells, the Stations of the Cross, the crucifixes, and so on, all tended to quicken the thought of Christ. And in the age of the Reformation our fathers sought to obtain the same effect by giving prayer a place in everything, by multiplying church services, and by sanctifying in God every event of life. Not only last wills and testaments but even contracts of rent were begun in God's Name. On coins the words appeared: "God with us," and wherever it was possible God's holy Name was brought to mind.

Thus an atmosphere prevailed which was impregnated with something from the higher spheres of holiness, sometimes even too much so. To this was added that in Asaph's time and in the days of our fathers, the religious undulation was far stronger, and religion took a far broader place in life.

But we have everything against us. In the broad circle of society and community life God's Name is scarcely ever mentioned. Bells are scarcely ever rung. An altogether different world of thought fills minds and hearts. One is called old-fashioned, if not scorned, when he attempts to hold fast to holy usages. A life divested of God and His Name is deemed most desirable. And as regards the religious backward and forward movement, it still prevails in small circles, but the tidal-wave of life goes purely materially for money and sensual pleasure.

In such times as these, to be near unto God demands double exertion. Nothing can be neglected that here may have effect, neither positively nor negatively. Positively every means must persistently be applied to cause our soul to exercise itself every day longer and more intimately with God; and negatively everything must be opposed and resisted that militates against our fellowship with Him.

Does the Church of Christ understand, is it felt in the Church of Christ what high issue is here at stake? Can it be said that there is an endeavor in evidence, at least within the church's domain, to realize this high ideal?

The Apostle points out to us, as one of the means to be near unto God, that we should *live in peace*. "Be of one mind," says he, "live in peace, and the God of love and of peace shall be with you" (2 Cor. xiii, 11).

And yet there is a continual disturbance of this peace.

Understand it well.   It is not said that no serious differences can arise, neither that with every difference salvation
can be sought in indifference. Even S. Paul did not do this.

No, it here hinges on the *spirit* in which differences are
faced and settled.

A twofold impulse can here arise. On one side the holy
impulse, when there is a point of difference at stake, to
be doubly on our guard that love suffer no loss and that
no unholy word shall proceed from our lips or from our
pen. And on the other side the unholy impulse, in so
much as there is now dissension anyway to allow one's
bitter mind free play, to give free rein to one's passion for
annoying and inflicting whatever pain one can.

With the first, one places himself in an atmosphere of
love and peace. With the second, one breathes in an atmosphere of bitterness and anger.

It is in the Church as it is in the family.

Between husband and wife, between parents and children, and among the children themselves, dissensions
constantly arise. This can not be helped. Interests, insights, efforts diverge.

But see what difference there is between one family and
the other.

In a family of high moral standing, each strives to *limit*
these dissensions, and a tone predominates which of itself
opens a way of escape. And where love thus dwells, the
Lord commands this blessing, namely, that the hearts
remain *one*.

Alongside of this, alas, how many other families we
find, in which no pains are spared to aggravate each dissension as much as possible, to put the sharpest, if not a
poisonous, arrow to one's bow, and where husband and
wife, parents and children, brothers and sisters again and
again, face one another like furies.

This is always the same contrast as that to which we have pointed. A world, a family, a Church, without dissensions, this sinful world does not bring us. But it all depends on this: whether the point of dispute in the family or in the congregation finds an atmosphere of love and peace, or one of bitterness and anger.

And now the Apostle points out to us that the cherishing of such an atmosphere of love and peace is not alone by itself a Christian duty which makes life sunny and comfortable, but that it is likewise a necessary requisite in order to advance the life near unto God.

Of course a child of God *can*, yea, he *must*, even when he finds everywhere around him a spirit of unrest and unpeace, be near to his God and live in close nearness to Him. And he who perseveres obtains this blessed end. But it is made unspeakably more difficult thereby.

Where the atmosphere that surrounds us is charged with evil electricity, and the tongue is not held in leash, and estrangement loosens the tie of love, and the passion of strife blazes forth, everything draws your heart away from communion with God. There "the peace of God that passeth all understanding" can not fill your soul. There you miss the calm and inward rest that comes from lifting yourself out from this earthly sphere into the world above and blessedly enjoying the nearness of God.

And then in a twofold respect harm is done. First it robs you of one of the most precious means of being near unto God; and secondly you become subject to the dominion of an element that with separating effect throws itself in between you and your God.

A gently tempered mind can with respect to this be a blessing to a whole family, to a whole community; and, likewise one mind that is poisoned as with the bitterness of gall, can entirely corrupt the tone and spirit of it, and cause the godliness in that family and in that community to suffer bitter loss.

For every unbecoming and unholy word, and equally for every bitter, irritable frame of mind, we must one day give account unto God.

For do not forget, nothing influences tone and spirit so strongly as the custom and the habit that form and dominate the condition and the temper of our mind and heart.

If you have once become accustomed to hold back and control yourself, and when Satan plays the poison into your hands, at once to reach out after the alabaster box of softening balsam, then gradually the fight becomes lighter, the effort to create stillness more lovely, and the joy of having nursed peace and love increasingly rich.

But if once you give way to your sharpness, to your passionate temper, to your bitterness of mind, then you lose ever more and more control over yourself and occasion for yourself and for your environment, indescribably much harm.

With insipidity, with not daring to speak one's mind, with letting everything pass—the "peace" which the Apostle here speaks of has nothing to do.

Indifference is no sacred art, but cowardice.

But this is sacred art, in everything to stand strong and courageous, and yet *so* to take hold of everything, *so* to treat, and *so* to bring to an end, that in your own mind no unholy spark starts fire, and, for no moment you disturb the inward peace in the minds of those who are around you.

He whose godliness is more semblance than reality cares for none of this. But he who strives unto the end in every way to maintain his hidden walk with God, and constantly to be near Him, *he* can not resist the stress of the apostolic word.

He realizes to the full that the atmosphere of love and peace makes him dwell near to his God, and therefore avoids, or seeks immediate escape from, a sphere of strife and unrest because it draws him away from Him.

A DECEIVED HEART HATH TURNED HIM ASIDE

THE world, our environment, our business, yea, and what not, lead us, as a rule, away from God. By this is meant that it costs us a positive exertion in the midst of our daily avocation and recreation to keep our thoughts and outpourings of soul directed toward God. There must have been days in your life when at night on bended knee, with shame to yourself you have had to confess that that whole day you had scarcely once lifted up your heart and mind to God. To make this seem more beautiful than it is will not do. So and not otherwise is the sad reality. With many whole days of their lives have been spent in which they have not so much as once thought of God. One was too busy, too much overwhelmed, too much abstracted, too much diverted the whole day long, to learn anything of the blessedness of being near unto God.

This is, of course, exclusively a result of the sinful character of our earthly life, for of itself nothing needed to draw us away from God. God does not stand by the side of things, but He is *in* all things—from Him, through Him, and to Him.

Diversion is necessary for our spirit, when it has been exercised too one-sidedly and too exclusively by *one* thing. This is noticed by the staring eye, by the expressionless face, and the constant return to the same subject. When soul and mind are directed too one-sidedly and too continuously to *one* thing, so that one thinks of nothing else, forgets everything, and whether one would or no, is always exercised again by the same thought, then there is the beginning of mental disorder, and diversion is the proper medicine.

But it is not so with thinking on God. In the creaturely world a number of things stand side by side, each with its own claim, and our mind is normal when in just proportion we pay due attention to them all. If this order is disturbed by too much thought of the *one* and too little of the other, then the equilibrium is broken and our spirit totters at length in its own confusion.

God, on the other hand, never stands *alongside* of created things. Hence it should never be ninety parts of your attention for the creature and ten parts for your God. Neither yet ten parts for the world and ninety parts for God. In everything, in the full one hundred parts, God is to be worshiped. Jesus says it with so much emphasis: "God thou shalt love with all thy *strength, all thy soul and all thy mind.*" And in the same way, you should let the one hundred parts of your strength operate in created things. But the two should so act as to enter into one another, penetrate each other, and together form *one* blessed life.

So it is in the Father-house. So it was in paradise. So it is sometimes here for *one* short passing moment. But as a rule it is so no more. There is division. There is what diverts. And the whole battle of our godliness is to work against this division, against this abstraction, against this diversion, and yet, at least *parts* of the day and *parts* of the night be near unto God.

But then it is important that with this we should have a correct view of *what* distracts. And in this matter, Adam is ever yet inclined to put it upon Eve, and Eve to shift it upon the serpent. Our wanderings away from and our life without God, are then explained by the world, the busy life, the many distractions. One is occupied from early morn till late at night and then from sheer exhaustion falls asleep, sometimes before he has prayed. There is no time left for God and for His service. Sometimes there is for one who can quietly remain at home, but, anyway, not for the man of business. And so one continues to put the fault upon life, upon the bustle and noise of the street, upon the ever enticing world.

Or one complains about his body. It is a feeling of being unwell, it is a headache, fever or other indisposition that keeps the spirit bound. Only this, it does not become a complaint about *one's own soul.* And it is against this that Isaiah (xliv, 20) enters his striking charge: *"Your deceived heart hath turned you aside."*

Assuredly the world has come in with its enticements, life with its many activities. Thereby you have allowed your heart to be deceived. And yet, it is not the world nor its busy demands upon your time, but your deceived heart, that has turned you aside from God; *so* turned you aside, Isaiah adds, that your soul can no longer save itself, can no longer escape from its own intoxication.

This Isaiah says of the man, who makes an idol for himself. A tree is dragged into the house. The knotty parts are sawn out and chopped off, and of the best part that remains the poor man makes himself an idol. And now it is not that idol that does the wrong, but it is the idolatrous thought that was in this man's soul and that took possession of his heart before he made his idol. That piece of wood, that image, is merely the expression of what went on in his heart. Not that image, but his deceived heart turns him aside, yea, it does this so strongly, that at length he sees no longer any difference between a piece of wood and God. Or as the Prophet puts it: "He is turned aside so far that he can not come to discover that there is a lie in his right hand."

And this same evil is at work today, not alone among the heathen, but equally as much, though in another way, among Mohammedans, Jews and Christians.

It is a human wrong.

The direct outcome of our sinful nature.

And how does this show itself?

Very promptly and clearly, just as soon as some object of desire makes its one-sided appeal to your heart, which attracts, arrests and holds your attention and which, involuntarily, of itself every time again excites your soul and senses, crowds your mind with thoughts, enlivens your conversation, and brings you into a fanatical state of mind.

Of course this does not mean the lively interest and activity of your spirit when your duty, your work, the course of conversation claims your full attention. On the contrary, then lack of attention, neglect of due examination of the matter in hand are a fault; can even be a sin.

No, the idolatrous turning aside of your inner self only becomes apparent when this special attraction continuously claims your attention and when the drawing power does not work from without but from one's own heart.

So there are people of whom, instinctively and by anticipation, you know when they meet you what they will talk about. There is but *one* thing of which they are always full, but *one* interest to which they are always awake. With one it is money, the idea of getting rich, of gain in every way. With another it is pleasure; sensual delight under all sorts of forms; passion to shine. With a third it is art, music, a concert, a piece of literature, a museum, anything as long as it is art and shows itself in an artistic way. Again with some one else it is the scientific problems which restlessly pursue him. For another still it is politics, or society gossip, or the hunt, or sport.

And in all this, spiritual sickness is symptomatically present as soon as you observe that this *one* interest, even without any particular occasion, keeps him engaged, enthuses and captures him, and makes him dense and unsympathetic with respect to everything else.

Then there is a one-sided concentration of his mind upon one given point. Then this one matter becomes to him supreme, something to which all the rest is made subservient. And this means that with him this one thing begins to usurp the place which in a normal mind and heart is accorded to God alone.

And so it becomes idolatrous.

He is full of it. He is never done talking about it. He deems no sacrifice too great in its behalf. He devotes himself to it with heart and soul. He knows and honors nothing higher.

He even forms a brotherhood for its sake as he is interested only in those who live for the same cause and whose minds are filled with the same interest.

With all those who so live, the equilibrium is broken, and in the highest place, which belongs to God alone, this other thing is put which they love with all their heart and all their mind and to which they devote themselves with all their strength.

Now it is self-evident that subjection to this idolatrous influence in this literal sense does not occur with Christians. This can not be, and in fact is not so. He with whom it has come to this pass may still claim to be a Christian, but a Christian he is not.

But from this it by no means follows that the child of God should not be exposed to a like danger. Even they who sought most earnestly after the hidden walk with God have confessed that no sin lies more constantly at the door of their heart than this very inclination to allow themselves by the working of their own heart, soul and mind to be drawn away from God to earthly things and to vain thoughts.

To be full of the Holy Ghost is to feel the rise inwardly from the heart of a constant, urgent desire that goes out after God and after things that are holy. He who has come to this never needs to repress other things from his thoughts in order to think of God, but instinctively he thinks of God, and of other things only by *intentional* application.

But what constantly happens, even with Christians, is the very opposite. Involuntarily he thinks of all sorts of other things, and not, except by an act of *the will*, does his soul engage itself with God.

If these are different things every time, the danger is not so great, because then it is not one special thing that engages the heart, and the worship of God then always far exceeds every other interest.

On the other hand, this danger becomes great when the heart allows itself to be attracted to one particular thing, or to a particular sort of thing, which fills us with enthusiasm and lays claim upon our heart, because then this is bound to take the place in our heart which belongs alone to God.

You can not be near to your God and in His hidden walk when unwittingly and as it were magnetically, ever and anon, you are turned away to something worldly.

Then your heart has deceived itself and the deceived heart has turned you aside from God.

And, therefore, when you are troubled, and feel that your life is not lived in nearness to God, then cease one-sidedly to enter your complaint against the world and your environment and your busy life as though it were these alone that turn you aside from God.

Rather turn in upon yourself, watch your thoughts, your conversations, your perceptions, study your heart, and when you realize that not only, not even mostly, from without, but from within arises the diverting workings which interrupt your fellowship with God, and prevent your living near to Him, then cast down this idol within and destroy it.

For Christ and Belial both, there is no room in one self-same human heart.

Do you not know your own selves, in the words of S. Paul, the mighty Apostle, *how that Jesus Christ is in you?* (2 Cor. xiii, 5.)

XCVIII

WHATSOEVER YE DO, DO IT
HEARTILY AS TO THE LORD

In His Word God absolutely forbids every inclination and every attempt to break up your life into two parts, the one part for yourself and the other part for Him. There must be no cleavage, no division. Not six week days for you and Sunday for God. Not an unconsecrated life interspersed with consecrated moments. Not an unhallowed existence into which at intervals a holy thread is woven. Not a life outside of religion sprinkled in parts with godliness. No, on this point the claim of Scripture is as inclusive as possible; and, though it may sound strangely to our ears, the obligation is imposed upon you that you shall pray *without ceasing*, that in *everything* you shall give thanks, that you must always rejoice in your God, and so also that whatsoever ye do, you shall do it heartily as unto the Lord (Col. iii, 23).

To the Thessalonians (I Thess. v, 16) S. Paul writes: "Pray without ceasing. Rejoice evermore. In everything give thanks." To the Philippians (iv, 4), "Rejoice in the Lord always." And to those at Colosse: "Whatsoever ye do, do it heartily as to the Lord."

You are never given a respite. Never an agreement is made with you. Never with less than your whole life does God take pleasure. Where faith becomes the rule of your life, it wills its rule to be *absolute*. No excuses, no half measures will do. He who as child of God, as servant of Christ, as inspired by the Holy Ghost, lives his life in this world must in everything be led and carried by his faith. He who divides and makes distinctions, robs God of a part that belongs to Him alone. If you are to love your God with all your heart, all your soul, all your mind and all your powers, every avenue of escape is closed against you, and the all-claiming and exigent character of the faith is founded in love itself.

Every division works harm in your life and in your religion.

He who divides and then undertakes too much in behalf of his religion, neglects his family or his calling. And he who divides, without being godly, gives the lion's share to the world, and skimps with a stingy heart what he professes to set apart for God in strength, time and money.

He who would choose to be near unto God and go through life in close fellowship with Him is not permitted to practise this fellowship at one time and to neglect it at another. With him in *everything he doeth* God must be known, God must be the end and aim, God must be prayed unto, and God must be thanked. Not formally with closing of eyes and folding of hands and muttering of words, but in that innermost part of his heart and in that hidden recess of his self-consciousness in which are the issues of his life as well as of his prayer.

This reacts against the idea that a clergyman can, and a merchant can not make this fellowship with God a constant reality in his life; that the man or woman who works zealously for missions, for philanthropy or evangelization, but not the father and the mother in the family are engaged in holy service in the eyes of their God.

What a clergyman, or missionary, or nurse does, is then called consecrated labor, and what the gardener, or merchant or seamstress or servant performs is then said to lie within the pale of unconsecrated ground; and it is just this false representation of the matter that works so much harm to the godly life and to vital godliness.

Of course there is no denying that he who directly ministers in the sanctuary is necessarily more busy with holy things, and herewith enjoys an uncommon privilege for which he shall give account before God. And equally little can it be denied that at the Exchange and in the shop and office, it takes far more effort and overcoming of self to always remain in everything near unto God. This takes the more effort, in connection with which God knows of what we are made, mindful that we are but dust.

But weighing against this stands the fact that the ministry in the sanctuary brings with it, in no small measure, the danger of becoming too much accustomed to holy things and of handling the same more and more with unholy hands; and, by sinning in and against the sacred calling, faces so much heavier a judgment. Ever and anon, in the best church and in the most excellent mission, the evil times have come back when priests and priestesses in the sanctuary have profaned themselves, and that not from among them but from among the humble patrons and working people and shop-keepers and merchants, the action arose which restored holy things to honor.

A godly pastor, a devout missionary, a consecrated nurse, and so, too, a truly godly warden, elder or deacon, represent a glorious power; but one makes a mistake when he thinks that of itself the office or the more sacred calling brings true godliness with it. Especially, young clergymen who have tender consciences are bound, again and again, to acknowledge to themselves that the godliness of many an ordinary member of their congregation puts their own religiousness to shame.

Likewise it must be granted that in our extremely defective condition, a certain intentional, a certain special consecration of a part of our life, of our strength and of our money, to religious works and interests appears necessary.

You can not *so* serve your God all the days of your life, but the day of rest continues to retain its higher significance. You can not *so* be near your God in everything you do, but the special seasons for direct prayer, for the worship in the Word, and for thanksgiving in spoken praises, remain for you a need of the heart. And you can not *so* practise justice and mercy in everything, but the setting apart of intentional gifts for the service of the Lord, is felt by you to be a blessed duty.

In the Jerusalem above this duality also shall fall away. The Church Triumphant above shall not stand in nor alongside of the life of glory, but shall be that life itself. Father-house and triumphant Church before God's Throne are *one*.

But it is not so here. Here it can not be otherwise than that the duality maintains itself. Your Church is something else than your family or your workshop. The mighty contrast between the things of this world and the things of the kingdom demands this.

But this should never bring it about that your religion, your godliness, should so concentrate itself within this sacred domain that it should give rise to a churchly life with godliness, alongside of a life without godliness.

Godliness may find a more exalted expression within the sacred domain and may strengthen you for daily life, but if your godliness shall be of the true and genuine type it must be a golden thread that maintains its glistening brightness throughout your whole life.

All this depends on whether you truly believe that your God is the Almighty, the Creator of heaven and earth. Thus also whether you believe and consider that every material which you elaborate is His creature; that every article of food and drink on your table is His creature and His gift; that your body and all your senses are His embroidery, and that He maintains the workings of them; that every power of nature wherewith you have to do is His omnipresent working; that every circumstance you encounter has been assigned to you by Him; that every relation in which you are placed by blood, by marriage, by appointment or from choice has come to you under and by His providential plan; that every exigency and difficulty in which you find yourself has been put by Him in your way; that every task or duty to which you are called comes to you for His sake and has a definite significance in His government; that you can not think of anything so high or so low on earth but it all forms a link, great or small, in the chain of His disposal; that no joy is tasted and no suffering endured but He measures it out to you; or, briefly, that nothing is conceivable in heaven or earth, and nothing can exist, but that God Who created heaven and earth maintains and governs it, has His holy purpose in it all, is in everything the Lord Who disposes and ordains it, and Who in all things uses His people— which includes you—to carry out His counsel to completion.

To except from this anything whatsoever, is *unbelief*.

When therefore the Apostle says: *"Whatsoever ye do,"* in words or works, *"do it all heartily as to the Lord,"* he says nothing but what directly flows from your profession, that you believe in God the Father Almighty, the Creator of heaven and earth. Then there is neither in your personal life, nor in your family life, neither in your study and labor, nor in anything that you do, anything that you can think of that should separate you from God, and that should not rather, provided it is rightly interpreted, lead you to Him.

Sin, yes, *that* you can not do as to the Lord. That separates, that breaks up the fellowship and throws you back upon yourself.

But for the rest, whether you stand behind the counter or work at your trade; whether you sit in your office; whether you lose yourself in study or devote yourself to art; whether you are at home with your family or other company—it can and must be all one working, one activity, with strength imparted to you of God, in things created by God, for a purpose that God has ordained with respect to it.

It is thus but the question whether your faith—not now in the mysteries of salvation, no—but your faith first of all in God as the Creator of heaven and earth floats upon your soul as a drop of oil upon the waters, or whether it enters into the whole of your life and is applied by you to everything.

If it is the latter, then there is no division anywhere. Then the man who plows and sows, the carpenter at the bench or the stone-mason, the mother who cares for her children and her home, in brief, no man or woman in whatever position in life is ever to do a work without God, but always as in His service.

Then to be near unto God, then the fellowship with the Eternal, the hidden walk with Him Who knoweth the heart is no sweet-smelling savor alongside of life, but the breath of life itself that breathes forth from your entire life its grateful savor into your nostrils.

In everything then you rejoice, because from everything and in everything the Majesty and the grace of God breathe forth upon you.

In everything then you pray, not with the lips but with the heart, because in whatever you do you feel your deep dependence upon His Almighty power.

In everything then you give thanks, because every success is the fruit of His grace, and every adversity is intended to stimulate you, with the assistance of ever more grace, to greater exertion of strength.

Yea, then you do everything heartily, not mechanically, not slavishly, not from necessity, but willingly and gladly, because you are permitted to do it *thus* in His service.

And so you come to a level of existence where godliness and fulfillment of duty are *one*, because in quiet and restful nearness to God whatever you do, you are permitted to do *as to the Lord.*

HOW EXCELLENT IS THY NAME IN ALL THE EARTH

In one of the last Hallelujah-psalms the closing verse sings of the children of Israel as of a people that is near unto God.

It says in full: "He hath exalted the horn of his people, the praise of all his saints; even of the children of Israel, a people near unto him" (Ps. 148, 14). Thus, the distinction here is, that not only may the individual soul find itself in closer fellowship, in more intimate communion, in more constant walk with God, but that, in a much vaguer sense, of course, this may also be true, under given circumstances, of a vast multitude of persons and even of a whole people.

This to a certain extent can be applied to the population of country districts, especially in contrast with the population of great cities.

The fairy-tale of the "Temple of uncarved wood" remains herewith under the sentence of its own unreality. In its hypocrisy this legend was never anything else than the poetic, pious talk of those who on Sunday would rather take a walk than go to Church.

No, what here is meant is the fact observed in almost every country, that the rural population taken as a whole has remained devoted to their religion, while, on the other hand, the great mass of city people, at least among what are called Protestants, have died to all home religion and public worship. It can even be said that this grave phenomenon increases in the measure in which the population of a city enlarges itself.

This does not mean that in these great cities there is no remnant of devout people. Sometimes, even, these people are very influential, their godliness in many ways is of a higher type than the rural godliness, especially in strength of purpose and buoyancy. This comes from the greater friction and fiercer conflict of city-life. He who in such cities remained faithful to the sacred traditions of the fathers, did this under protest, had to suffer for it, had to fight for it; but he who in this conflict held his ground, came out of it better disciplined, fortified, strengthened, and felt himself better equipped against unbelief and indifferentism.

But apart from these relatively small exceptions it can not be denied that in rural districts reverence for religion is more firmly rooted, and that in city life this reverence wanes; especially where there are great industries, much commerce, and much speculation at the Exchange. Indeed among factory owners and factory hands, among merchants and office clerks, among the members of the Exchange and capitalists there are also truly consecrated children of God, but they are white ravens among the black flock.

Sundry causes have brought this about. In the country, with weather and wind, with harvests and failures of crops, with cattle and land plagues, one is far more dependent upon the direct doings of God. In the industrial world it is more the human factor, the machine-invention that exercises dominion. Also in the country temptation is less brutally on exhibition. There evenings are shorter and people rise earlier. People know one another personally, and hence the discipline of public opinion is more effective. A church has fewer members, so that supervision is more general. A number of causes here co-operate, the greatest among which will ever be: *life in the country itself,* and the consequent influence of nature, *of the visible creation of God* that surrounds country-people. From which it is to be inferred that he who seeks the nearness of God loses considerable power when he does not open eye and ear to the impression of God's nearness which the visible creation can give us.

How necessary this opening of eye and ear is, you readily see in the large numbers of city folk who in summer go to the country, but who, when there, look for nothing but fresh air and recreation, and return as estranged from God as they came. But it remains a fact that the city man misses nature. Parks and boulevards compensate something, but the great masses, especially of working people, only come home when it gets dark. Yet truly even above our cities the glory of the stars glistens in the firmament, but who among the many that walk the busy streets by night lifts up his eyes on high to see who has created all these things, bringeth out their hosts by number and calleth them by name?

In our villages one has nature all about him, whether he wills or not. It forces itself upon the inhabitants. In our cities, on the other hand, one is shut off from nature, and he alone finds it who seeks it above or outside of the town.

In the country, God's voice comes to us from within and from without; in our cities it comes to us alone from within, while in all manner of ways the voice of man loudly resounds to deafen the voice of the Lord, even in His starry heaven and in His thunder.

They who are advanced in years and whose life's work is done, seek the country to make good their loss; but by that time, in most cases, they have lost their susceptibility to nature and remain isolated from their surroundings.

Now in the face of this take the Scriptures.

Man comes up in a glorious paradise where all nature brings him a pure address from his God. And even after the Fall there remains so much glory in broken nature that the invisible things of God are understood from created things, both His eternal power and Godhead (Rom. i, 20). "The heavens declare the glory of God, and the firmament sheweth his handiwork. Day unto day abundantly uttereth speech and night unto night sheweth knowledge. There is no people or land where this voice of God is not heard" (Ps. 19). "Glorious is his name in all the earth. The voice of the Lord is upon the waters. The God of glory thundereth. The voice of the Lord is powerful. The voice of the Lord is full of majesty. The voice of the Lord breaketh the cedars, even the cedars of Lebanon" (Ps. 29). And so it goes on through all the Psalms. Read and reread the one hundred and fourth Psalm. And then at the end of the Psalter we have a striking description of nature in the hundred and forty-seventh and hundred and forty-eighth Psalms. And even before the Psalter, is Job with his magnificent descriptions of the Behemoth, the horse and the pleiades. It is all one mighty call in the greatness and beauty of nature to behold the glory of God.

And when in Scripture you have come to the appearance of the Son of Man, by His sayings: "Consider the lilies of the field, how they grow!"—"Behold the fowls of the air!"—light is thrown upon the mysteries of the kingdom from what is seen in the sower and the shepherds, and in the end there is the touching comparison of Jerusalem with the hen that gathers her chickens under her wings.

The whole of Revelation, the whole of Scripture is aglow with the glory of nature. God's ancient people was a rural people, and the holy land which God had given to them was then, though no longer now, a fertile region of unequaled beauty.

The new earth under the new heaven shall be a return of paradise. The wilderness shall blossom as the rose. And when our times know the honors lavishly conferred upon the landscape painter—because of the enchanting scenes which, with depth of glowing color and life, as by magic he works before our eyes—then what dullness of the spiritual eye it is that these same times have no eye, no perception for the thousandfold higher beauty in the handiwork of God, the greatest Artist?

For this very reason, therefore, it affects one strangely, when among Christian people he often finds so little, if any, appreciation of the glory in nature.

Undoubtedly the voice of the Herald of Peace rises far above the many voices of nature. "In his temple," says the Psalmist, after he has described God's mightiness in nature, "in his temple doth everyone speak of his glory" (Ps. 29, 9). And in the Hallelujah-song of Psalm 147 it is said that Israel is highly exalted above the primitive peoples, because the Lord hath made known His words unto Jacob. And then it says: "He hath not dealt so with any nation, neither have the heathen knowledge of his laws." In the congregation of believers, when the Word is rightly proclaimed, there is spiritually a far higher beauty, than the beauty of nature can ever provide.

But shall we, therefore, be one-sided, and allow one half to be lost?

"From two sources," says one of our creedal Confessions, "have we knowledge of our God. From His Word very surely, but also from the creatures, who are as letters in the book of creation to make us understand God's Mightiness and Majesty."

Godly conversations, Christian gatherings, edifying books, are all excellent, but may you therefore leave the great book of creation to remain closed to your soul's eye?

It is all for the sake of impressions on the collodian-plate of our heart, for the sake of impressions which go out far above those of our daily life, and above the impressions which we receive from man.

We will not, we may not, live under the impression that the Divine could ever shrink to the measure of the human. We will not degrade and minimize God to our dimensions, but rather lift ourselves up to the measure of His Majesty. Not a God after our image, but ourselves created after the Image of God. And this your books will not give you, your mutual conversations will not provide.

All this remains within the pale and within the measure of our small proportions. So altogether different from a rising and a setting of God's sun. So altogether different from the light of a lightning flash or from the thunder that reverberates in the clouds. So altogether different from the starry glory that arches itself above you, and from the mighty forest, or from the lion that roars for prey.

What we have here is the sublime, and therein is the Divine outpouring of the super-beautiful and the glorious.

The sublime! A majesty that is elevated far above the small dimensions of our economy and of our making. By which you know and understand that you are not in touch with the bungling works of man, but with the glorious high art of the Creator of heaven and earth.

Of course this glistening, glittering nature can not disclose to you the way of salvation, the spiritual mysteries.

For this, God in His compassion has given you His Gospel.

But what the outshining of God's Almightiness and Divinity in nature does, is, that it broadens, expands and uplifts all your ideas to a higher sphere than your own seeing can give you.

This, that it lifts you up from the insignificant-human to the Divinely-great.

To the sublime!

And so brings the High and Lofty One nearer unto you.

C

THOU TRIEST MINE HEART THAT IT IS WITH THEE

DISTURBANCES in the hidden walk with God can have more than one cause.

The most mysterious to your devout feeling is when God's Face withdraws itself, in order by the deprivation to make you thirst more truly after Him. The most common is, when earthly interests so occupy and exercise you, that your soul, as it were, is ensnared by them. And the one that most offends your soul is, when a newly committed sin came in the way, which not only broke the fellowship with God, but also remained a hindrance to your return into the nearness of the Holy One.

Only of a committed sin is mention made here, of a word, a deed, which you felt, when you faced it, would be a sin to you, and which yet you failed to evade.

A sinful inclination, a sinful mood, especially a sinful desire, can also very seriously affect your fellowship with God, but thereby the working is of another sort. For on this side of the grave this sinful intermingling will ever continue with you, and this by itself, provided you do not cherish it, does not prevent your hidden walk with Him. Your hidden walk with God is always in Christ, and this itself is the avowal that you do not come to Him as a saint, but as one who is in himself a sinner.

But with a sin that you have consciously committed it is altogether different. Then there was compliance, yielding, the doing of it; and then at once the light of God's benign Countenance is dimmed; then it becomes dark to you from His side, and there rather comes up in you an inclination to flee from Him than to be near unto Him.

We perceive this turn in the disposition of our soul at once clearly and most painfully when it was a sin that suddenly laid hold on us; a sin which, once committed, overwhelmed us, and for which we would sacrifice anything if we could immediately remove the stain of it from our soul. When, to say it plainly, it was a grievous sin.

For in nothing is our degraded moral viewpoint so pitifully evident as in the fact that we have scarcely any knowledge of our minor daily sins. Neglected duties; unloveliness; assertions of egotism, of pride, of vanity; tiny untruths, trifling dishonesties, and more.

This is still something altogether different from what David calls the "secret sins." These are faults that leave a stain upon our garment, but yet too trifling for our lustful eye to discover it to us.

This refers to sins of which we have no knowledge yet, and the sinfulness of which will only be realized with a more advanced development of the life of the soul.

But of our sins which we call "not so very bad" we have this knowledge. Only, we became accustomed to them. They trouble us no more. Our soul no more reacts against them.

And also of this sort of sins it is certainly true that they hinder your hidden walk with your God, but do not prevent it. They do not break off what existed, but they make your hidden walk with God very defective, so that it remains a fellowship from a distance, which keeps you from the deeper enjoyment of this communion.

Interruptions in this fellowship with God through your sin only occur when ordinarily you live near to God, know Him in all your ways, and have been initiated into the secret of salvation, and all unforeseen you commit a sin that overwhelms and lays hold on you, and brings it to pass that a dark cloud draws over your sky, and you are thrown back upon yourself, and you feel that you have lost your part in the satisfying walk with God.

Of such an interruption David speaks in the thirty-second Psalm, and he confesses that this cessation continued *because he kept silence.*

"When I kept silence thy hand was heavy upon me day and night."

But finally he breaks that silence.

"I said I will confess my transgressions unto the Lord."

This he does, and now at once the disturbance is removed. Now he seeks and finds his God again, and now he jubilantly sings: "For this shall every one that is godly pray unto thee in a time when thou mayest be found. Thou compassest me with joyful songs of deliverance." Yea, now he meets God again, and this God does not repel him, nor put him back, but he hears it sweetly whispered in his soul: "I will instruct thee, I will guide thee with mine eye."

And in truth there lies in this Davidic experience of soul the only correct diagnosis, and the only effective medicine.

When we are so weak, nay so wicked, as willingly and knowingly to commit a sin, the first impression it makes upon us is, that we want to hide ourselves from God, that we are afraid to appear before His presence, and that with the bitter remembrance of our sin we draw back within ourselves.

Not from enmity, but from fear. Not from lack of will, but from shame. We then know well that we must get back to God, but we postpone it. We would like to pray, but we rather allow some time to intervene.

We keep silence.

And it is in this heavy, this soul-distressing silence that we get ever farther away from God.

This is the diagnosis, the correct explanation of the wound from which at such a moment our soul bleeds.

And the only proper medicine is that you immediately break your silence, that you allow no time to be lost, that without delay you seek solitude, and in this retirement you fall upon your knees, and, without sparing yourself, candidly and openly confess before God the sin that you committed, and call upon Him for forgiveness, yea, implore Him not to take away his Holy Spirit from you.

Truly, this costs pain, for which at such a time you must do violence to yourself; you then feel the sting of God's anger, and across this anger you must reach out after the mercy.

But the effect of this is always surprising. It is just as David said. It breaks at once the ban which your sin put upon your heart.

Something melts within your soul, and in this melting comes the liberation, comes the redemption, comes the reconciliation, and God approaches you in His faithfulness, even as Jesus pictured it to us as the shepherd with the lost sheep. Yea, it seems as though God in such a moment comes nearer to you than ever, in order to cause you to believe in His infinite compassion.

Satan whispered in your heart: "Stay away from God." But your Father in heaven called out to you: "No, come to Me, my child."

And in this mutual approach of your guilt-confessing heart to your God and of your God to your soul, the interruption that intervened comes to nought.

And then it is good for you, so unspeakably good, again to be near unto your God.

And what now is the secret of this work of healing the soul?

Is it not in what Jeremiah exclaimed: "Lord, thou knowest me, Thou seest me, Thou triest my heart that it is with Thee" (xii, 3).

What with Psalmist and Prophet makes the outpouring of soul so touching is that their whole life and their whole existence is interpreted within the scope of a conflict for or against God.

A conflict between God and Satan, a conflict between God and the unholy powers of the world, a conflict with God in every sin. With them is never heard the weak, cowardly language of a self-developing and degenerating moral life. No, everything is put into immediate, vital relationship with God, as the center of all things.

A conflict between all sin and unrighteousness and God, and a conflict on the part of God with all sin and all unrighteousness.

A conflict of the ages, from paradise on, and continuing until the end of time when God in Christ over the last enemy shall triumph.

And in this conflict every one of us is involved and concerned. If we sin we battle on the side of Satan against God. When we live by faith, we battle on the side of God, against Satan.

Such is the interpretation of life on the part of Prophets and Apostles, and such, also, must be ours, even the profound and striking interpretation of life on the part of every child of God.

And what now is a sin that we commit? What other can it be, than that in an evil moment we lend our support to the power of evil against God, and with Satan militate against Him?

And if this is so, what is to make confession of your sin other than that, realizing this, you immediately desert again the ranks of Satan, in order to return to the ranks of God, beseeching Him that you may be counted worthy to fight in His ranks, and to be found again on His side.

And now comes the appeal of your heart to the omniscient knowledge of the God of all compassions.

Did you mean to run away from the ranks of God to join the ranks of Satan?

No, thrice no.

You did not intend to do it; the thought of such an evil did not rise up within you. You allowed yourself to be taken unawares. You slipped without realizing the dreadful wickedness of your deed.

And now that you realize that this is what you did, you make your appeal to God Himself.

In the deepest depth of your heart you did not will to desert God; and the sorrow of your soul, your remorse, your self-reproach is that in the face of it you have nevertheless incurred the guilt of an act of enmity against Him.

And therefore you now plead with Him, the Knower of your heart, and ask, whether: as He tries your heart He does not see, that, notwithstanding all, in its deepest depth it is still *with Him* and not with Satan.

GET THEE BEHIND ME, SATAN

It can not be denied that in former times, especially in the Middle Ages, people strongly exaggerated Satan by dragging him, wisely or unwisely, into everything. But does it not seem that our times rather incline to the opposite extreme, and forget, if not deny, the very existence of the Evil One?

With this denial, self-conceited freedom in matters of belief makes singular shifts with the Gospel of our Lord.

It is then said that one feels himself detached from the Old Testament, and for this very reason holds himself the more closely to the Gospel. These people who are amphibious of spirit are not concerned with Moses but with Jesus, and oftentimes do not scruple to criticize you, who hold to the whole Scripture, as being too old-testamentish and, therefore, only half Christian.

But now see how these very people who are so loud in their praises of the Gospel, themselves deal with the Gospel.

It is true that almost no mention is made of Satan in the Old Testament, and that on the contrary he is broadly and amply dealt with in the Gospel. And not this alone but that also Jesus Himself, in His words as well as in His works, ever shows that He reckons with Satan. Only think of the Temptation in the Wilderness, of the constant casting out of devils, of the whole conflict of evil spirits with the Saviour; then of all He spake concerning the Prince of this world, yea, how He understood all His suffering and dying as a combat with this Prince; and then, not to mention other instances, think not least of this, that in the short "Our Father" He interwove for all His people as a final prayer the petition: "Deliver us from the Evil One."

But all this is of no avail. The half friends who have put the Old Testament aside in order to hold themselves alone to Jesus and His Gospel, do not scruple to reject this whole matter of Satan's influences, part and parcel, from their Gospel. And so here, too, is shown how such effort is always bound not to fashion their own mind and thoughts after the Gospel, but to frame the Gospel after *their* world of thought.

And with respect to this, there is even guilt among those who are more faithful to the truth; not by denying but by forgetting Satan's real working.

Is it not extremely rarely that in the spoken address or written essay, in psychology or in the revelations of the inner life, the Evil One is reckoned with as a real factor?

Now in connection with this you should bear in mind that Satan is like a thief; he prefers that you should be unconscious of his presence and of his doings.

In the very circles in which his existence is denied or ridiculed he has his hands entirely free to murder souls to his heart's content. And that he can be so strangely forgotten by those who are more inclined to believe the Gospel, also offers him the most wonderful chance to poison souls.

You may be quite sure, that in all this denial and in all this forgetting of the actual existence of Satan, there operates effectively a trick of Satan himself.

When the mighty Spirit of Christ operated upon the life in Palestine, Satan had no success in this for a moment, and Jesus compelled him to show himself.

But now he does succeed in keeping himself concealed, and from the ambush unseen and unnoticed, he infuses his character to better effect on this very account.

How the working of Satan goes on is not revealed to us in detail. Only we know that our human world is not the only world of conscious beings, but that there exist myriads of other spiritual beings which are called spirits, angels, cherubim, seraphim etc.; and it is equally certain that this world of spirits is not separated from our human world, but exists alongside of it, is related with it in all sorts of ways and strongly affects it.

In addition to this, it is revealed that the antithesis between holy and unholy has also broken out in this world of spirits, even at an earlier date than on this earth, and that from this world of spirits it has entered into our human world.

Hence there is a certain alliance between good spirits and good men, and also a conspiracy between unholy spirits in the invisible world and unholy spirits in the visible world. Joy among the good angels over one sinner that repenteth, and a sardonic grin among the evil spirits when the fall of a lost soul is successfully brought about.

It is all *one* conflict, *one* warfare, *one* struggle *with* Christ as the Head of the holy spirits on this earth, and outside of this world against Satan as the head of all unholy spirits among men and devils.

All this is clearly, broadly and exhaustively brought to our knowledge in the Gospels, in the Epistles and in the Book of Revelation. This we know, this we believe, and in accordance with this we must direct our doings and non-doings.

But how this working of unholy spirits operates upon our human world, remains for us wrapped in shadow, so that only a few vague features give direction to our thoughts.

Yet it is sufficiently certain that a threefold working outlines itself severally with sufficient clearness.

There are workings from the unholy spirit-world which, without any definite attack, of themselves find vehicles that are observable by us in public opinion, in usages and customs of life, in sinful human nature.

This is the ordinary, the everyday, the ever continuous working from the unholy spirit-world which, as it were, is in the air, and of which we all undergo a certain influence.

There is a second, more grievous working, when one of the many evil spirits takes possession of the spirit of a certain class of people, or of the spirit of an individual person. Sometimes several evil spirits do this at the same time. Just recall Jesus' parable (S. Matt. xii, 45).

And, finally, there is a third, still more painful, yea the most painful working, when Satan does not send out one of his satellites, but girds himself for battle, to assault a chief stronghold in the spirit-world.

In accordance with the conditions of the times and of the persons the first, second or the third working appears in the foreground.

You see it in Jesus' days.

The main question at issue had then to be fought out, and consequently all these three workings came powerfully into play.

Satan himself against Jesus and His Apostles, evil spirits against elect victims, and the ordinary workings among the rank and file of the whole people.

Escape then was no help. Hiding did not do. The conflict was in the open.

So altogether different from now.

Yet even then—and this is so full of instruction for us—Satan tried to hold himself concealed.

Peter with his sensitive temperament and impetuous nature was bound thereby to serve as an instrument. "His Jesus to die on the cross! Never!" Love alone was the motive in contending against this dreadful thought in Jesus. And so we read that Peter *rebuked* Jesus, saying: "Have pity on thyself! This shall in nowise be unto thee!" (Matt. xvi, 22.)

Herein Satan's working concealed itself. Peter did not realize this. But Jesus immediately saw through it, and now in turn *rebuked* the disciple, who was adrift upon his feelings, instead of being at rest upon the prophesied plan concerning the Man of Sorrows: "Get thee behind me, Satan, for thou savourest not the things that be of God, but those that be of men."

So Satan did not gain an inch. Jesus unmasked him at once. Even by his attack from the ambush he could advance nothing against Jesus.

But for us this event is of incalculable benefit.

It shows us that under the most lovely forms of feeling, when apparently no evil intent can in anywise be surmised, and when we have the impression of walking very tender ways, nothing less than a direct assault of Satan can be concealed under it.

This does not say that Satan ever attacked you yourself personally. It is very possible that thus far he confined himself to influence you by one of his subservient spirits. It is even conceivable that he never influenced you otherwise than by his general workings in the spiritual atmosphere.

But this incident with Peter shows nevertheless that you might be mistaken. That there might be an assault of Satan himself, where you did not in the least surmise it.

And in any case, that the daily prayer: Deliver me, "deliver us from the Evil One!" can for no one of us be a superfluous wealth.

Looking back from behind, long afterwards, altogether objectively, upon a temptation that we endured, the question can sometimes present itself: "Was not this an assault of Satan himself upon my heart, and was it not my God Who delivered and saved and preserved me?"

This applies not always to the temptation to commit one particularly great sin. See it in the case of S. Peter. He rather deemed that he was doing good.

But this is certain, that what obstructs most effectively the way to the evil world of spirits is your seeking and striving to be near unto God, to live in His hidden walk; in vital, conscious fellowship with God to choose your path and to pursue your way through life.

And for you yourself, on the other hand, there is no safer stronghold within which to spare yourself these unholy influences than in being much of the time near unto your God. This is the reason why Satan is ever intent to interrupt this communion with God in your heart.

That you seriously seek the hidden walk with God is a reason for Satan to attempt an assault upon you in a particular way, by no means always to entice you to a great sin, but very often, as with S. Peter, by giving you diverting workings of the affections.

Be, therefore, on your guard.

As soon as you observe spiritual coolness, as soon as you perceive that, whatever it may be makes it difficult for you or hinders you to be and to remain near God, then see to what influences you are exposed, what unnoticed influences take place in your soul, and shake everything off, and rest not until you have found your hiding place again near to the heart of your God.

Hesitation, procrastination, is not tolerated here.

Jesus broke the spell, immediately, on the spot; and repulsed S. Peter and threw him off from himself with the first word that came to his mind.

"Satan, get thee behind Me!"

Brief, strong and aggressive! So alone the snare breaks and you can escape.

OH, THAT THOU WOULDEST REND THE HEAVENS!

THE day of Ascension is a Divine memorial day!
So glorious because of our Saviour.

The work of Redemption that had to be accomplished
on this earth was now finished. Not only His bearing the
form of the servant. Not only the course of the Man of
Sorrows. Not only the entering into eternal death. But
also that sojourn of forty long days on this earth, in
order to consecrate His Apostles to the holy, gigantic
task which now awaited them.

These forty days were once again an offering of love on
the part of Jesus.

The glory of heaven beckoned to Him. He was called
and drawn toward the place at God's right hand in the
heavens. There the crown awaited Him.

But yet He lingered. Yet He remained for days together in the sphere of this world. Not because the
world attracted Him. On the contrary, between the
risen Saviour and that world still submerged in misery,
every tie of fellowship was severed. With respect to that
world He had ceased to dwell in its midst. He had died
unto it, and His Resurrection had restored Him not to
that world but only to the circle of His saints.

This lingering on the earth for forty more days was
rather something unnatural for Him. He belonged to it
no more. He had become estranged from it, and it from
Him. Even though He still tarried in it, that world would
see Him no more. He would still be Himself, but outside
of it. Belonging no more to it, but to a higher sphere, into
which He had actually entered by His Resurrection.

But Jesus loved His disciples. The tragic parting from them in Gethsemane, the parting from S. Peter in the Court room, the parting from S. John on Golgotha, could not be *the* farewell. Not the world but *they* must see Him after His Resurrection. They must be initiated into their new relation to their Lord. Regenerated in His Resurrection itself, they must receive the apostolic anointing. They must be prepared for the transition into the new relation, when they would be alone on earth and their Master in heaven.

And to this end Jesus had also brought this last sacrifice of not ascending into heaven immediately after His Resurrection, but only weeks afterwards, and of foregoing during all these days the glory that awaited Him on God's Throne.

But this could not continue. It had to come to an end. It was a holy pause in His glorification, entered upon from love, but which had to be as short as possible.

It could not be, and could not be allowed to be, a continuous intercourse with His own during all those days. Then it would not have answered His purpose, then it would not have accustomed them to the parting that must follow. And so there was nothing but an appearance now and then, in order presently to withdraw Himself again. At first, more frequently; after that, more rarely; and, finally, the entire break—though again at Damascus and on Patmos He showed Himself for a fleeting moment.

And in between these, lies the final parting. The last meeting on the Mount of Olives, with Gethsemane at its foot, Jerusalem broadly spreading itself behind it, and, back of Jerusalem, Golgotha and the cave from whence He rose.

His last orders Jesus had given them. The moment of parting was now at hand. And then from the top of the

Mount of Olives He lifted Himself from their midst, and ascended, so that they saw Him rise higher and higher until a cloud of light received Him out of their sight, and angels from the midst of it became manifest, who brought His disciples the parting word of comfort: "He is gone from you, but one day to return. One day the whole world shall be His."

Where those heavens are whither Jesus went, remains a mystery to us. We seek them above, and all Scripture tells us, and our own heart returns an echo to it, that the heavens of glory arch themselves above us.

It is to us an inborn necessity of soul to seek the Throne of God not around and with us, nor yet underneath us, but above. The heavens are God's Throne and the earth is His footstool. To those heavens we look up, from whence comes the light to us, where God's stars sparkle in the firmament, from whence the rain descends and waters the earth and spreads blessing all around us. But dimensions here do not count. The heavens of God are not of our materiality. They are not to be reckoned by our distances. They are not comprised in the measure of the finite.

One day they will disclose themselves to us where we did not surmise them to be. They will not be where we imagined them. But in unknown glory they will open their gates to us. And it is into *this* glory that when He ascended Jesus entered.

"*Oh, that Thou wouldest rend the heavens!*" exclaimed Isaiah (lxiv, 1) in great distress of soul, for taken in its deepest sense this was our misery, that by its sinful degeneracy our world was closed off from the heaven of God. The holy above; the unholy, round about us and in our own heart.

And then ever and anon a looking up above, to heaven,

which seemed like brass, and whose closed windows and gates scarcely let our prayers pass through.

To that heaven we were disposed, for that heaven we were intended; only a life in communion with that heaven could add to our existence here on earth the luster which God intended.

We could not clinb up to those heavens in order to unlock their gates; all we could do was to look up to that heaven, gaze at it, and call to it and supplicate that God, Who alone could do it, would rend it, and disclose to us again the access to it.

And this prayer has been answered in Christ. First in that He descended from that heaven, and then, in that He ascended to that heaven.

By the latter even far more than by the former. For very surely, when Jesus was on earth, there was above Him always an opened heaven, and the angels of God ascended and descended above the Son of Man. But through Jesus' Ascension, the communion between heaven and earth has been established on a broad scale, durably and permanently.

He ascended not as He descended, but in Himself He took up our human nature. As the Son of God He came to us, as the Son of Man He entered heaven.

His Ascension is no break in the fellowship with His own, but rather a fastening forever of the tie that binds Him to His saints on earth.

Wonderfully mutual is this fellowship. He, our Head, and in Him our life hidden with God; and also He, our Saviour, taking up His abode in the hearts of His own and forever abiding near them with His Majesty, His Grace and His Spirit.

There is now no moment more of breaking off, far less of dissolution of the tie that binds earth to heaven, but in the holy mystery it is an ever continuing, living, holy out-pouring of light and splendor, of power and mightiness from the High and Holy One toward us. And over against this, in an equally holy mystery, a ceaseless ascent of our faith, our love and our hope to the Throne of Glory.

By ascending up to heaven, Jesus has not become far-ther distant, but has come closer to us.

What now vibrates and lives and works is a fellowship between the King of Glory and His saints on earth, no more bound to the upper room, no more limited to a mountain in Galilee, but extending throughout this whole world as far as there are souls whom He has redeemed and saved, and who in supplication go out to Him.

It is now an invisible, unobservable, but nevertheless a powerful and systematic Divine regime which Christ as our Head makes operative in all the earth.

In the wilderness Satan showed Jesus the kingdoms of this world and showed Him in a dazzling light a diabolic rule over these kingdoms. This, Jesus refused, and for what He then refused, He now received, as the crown upon His Redemption-work, the spiritual and Divine government over all peoples and nations. Thus won-drously and majestically He brings to perfection in all parts of this world, that gradual preparation of spiritual con-ditions which will one day bring about the consummation, in order then to establish His eternal kingdom completely in this selfsame world from whence He ascended.

So have the heavens been rent, so have the windows and gates of heaven been opened, never to be closed again, nor even to be veiled.

He who now with his prayers still stands before a heaven of brass has nothing to attribute this to save his own un-belief and his own unspirituality.

But for him, for her, who believes, the heavens are

opened, and from this opened heaven shines out into the darkness of this world and into the darkness of our own heart a soft, blessed glow of light, love and life. And the soul that is cherished by it already now "walks above" among God's saints, and with a joyful smile watches the hour approach, when having finished his earthly course, he, too, shall enter into that full glory.

The early Christians realized this, and, therefore, amid glad songs of jubilation, clothed in white garments, they carried to the grave their dead who had fallen asleep in Jesus.

We, at a farther distance from the Mount of Olives, follow other usages, only be it never with a less firm hope in the heart in behalf of our beloved departed.

WITH ALL SAINTS

EVEN in your most exalted frame of mind and in the urge of your soul to be near unto God you must not appropriate the Lord your God unto yourself. And yet this is a sinful abuse, which, from very intensity of devotion, is so readily committed.

In the *Our* Father stands a *plural*, where we, left to our own impulse, so readily would use a *singular*. It does not read: My Father, but "*Our* Father, who art in heaven," and that plural form: *us* is used in the Our Father to the end.

Of course this does not mean that in our supplications we may not also use the singular. In the *Eli Lama Sabachthani* Jesus himself borrowed this form from the twenty-second Psalm, and obviously with Jesus there could be no mention of a plural in His own prayers, as often as it was the Son of God Who held communion with the Father. As such, Jesus stood solely alone in holy isolation. And though it is not so with us in that exalted, unique sense, in which it was the case with Jesus, yet with us also arise conditions and soul's experiences that isolate us, and of which we do not know that we have them in common with others. Then it is a personal case, from which we call upon God, and it is natural that in the singular we speak of: "*my* God and *my* Father."

Only, this can not be the rule, it may not be the ordinary tenor of our prayer. Of itself it is not this when we pray together, but it should not be this even in our ordinary quiet, secret and personal prayer.

With respect to common need, even though one prays alone, we feel of ourselves that this is not seemly. In a shipwreck, this has often spontaneously shown itself. If among the more than thousand miners who perished at Courrieres there were some who could pray in that dreadful subterranean hell, it probably was not otherwise. And when lately Vesuvius vomited fire and sulphur, the devout people did not each by himself remain at home to pray, but all gathered together for prayer in the churches.

So and not otherwise it is with us men before our God in the common need of our sin and misery.

With each of us this common need may assume a form of its own. With each of us sin may bear a special character, and with each of us the misery of life may present itself in a special manner. Yet this does not do away with the all-dominating fact that all sin and misery flows from *one* common source, makes us all sharers of one common lot, and must move us to a collective calling upon God for redemption and deliverance.

If this is so with our supplication in time of need, it is not different with our thanksgiving for grace and with our prayer for protection by this grace.

Every man's salvation and deliverance is from Bethlehem and Golgotha and the opened grave. To the grace of every man the selfsame Satan seeks to do harm. And the safe-keeping of all by the grace of God flows from the influence in our hearts by one selfsame Holy Spirit and from one selfsame glorious rule of Christ as our King.

If thus in sin and misery we stand in one common lot with all mankind, in the sphere of grace we stand in one common lot with all that have been given by the Father to the Christ; and our spiritual position in holy things may and can, therefore, be no other than that we know and feel, that "with all saints" together we make our approach to God and that "with all saints" together we stand before our God.

Now notice that the Apostle says: "With all saints"
(Eph. iii, 18).

Some devout souls well know the fellowship with the
devout in their home town, but they forget that the *devout* and the *saints* are not the same, and they largely
lose sight of this distinction.

This does not say that it can not be good and excellent
to have daily fellowship with the devout in one's home
town, for the upbuilding of faith and for mutual edifica-
tion. Only this common fellowship "with the devout"
is something so altogether different from the sense of
sharing a common lot "with all saints."

With "the saints" Scripture does not refer to sub-
jective personal piety, but to objective sanctification by
Christ and in Christ. The "saints" are the redeemed,
those that have been drawn unto eternal life. Not *your*
choice, but the choice of your God here counts. Not a
communion with those whom you hold to be godly, but
communion in the common lot with all those who have
effectually been called by God.

The circle therefore is not narrow, neither is it temporary; nor local, but a multitude which no one can
number, in all parts of the world, here and above, from
paradise on until now, and from now on to all eternity.

So alone comes this "with all saints" to its own.

So in the *Te Deum* the jubilant choir sings to Christ:
"The holy Church throughout all the world doth acknowledge Thee."

"With all saints," therefore, means fellowship with the
redeemed through the blood of Christ, in your surroundings, in your whole country, in your church, in other
churches, in other lands, of the present and of the past, of
now and of later. It is the whole "Body of Christ" with
all its members, not one excepted. With the patriarchs

and Prophets, the Apostles and martyrs from of old, with your redeemed family members and acquaintances who have gone before you into eternity, and with those who still continue with you; with those who grow up from among the children of the church; with those that are still hidden in the seed of the church; and with those who shall be brought into the church from without.

Not one whom God included may you exclude.

And that this refers not only to your salvation, but also to your fellowship with the Triune God and to your being near unto God, is clearly evident from what the Apostle writes so enthusiastically, that you *"with all saints* may be able to comprehend what is the breadth and length and height and depth in the mystery of the grace of your God."

Especially in behalf of practical benefit this expansion of your holy sense of fellowship is deeply significant.

If you accustom yourself to limit the multitude which no one can number to the few godly people whom as members of your own church you know personally, then your sacred horizon becomes pitifully small and narrow. Then the people of God sink away to a few hundreds, and all the rest of the world presents itself to you as a lost mass.

If, on the other hand, you picture to yourself the broad circle of all God's saints, of those near by and of those afar off, of the present and of the past, of those who are on earth and of those who are in heaven, and of those who are yet to be born, then at once all the saints of the Old Covenant come nearer to you, then you live in fellowship with Apostles and martyrs, and you have an innumerable multitude of brothers and sisters above, and then you expect from the rising generation and from those who shall come after them an ever steady increase of the Body of Christ.

Then recedes the dejected and depressed feeling, to give place to a feeling of triumph and endless glory. Then your case stands no more alone by itself, but thousands have shared it with you. Though other thousands have been far worse off than you, yet they have entered into eternal life.

You, too, undergo the glorious effect of the magnitude of the work of grace. Hence you do not belong to a small, forgotten group but to a multitude without end, a vast company which no one can number, to an innumerable multitude which already stands before God, or is on the way to the Father-house, or presently from God's Al-mightiness is to be born.

Your God and the work of grace then becomes so infinitely great to the eye of your soul. Everything little, everything that is limited falls away, and you journey on as a pilgrim, not complainingly nor mournfully, but jubilantly in the salvation of God and with your feet already here standing in the gate of the heavenly Jerusalem.

And this is the mood that equips you for the hidden walk with God and makes you be near unto Him.

So long as it remains a purely personal fellowship with God, as though with only a few fellow-believers you came to Him for hiding, the Majesty of the Work of Grace escapes you, and with it the Majesty of His Divine Being. Then the narrowness of your own soul's condition and of your outward need, limits also the length and breadth, the height and depth of the majestic doings of God. Then you transfer so readily your insignificance to the Eternal.

But when you feel that you yourself are a living member of the whole living Body of Christ, that you are one of the multitude which no one can number, that you are bound to all the saints above, to all the saints of God in the whole earth, and to all God's saints among the little

children and among your children's children, then the
pinnings of the sacred tent are widely set out, your outlook is enlarged, your love is extended to ten thousand
times ten thousand, your faith is deepened, and your
hope begins to glisten before you in the glorious radiancy of
victory.

The heart of God is so wide of conception that nothing
estranges you from that Father-heart but your own nar-
row-heartedness.

"The glorious company of the Apostles: praise thee.

The goodly fellowship of the Prophets: praise thee.

The noble army of Martyrs: praise thee."
as it says in the *Te Deum*.

Sometimes the desire takes hold of you that you might
have lived in the days of an Isaiah, and might have com-
panied with a S. John, and might have witnessed the
courage of dying martyrs. And then you dream that all
this has sunken away in an inaccessible past.

Well then, live in the sense of fellowship "with all the
saints," and they will all come closer to you. They are all
your brothers with whom you are included in the Body of
Christ.

And the nearer you come to that company of God's
saints above, the closer you will find yourself in the nearness of your God, Who has included you with all these
saints in one selfsame bundle of life.

THE GRACE OF OUR LORD JESUS CHRIST, AND THE LOVE OF GOD, AND THE FELLOWSHIP OF THE HOLY GHOST, BE WITH YOU ALL

THE apostle from whose hand the richest epistolary legacy has come to us was in the habit of beginning and ending his epistles with a benediction-prayer.

The benediction-prayer with which he began was almost always: "Grace be with you and peace from God our Father and from the Lord Jesus Christ;" and the prayer with which he ended mostly read: "The grace of our Lord Jesus Christ be with you all."

Only by way of exception S. Paul departed from this custom at the end of his Second Epistle to the Corinthians, where he expanded his prayer, and said: "The grace of our Lord Jesus Christ, and the love of God, and the fellowship of the Holy Ghost be with you all." A closing prayer which is particularly noteworthy, because the Church of Christ has used it almost everywhere as the Apostolic benediction at the close of public worship. Millions and millions of times these sacred words, so rich of content and so tender of import, have been repeated, after S. Paul's departure, and for the most part it is still under the influence of these words that congregations of believers from the place of prayer turn homeward.

In this habit of S. Paul, of beginning and ending his epistles with such a benediction-prayer, one can see the aftermath of the manner of the East, and on this ground see nothing in it but a phrase, nothing but a formula of

politeness, which, as such, is devoid of all spiritual significance, at least for us. But is not this superficial?

The people of the East had from of old, and still have
to this day, the habit in meeting and taking leave of one
another, of using fairly lengthy formulas of greeting and
valediction; and it is true that this greeting and this
valediction mostly consist of wishes for blessing from
above.

But how can it follow from this that such an expression
of desire could merely be an empty phrase? And is not
this practice the same all through Scripture? Did not the
Lord Himself after His resurrection appear to His disciples with the benediction-prayer: "Peace be unto you!"
And, again, is it not by constant use in apostolic writings
that this ancient custom has been adopted as a real integral part in mutual Christian fellowship? Adopted not
merely in the Church of the East, but transferred to the
Church of the West, and there consecrated by the custom
of almost twenty centuries?

And if, moreover, as for instance in Jacob's blessings of his sons, even prophetic revelation has employed
this benediction-prayer to throw light upon the future,
is it then not superficial and thoughtless, to see in
such an expression of desire for God's blessings nothing
but words and sounds, and to empty it of all *real* significance?

Over against the *blessing* stands the *curse*, and to the
curse also in Scripture cleaves such serious significance.

Not to every curse. Not to the curse of hatred and
anger. Not to base-hearted meanness, which employs the
curse as a poisonous weapon wherewith to wound. But
truly to the curse of him who is justified in its use, to the
curse of a father, of a mother, of him who is clothed with
spiritual authority.

Then such a curse was valid as spoken under supreme responsibility, under inspiration from Above, and such a curse was fulfilled.

And where over against this curse there stood an equally sharply defined address of blessing, and this address of blessing likewise borrowed its words and significance from the person, the place, and the occasion through which and under which it took place, it is evident that in this most noteworthy phenomenon of blessing and curse there lies concealed a spiritual avowal, for which in our Western lands and in our unspiritual times the sense and the receptivity have all too far been lost.

Of the curse there is almost nothing more left among us than the blasphemous language of profane persons who abuse the holy name of the Lord by using it as an expletive and in the outpouring of wrath; and of the benediction-prayer little else remains but the *good wishes* at the entrance of a new year, at a birthday or at a wedding.

Just in this mighty difference between a wish and the ancient address of blessing the weakened and abated character-trait of our utterance of life depicts itself.

Even upon the death-bed, little more is heard of such a blessing of one's children. The only thing that is now noticed at a death-bed is, whether one passed away quietly and calmly, without any perceptible death struggle.

In most cases nothing more is heard.

Yet in spite of all this, the Churchly usage has been maintained, and the congregation of believers comes together under the holy salutation, and turns homeward under the address of the blessing of the Lord. For this closing benediction the congregation even kneels, or stands with head reverently bowed, and in all seriousness listens to the words of this address of blessing, closing with the word: *Amen.*

This is highly encouraging, and the minister of the Word does well to heighten this last act of dismissal by restful calm and stateliness of tone.

The preceding use of the words: "And now, receive the blessing of the Lord," is an introduction that tunes the heart, and anoints and uplifts.

What expresses itself in salutation and in final benediction but the glorious sense that the Church of the living God stands in living contact with a higher order of things than this world offers, and with Him Who in this higher order of things has established His Throne?

He who stands in the faith knows that he lives in a two-fold world. In the common world together with unbelievers; and in that higher world together with the saints around God's Throne, with the good angels, with his Saviour and King, and in his Christ with his Father and his God.

These two worlds are dove-tailed one with the other. From the higher order grace, peace and life, power and mightiness, have come down into this visible world, have attached themselves, and now in Christian lands cleave to all sorts of Christian ordinances and usages. But the real, the actual merging of these two spheres only takes place in believers, who, while they live in this visible world, carry the higher world in their heart; the latter expressing itself in their fellowship with the Holy Ghost.

And as often as this preponderance of holiness in believers comes to clear expression through the word, there is the holy salutation, and presently, at parting the address of blessing.

But thereby arises in our life a *twofold sphere*. The one sphere of the unbelieving world, the other the sphere that is breathed in from the higher order of things.

You feel this at once, from the difference in your sensation as you find yourself in the company of God's children or in the company of the children of the world. In both circles, in both spheres, a different tone prevails, a different language, a different love. Among the children of the world the flower of your inner life inclines to close itself up; among the children of God this calyx opens of itself.

This gives you no cause to withdraw yourself from the visible world. On the contrary, in it God has given you your calling, your work. You should even be on your guard not to lift yourself up in spiritual pride before the children of the world. What better were you than they, and what is your higher life more than pure *grace?* Indeed, you should never forget your calling to give yourself like your Saviour, to this world, to minister unto it, to bless it with your love and to influence it for good.

But the salvation of your spiritual life is and remains, that you continue to feel deeply and keenly the antithesis between the world and the higher order of things, and continuously cherish, strengthen and feed your fellowship with that higher order of things, removing everything out of the way that might hinder or weaken your fellowship with it.

This does not come to you from yourself, nor from your brothers, but only from God.

What maintains your vital relation with that higher world is exclusively the grace of Christ, the love of God and the fellowship of the Holy Ghost.

And therefore it is, that as often as the congregation comes together, the minister of the Word salutes it with the promise of this, and at parting dismisses it with the same, in the name of the Lord.

To be near unto God is the strength of the life of all believers. This alone; nothing else. He who wanders away from his God, and estranges himself from Him, weakens himself, spoils his inner life and becomes absorbed again in the world. On the other hand, he who remains with God and lives in His hidden walk, drinks in anew every morning the powers of the kingdom, thrives in spiritual things, and is breathed in upon from on High.

And now, this salutation with blessing and that parting with blessing is always the repeated assurance of the Triune God, that His grace, His love and His fellowship shall continue to incline itself towards you; that He wills to be near unto you in order that you may be near unto Him; and that it is your sin alone that makes you lack this blessed fellowship.

I THE LORD THY GOD AM A JEALOUS GOD

"Say to my people," spake the Lord in the ear of Eze-kiel (xi, 5), "I know the things that come into your mind, every one of them. Thus also what ought, but does not, come into it."

The all-seeing eye and the all-hearing ear of the Holy One of Israel are never impeded. The look of that eye bores down through everything; the hearing of that ear escapes no single vibration.

In one of the marble tombs at Syracuse the tyrant Dionysius managed to effect a wonderfully far-carrying echo, that he might overhear every conversation of his imprisoned opponents. Even now this echo returns most clearly the crackling sound of a sheet of paper at a distance of several hundred feet; and, as the story runs, nothing so kept these prisoners in check as this so-called "ear of Dionysius." They could not put it out of mind. They thought of it with every word. It dominated their spirit and their existence.

This is what these wretched prisoners did for the sake of the ear of a man, but what do we do for the sake of the holy ear of that all-hearing God?

For Him Who not only sees, and sees through, every-thing we do, but to Whom, also, every word is known before it passes over our lips. Yea, Who scans every one of our thoughts which we will never put into words, and Who becomes aware of every impulse, every movement, every thrill, which will never crystallize itself into a thought within us, but which yet comes into our mind.

He who does *not* believe has no impression of God's all-knowing and all-hearing perceptive character; is not influenced by it; its power does not dominate him. He acts, speaks, thinks and lets his disposition operate as though there were no God Who watches him, overhears and inwardly penetrates him with His look.

But he who believes can not be so. With him the fear of the Lord is identical with every awakening in the life of his soul; and when he thinks of God he avoids the evil deed for God's sake. He shuns the unbecoming word, suppresses the unholy thought, and checks everything sinful or demoniacal, that would enter into his spirit.

Only his soul is not always so fully awake in him. It is as though faith in him slumbers through whole parts of his life. And then he does not think of God, does not concern himself about God, and is almost insensible as to what God observes of his commissions and omissions in his inmost self—all of which leads to sin, till the conscience comes to act again, and God Himself awakens him.

Is then our faith-life derived from fear alone?

No, it is born *from God-fearing love.*

For already from Horeb it had been proclaimed to God's people; "I the Lord thy God am a zealous (a jealous) God, visiting the iniquity of the fathers upon the children" (Exodus xx, 5).

For us it is a blessed privilege, if we may be near unto God, if we may enjoy His nearness and fellowship and may taste His hidden walk; but here, too, God responds to our spiritual feeling with a like feeling on His part.

For Him Who loves us more tenderly than a father it is a Divine joy when His child is mindful of Him, thinks of Him, goes out after Him, and seeks His holy fellowship. Then too, on the other hand, the love of God feels hurt when His child can forget Him, not think of Him, and is busy in mind with everything save with Him.

When He, so far as it depends on us, is the forsaken One!

For, in order strongly and deeply to impress upon the heart that outgoing of God's Father-heart after love's fellowship with His child, God in His Word does not hesitate to picture this love to us in the image of conjugal love.

With conjugal love enters zeal, the passion of jealousy which can not endure nor tolerate to be forgotten or forsaken by the object of its love.

In the love-picture of Ezekiel (xvi) the continual message is that Jehovah hath betrothed Himself unto Israel; and so also in the bride-picture of the Church, time and time again the passionate love which finds its unfolding in the relation of husband and wife is applied to God and His people.

Like as a bride lives for her husband alone, so must God's people live and exist alone for their God. And like as the desertion on the part of bride or wife most deeply hurts, insults and wounds the heart of bridegroom or husband, so that jealousy arises irresistibly, even jealousy burning like a fire, so, too, the Lord our God avows that He is moved by holy jealousy when His people, when His redeemed can forget Him, wander away from Him, and desert Him in His love.

Yea, even the wrath of quickened jealousy is not held back: "Who visiteth the iniquity of the fathers upon the children unto the third and fourth generation."

So "to be near unto God" has its terrible reverse side. He who is not near unto God is near unto something else, turns his heart towards something else, gives his love to something else. And this provokes Divine jealousy.

Whether you then pawn away your love to your own self, to a human being as your idol, to the world, or to demoniac spirits, the Scripture condemns this always and unconditionally as a withdrawing of yourself from God, a violation of fidelity to God, a wandering away from the Holy One, a deserting of Him Who alone is worthy of all your love.

There is here no neutral ground. It is always a being busy in your heart with something, a giving of your heart to something, an allowing to enter into your spirit of something that does not extend itself after what is God, but what is God's creaturely competitor, and what, therefore, in the holy domain of love and affection is God's enemy and opponent.

And this awakens the holy jealousy.

Of course not as though there were ever passion in God; but instead of this there is in God an exquisite sensibility which in the mightiness of its working far exceeds all human passion.

With conjugal love among men what is known and observed hurts, but there is so much that is not known and therefore does not hurt. With wedded love among men there is also successful misleading, successful deception. And then, too, there is what does not hurt because it is not known. No bridegroom on earth can scan his bride to the center of her inner life and existence. There is here a broad domain that does not come into account.

But all this is unthinkable with the Lord your God. Nothing escapes Him in your doing or not-doing, in your thinking or speaking, in your inward ponderings or perceptions. He enters unceasingly, always more deeply into your being than the brightest beam of light into the bed of the stream.

And here no misleading avails, no putting forward of

yourself other than you are, no hypocrisy. His all-pene-trating look pushes every covering aside.

And these two taken together bring it about that the sensibility of the holy love in God is far more strongly aroused to jealousy than the strongest passion among men can ever quicken brooding envy.

Among friends it troubles us when no one thinks of us; but far more seriously does it hurt the bridegroom when he perceives that his bride is filled with other thoughts than of him.

This most tender love demands that we be interested in one another, that during temporary separation we shall live with one another in thought, and, while the separation lasts, cherish no other purpose than to seek one another again, to find one another again, and in each other's company to feel ourselves rich, happy and blessed.

Now apply this to your love for your God, to your avowal that it is good for you to be near unto Him. For that love, too, is unique. It is no love alongside of another love, but a love that far excels every other attachment, every other affection, and every other union of mind and heart, and must dominate them all.

Not, to love your wife, your child, your country *and* your God; but to love your God solely and alone; and *from* this love let the cherishing flow forth wherewith you also love wife and child, Church and native land.

And is it, then, too much that God asks of you, that you shall always be concerned with Him, that you shall always think of Him, that with your heart you shall always go out after Him, and that in your spirit you will repress everything that rises up within it to lead you away from Him, and induce you to forsake Him?

Is not this jealousy of your God for your love, your very honor, your greatness, your glory? And is it not dishonoring to both yourself and to Him when you discard this holy urge of love, play with it, and for the sake of religious recreation spasmodically return to it, but for the rest withdraw yourself from it again, in order in your innermost soul to be busy with all sorts of things except with God?

The wound thereby inflicted in His holy love would not be so grievous, if your God could for a time forget you, like as you forsake Him. But that He can not do. Before there is yet a word on your lips, behold, He knows it altogether. Your God Himself has said it: "I know every one of the things that come into your mind." Hence, let it be here repeated, every one of the things that *ought* to come into your mind, but remain away.

He knows, He feels it, every moment that you do not think on Him, are not engaged with Him, do not seek Him, do not crave His nearness, and shamefully live along outside of His hidden walk. And when, in the face of all this, you yet sing together with others: "But it is good for me to be near unto my God," is there then not something of a provocation that offends and *must* wound?

And if this is the reverse of desiring to be near unto God, confess, does there not go out from this an altogether unexpected, an altogether new impulse, to make your seeking of God's nearness an ever broader reality in your life?

So long as you view this being near unto God from your side alone, you can comfort yourself about any temporary loss of it, by calling to mind the rich blessedness of the single moments of its enjoyment. But when you view this being near to your God, this thinking of your God, this being engaged with your God, also from the side of

Him Who loves you, then there mingles itself in this love-song an altogether different note.

Then you must not, then you will not grieve the Holy Spirit. Then it is not your soul alone that seeks God, but, far more, God Who awaits the love of your soul.

God Who, with holy jealousy is vexed every moment that you withdraw yourself from His seeking love.

CVI

THE SIGNS OF THE TIMES

TIMES differ. It is not, age upon age, one monotonous sameness. Rather there is constant alternation and ceaseless change. And even to a century like the one that has just ended, which as the nineteenth century almost imagined itself to have been the discoverer of the abiding light, it is already evident that Psalm 102 (vs. 26) can be applied: "It shall wax old as doth a garment, and shall be changed."

From this difference comes the "difference of signs" not unlike to difference in the weather. Sailor and farmer, both dependent upon the weather for navigation and agriculture, learned from their youth up to observe these signs. Not as wondrous signs of something that had never been seen before. As already the preacher at Jerusalem exclaimed: "That which *has* been is *now* and that which *is* to be hath *already* been" (Eccl. iii, 15). These "signs of the times," even as the signs in the weather, show themselves for the most part exclusively in a different degree of intensity from that with which the ordinary phenomena appear, and hence in their mutual relation. Whether the sky in the evening shows itself bright red or dull red depends upon the greater or lesser density with which mist or vapor places itself between our eye and the red glow of the setting sun. And so in the spirit world, also, an altogether different constellation presents itself according as the cloud of religion enters into the life with fullness of weight, or remains suspended, light and extremely transparent over the waters of life.

The difference in this respect between age and age becomes evident.

In the age of the Reformation the dreadful controversy of religion filled almost all of life. In the court room, in the council of princes, in public opinion, in the pulpit, in the market place and especially in the family, religion was then more than anything else the deciding factor. From every side the sky glowed a bright fiery red.

And compare with this the eighteenth century. How dull its red was then. All brightness had paled, all warmth of religion had withdrawn within a single mystical group, and, moreover, in public life religion was debased to trivial reasoning, stupid self-conceit, laughter and scorn.

Then came the nineteenth century, by revolution and Napoleonic war strung to a higher seriousness. Within the religious domain it brought us three signs: first, in the Christian domain and in a very limited circle the *Reveille;* secondly, as a new find, the quickly exhausted modern theology; and, thirdly, alongside, and on account of this, within the broad domain of science, endless doubt or proud materialism, and in society cold unbelief and a breaking with all religion.

Now, on the other hand, in our twentieth century the table turns again. There is once more a *reveille*, but not in the Christian domain. A reveille far more of the mystic religious feeling. Altogether outside of Christianity. Mostly rejecting the way of truth and seeking ways of its own. And so of itself falling back into the ways which in earlier times man himself had discovered. Spiritism, Theosophy, Buddhism are now the asked-for articles. A few (though this is the exception) even fall back upon the Crescent again. What alone is *not* observed is return upon a broad scale, to the Man of Sorrows. One wills to become religious but must be permitted to remain anti-clerical.

In the eighteenth century, the falling into slumber. In the nineteenth century, the pouring out of the spirit of deep sleep. At present, in the twentieth century, a gradual waking up of religion, but still dozing in false mystical dreams.

The Christ and His Cross are passed by.

To such "signs of the times" the pharisee pays no attention (see S. Matt. xvi, 3). He thinks, and continues to think, that in his more limited circle everything is good and healthy, and everything outside of it is evil and unholy, and he does not even surmise from afar the influence which the change in the spirit of the times exerts upon him and upon his circle.

But the true disciples of Jesus do not do so. They know better. They feel and understand right well that in spiritual concerns also the waters of life continually flow into one another. They observe it in themselves and they see it in their family and in their surroundings, how general conditions of spirits influence one another on every side. And with every new change they ask of themselves to what criticism this must urge them, to what discharge of duty this must constrain them.

They hold their ground. Naturally! They do this by virtue of the grace that is in them, by the Spirit's urge that operates in them. Though they should have to die for Jesus, they can not let go their hold upon His Cross. With ties which they can not loosen, that Cross lies bound upon their heart.

They feel themselves as in an oasis around which, as far as eye can see, grins the grey spiritual barrenness of the desert.

In this oasis they rejoice. In it they drink from the fountain, they enjoy the bread and the shade of the palm trees. They make their children enjoy it with them. They give thanks, they glory, they jubilate.

Only nothing in themselves makes boast of this. God Almighty has brought them into this oasis. And that, not

because of any good that was in them. In nothing do
they know themselves to be better than any one else.
They rather dress each day again the bleeding wound of
their own heart. It is grace and nothing but grace. A
grace which in its entirety was, and remained, nothing but
grace.

But the desert round about this oasis troubles them,
nevertheless. The sand-wave from it flies upward. The
hot wind travels through it. And then, they that there
wander about in that desert, are they not in many respects their fellow-countrymen, not infrequently of their
own family? Sometimes their own friends. And also
apart from this, what talent, what civic virtue, what
noble sense, does not frequently mark those wanderers.
Much that is low, much that is common, much that is
coarse that is true. Many are so, but not all.

And prayer, also for these wanderers, again and again,
involuntarily ascends from their perplexed hearts.

Even in the deepest depth of the life of their soul
they undergo the perceptible influence of this change in
the signs of the times.

To be near unto God, and to remain near unto God, is
so much easier when everything round about you warmly
calls for the honor of God, than when the spirit of the
times opposes everything that is holy. Herein hid the
godly secret of a long period in the Middle Ages, the
secret also of the fifteenth and part of the sixteenth
century. Almost everything then pressed after God's
nearness. Religion was the atmosphere which of itself
was breathed in everywhere. Hence from both these
periods came our over-pious traditions.

But, ever since, the thermometer has gone down. First
it became cool, then cold, then ice-cold. Then everything broke down, everything put itself in the way

when the soul went out to seek the nearness of God.   So much that blossomed before, now froze!

Thereby the seeking of God and your approach to His nearness now demanded an effort before unknown. It became a struggle. A climbing with hands and feet in order to scale the holy mountain. And when the top was reached what mists still intervened that cut off the outlook from you, what effort it took to keep your standing there. And above all, what painful distance between that high mountain top and that world below at the foot of the mountain, which yet remained your world and into which your daily task called you.

Surely there is a gain. That which results from such constant, serious and holy effort goes deeper, is richer in its enjoyment, and gives you more intense blessedness. He who in spite of contrary current and storm yet drops anchor in the harbor knows the joy of a higher order than he who drifted with weather, wind and tide.

But it brings weariness. It exhausts the mind and the heart. And it is the aftermath of this exhaustion that involves the danger of the spirit of the world outwitting you, and makes you dread still more a new course, attended with danger, perchance of death.

If you stand true, then, to be near unto God in such times is more blessed, but the enjoyment of it less constant.

And more times of wandering away and of estrangement come in between.

And, *moreover*, this unfavorable change in the signs of the times brings new *duties*.

The captain who himself through current and storm safely made the harbor can not be indifferent to the other sailors, who less fortunate, out at sea, still struggle with death. Or, likewise, he who himself reached the oasis, quenches his thirst and satisfies his hunger with good things, must not be indifferent about the long caravan, that still wanders among mortal dangers in the desert.

And so also, you who by grace, and by nothing but grace, refresh yourself in the nearness of God, you may not, you can not, if rightly disposed, be indifferent about those thousands and thousands who, lost in the byways, know not the Christ, understand not the Cross, and, therefore live without God in the world.

For them, therefore, no hardness, but in your soul a deeply implanted divine compassion. No pity that spitefully scorns and repels, but a compassion that by valor invites and as a holy magnet attracts.

Never hide or cloak your own religion. Never let there be a guilty silence, or a putting on of manner as though you were one of them. Never the cowardice that deems itself love.

But by all means understand them, enter into their condition, show them not your wisdom but your heart. Always show them that you *care* about their eternal salvation.

And in order to be able to do this, do not hold yourself aloof, but take part in actual life. Be at home in what the things of the world, under God's providence, produce of interest and of beauty. Always keep open a ground on which you can meet them, discover yourself to them, and converse with them.

Surely their estrangement can become ill-will and resistance. There can come a moment when you, by forgetting yourself, might cause the holy to be made a laughing-stock. And then breaking away can become duty.

But as your Saviour on the way to the Cross ever had His eye upon the world, and on the Cross still prayed for the forgiveness of those who knew not what they did, so shall the eye of your seeking love ever remain upon those who have wandered away from God, and your prayer continually rise in their behalf.

Moreover in this seeking love and in that prayer you will have the surest token that you are not mistaken, but that in all reality you yourself are *near unto your God.*

CVII

WHEN I WAS A CHILD

OUR hidden walk with the Eternal Being follows no fixed, uniform model. What presents itself in this exceedingly holy and intensely fervent domain in *imitated* form arouses by this very imitation the surmise of hypocrisy. Already in human fellowship, all friendship of the more intimate kind seeks escape from the stress of conventional usage. Uniformity in association and fellowship prevails, and may only prevail, with that superficial contact on a broader scale which has the smile of kindness on the face but does not let it rise from the heart.

Our life with God can not subject itself to the mechanical. Even as in nature, so also in this spiritual domain, the expression of life is organic. And as every tree unfolds a different leaf, and every stem a flower-bud of its own, so every human heart discloses itself to God in its own way, sings before God its own song with its own melody, and tastes in the hidden walk with the Almighty an intimacy of enjoyment which altogether responds to the peculiar need of its own inner existence, and by no other can so be enjoyed.

If anywhere, it is here that the apostolic word applies: "With one after this manner and with another after that." Sex exerts an influence upon this, and temperament, conditions of life, nationality, disposition and character. And even where these data show themselves almost exactly alike in the members of the same family, yet in personality there is such a strong divergence, that the exception is extremely rare when two brothers or two sisters are entirely alike in their religious nature.

But not merely between two or more persons does a sharply defined difference in most cases show itself with respect to this; a similar difference, likewise, shows itself with the *selfsame person*.

Your own holy experiences in your endeavor to be near unto your God are by no means always of like nature. It is self-evident, moreover, that they differ in *degree* as to clearness of impression. But that is not all. They also differ in *character* and *nature*. They are altogether different in moments of intense joy from what they are in moments of dire need and great anxiety. Robust health or wasting disease puts an altogether different stamp upon your inner existence. After overcoming self in the hour of temptation, your fellowship with God is a something altogether different from what it is after yielding to sin, and falling.

Under all this it is always the selfsame organ in your heart, but entirely different combinations of registration are opened every time, and continual changing of harmony.

And this endless process of change and modification must continually be recalled, because in imitation, in sameness, in uniformity, death reigns; while the rich, full, blossoming life of piety only thrives in endless variety.

Especially upon one difference too much emphasis can not be laid; namely, upon the difference in age.

The Apostle describes it accurately: "When I was a child, I spake as a child, I understood as a child, I thought as a child" (I Cor. xiii, 11). But it did not continue so. Later on it was altogether different. "When I became a man, I put away childish things." And note carefully how the Apostle emphasizes this difference between the existence of a child and of a man, while he treats of the personal knowledge we have of God.

Naturally this difference operates very delicately.

The Apostle only places the child over against the full-grown man for the sake of brevity; but it needs scarcely to be said that the lad and the young girl exist differently from the youth and the young maiden; that the man in the strength of his years exists differently from the man in his declining days; and that at the end of the pilgrim journey the grey-haired man exhibits again an image correspondingly different.

Of all these transitions in age and conditions of the inner life our fellowship with God undergoes of itself the necessary influence. What comes, develops itself from what went before. So with the regular, undisturbed development of person, there is a constant enrichment, strengthening and deepening, and, moreover, every new phase of life adds to what went before a newness of self-expression, even in so strong a measure that the aged man finds it almost impossible to think himself back into the bitter struggles of passion in which in those early days he had to defend or to recover his fellowship with God.

But though the modification, change and reformation of the hidden walk with God goes on continuously until the end, yet Christ pointed also to the fact, that with respect to this there is a striking difference between the child and the man, which lends to the inner life of each an altogether different type. Not to recognize this radical difference, so often spoils fundamentally the Christian training.

Provided family and other environment do not from the first choke the seed of religion in a child, the child mind is normally religious. Not by outward show but by receptivity of holy impressions and by a hushed reverence before the Eternal Being. To teach a child to pray, if done under pious guidance and not mechanically, is a beautiful and tender joy.

This does not find its cause in knowledge of the holy. Even when the child can not yet read, far less is able to follow the catechism, let alone to understand it, he stands instinctively in fellowship with the world of hidden things. He gives himself no account of this. He is himself not conscious of this. He does not know how to explain this, but it is so. It is even evident in his fear of darkness or of strange phenomena.

This anxiety shows that the child has knowledge and feeling of the existence of another world than that which he sees before his eyes. Hence his faith in the reality of the phantoms that create his fear.

This sense of the existence of a mysterious world, and the feeling that this mysterious world can unveil itself, directly governs the inner life of the child. His delight in fables and fairy-tales is immediately connected with this and works upon his imagination, makes it taut, and gives to the inner existence of the child that intensity and depth, that with such captivating charm addresses you from his eye.

And it is by this selfsame trait that the child instinctively opens his young heart to religion. It is an unseen working that goes out from the unseen world to the heart of the child. It is God Himself Who thus plays upon the delicate harp in the child-heart.

This natural piety of the child has an even more intimate relationship with the life of the blessed, than the religion of us who are full-grown.

With us a whole world of thought, a world of reasoning and of consequent doubt, enters in between, which only at our death is lifted out again.

Hence Jesus' word, that to become as *a little child* is the regeneration of our person, through which to enter into the kingdom of heaven.

Nothing, therefore, is so cruel and so painful, as to see such a little child abandoned to a leading and a training which has no understanding of this whatever, and will treat the child as a miniature adult, killing and destroying the child-type in the child-heart.

Cruel and painful is the mechanical way in which the child is taught to pray, with a voice devoid of feeling, as a something that must be done, without entering with him into the holy devotion, so that he feels himself rather bewildered in his religious earnestness than guided and encouraged.

Equally cruel and painful it is, in the presence of such a little one to be unsympathetic, untactful and impatient in regard to holy things. This hurts the child-heart, and then it does not take long for the tender germ of religion in it to be choked.

It is also cruel to let the years of childhood pass by, without training the child in holy things, and to think that somehow religion will come to him later on. These first years of life are the appointed time in which to let the foundation of all religion in the fellowship with God crystallize in the heart of the child.

There is in the child's heart a natural receptivity, which, guided and fed in a reverent manner, gives a bent to the heart, whose effects will operate beneficially throughout all the later life. And conversely, if this is not attended to, and this first receptivity is brought to naught, then all the life long, the religious sense, even though it awaken later on, will lack that very fervor and tenderness which Jesus asks for in our child-likeness.

This danger can only be averted by bringing the little child at once in his own way, after his nature and type, into fellowship of soul with God Himself.

Of course, the little child must likewise learn sacred history, must learn to know the sacred truths, and identify himself with sacred songs. All this is excellent. But all this will avail nothing, if, first of all, in the little child his instinctive sense of a mysterious world does not unfold into an immediate sense of his fellowship with the all-seeing, omniscient, omnipresent God.

MAKE ABODE WITH HIM

THE sublime note of joy with which the Apostolate went into the world focused itself in the confession: "The Word became flesh and dwelt among us."

The Gospel did not first come in Bethlehem. The Gospel was already proclaimed in Paradise. And it is a misappreciation of both Moses and the Prophets when you allow the Gospel of Grace only to have begun with the Apostolate.

The Israel of the Prophets already had the very same Gospel as we, and you need but turn to the writings of the New Testament Evangelists and Apostles to find yourself, again and again, referred back to the Old Testament to see the proof of the truth drawn from this ancient source, and to find accurately outlined, and, to us, often surprising indications that the whole treasure of the New Covenant had been deposited ages ago in the Old Covenant, though, at first, in germ form.

No, the difference and the antithesis between what lies back of Bethlehem and what came after it, hide altogether in something else.

Undoubtedly there is a definite and an absolute difference between the Gospel *before* and *after* the Manger mystery, but this difference does not lie in the larger or lesser riches of the Old Testament or the New Testament Gospel. No, the Old and the New Covenant differ in this one particular alone, that the Old Testament lacks the reality, and that the New Testament has it.

This was generally indicated by speaking of the dispensation of shadows and the dispensation of fulfillment;

but this states it far too weakly. You can express the difference far more accurately by saying that in the Old Testament the Image has been shown, but that in the New Testament the reality itself has appeared in the Person of Christ.

That the law is given by Moses (S. John i, 17), is a statement which does not refer to the Ten Commandments. The law here is the name of the whole Old Testament taken as an instruction, a revelation, as a word of God that has gone out to Israel. This Word, this Revelation, this instruction which God gave in figure, begins with Moses to *obtain* form, but when Bethlehem sees the birth of the *Holy Infant*, then there comes something altogether different; then there comes not mere instruction and prophecy, but *truth*, and truth here means what we call: *reality*. Not the Image is the truth, not the shadow is the truth. Image and shadow are in themselves unreal, and the real comes only when in tangible reality *He* appears Whose Image has been seen from afar and whose Divine Shadow fell upon Israel.

This is why the Apostles put so much emphasis upon the fact that they have *seen* Jesus, that they have *heard* Him, that they have *handled* Him. The emphasis on this, that the Word now had received *flesh*, earthly reality. There was an emphasis no less upon the fact that Jesus had truly been foretold, that He had appeared and disappeared again, but that now He was come in full reality, and from Bethlehem to Golgotha had *dwelt* among us.

To dwell is really and continuously to tarry. Not only to come but also *to stay*. Not once in a while to turn in for the sake of passing the night, but by staying continuously to make one's presence known.

Now God dwells in heaven and His abode is in the light.

But though Scripture declares that God dwells on high, at once it adds that that same God looks low down upon the children of men on earth.

Heaven and earth are not intended to be apart, but to form a higher unity, so that the Lord our God simultaneously dwells both in heaven and on earth.

It began with this.

In Paradise dwelt God, and originally the fellowship of man with his God and of God with His creature was a very real and undisturbed communion.

The separation only came when by his sin man expelled God from this earth, drove Him out from His own creation, dismissed Him from fellowship with His own highest creature.

But God abandons not the work of His hand. Expelled by sin He comes back in seeking grace. "Adam, where art thou?" is the call with which God returns and claims His world again.

In the end, God regains His abode on this earth. Provisionally already in the cloud, column of fire and in the Tabernacle, but in the fullness of symbolism only upon Zion. "This is my *habitation*," said the Lord, "this is my *rest*, here will I dwell" (Ps. 132, 14).

Zion over against Bashan indicates that God continues to be expelled from His own wide world, but that in Zion He has prepared for Himself a place of rest again, an oasis of grace, a habitation of His own.

This holy symbolical return of God to this world, this is what prophesies age upon age in advance the glorious Bethlehem. And when, finally, the fullness of time is come and the Babe is born in Bethlehem, then God no longer dwells symbolically in Zion, but in full *reality* in the Christ.

And that is why the Apostles proclaim so jubilantly

that God is revealed in the Flesh, and in the Flesh (in reality *revealed*) has dwelt among us.

Hence, this is Bethlehem, the real and actual return of God to this earth, in order now *to dwell* continuously upon this earth with and among us.

Restoration of what was real in Paradise.

Now does this end with Golgotha, or if you please, with the Ascent into heaven?

By no means.

Rather the dwelling of God upon this earth becomes possible in the fullest sense only through Golgotha and the Ascension.

Between Bethlehem and Golgotha there was a real dwelling of God upon earth, but in an extremely limited sense. A dwelling limited to one people, and among that one people limited to the narrow circle of those who adhered to Jesus.

The need, on the other hand, was that God should dwell on earth among *all* people, in every part of the world, accessible age after age to every soul that feared Him.

And this full, this extended, unlimited, permanent, ever-continuous, and ever expanding dwelling of God among the children of men only became possible when Jesus was no longer seen, heard, handled among *one* people in a narrow circle, but was exalted and glorified upon the Throne of Grace, whence He could extend His working to every people and to every heart.

For this reason, Jesus repeats again and again in the ear of His disciples: "It is expedient for you that I go away;" but then also adds: "When I shall have gone away, I shall come again, and with the Father make my abode with you" (S. John xiv, 23).

Thus a threefold dwelling of God upon the earth.

First symbolically in Israel on Zion. After that in the reality of the flesh when Jesus walked about on the earth. And now, in the third place, the dwelling of God among us, and in us, in all parts of the earth. Our heart has become a dwelling-place of *God* in the Spirit. Our heart is the real Zion, and therefore our redeemed human heart is His temple wherein He dwells.

Sin expels God. In grace God resolves to return and to dwell again among us and in us; and therein lies all the mysticism of genuine Godly piety.

Piety does not begin with this. Rather it begins with the outward confession that it knows God alone as the One Who is above, and is always conscious of a fatal distance between itself and the Most High God.

But grace for grace gradually brings about a modification in this, and makes internal what began by being external.

To have the Spirit is to carry God Himself about in one's own heart, in one's own soul. And the new commandment of brotherly love is nothing else than the commandment that as you yourself carry God about in your own heart, you must discover this same God as dwelling also in the heart of the brother, and now to join heart to heart because it is one God that fills the heart of both.

But although this is so, most people dare not face it. Though God dwell in their heart, they constantly push God back into the corner of their heart, so that they feel at a distance, and for the greater part again withdraw that heart from God. And this is the sin of the saints.

But grace holds on. God does not let you go. From the corner of your heart into which you push Him back he comes forth continually to recover again a part of your heart, until at length you give up the fight, open your *whole heart* to Him, and now experience with joy that in Christ He really has taken up His abode with you.

And this now is the perennial Christmas Gospel.

Not a Christmas Gospel that remains standing by the manger, but such a one as passes from the manger over into your own heart.

First the jubilant note of the Apostolate: "The Word is become flesh and has dwelt among us."

And then the anthem of praise on the part of God's saints: "The Word is become flesh and *has taken up His abode* in mine own heart."

CIX

WHOM HAVE I IN HEAVEN BUT THEE?

THE refreshment of grace is particularly abounding when in its departure from this world the soul is privileged to be *near unto its God.*

On the death-bed higher bliss has more than once been tasted. Many have fallen asleep not alone in firm faith and in higher clearness of mind, but also in the foretaste of blessed enjoyment.

You can frame no rule for this, and it must be denied that a blessed death-bed is always the reward of holier-mindedness and deeper spirituality. Not infrequently a God-glorifying death-bed has been seen with one who in his life had wandered far off; and over against this, a painful struggle in distress and agony on the part of him who long years had been initiated into the hidden walk with his God.

This depends of itself as a rule, upon all sorts of things that have nothing to do with a devout frame of heart. First, upon age, upon temperament, upon the nature of the disease, upon the degree of weakness, upon the tension of the nerves, upon freedom of speech or diffidence, upon longer or shorter duration of the process of dying.

Also, in part, upon the physician, whether he conceals the certainty, or least the probability of the approaching end, or whether he frankly and honestly tells the patient the exact state of the case. And then again upon family and friends, and those who nurse the sick, whether they are spiritually inclined and helpful to the patient in his holy meditation, or whether they provide so-called diversion, and keep his mind filled to the end with all sorts of earthly concerns.

If, then, it sometimes happens that all this works for good, and that he who is about to be called of his God lies, at least for a few days, as with a waiting heart at the gate of eternity, looking that it might be opened unto him and meanwhile bearing witness to the powers of the everlasting life, sometimes in terms that far exceed ordinary speech— then in such a dying person operates special grace. And the Lord imparts this special grace to him, yea, *truly* to comfort him in his dying, but far more to glorify Himself and to make a testimony of striking power to go forth from so glorious a death-bed.

The passion to pose even in one's piety is a sin which in its more refined forms cleaves to almost all religion, and has sometimes been observed even with martyrs. And this passion would very certainly be more generally evident in dying, if God the Lord did not prevent this by weakness and disease. And in this cutting off of the chance of making a show of one's piety upon the death-bed we are bound to recognize grace.

But there are times when at death grace exhibits itself in a higher form, when something of almost prophetic inspiration takes hold of the dying saint. This was strikingly evident with Jacob the Patriarch. But though, perhaps, in measure less strong, occasionally such a higher inspiration is still witnessed among us.

Such a death is not alone a dying in the faith; not merely a falling asleep in Jesus; but an active entering with open eye through the gate of eternity.

And then it is clear consciousness, and from this clear consciousness a holy testimony, because he who dies knows and feels himself until his latest breath near unto his God.

Never, on the other hand, should it be inferred from this that he who dies less triumphantly was, therefore, deprived of the nearness of God.

All too frequently the weakness of the body so affects the mind, that little shows outwardly of what inwardly goes on in the spirit.

God is mighty to do much in and on behalf of the soul, of which a third person observes nothing.

When a few months old infant is carried from the cradle to the grave, you would not say that God was unable to minister grace unto that little child; but you saw nothing of it, and the little one himself knew nothing about it.

The same can take place in sleep. Would any one assert that while we sleep God's ministering grace in our heart is excluded for the space of those seven or eight hours? In serious illness one can be deprived of his consciousness for several days together; does God then stand all those days helpless before this stricken soul? And to what else does it come with the young child in sleep, or in sickness, save to this, that a gracious ministry to the soul can take place on the part of the Holy Ghost, which through some physical disturbing cause is not shown outwardly, but remains concealed within?

And in most instances, when the end draws near, this physical hindrance enters in. Particularly with those who pass away in unconsciousness; and with the sick whose pulse is almost imperceptible, and whose breathing can scarcely be observed. With such, no one may say that on account of these causes their soul passed away in secret and was estranged from its God. Almightiness and grace can here perform in holy stillness what no human eye or human ear can trace.

And as regards the sick person who died, surely, from the nature of the case his consciousness depended upon the power that still operated in his brain. But suppose the brain refuses to respond, should the inner life of the soul have to be deprived, therefore, of grace? And presently the brain refuses to function altogether. Yet without this disturbed brain the soul will know its God and glorify Him forever.

What else is it then to be near unto God in dying, though no one may observe it, save already here to have an entrance in part, into what after death becomes true altogether?

A beginning of that new condition when our person, altogether separated from our body, wholly incorporeal, is with God and companies with Him.

But, also, apart from this, the while we continue our pilgrim journey here on earth, this Divine ministry in our dying is so deeply significant to us as a *memento mori*. This was implied in Asaph's inquiry: "Whom have I in heaven but Thee?" (Ps. 73, 25).

By itself this means that we are to set store by nothing in heaven but God. And this is altogether the same thing as to love God with all the soul, mind and heart. But Asaph's question puts the matter still more clearly before us.

For the struggle of our heart consists in this, that it goes out after all sorts of things as well as *after God*. This struggle has been laid upon us because God Himself has related our heart to all sorts of persons on earth, and has endowed our heart with power to appreciate the glories of nature, and has given us all sorts of inclinations and callings to go out after visible things. The Stylist who withdraws his eyes from all earthly things, in order that, with nothing around him but the air, he may seek God evades this struggle and becomes unnatural.

The holy art of the child of God is so to possess the things that are seen, that he can truly say that nothing on earth delights him but his God. This means, of course, that in all the things that are seen he sees nothing but things that are God's, nothing but things that exist purely for the sake of God, and which, therefore, must render service to God, so that in all the pleasure which he takes in God all these other things are embraced and included, but *so* included, that they only come into consideration in the measure in which they are subject unto God and are revelation of his Divine power.

Whether in very deed and truth this is the case with us is only evident at the time when we come to die, when all these other things fall away from us and God alone remains.

It has been tried to transfer our earthly desires into heaven by picturing to ourselves all sorts of persons and pleasures there, other than God. The Mohammedans have gone farthest in this; but even among Christians there are not a few whose thought of heaven connects itself first of all with their dead with whom to resume their former life again, and thus even in heaven to imagine for themselves a whole world apart from their God. And this is confusing to the mind. For he alone who in dying expects nothing in heaven but his God, shall find also, through and under God that other Fellowship in the Father-house above, which shall and can have no other purport than, in unison and with one accord, the better to glorify the God and Father of all in Christ.

And this very thing must here be applied to our hidden walk with God, and again and again we must put the question to ourselves: "If now you had nothing, absolutely nothing, aside from your God and your God alone, then would the wealth and the riches of your soul be complete?"

When you seek and endeavor and strive to be near unto your God, is it then that you might rest in Him and in

Him alone, with all your heart, or is it perchance merely to seek in Him the helper who can assure you all sorts of other desired things after which your heart goes out really more strongly?

Never let it be said that he who has God and God alone has *nothing* but God, for he who has God, has in Him *everything*. But in order personally to test the sincerity of your piety, you should know for yourself whether you are so concerned about God that, though the other things are added, you are really intent upon Him alone; or whether your heart really seeks the other things and, in addition to them, God, in order that through Him you might obtain those other things; or, finally, whether you are intent upon becoming partaker of both, having your God and, next to Him, having all those other things too.

And in behalf of this test, anticipation of the hour of your death has uncommon value. That you imagine to yourself the moment when everything on earth shall fall away from you and abandon you and, shall cease to exist for you. And when you enter upon the thought that in heaven you will forever have nothing *beside* the Triune God, whether this lifts your heart up to the highest foretaste of holy enjoyment, so that in all sincerity you can say that it is good for you to be near unto your God, because aside from him you have nothing in heaven, and aside from Him nothing can satisfy you on earth all the days of your pilgrim journey that still remain.

CX

AS THE HART PANTETH AFTER THE WATER-BROOKS

Not twenty centuries and more have been able to darken the golden glow of the immortal song that has come to us in the forty-second Psalm, and, with all the bitter estrangement from God that in large circles characterizes life in our times, the praises of the priests of art even yet join heartily with the lauds of the redeemed of the Lord in giving the song of the "hart that panteth after the water-brooks" a place far above all other lyrics in which the home-sickness of our human heart cries after the Source of our life.

What here grips so mightily is the ardent fervor that breathes throughout this whole psalm, the passionate outpouring of soul that makes this glorious song to expand.

To be near unto God is our most blessed experience, and in the face of distraction and temptation our soul on the point of fainting can yet turn away from the world unto God, inasmuch as a voice within whispers that he who forsakes God disturbs the peace in his own heart.

Time after time we have turned back to God, and have knocked at the door that we might be admitted again to the hidden walk with Him, after we had discovered in hours or days of wandering that worldly pleasures are vain and that worldly glory deceives.

At another time we have let ourselves, as it were, be taken along to God by one who "holy, and humble of heart" drew us to God.

Again at another time a wound inflicted in our heart, a great anxiety against which we battled, or a distress in which we almost perished, impelled us to seek help and comfort in the holy nearness of our God.

The paths along which our human heart came to God wind themselves through all of our life, and disclose themselves, however oft abandoned, every time anew.

And yet, with all this, there was no ardor. Rather in such moments our heart, if left to itself, would not have inclined toward God, and it was a pressure, an impulse, a stimulus from without, which drove the half-unwilling and self-sufficient heart out after Him.

But in this Psalm the heart itself pushes and drives. It is not from without but from the inner chamber of the heart that the home-sickness after the living God irresistibly wells upward.

It is here no accidental happening; no cause that operates from elsewhere; no bitter experience, no enticing voice from without; not the stimulus of conscience; not the urgency of need; far less, sagacity and calculation; no, here it is from nature, from the re-born nature of our heart itself that the pressure after God, the not-being-able to do without God, the impetuous hastening after the living God springs.

Even S. Augustine's exclamation: "My heart continues restless within me, until it rests in Thee, O, my God!" pales here in loveliness of glow.

Here it is a *thirsting*. A thirsting after the living God, even as the dried-up blood, after exhaustion, in man and beast does not merely call for moisture, for quenching, for water, but in agony cries out for it, so far as the parched palate still permits this crying with husky throat, this moaning with audible sound.

The imagery goes back to the animal world, where there can be no idea of reflection, or pious intention or crying from set purpose. The exhausted hart, no more able to endure its suffering, moans as in despair, because, having at last reached the stream-bed, finds that stream-bed emptied of water; and now, from the pure impulse of nature, at the point of dropping to the ground, and no longer able to go without water, breaks the air with his agonizing cry for *water, water;* and must presently succumb, unless water comes.

In this impulse of nature, in this passionate longing, in this ardent fervor, in this almost dying of thirst after God on the part of the soul, in this consuming home-sickness after the living God, lies what exalts, what grips, what enchants, and what at the same time puts us deeply to shame.

How many have been the moments in your life, when, apart from the pressure of necessity, apart from the voice of another who invited you, or the sting of the conscience that troubled you—from a purely natural impulse of soul you have thus thirsted after the living God.

You feel, you perceive as you listen to this silvery melody, as you join with others in the singing of this glorious forty-second Psalm, that such, not sometimes but always, should be the state of your heart; that to this end God created you; that His plan concerning you includes the intention of such a glorious longing in you after Him; that you failed of the high possibility of your nature every moment that this plan ceased to be operative in you; and that you sin against grace when, at least in your re-born nature, this longing, this thirst, this home-sickness after the living God, can keep silence.

Even as blood, by dessication, calls for water, and, if the moisture does not come, ceases to circulate, so likewise you obtained a nature from God which, normal and uninjured, must cry out in your soul after Him, or collapse.

Piety which has sometimes imagined itself to be of a high order, here feels itself sink away, because it has so rarely reached that fervor, that ardent passion, that consuming home-sickness after God.

It is your holy exaltation, an illustrious evidence of your human nobility, that your nature has so been created, that so it should be, and that so it can be; but it is at the same time your deep self-humiliation, that this nobility of higher origin exhibits itself so extremely rarely in you with all the fullness of its strength.

But then it is also a stimulus which leaves you no rest, which makes you turn in upon yourself and deepen your thought, and which, under this changing impression, makes you feel the thirst after the living God, and as soon as it is felt, makes you experience, so blessedly, its quenching power, because God makes His approach to your soul.

"So panteth my soul after God! My soul thirsteth for God, for the living God!"

The word "living" is also here an image from nature.

There is water that is stagnant, is marshy and poisonous, and thereby is unfit to refresh the life-blood of man and beast. Therefore the hart does not merely pant after *water*, but after the *water-brooks*, after the fresh, leaping, rushing water that is alive.

And so also, says the Singer: "My soul pants, yea, *thirsts* after the *living* God." Not after a Creed regarding God, not after an idea of God, not after a remembrance of God, not after a Divine Majesty, that, far removed from the soul, stands over against it as a God in words or in phrases, but after God Himself, after God in His holy outpouring of strength and grace, after God Who is alive, Who in His life makes advances towards you, with His life penetrates you, and in holy exhibition of love reveals Himself to you and in you as the *living* God.

You feel that here all learning falls away, all dogma, all formulas, everything that is external and abstract, everything that exhausts itself in words, in order in the word to dry up and wither. It is not your idea, not your understanding, not your thinking, not your reasoning, not even your profession of faith, that here can quench the thirst.

The home-sickness goes out after God Himself, until in your soul's transport of love you feel the warmth of His Father-heart in your own heart. It is not the Name of God, but God Himself Whom your soul desires, and can not do without, God Himself in the outshining of His life; and it is this outshining of His life that must penetrate you and must be assimilated in the blood of your soul.

The Psalmist seeks this in the sanctuary. He was from Israel, and for Israel the clear, rich, full enjoyment of God's Presence was bound to Zion. It was Zion that God had chosen unto Himself, in order in this fullness to give the enjoyment of Himself to His people.

The life of the world then drew too mightily away from God. It was idol after idol that filled the world, and therefore the Presence of the Lord Jehovah was concentrated symbolically between the Cherubim on Zion.

To apply this to the congregation in the church building is to cut the nerve of the song. For though it is true, that there is much in our sanctuaries that draws us to God, and that there is much in the world and even in our homes that draws us away from the living God, yet this again would be the stimulus from without; while what this Psalm wills is the *thirst* in the heart itself, and panting from the blood of the soul after God.

Zion is not your prayer-cell, Zion is not your church building, it is not even godly company; what Israel found on Zion alone, and at that time symbolically, is for us, and now really, in Christ; in your King, Who is Himself God, to Whom be glory for ever and ever, Amen!

Now he who is redeemed is in this Christ, and Christ is in him. Wondrously has he been woven as a living member into the mystical Body of Christ. His re-born nature has melted together with Christ in the most intimate way, and it is in that mystical life with Christ alone that the heart that thirsts after God, drinks in the life from God.

And therefore the being near unto God, yea, the drinking in of the life of God with all the ardor, all the thirst of our soul, is not bound for us to any place, to any presence of others, to any altar or to any priest.

Every place wheresoever, can at any moment become a Zion unto us; depending on this alone, that you approach your God in Him through Whom there is access, and Who ever liveth to make intercession for us (Heb. vii, 25).

TEXTUAL INDEX

677